KEVIN O

# KEVIN O'HIGGINS
## Builder of the Irish State

### JOHN P. McCARTHY

IRISH ACADEMIC PRESS
DUBLIN • PORTLAND, OR

*First published in 2006 by*
IRISH ACADEMIC PRESS
44 Northumberland Road, Dublin 4, Ireland


*and in the United States of America by*
IRISH ACADEMIC PRESS
c/o ISBS, Suite 300, 920 NE 58th Avenue
Portland, Oregon 97213-3644

## *Website:* www.iap.ie

British Library Cataloguing in Publication Data
An entry can be found on request


ISBN 0-7165-3413-4 (cloth)
ISBN 0-7165-3414-2 (paper)


Library of Congress Cataloging-in-Publication Data
An entry can be found on request

Typeset in 11pt on 13pt Sabon
by FiSH Books, Enfield, Middx.
Printed by MPG Books Ltd., Bodmin, Cornwall

To the late Sister Mary Patrick McCarthy, GNSH,
A loving sister,
A devout religious,
And a selfless educator.

# Contents

# Acknowledgements

I WISH TO ACKNOWLEDGE the assistance, encouragement, and interest of numerous institutions and individuals in my researching and writing this book. A Fordham University Faculty Fellowship and grants from the American Philosophical Society and the American Council on Economics and Society were extremely important in facilitating my research. Seamus Helferty, the Principal Archivist of the Archives Department at University College Dublin and his staff were very gracious and helpful, as were the staffs of the National Library of Ireland, the National Archives, and the library of the American Irish Historical Society. The late Una O'Higgins O'Malley was kind and hospitable in enabling me to see her father's letters in her home and various other documents and materials related to him. Lengthy conversations with her and her husband Eoin were very useful to me in appreciating her father and the general milieu in which he operated. I regret this book had not appeared before her death. My perspective on twentieth-century Irish history and the era in which O'Higgins lived was broadened by conversations with many others, both in public life and the academic world. They include Conor Brady, John Bruton, Conor Cruise O'Brien, Perry Curtis, Mary Daly, James S. Donnelly, Ronan Fanning, the late Tom Flanagan, Richard B. Finnegan, Tom Garvin, Dermot Keogh, Michael Laffan, Emmet Larkin, Joe Lee, and Cormac O'Malley. Sinead McCoole and John M. Regan have been very gracious in communicating with me with regard to our interest in Kevin O'Higgins, although no doubt they may not agree with my interpretations and emphasis on various matters. Students of O'Higgins's career and times who have let me see their work are Frank Bouchier-Hayes, Richard Egan, Jason Knirck, James Eoin Lynch, Kevin Matthews, Gillian McGoey, and Mary Frances McKenna. Others who were helpful in different ways were Terry Golway, Annette Kirk, Andrew Lynch, and Gerry Torsney. I wish to express a special appreciation to the late Professsor Maurice R. O'Connell, my colleague at Fordham, for his contribution to my understanding of Irish history. I want to thank my wife, Catherine, for her encouragement and for her patience, and my family for their support, during the hours, days, and, indeed, years, in which what may have seemed an inordinate amount of my attention was turned to this project. My daughter, Kathleen McCarthy O'Connell, had a very keen sense of inappropriate wording in earlier drafts she read. Naturally, I claim sole responsibility for the work, and exempt those named from any criticism it may encounter.

John P. McCarthy
Co. Kerry, Ireland
30 January 2006

# Illustrations

All photographs courtesy of the Archives Department at University College, Dublin.

1. Young Kevin O'Higgins surrounded by brothers Jack, Tom and Michael.
2. Brigid and Kevin O'Higgins.
3. Kevin O'Higgins at his desk.
4. Dairmuid O'Hegarty, Kevin O'Higgins, Desmond FitzGerald, Joseph Walshe and Michael McWhite.
5. Treaty supporters, including Kevin O'Higgins.
6. Group photo at the wedding of Kevin O'Higgins and Brigid Cole in 1921.
7. The Free State Cabinet (1923).
8. Mrs and Mrs Kevin O'Higgins at the RDS.
9. Wedding picture with Eamon de Valera and Rory O'Connor.

# Introduction

THE STORY OF the Irish state can be read in many ways. Two views, however, have dominated. One popular view looks upon the War of Independence (1919–21), as the near fulfilment of the 1916 sacrificial act of national redemption, with the ultimate unification of the island remaining as the concluding chapter. The civil war, according to this view, was a tragic diversion attributable to either compromisers on one side or zealots on the other. A second view sees modern Irish nationhood having been virtually realized in the late nineteenth century with the successful alliance of Charles Stewart Parnell, the Irish Parliamentary Party, and the Catholic hierarchy, which acquired control of Irish political life, including over most of the Irish delegation to Westminster, local government and education. Nationhood was further enhanced with the commencement of land purchase transforming the island from one of tenants to one of small holders. In this second view the violent events of 1916 to 1923 are an exception to a story of constitutional evolution towards self-government, to which path Ireland returned with the conclusion of the civil war. Indeed, in remaining on that path, Ireland has been almost unique among many newly independent nations of the twentieth century.[1]

The life of Kevin O'Higgins encompasses both views. As the Vice President and Minister for Justice in the Irish Free State, he has to be considered one of the founding fathers of modern Ireland. While his name is not as easily recalled as that of Éamon de Valera or Michael Collins, whose dramatic stories are more familiar and hold a place in the popular imagination, O'Higgins' contributions to the formation of the Irish state are comparable to those of de Valera and Collins. An example of his being overlooked is the most recent issue of a standard general history of Ireland, *The Course of Irish History*, edited by T.W. Moody and F.X. Martin, in which no mention is made of him other than the notation of his assassination in the chronology at the end of the book.[2]

While O'Higgins participated in the revolutionary pursuit of

national independence, he played a conservative role in consolidating the institutions of a new state after the Anglo-Irish Treaty of
1921. His work in a short period of five years ensured the solidity
and survival of constitutional democratic institutions in Ireland in a
century when such survival was scarcely guaranteed and when
societies confronted with comparable problems have descended into
authoritarianism. Particularly notable accomplishments were his
formation of an unarmed police force and his expulsion of private
factions within the national army. His tragic assassination on 10
June 1927, when he was only 35 years of age, robbed Ireland of one
of its most constructive political figures. In his essay, 'On the Boiler',
Yeats placed O'Higgins along with Swift, Burke, Grattan, and
Parnell, as being among 'the true Irish people, and there is nothing
too hard for such as these'.[3] The personal tragedies and the great
moral confrontations that O'Higgins experienced confirm that
capacity of endurance in the pursuit of tasks, which in his case, was
nation-building.

O'Higgins was a leading proponent of the pro-treaty position, an
ally of Michael Collins and opponent of Éamon de Valera in the split
within the Sinn Féin movement which would culminate in the Civil
War of 1922–3. He was Minister for Economic Affairs in the treaty-
mandated Provisional Government that Collins led. When Collins
was ambushed two months into the Civil War, the Provisional
Government was reorganized and O'Higgins became Vice President
of the Executive Council, as the cabinet was called, and Minister for
Home Affairs, later re-entitled Minister for Justice. Five years later
he was assassinated by IRA members, embittered at his role
opposing them in the civil war and after, and became, like Collins, a
martyr figure for those in Ireland adhering to the pro-treaty position.
Fine Gael, the contemporary Irish political party that has evolved
from that tradition, lionizes both men.

O'Higgins came from a professional family; his father was a
medical doctor from 'strong' farmer stock in the Boyne Valley and
his mother the daughter of a Dublin Lord Mayor who was a leading
figure in the Irish Parliamentary Party. He had some Jesuit education, had been a seminarian, graduated from university and was
called to the Bar. O'Higgins' role during the War of Independence
was primarily political, directing the local governmental bodies that
supported the national cause in the harbouring of resources made
scarce by British punitive action. While he regarded the treaty
settlement as imperfect, he celebrated its giving to Ireland the ability

to self-govern. He took an uncompromising hard line against the opponents of the treaty during the Civil War and after, and has to be seen as a central figure in the restoration of post-revolutionary political and constitutional normalcy to Ireland.

O'Higgins' concern was that the writ of the law, law sanctioned by a self-governing Irish parliament, prevail against a spirit of lawlessness and disorder engendered by insurrection and civil war. He was also anxious that revolutionary forces be curbed, that the national army be under the control of civilian authority, and that a regular judiciary replace the revolutionary courts of the War of Independence and the martial courts of the Civil War. His political perspective emerged from the narrow revolutionary sectarianism of Sinn Féin to a more politically ecumenical position that viewed the government as responsible to all who lived in Ireland, regardless of whether or not they had been supporters of the Sinn Féin insurrection. Such was the broadness of his vision that had O'Higgins survived he may well have kept Ireland from lapsing into the era of political and cultural isolation and socio-economic stagnation that characterized it in the mid-twentieth century.

O'Higgins developed a practical, rational attitude toward the question of the partitioned Northeastern section of the island, as he argued that political unification would only follow cooperation and cordiality rather than demands and threats. He came to have a positive attitude toward Irish membership of the British Commonwealth, within which he advanced a clearer pronouncement of the sovereign autonomy of the dominions like Ireland.

An American parallel for O'Higgins and associates in the Cumann na nGaedheal Party, which was what the Free State government supporters were called, can be drawn with the Federalist Party. Led by John Adams and Alexander Hamilton, the Federalists were the late eighteenth and early nineteenth century political faction that formulated an enduring American constitution. The Federalists realized that the new American nation had to draw for its own development on the heritage of what had been the 'mother country', particularly the common law and gradual evolutionary change. They identified with England in opposition to the revolutionary forces emanating from France. Like Cumann na nGaedheal, the Federalists did not survive as a political party, in part because of the loss of a significant leader, Hamilton who, like O'Higgins, died violently at a young age. Their opponents, the Jeffersonians, who had preached the need for periodic revolutions, then came to power. Although they dominated American politics for most of the next half century, they did not depart from what the Federalists created. In the same manner, soon after O'Higgins' death, former armed enemies of the Free State reorganized as the Fianna Fáil Party and entered constitutional politics. Coming to power in 1932, Fianna Fáil has governed Ireland more than two-thirds of the time since, in substantial accord with the constitutional and democratic agenda that O'Higgins had espoused. In this perspective O'Higgins forgiveness of his killers and his wish that killing end in Ireland can be seen as having been fulfilled.

O'Higgins' work and contribution to Ireland should be appreciated in a new century when the bitterness of the Civil War and its aftermath are long past. Even the contemporary steps towards peaceful resolution of the Northern Irish question, especially the promotion of respect for both traditions, can be seen as a confirmation of the intuitions he had three-quarters of a century ago.

This book will emphasize the fine detail of political issues rather than the psychological motives or personal lives of the main characters, and concentrate on O'Higgins' political policies and his own justifications and rationale for them, and the perspectives of those, especially members of the Dail and Seanad, who opposed, criticized, or sought to modify his programs and positions. It is hoped the book will give an understanding of a much forgotten era in Irish history, the early years of the Free State, especially regarding issues like public security, intoxicating liquor legislation, censorship, and divorce. These issues, as well as the major theme of state-building, still echo in the contemporary Ireland in which more liberal attitudes predominate.

There has been only one book on O'Higgins, written in 1948 – a commendable and favourable biography by Terence de Vere White.[4] But since then many government documents have become available and there has been an enormous amount of thoughtful research on modern Irish history by recent scholars. The first biography appeared at a time when unreconstructed nationalist republicanism was in the ascendancy in the Irish popular mind, as evidenced by the confidence that an anti-partition campaign could get international sympathy in the aftermath of World War Two and the onset of the Cold War. A generation later a revisionist historical view coincided with disapproval in the Republic of Ireland of the irredentist campaign of violence being waged in Northern Ireland by the IRA and viewed O'Higgins favourably. The historical wheel has turned again in our time, as some younger historians are alert to nationalist grievances of earlier times and less approving of those who accepted less than the full republican mandate. The newer views are partly a consequence of social liberalism that inaccurately attributes the conservatism and moral puritanism of mid-twentieth century Ireland to the Free State, when in fact, most of its republican opponents shared the same social and moral perspective, but only differed on the national question.

John M. Regan's book, *The Irish Counter-Revolution, 1921–1936: Treatyite Politics and Settlement in Independent Ireland*, is an excellent example of the latter. In a finely researched and comprehensive study of the 'pro-treaty' political forces in Ireland, he employs confusing concepts in picturing so many of the central figures like O'Higgins as counter-revolutionaries. The very definition of counter-revolution with which Regan begins his book, 'a revolution opposing a former one or reversing its results', seems inappropriate in describing the role of O'Higgins, which was the consolidation rather than the reversal of the national struggle. Indeed, his work consolidating institutions was generally accepted by even his political opponents.

Regan says that violence was 'the only truly radical and revolutionary aspect of what should be accepted as the Irish revolution'. This view could imply that the 'revolution' which was countered was not any radical program or further progression, but the simple employment of violence.[5] But the desire to stop violence scarcely merits the label of counter-revolutionary. If the major goal of the revolution, like the major goal of the constitutional nationalists, was self-governance, then those like O'Higgins, who worked to consolidate the institutions of a self-governing Ireland, were scarcely counter-revolutionaries. This was especially the case when it is realized that many of their opponents among the irregulars and later Fianna Fáil shared much of the same relatively conservative socio-political outlook on many issues.[6] O'Higgins' assertion of near ascendancy within the Cumann na nGaedheal Party, his refusal to cater to the elements within the party who had not abandoned the Sinn Féin mindset despite their acceptance of the treaty, and his efforts at getting the acceptance and support of the many elements in Ireland who had not been part of the Sinn Féin movement suggest political ecumenicism more than counter-revolution.[7]

Hopefully, this book, by concentrating on O'Higgins' political achievements, examining the issues confronting the newly independent Ireland, and exploring the debates of the time will open a window into a critical time for the foundation of the state and confirm his role as a state-builder. Not only ought his position in Irish history be better appreciated, but his work might well serve to guide those seeking to establish democratic and constitutional institutions in the developing world and in nations recently liberated from totalitarian domination.

NOTES

1.  Emmet Larkin of the University of Chicago is the foremost proponent of this view, which he has made his life's work in the several volumes of his study of the Catholic Church and Irish politics in the second half of the nineteenth century. A brief introduction and summary of his work appears in the introduction of a festschrift to him, Stewart J. Brown and David W. Miller, 'Introduction', *Piety and Power, 1760–1960* (Notre Dame: University of Notre Dame Press, 2000), pp. 1–15.
2.  T.W. Moody and F.X. Martin (eds), *The Course of Irish History* (Dublin: Mercier in association with Radio Telefis Éireann, 2001 edn.). A sign of possible renewed interest in O'Higgins was the appearance of a documentary on him on RTE on 16 November 2004 (Ted Dolan, Orpheus Productions for RTE).
3.  W.B. Yeats, 'On the Boiler', *Explorations* (New York: Macmillan, 1962), p. 442.
4.  Terence de Vere White, *Kevin O'Higgins* (London: Metheun, 1948; Dublin: Anvil, 1986).
5.  John M. Regan, *The Irish Counter-Revolution, 1921–1936: Treatyite Politics and Settlement in Independent Ireland* (Dublin: Gill & Macmillan, 1999), pp. xii–xvi.
6.  Jason Knirck, 'Afterimage of the Revolution: Kevin O'Higgins and the Irish Revolution', *Eire–Ireland*, Vol XXXVIII, Nos 3–4 (Fall/Winter 2003), pp. 212–43.
7.  Regan, *Irish Counter-Revolution*, pp. 244–73.

# Republican Dissenter in a Parliamentary Family

Kevin o'higgins' family background would not suggest his becoming a supporter of a violent nationalist insurrection. He might well have been part of that early twentieth-century elite of university-educated Irish Catholics 'prepared for the future leadership of Ireland under Home Rule', but for revolutionary nationalism gaining popular ascendancy between 1916 and 1921. Most of that elite 'actively espoused the policies pursued by the Home Rule party and anticipated the development of Ireland into a pluralist, liberal and self-governing nation', and looked upon the era as 'one of preparation, not for independence, but for Home Rule and a central role in the Empire'.[1]

His father, Thomas Higgins,[2] had studied at a Jesuit College at Tullabeg and then at the Royal College of Surgeons, qualifying as a doctor in 1881, and becoming the dispensary doctor in the Laois village of Clonaslee. He was elected in 1882 as coroner for Queen's (Laois) County, which post he held until his death in 1923. In 1883, he transferred to Maryborough (Portlaoise) and two years later became the dispensary doctor at Stradbally. The grandfather, John Higgins, was a strong farmer able to provide his family with secondary and medical school education, as must have been the great-grandfather, Michael Higgins, judging by the still-standing substantial shell of Michael's farm house in Athboy, County Meath.[3] In 1887 Thomas Higgins married Anne Sullivan, the daughter of T.D. (Timothy Daniel) Sullivan, the then Lord Mayor of Dublin. T.D. Sullivan and his brother, A.M. (Alexander Martin), were leading members of the 'Bantry Band', a faction within the Irish Parliamentary Party whose nickname was attributable to their roots in the Bantry area of County Cork. Both Sullivan brothers and their relation, Tim Healy,[4] were supporters of Charles Parnell in the supplanting of Isaac Butt as leader of the Irish parliamentary movement in 1879. They were vigorous champions of the interests of the Catholic Church and, as such, were an important component of the disparate Parnellite alliance.[5]

T.D. Sullivan and Tim Healy strongly opposed Parnell's successful effort to force the candidacy of Captain William O'Shea, the husband of his mistress, on the Galway constituency in 1886, dissented from Parnell's 'conservatism' on the land issue when they supported a renewed land agitation later in the decade in the form of the Plan of Campaign, and permanently split with him in late 1890 after he refused to step down as leader after having been named co-respondent in the O'Shea divorce case. T.D. Sullivan, who had been elected to parliament in 1880, remained in office until 1900, when John Redmond and the United Irish League had become strong enough in the Parliamentary Party to make things uncomfortable for the unreconstructed anti-Parnellites.[6]

Dr Higgins and his wife Anne had fifteen children[7] of whom Kevin Christopher, born on 7 June 1892, was the fourth son. The family size necessitated the purchase of an eighty-six acre farm called 'Woodlands', a few miles outside Stradbally. A grandson, Justice Thomas O'Higgins, writing in 1996, described the house as a deceptively large residence and noted that the farm provided a source of supplementary income. The name of the farm came from a wood on its northern side. The property contained an orchard and a stream in which trout ran.[8] Rural life as a member of a large family no doubt had a conservative influence on Kevin O'Higgins that was borne out by his rejection of revolutionary absolutism after the Anglo-Irish Treaty.

His early education was first at a convent school and then at an Irish Christian Brothers' School in Portlaoise. Afterwards he followed his older brothers to the more exclusive Jesuit school, Clongowes Wood, in Kildare. But when he was fifteen, he indicated an interest in the priesthood and transferred to Knockbeg College in Carlow as a preliminary to entering Maynooth College, then exclusively a seminary. Although he shone academically, particularly in the classics, O'Higgins was asked in 1911 to withdraw from Maynooth for disciplinary reasons, specifically his disregard of the rules against smoking. A sympathetic instructor at Maynooth convinced a bishop to sponsor O'Higgins in another seminary in

Carlow, where tolerant priests allowed him to smoke in their quarters. There he did not perform as well academically, as he failed exams taken as an external student at the London University. When he was caught using the liquor and the cigars of the President of the seminary, the keys to whose office he had copied, he was expelled.

His cousin, Maurice Healy, Tim Healy's brother, offered him a position as a solicitor's apprentice in his Cork office. But before undertaking this position, O'Higgins began to study at University College Dublin (UCD), for an arts degree. He completed his studies with an unimpressive passing degree that scarcely measured up to his potential. He spent much of his time in public houses, where he often wrote short articles and poetry for newspapers to replenish his drinking money. Where O'Higgins did manifest his brilliance and future political role was in the proceedings of the Literary and Historical Debating Society, 'where he was considered one of the wittiest speakers in the University' and 'most noted as an impromptu speaker'. He was one of the first among the small minority among the university 'elite' who became 'eagerly interested in one or other of the aspects of the Volunteer and Sinn Féin Movements'.[9] This suggests, as did his biographer, de Vere White, that the prospects of a solicitor's life and preparing for the requisite law exams in Cork after completion of his B.A. did not excite him.[10]

But O'Higgins was excited by the oratorical appeal made in 1915 by Padraic Pearse at the graveside of the old Fenian, O'Donovan Rossa, whose remains had been brought back from the United States for a classic Irish revolutionary's burial at Glasnevin in Dublin. This was the speech in which Pearse referred to the British authorities as 'The fools, the fools, the fools – they have left us our Fenian dead, and while Ireland holds these graves, Ireland unfree shall never be at peace.'[11] A year after O'Higgins' death, his sister Kathleen recalled his weekly visits to her at that time when she was in a Carmelite novitiate in Rathfarnham: 'It was in those talks I learnt to know him best and I can still see his face as he told me of Pearse's speech by the graveside of O'Donovan Rossa.'[12]

Kevin O'Higgins' assumption of a revolutionary role between 1916 and 1921 was reflective of the disappointment felt by some at the tail end of the 'preparatory generation', especially students at University College Dublin, when home rule was postponed at the outbreak of the First World War. The turn of events intensified a desire 'to define and understand Irish nationality' and made him susceptible to the revolutionary and separatist appeal.[13] Yet, two of his older brothers served in the British forces in the war: Jack, a doctor, was surgeon on a naval vessel and Michael died in Flanders.[14]

O'Higgins joined the Irish Volunteers. They were a small minority of the earlier group formed in late 1913, as the overwhelming majority had followed the appeal of Irish Parliamentary Party leader, John Redmond, to call themselves National Volunteers and support the British war effort in the First World War. The smaller group, who retained the name of Irish Volunteers were led by Eoin MacNeill, a University College Dublin historian, and took a position that they would not support the war, although agreeing not to engage in violent action unless needed to defend nationalist societies should they come under attack from the authorities. However, the military council of the Irish Volunteers, dominated by the Irish Republican Brotherhood, the secret conspiratorial group committed to the violent achievement of an independent Irish Republic, prepared for armed insurrection. Despite efforts by MacNeill to countermand orders for a rising, this began on Easter Monday 1916 in Dublin. O'Higgins, a young Volunteer at his home in Stradbally on Easter break from his studies at UCD, was unable to get to Dublin upon hearing of the rising because the military restricted movement to the city. However, he continued his involvement in the Volunteers and in what would increasingly become its political arm, the Sinn Féin Party. Indeed, O'Higgins' oratory on behalf of Sinn Féin, and against British recruitment efforts for the war, got him imprisoned for five months, first in Mountjoy Prison, Dublin, and then Belfast. He was released in October 1918.[15]

Imprisonment gave O'Higgins time to turn to poetry. He wrote a tribute to Pearse that would have made his maternal grandfather and grand-uncle proud, even if they would have had reservations about the anti-constitutional path he was taking:

> Peace to your soul! for one short glorious week
> You cast defiance in the Saxon's teeth
> Not all the bloody vengeance they can wreak
> Can rob the patriot hero of his wreath.[16]

As a student, as a prisoner, and as a Sinn Féin activist, O'Higgins lionized the Easter Week rebels. However, he used the language and poetic idiom of Victorian-era Irish poets who were not necessarily Fenians nor even political separatists, but who did celebrate earlier Irish warriors, including the 1798 rebels. In some ways O'Higgins saw the Easter Week rebels as being part of a continuum of Irish patriots, being the latest model of a long-storied line. For example, a poem from his student days, while scarcely of extraordinary literary quality, illustrates that his turning toward Sinn Féin was more a natural progression than a departure from his familial nationalist heritage:

> "We won the fight" the Saxon said
> And Ireland's soul is dead
> The Gael content a slave to be
> No dreams of liberty
> But Easter Week has shamed the lie
> And shown that nations cannot die
> The Race from which these martyrs came
> No British power can ever shame.[17]

The remarkable collapse of the Parliamentary Party had begun with the North Roscommon by-election of February 1917 when Count George Plunkett, the holder of a Papal title and the father of the Easter Week martyr, poet Joseph Mary Plunkett, became the first Sinn Féin-endorsed candidate to win a parliamentary seat. That election prompted O'Higgins to wax poetically:

> As surely as the crop springs up from seed
> So Ireland, honouring their noble past
> Now takes the stricken father to her heart.[18]

Having demonstrated his political talents in campaigning on behalf of Dr Patrick McCartan, the successful Sinn Féin candidate in a by-election for the Offaly seat in parliament in 1918, O'Higgins himself ran for the Laois-Offaly constituency in the December 1918 general election. His was one of the seventy-three seats gained by Sinn Féin of the total 105 Irish seats in the Westminster parliament. The Irish Parliamentary Party won only six seats, four of which were from some Ulster constituencies where Sinn Féin had not seriously competed to avoid splitting the nationalist vote.[19] The Sinn Féin victors followed their electoral pledge and refused to take their seats at Westminster. Those who were neither in jail nor on the run gathered the next month, January, in Dublin's Mansion House and labelled themselves Dáil Éireann, or the Assembly of Ireland, and formed a revolutionary government. O'Higgins was appointed assistant to the Minister for Local Government, William T. Cosgrave, a man twelve years his senior, a veteran member of Sinn Féin, an Easter Rising participant, and a member of the Dublin Council.

SINN FÉIN ACTIVIST

The Sinn Féin triumph in the parliamentary election reflected the sea change in attitude on the part of a decisive portion of the Irish population. Home rule, that is, local governance or devolved power within Great Britain, that earlier seemed to be the highest Irish popular aspiration, was no longer sufficient as a popular objective. The Easter Week leaders were transformed by their brutal executions from extremist zealots to martyrs. In 1918 an attempted imposition of conscription on Ireland, the arrests of Sinn Féin leaders, and the imposition of a coercion policy under the Defence of the Realm Act which allowed the banning of meetings and even fairs, all at the behest of Lord French, the new Lord Lieutenant who had been Commander-in-Chief of the British Expeditionary Forces, 1914–15, and of the Home Forces, 1915–18, made popular sentiment increasingly desirous of separation from Britain.[20] While it remains uncertain that such a view encompassed endorsement of armed insurrection, which began simultaneously with the formation of Dáil Éireann (but without that body's endorsement),[21] there was no doubt but that the postponed goal of home rule would no longer satisfy the Irish public.

A series of articles by O'Higgins in the provincial weekly, *The Nationalist and Leinster Times,* between May and July 1919 reflected this change in attitude away from the Parliamentary Party. The first article, provocatively entitled 'The Disloyal Irish', discussed the leaders of the Parliamentary Party, especially John Redmond, who had died in April 1918, and his successor, John Dillon, who had been defeated almost two to one by Eamon de Valera in East Mayo in the general election of December. The disloyalty to which O'Higgins referred was not the party's attendance at the Westminster parliament, but rather its placing of limitations on the ultimate aspiration of Irish self-governance, that is, 'Ireland's right to the fullness of national life, to absolute separation from England'. Ironically that would be the same criticism radical anti-treaty Republicans would later levy at O'Higgins himself and his colleagues in the Irish Free State government.

O'Higgins saw Redmond and Dillon as having diluted the nationalist aspirations in the way they celebrated the 1914 Home Rule Act. Redmond had accepted it as 'a full, complete and final settlement of Ireland's claim', and John Dillon had said he would use his energies to see 'that no man used that Bill as a leverage to secure more, for that would be treacherous and dishonourable'. In making those statements, both men, in O'Higgins' eyes, 'publicly challenged their country's right to the fullest freedom and constituted themselves leaders of sedition and disloyalty in Ireland'. Those statements by Redmond and Dillon alone, never mind their acceptance of British military recruitment and additional taxation in Ireland, justified national rejection of the Parliamentary Party. Extravagantly interpreting the position of the party as 'a swift course of national degeneracy from the proud day when Grattan saluted his country as a nation', he saw the party's central flaw in its asking 'from England of something less than that to which we were entitled'. Requesting home rule or any other amelioration was akin to asking a favour of England. Instead, the only thing Ireland should ask from England is 'the recognition of her absolute independence'.[22]

O'Higgins said the Parliamentary Party had lost its idealism when it entered a pact with the English Liberal Party in 1911. The equal strength of the Conservative and Liberal parties in Parliament made the Liberal government reliant on the support of the Irish party for legislation such as the reform of the House of Lords. In turn the government advanced home rule. But from that point, in his view, the party activists gave themselves over 'to an orgey [sic] of jobbery'. The 'leaky old bark' of the party was kept afloat, but recent times have tested vessels stouter than 'the corrupt and emasculated Parliamentary Party of Ireland'. He sarcastically suggested that it must have been soothing to Dillon's vanity 'that his fall synchronized with that of kings and emperors [Wilhelm II and Nicholas II] and that his party disappeared amidst the crash of dynasties in many lands'. Abandoning its support of the party, Ireland had been moved by the 'sublime protest' of 1916 'to uproot and cast aside the poisonous growths of Anglicisation that had flourished in the genial atmosphere of "constitutionalism"', and to regard herself as 'an invaded country'.[23]

O'Higgins' rhetoric might appear extreme, but it did not deviate very much from the standard oratory of Irish nationalist spokesmen throughout the nineteenth century, whether that of O'Connell at the height of the repeal movement or Parnell and associates in the

1880s, when appealing to mass audiences and, especially, to Irish-American supporters. O'Higgins condemned the Parliamentary Party leaders in the last stages of their party's existence, but he did not condemn the tactic of parliamentary politics itself. Significantly, he made no reference to Wolfe Tone, the major theorist of Irish revolutionary nationalist separatism, alluding instead to Grattan, O'Connell and Parnell.

Too sharp a distinction should not always be drawn between the revolutionary and the constitutional tradition in Irish nationalism as many individuals had a foot planted in both camps. At a minimum, nationalist rhetoric was often resplendent with military imagery, even if the figures in its pantheon might actually have been royalists scarcely fighting for anything like a modern Irish republic. There was a rhetorical ambivalence in that same tradition: constitutionalism was preferred, but some violence was tolerated. A distinct sense of Irish nationhood and an historical memory of conquest and domination by the foreigner were central to the perspective. In his memoirs, T.D. Sullivan said that two doctrines inspired him and his brother in their direction of *The Nation* from 1855. One was 'that a re-establishment of the Irish Parliament could be won by constitutional agitation, vigorously and wisely carried on'. The other was 'that, war or no war, pike or no pike, there should be no recourse to secret conspiracy' for the pragmatic reason 'that in the existing condition of the country no widespread conspiracy could be safe from governmental spies and informers'.[24] Furthermore, the conservatism of parliamentary nationalism – concerned mainly with asserting full equality for the Irish in essentially English structures – was compatible with the romantic conservatism and ideological agrarianism of the Celtic revival of the time.[25] However, among the revolutionary separatists a distinction must be made between those who considered themselves as the elite vanguard – able to express what the nation would eventually come to see as its general will – and those whose views were in response to the changing temperament of the people at large. O'Higgins belongs to the later category: his views evolved with the people. Certainly this would explain his position a few years later following the Anglo-Irish Treaty of 1921.

In later columns in *The Nationalist and Leinster Times* O'Higgins insisted on the centrality of the policy of abstentionism, that is, non-attendance at the Westminster parliament, to the Sinn Féin or Irish case. He argued, much like his own anti-treaty opponents would three years later, that:

To take the oath of allegiance to England's King and a seat in England's Council chamber means that you recognize and accept the sovereignty of England, that you look to her Parliament as a fit and proper tribunal to decide the question of Ireland's status, that you look for redress to no other tribunal. Such oath taking would mean the abandonment of the claim of independence. It would imply that the issue was a domestic question between Ireland and Great Britain, and not, as Dáil Éireann claimed, an international issue deserving of world attention, specifically the attention of the International Peace Conference then meeting at Versailles.[26]

In other columns O'Higgins discussed unionism and the attitude of Sinn Féin toward Ulster. He challenged the suggestion that the unionists be seen as 'natural conservatives', who desired to preserve the institutions of one's country 'against innovation and change'. Instead, he construed their beloved 1800 Act of Union as a rejection of a nation's history rather than a conserving measure, and he repeated Daniel O'Connell's description of a defender of the Union as being comparable to that 'of the receiver of property which he well knows to have been stolen'. He regarded the Act of Union as having been fathered by bribery and corruption, and blamed it for the depopulation of Ireland, the inhibition of its industries and trade, and the disproportionate taxation of Ireland for the imperial exchequer.[27]

Sharing a view that was pervasive in Ireland in the early twentieth century and even later, O'Higgins depicted the unionist community of Ulster as descendants of a 'ruthless confiscation and plantation' of three centuries before and as a minority 'standing in the path of national unity and national progress'. Nonetheless, he was convinced that Ireland, with its 'good digestion', would 'long since have assimilated the Orangeman', as she had the Norman and the Dane, but for the British government's exploitation of the flames of religious bigotry. Even though 'nationalists look coldly on Protestants because for the most part they stand and have stood against our national aspirations', he insisted that 'a self-governing Ireland would never persecute or discriminate' against the Protestants. As for partition or the separation of the Ulster unionists from the rest of Ireland, O'Higgins emphatically asserted that:

The leaders of Sinn Féin will never temporize with or pander to the forces of disloyalty in Ireland whether before or after the recognition of the Irish Republic. They will never admit the right of any portion of Ireland to secede from the Irish nation. If those who were planted in Ireland three centuries on the confiscated territory of the native Irish are not prepared to live in loyalty and obedience to the government then they can leave the country and the Irish government will be prepared to acquire their interests not by confiscation, but by purchase. That is the attitude of Sinn Féin to that which Sir Edward Carson, with considerable audacity, calls 'Ulster'.[28]

Such assertions would be a far cry from the nuanced analysis O'Higgins would make six and a half years later in the wake of the failed effort of a commission to rectify the boundary between the Irish Free State and Northern Ireland.

### BRITISH RESPONSE

Before attempting to understand Irish republican separatists like O'Higgins in 1919–21, an examination of the British position on developments in Ireland is in order. The 1918 general election, in which Sinn Féin achieved an overwhelming victory in Ireland, returned a massive Conservative–Unionist majority to the Westminster parliament. The Prime Minister, David Lloyd George, was a Liberal, but one who had abandoned his own party to lead a predominantly Conservative coalition. Most of his cabinet colleagues were Conservatives, and many, such as Andrew Bonar Law, Arthur Balfour, and Walter Long, were closely associated with the interests of Irish unionism, had opposed the Home Rule Act, and frowned on the disloyalty of the Irish who now supported a movement that had been treasonous during the war. The new government could pride itself on victory in a ghastly war and on the expansion of British imperial authority, admittedly as a League of Nations trustee, to large parts of the old Ottoman Empire and to the overseas German Empire. Accordingly, commitment to the maintenance of the British Empire meant that Irish matters would be weighed in terms of their possible implications on potential nationalist aspirations in other parts of the empire.

On the other hand, there had been considerable evolution in British opinion on the Irish question, even within the ranks of the governing Conservatives. The Home Rule Act had been passed and its application had been delayed only because of the war. The 'post war' peace conference enabled its application to be further postponed until the signing of the last peace treaties with other belligerents. The Prime Minister remained too preoccupied with other issues to give primary attention to Ireland, and took the attitude that the violent campaign that the Volunteers or the IRA had started in Ireland would have to be brought under control before any steps toward home rule could be taken. That effort was considered to be one of law enforcement more than a military campaign, as it was assumed that the IRA, and even Sinn Féin, was not truly reflective of Irish popular wishes. James MacPherson, the Chief Secretary and a home rule Liberal, wished that Sinn Féin be proscribed as an illegal organization. The idea was opposed by Long, the First Lord of the Admiralty, who had earlier been a leader of the Irish Unionists, and chair of the cabinet committee on Irish legislation, who thought it would be impossible to enforce, and H.A.L. Fisher, a Liberal member of the coalition and President of the Board of Education, who argued that the movement was not composed entirely of physical force supporters and had popular Irish support. Regardless of such reservations, the government agreed to proclaim Sinn Féin as illegal in June.[29]

In October 1919, a cabinet committee, chaired by Long and including F.E. Smith (Lord Birkenhead) and Lord French, the Lord Lieutenant, and Macpherson, the Chief Secretary, not being able to 'recommend the policy either of repealing or of postponing the Home Rule Act of 1914', suggested giving home rule to two separate parliaments, one for Northern Ireland and one for Southern Ireland. The measure, which could be seen as the Fourth Home Rule Bill, was ultimately passed in December 1920. The split form of home rule was designed to meet the opposition of Ulster Unionists to inclusion in a Dublin-based home rule system. The Conservatives in government, realizing that resistance to home rule for all of Ireland had become impossible, even among the British electorate, sought an accommodation that would satisfy Ulster Unionist anxieties. Suggestions of an Ulster-wide home rule were abandoned in response to an Ulster Unionist desire to limit the area of Northern Ireland to just six counties, as the inclusion of the whole province would have made the Unionist majority too narrow for comfort. On the other hand, home rule by now had become clearly insufficient for nationalist opinion that had gone much further in its aspirations. It was obvious that Sinn Féin would control the home rule parliament for Southern Ireland and insist on separate and republican status. But the government's imperial concerns foreclosed consideration of anything that would allow further separation.[30]

Still the government remained uncertain as to its proper approach to the IRA insurrection. Chief Secretary James Macpherson hoped to rely on 'all law-abiding citizens here – whether nationalists or unionists' to counter criminality, but to also be conciliatory toward nationalist sentiment.[31] Such a policy assumed that criminalization of the armed insurrectionists would lead to their isolation, but the opposite happened as repressive measures were both damaging to the general public and ineffective against the rebels who seemed to gain support as a result of the public's discomfort. Rebel attacks were able to virtually break the authority of the police, but the government continued to hold back from pursuing a whole-hearted militarization of the situation.

In late 1919, it had become apparent that the RIC, which had borne the brunt of the IRA attacks, needed to be strengthened in personnel and in arms. Some, including Walter Long and the Viceroy, Lord French, supported a military solution, which would entail the option for martial law. Even the Liberal Macpherson moved toward that attitude. But the full employment of the army would be difficult in view of its lowered numbers following 'post war' demobilization, its numerous overseas commitments, and its possible need should domestic disorders erupt from increasing unemployment. However, from January 1920, the army was employed in accord with the Defence of the Realm Act in policing action against committers of outrages and in searches of individuals and buildings.[32]

In April 1920, Hamar Greenwood, another Liberal replaced Macpherson as Chief Secretary, and Neil Macready, who had been Commissioner of the London Police, became the commander of the army in Ireland. Both shared the same view that 'all out warfare' should be avoided and the pursuit of criminality enhanced. As a conciliatory gesture, even hunger-striking prisoners were released. However, in the campaign against the IRA insurrection, the inadequacy of both the RIC and the military employed to assist them was increasingly evident. But since the alternative of massive military reinforcements was regarded as politically unacceptable in Britain, the RIC was reinforced by new recruits from Britain, many being demobilized soldiers. These new members, for whom there was an inadequate supply of police uniforms, had to wear Black RIC hat and army khakis, which earned them the nickname of 'Black and Tans'. Their total numbers would amount to between 2,000 and 3,000 in a force of about 11,000 to 12,000. In addition, in July, a new force, a special 'gendarmerie' of ex-army officers, was recruited to become an auxiliary division of the RIC. The concept was championed by Winston Churchill, the Secretary of State for the Colonies, at a joint meeting of the cabinet and the Irish executive on 23 July 1921. The group, the 'Auxiliaries', which ultimately numbered almost 1,500 and were under the distinct command of General F.P. Crozier, would become as infamous as the Black and Tans in their repressive behaviour, particularly their pursuit of a policy of reprisals.[33]

The following month a Restoration of Order in Ireland Act established a system just short of complete martial law. Dublin Castle called the act 'a strong measure', but the army found it 'too slow and cumbrous to be really effective'. It allowed the army to use martial courts in certain situations, but did not give it control over the police.[34]

### REVOLUTION AND COURTSHIP

It was in this atmosphere and while being an official in a revolutionary government waging a war of independence, that O'Higgins undertook the successful pursuit of the hand of Brigid Cole. A Dubliner, one of two daughters of a twice-married widow, and a cousin of the Provincial of the Carmelite Order in Ireland, she taught English at St Mary's College, Knockbeg, Co. Carlow. He got to know her through his Sinn Féin activism. The rector of the school at which she taught, Father Patrick Doyle, one of the seminary instructors who had allowed O'Higgins to smoke in their quarters, had permitted him and other Sinn Féiners to use Knockbeg as an occasional hiding place. One faculty member, an instructor in Irish, was Gearoid O'Sullivan, subsequently one of Collins' right-hand men and later Adjutant-General of the Free State Army.[35] O'Sullivan also was attracted to Brigid Cole. She preferred O'Higgins, but O'Sullivan's continued interest caused her great anxiety and was a potential cause for bad relations between the two suitors. O'Higgins advised her to tell O'Sullivan where things stood: 'It is your affair primarily. But you should do what you think best for *yourself*. If you do that no one in the picture, or out of it, will have any right to complain.' Obviously O'Sullivan was disappointed, as O'Higgins noted in a letter a month later:

> I am sorry that he has taken it that way – the suggestion that I sought your 'arbitration' is just a bit bitter and unjust. However it lies with him to define what future relations are to be – I could not think of going on the defensive in this matter. I risked my life's happiness in my scrupulous care to avoid what he holds me guilty of, and with a pretty clear conception of his present condition. I believe that to lose would have meant much more to me. I am sorry for him from my heart and unless he makes it impossible for me I will be as good a friend to him as he has in the world.[36]

Later O'Higgins and O'Sullivan would be antagonists in the 1924 crisis that grew out of the Army Mutiny, as O'Higgins would force the resignations of O'Sullivan and his colleagues in the Army Council of the Irish Free State Army. (See Chapter 5.)

Kevin O'Higgins' letters to Brigid Cole indicate his reaction to major developments in the War of Independence. In one he interpreted a press interview given by Lloyd George as showing that the other side (the British) had 'degenerated into the blustery stage with a suggestion of hysteria'. As for the Sinn Féin–nationalist side, he insisted 'we'll hold the line – with a few stones in our pocket for the psychological moment'.[37] In response to Brigid's asking if he could understand the position of those who had not taken a side in the struggle, 'the man on the hedge', he noted: 'I think I can just glimpse it, dearie, but I haven't much sympathy with it. There oughtn't to be any man on the hedge at present, and if there weren't the load wouldn't be cutting the hearts of those who are pulling it.'[38]

In late September and early October, 1920, General Macready and Field Marshall Henry Wilson, the Chief of the Imperial General Staff, suggested a policy of reprisal against communities that sheltered IRA members who had committed attacks. While the Prime Minister in first reaction thought no government could take responsibility for such, within a short time there appeared official directions ambiguous enough to allow such. The Chief Secretary, Greenwood, argued that reprisals were not taking place, but the reality was such that even Churchill agreed to ask the cabinet to regularize a policy of reprisal in order to inhibit the troops doing such on their own. In late September Macready had produced a strategic plan to intern all IRA members and to clear all the major cities, then the railway lines, then troublesome areas of the southwest, and finally the remaining rural areas. However, soon after the government recognized the futility of such and remained satisfied with applying the Restoration of Order in Ireland Act and hoped for a popular acceptance of the Government of Ireland Act.[39]

In a letter to his fiancée, O'Higgins categorized this British campaign, which he referred to the 'Big Push', as 'a dismal failure'. Even though the RIC had conducted a reprisal raid on Balbriggan for the killing of a popular officer on September 20 and similar episodes occurred in Lahinch, Miltown Malbay, Ennistymon and Mallow, O'Higgins remained as certain: 'we are right and we are going on even if it snows ink. Furthermore the blood of brave men has been worth Independence in every land, in this land it is not going to be sold for "Home Rule".'[40] A month after the death of the imprisoned 'hunger striking' Lord Mayor of Cork, Terence MacSwiney, three weeks after the hanging of medical student Kevin Barry for his participation in an IRA ambush in Dublin, and the day after Bloody Sunday, when Michael Collins' special squad killed fourteen suspected British secret service agents and the Black and Tans fired on a crowd at a football match in Croke Park killing twelve, O'Higgins noted that ''tis a long lane that hasn't got a turning, if only the "plain people", to use a Wilsonism, keep a hoult o'themselves. We have not good qualities for this kind of fight – too clever, too imaginative, and too ruddy cynical.'[41]

O'Higgins, writing at the most intense period of the War of Independence, was unsympathetic to various peace feelers then emanating from the nationalist side. Some members of the Galway County Council called for a truce and a peace settlement. The Galway Urban District Council did the same. Members of the Catholic hierarchy had written to newspapers and to British government officials calling for a truce, as did Roger Sweetman, a Sinn Féin member elected for Wexford North, who proposed a conference that would include representatives of the Irish and the British Labour Parties, the Catholic hierarchy, and members of a private group, the Irish Peace Conference, but not necessarily Dáil Éireann representatives. Even Father Michael O'Flanagan, an important figure in the earlier history of Sinn Féin who was often silenced by the hierarchy for his political radicalism, telegraphed Lloyd George on December 5 calling for a truce.[42] O'Higgins was dismissive of these proposals and alluded to the scriptural warning 'against the kind o' fool that cries "Peace! Peace! when there is no Peace"'. In his eyes such premature peace advocates were as dangerous 'as the real murder gang for many will die of (or because of) their flatulence – alias windiness'.[43]

O'Higgins himself had one particularly narrow escape during that fearful November. His local government staff was using as a temporary headquarters an upstairs room in the Dublin County Council offices in Parnell Square. One day about noon Auxiliaries raided the building and ordered O'Higgins and his staff to come to the downstairs hallway where they joined the county council staff standing in a silent group under a heavily armed guard. Everyone's name and address was taken, which for O'Higgins and staff meant giving the fictitious names and identities used in the quarters where they lived. O'Higgins' pseudonym was Frank Wilson and it was assumed in his boarding house in nearby Gardiner Street that he was a law student. They were kept in the hall for over two hours while the Auxiliaries searched the building. One very tall and brutish Auxiliary in the interim occasionally struck some of those under guard. He asked O'Higgins if he'd like to get the contents of his revolver. O'Higgins' sarcastic reply, 'I'd hardly feel the last half dozen', provoked the Auxiliary into striking him in the face. At any rate the Auxiliaries did not find whatever they were looking for, probably some Dublin Council account books, and departed, unaware that they had had under their control 'the whole Local Government of Dáil Éireann with all the documents, records and staff'.[44] He noted to his fiancée that he 'had a stroke of luck today, if you can call it luck, was in the hands of our friends for over an hour and by an extraordinary fluke got clear'. He noted the necessity of a changed identity by telling her that Wilson was dead: 'he was a fellow of infinite jest but even his buoyant spirit could not contend against the prevailing gloom.' He added that Wilson's place would 'be taken *pro-tem* by a man named Hennessy' whose address would be the same as his predecessor.[45]

By this time, even O'Higgins' father, who shared the parliamentary nationalism of his wife's family, had, like most in Ireland, approved Sinn Féin's mandate. What expedited this evolution in his political attitudes was having his home frequently raided by the authorities in search of Kevin, as well as his sons Thomas and Brian, both active in the IRA. When the sons were not found, the father was apprehended and imprisoned at the Curragh. Brian joined him there soon after. His father's arrest did not leave him 'too depressed'; as he reckoned that 'our old clan can stand its share of the racket without putting up a whine abaht it'. He boasted: 'Proud I am of them all for the way in which they have risen to the big test.'

Also imprisoned was O'Higgins' assistant, Rory O'Connor, a

young engineer educated at Clongowes Wood and at University College Dublin, who had worked in Canada for four years, and who, in addition to being O'Higgins' assistant in Local Government, was the Director of Engineering for the IRA during the War of Independence and had directed a number of jail escapes in Britain and in Ireland. O'Higgins had great confidence and regard for him, as would be demonstrated by his later having him as his best man. Upon hearing of his friend and colleague being imprisoned with his father, O'Higgins told Brigid that she would 'be interested and a little amused to hear that R [Rory O'Connor] and "Pa" have coincided – verily strange bedfellows – R says that Pa is very well and healthy and that he was glad to strike on someone that knew and had worked with K [Kevin O'Higgins].The acquaintance will be good for the old man as R is certainly amongst the best we can show.'[46]

O'Higgins contrasted his family's 'patient and dignified sufferings' with 'the mean-spirited effusions of the Bishop of Cork and many of his colleagues'. Those members of the hierarchy were unsympathetic to a revolutionary struggle whose moral value O'Higgins found 'unquestionable' and whose idealistic endurance had been unmatched in history 'since the persecution of the early Christians'.[47] Ironically, O'Higgins' outburst of anti-clericalism was directed at a bishop who was a cousin and namesake of Judge Daniel F. Cohalan, the leader of the American support organization for the uprising, the Friends of Irish Freedom. Bishop Cohalan had rejected the legitimacy of Dáil Éireann and had excommunicated IRA members who had killed police or soldiers. Cohalan's outright opposition was not characteristic of the hierarchy. While they did not give formal support to the War of Independence, most were severely critical of British policy and muted in their criticism of IRA actions.[48] Nonetheless, O'Higgins shared the disappointment of many Sinn Féiners in having not received formal endorsement from the church, as he lamented that 'the Catholic Church has not the courage of its convictions – never had. It has bowed the knee to force, always muttering "render unto Caesar" without any inconvenient inquiries as to the basis of Caesar's power.'[49]

In December, the government finally accepted the concept of waging a full-scale military campaign and proclaimed martial law, although limiting it to four Munster counties, Cork, Kerry, Limerick, and Tipperary. Martial law was supposed to bring unity of command and ostensibly bring the unrestrained Black and Tans and Auxiliaries under military control. It allowed the military to try and impose heavy penalties, including capital punishment, on those in possession of arms or harbouring rebels, to restrict popular movement, control the press, and intern suspects at discretion.[50] However, concurrent with martial law was increasing popular criticism of Irish policy within Britain that would eventually move the Prime Minister to seek a negotiated settlement with Sinn Féin that would go beyond home rule to a different level of autonomy – dominion status. But before examining that, let us look at O'Higgins' role as part of the revolutionary Dáil Éireann government.

### O'HIGGINS IN LOCAL GOVERNMENT

His work as assistant to William T. Cosgrave, Dáil Éireann's Minister for Local Government, dealt with the bricks and mortar that enabled self-governance to succeed in Ireland. Only in recent years have scholars begun to turn their attention to this subject.[51] But to understand the task facing Cosgrave and O'Higgins the significant developments in local government in the previous quarter century must be appreciated. The Local Government Act of 1898 had abolished the landlord-dominated grand jury system of local government and replaced it with county and borough (city) councils elected by the ratepayers, as well as, on a more local level, rural district councils and urban district councils for the middle and smaller towns. Furthermore, the various land purchase acts, which provided state-backed mortgages, had enabled many tenants to become owners and ratepayers, therefore eligible to vote. As a consequence, Irish local government had become virtually democratic (equal suffrage for women had not been realized in Ireland or Great Britain and non-rate-paying males, such as adult sons, agricultural labourers, etc., could not vote). The elected councils were financed in part by local rates, but also received generous grants from the British government through the Local Government Board headquarters in the Customs House in Dublin.

The major objective of William T. Cosgrave and his assistant minister, Kevin O'Higgins, was to have the local elected bodies formally recognize the Dáil Éireann government. Their recognition was as important as, and a vital preliminary to, gaining recognition from other nations in demonstrating the legitimacy of Dáil Éireann. An opportunity to achieve such came when the British government decided to have Irish local government elections in Ireland. Those elections had been scheduled for 1917, but were postponed because of the war. The authorities finally called them for 1920. Assuming that Sinn Féin's following was small, and that the revolt could be dealt with better politically than militarily, they expected the local voting would demonstrate the shallowness of Sinn Féin's popular support. The voting employed the use of single transferable voting (the form of proportional representation still used in the Irish Republic), which it was hoped would even more clearly indicate Sinn Féin electoral weakness.

The voting for the city corporations and urban councils, where Sinn Féin support was weaker, took place in January, while voting for county and rural councils, where Sinn Féin support was stronger, would not be until June. The Sinn Féin performance in urban areas was expected to be weak and possibly to discourage support for the party in the June polls for the county and rural councils. But in the January election Sinn Féin did much better than anticipated, as 560 of its 717 nominees for the 1,816 seats were elected. The Irish Labour Party got 394 of its 595 candidates returned and many of them were on amicable terms with Sinn Féin. The Parliamentary Party candidates won only 238 seats, other independents 269, and Unionists 355. As for the control of the various councils, Sinn Féin and/or nationalists had a majority in nine of the eleven corporations (cities) and sixty-two of the ninety-nine urban councils (middle and small size towns).[52]

The revolutionary Department of Local Government had asked those councils having a clear Sinn Féin majority to pass resolutions of allegiance to Dáil Éireann, while those whose majorities were a combination of Sinn Féin and other nationalists were asked to pass more limited resolutions calling for the recognition of 'such form of government as the majority of the Irish people may select'.[53] However, the municipal bodies were hesitant to pass any motion 'pending the result of the County and Rural Council and Poor Board elections' scheduled for June. The department itself was reluctant to pressure the councils to take any action that might be used by the British to justify postponing the June elections. Accordingly, it modified its instructions to the local bodies, telling them just to withhold information that would facilitate the collection of income tax by the British authorities and to strike no rates on land or property to meet malicious and criminal injury claims awarded at local government expense because of IRA activity.[54]

On 19 April 1920 O'Higgins had to take over as substitute

minister when Cosgrave was arrested. In this position he took part in Dáil Éireann cabinet meetings. He displayed impatience at the cabinet's failure to make any definite decision about 'the future attitude of Republican Boards and Councils to the English Local Government Board'. In an effort to develop an appropriate strategy, O'Higgins held a meeting in Dublin on 11 May 1920 with eight people who had practical experience in local administration, including the Lord Mayors of Cork and Limerick (Terence MacSwiney, who would later die on hunger strike, and Michael O'Callaghan, who would be murdered by the Black and Tans), the accountants of the Kerry County Council and of Dublin City, and the secretary of the Monaghan County Council, and a report was prepared. Some proposed what O'Higgins labelled the 'clear-cut' republican approach: to cease contact with the Local Government Board. While he regarded that approach as ultimately 'eminently desirable' and 'the dignified consistent Republican course to adopt', and one which 'circumstances would render it inevitable', he thought it inappropriate at first since 'no adequate preparation has been made for its immediate application'. He argued that a uniform scheme of cost saving had to be developed for the councils to follow in order to be able to function independently of the subsidies from the Local Government Board. However, the Dáil government did not have adequate time to deal with the report of O'Higgins' committee and 'no decision was arrived at' as to what approach to take.[55]

In his report to the Dáil Éireann government on 2 June 1920, O'Higgins was cautious. He presented several reasons why the local bodies should avoid the clear break with the Local Government Board and the consequent loss of subsidies. First, the councils consisted 'for the most part of men with no experience of local administration'. The Local Government Board would probably declare illegal any rate increases the councils would levy to offset the loss of government grants. That in time would give a justification to political opponents of Sinn Féin (who probably paid a dispro-portionate portion of the rates) to not pay. Furthermore, banks would not allow customary overdrafts if the public bodies were in open revolt with the Local Government Board. Lastly, refusal to forward minutes to the latter or accept their auditing would allow that body to refuse to sanction loans by the local bodies from the Board of Works or the British Treasury for housing, drainage and other public works, which in turn would alienate organized labour.

In O'Higgins' eyes, a much better approach than a clean break would be 'to endeavor to manouver the enemy into taking over the burden of local administration'. Failing this, the 'Boards and Councils should carry on until by the stopping of grants etc., the financial position would have become hopeless' and, at that point, 'simultaneously cease to function'. He anticipated the British would employ criminal and malicious injury claims as a means of disciplining local bodies. When the latter would not strike rates to meet such claims, the British government would seek to take the funds from the bank accounts of the local bodies, as well as from any grants-in-aid. But since the councils had until April of the following year to strike any rate required to meet injury claims, this gave them time to take a number of steps that could minimize expenditure before being confronted with a punitive loss of grants.[56]

Accordingly, after the June elections in which Sinn Féin gained a majority in 29 of the 32 county councils and in 182 of the 206 rural councils, O'Higgins sent instructions that fell just short of formally severing all ties with the Local Government Board. However, the local bodies were told to pass resolutions acknowledging 'the authority of Dáil Éireann, as the duly elected government of the Irish People', not to provide the British authorities with lists of ratepayers or council-paid salaries and wages that would be helpful in preparing new income tax schedules, nor to strike any rates to meet criminal and malicious injury claims. In addition, they were to refer wage disputes to Dáil Éireann Courts (bodies that had been formed throughout the country as an alternative to the existing court system), to settle disputes with contractors in Dáil Éireann Courts of Arbitration, and, where possible, purchase only Irish materials and appoint 'only loyal citizens of the Republic' to the public service, giving preference to candidates having 'a knowledge of Irish'.[57]

In a Dáil Éireann debate on June 29, O'Higgins repeated his apprehensions about a premature break with the Local Government Board by the local bodies 'when they were in a state of unpreparedness'. To advance their readiness for the break, he moved that a commission of experts be set up to 'enquire into the possibility of carrying on local administration without financial aid from the English government', and 'to report as to reforms and economies in local administration and particularly in the Poor Law system that would enable councils to meet altered financial conditions if it is decided to break with the English Local Government Board'.[58] That commission, which O'Higgins chaired, and of which his assistant, Rory O'Connor, was secretary, first sat on July 27. Among the

sixteen other members were Terence MacSwiney, Michael
O'Callaghan, James MacNeill, the brother of Eoin and later the
second Governor General of the Irish Free State, and future Free
State ministers, Joseph McGrath, J.J. Walsh, and Eamon Duggan.
Meetings were held on August 3 and 4, after which an interim report
was submitted to the Dáil.

But on July 29, the Local Government Board itself forced the issue
which the commission was considering – the relationship of local
councils to the Local Government Board – by insisting that the local
councils submit their accounts, 'to audit and be prepared to conform
to the rules and orders of the Local Government Board', or, in failing
to do so, risk the loss of loans and grants for housing, road
construction and public health improvements that would be drawn
from the Imperial Exchequer. Most of the councils, aside from those
dominated by unionists, refused to comply. This made more
immediate the problem that the O'Higgins-chaired commission was
examining: how to finance themselves with the loss of grant monies
amounting to about one-fifth of their annual income.

The interim recommendations of O'Higgins' commission were
that the local bodies take necessary steps to safeguard what funds
they had at present, by ceasing to deposit money into banks
designated as treasuries by the Local Government Board, and
instead follow a technique devised in County Clare of working with
collaborating bankers to place the funds in private accounts free
from official scrutiny. The local bodies themselves were also directed
to economize by abolishing workhouses and making collective
purchases of supplies. Organized labour was asked to restrain its
demands for wage increases from councils and to prevent
transportation of property seized by the British from local bodies or
citizens. The local councils were also asked to keep duplicate copies
of their rate books and documents and to safeguard them. Naturally
they were expected to 'formally cease all further connection with the
English Local Government Board, by refusing to communicate with
them or to admit their auditors or other servants to the premises of
the Council'.[59]

The commission continued to have additional sittings in August
before issuing a final report in which it gave more specific
instructions as to how to meet the loss of income from grants. The
recommendations reflected not just an effort to deal with the
shortfall being experienced by the denial of the Imperial subsidy, but
also gave an opportunity to force reforms on local government,

specifically the imposition of economy and efficiency, against a tradition of jobbery and localism. Tom Garvin describes the mindset of the Dáil Éireann Department of Local Government, that is, the department of Cosgrave and O'Higgins, as having

> a general and sometimes intense distrust for the personnel in local government... commonly coupled with a contempt for the Edwardian Irish political system's characteristic plethora of small, parasitic and idle representative bodies. Sinn Féin, very much a party of youth, had its roots in a puritan and patriotic reaction against the Irish Party, which, in the view of the separatists, had demoralized and corrupted political culture and contributed mightily to the psychological enslavement of the Irish people.[60]

The commission had hoped to make the largest immediate savings in the refusal of local bodies to pay interest for outstanding loans from the Imperial Exchequer, as well as other common fees and payments for imperial agents and services such as sheriffs, courtroom rents, etc. Other savings were expected from the abolition of workhouses, the return of some asylum inmates to their families, and the reduction of TB patients in hospitals, the amalgamation of hospitals, the purchase of cottages by tenant labourers rather than public subsidization of their rents, a general economy in administration, and a pooling of public contracts by the local bodies. All these savings, it was anticipated, would meet about one-half of the loss from the denial of the Local Government Board's subsidy. Since it was considered 'most inexpedient and possibly not practical' to try to meet the remaining deficit by raising rates, public bodies were urged 'to reduce expenditure and carry out the reforms'. Assistance from national revenue (that is, the revenue received in various ways by Dáil Éireann) could be made available in specific cases. But any additional burdens on the national revenue should be met by diverting funds that ordinarily went to the British Exchequer, such as annuity payments consequent on the land purchase programmes, estate and death duties, and fees for various licences for public houses, dogs, auctioneering, guns, and the sale of sweets, and directing them to the Dáil Éireann treasury.

The final report made very detailed recommendations about how the Local Government Department of Dáil Éireann should replace the Local Government Board 'as the agency constituted to supervise and control local bodies in the interests of the ratepayers'. To that end it called for the establishment of an inspectorate in housing and public health, and the appointment of a substantial number of auditors to supervise the various levels of local government and of clerks for 'examining minutes, returns of rate collectors, and other statements' that had to be furnished to the department by the local bodies.

The ministry was attempting, in the midst of a revolution and while under police scrutiny and intimidation, to function as a normal government department. In other words, they were acting not just as leaders of a protest or abstentionist movement, but were actually taking on the work of governance. O'Higgins' efforts in these ventures were a foretaste of the role of state-builder he would play from immediately after the Anglo-Irish Treaty of December 1921, through the Civil War, and in the years immediately after.[61]

There were other weapons the Local Government Board could take against the pro-Dáil Éireann local councils besides the denial of grants and loans. One was legal action against rate collectors if they did not deposit their receipts into the banks designated as treasuries by the Lord Lieutenant. Failure to do so could jeopardize the personal sureties the rate collectors had been required to deposit upon appointment to their positions. Another instrument was the use of garnishee orders subjecting the funds of local bodies to the claims for violent and malicious injury caused by the actions of both the IRA and the Crown forces. In addition, the local bodies had to contend with the simple resistance from ratepayers. The non-complying ratepayers were not necessarily unionists, who often were faithful payers even though they had philosophical reasons not to pay, but Sinn Féiners themselves either filled with an anti-government mindset or resentful of possible economic reforms that the Dáil Éireann ministry had imposed in their local areas.[62]

Cosgrave reported to the Dáil about such difficulties being encountered, such as garnishee orders to collect malicious damage awards from the rates and *mandamus* writs against rebellious local authorities, which would force them to either go on the run or face imprisonment. In suggesting how to deal with these difficulties, O'Higgins had a more radical attitude than the more conservative Cosgrave. He saw as a major problem the reluctance of the rate collectors to jeopardize their personal bonds, which could happen if they did not lodge rates into officially designated accounts. Believing that 'nearly all the rate collectors were timid', and likely to not deposit rate receipts deposited in secret accounts with cooperative bankers, but rather put them in the officially designated accounts, he suggested dispensing with them altogether and using the IRA to collect the rates.[63] He doubted the British authorities would proceed against payers who had receipts given by the IRA, or that *mandamus* orders would be carried out or enforced. The garnishee orders were a more serious danger, and he suggested 'direct action against the parties securing the garnishee order or the parties who paid', in contrast to Cosgrave's belief that it was unjust to attack a man who made a payment on a garnishee order as obliged by English law. O'Higgins insisted it had to be seen as 'a question of a trial of strength between two governments'. Such an attitude was reflected in a circular sent out to the pro-Dáil Éireann local authorities warning that 'it would be a treasonable practice to have any communication with the Enemy Department', and such 'would be dealt with accordingly'.[64]

The temperamental differences between O'Higgins and his ministerial senior, Cosgrave, which persisted into the Free State era,[65] were obvious at the time. O'Higgins noted upon Cosgrave's return from brief imprisonment in 1920:

> things is wuss stead of better with C. back – he really gives very little attendance messing about to corporation meetings, etc. – and then when he does blow in he'll take up some business at random, give some wholly outlandish ruling on it and blow out again most complacently, feeling that he has saved the state sufficiently for one day. So my attendance now has the positive side of getting through work and the negative side of stopping old C. from doing things hopelessly reactionary... the man is only fitted to drive his wife about the countryside in a smart pony and trap and return the salutes of the peasantry with the proper mixture of graciousness and bonhomie. His corporation reputation is the kingship of the one-eyed man amongst the blind.[66]

At one point O'Higgins even came close to resigning and the Dáil Éireann cabinet expected Cosgrave to recommend a new assistant minister.[67]

Regardless of their temperamental differences, Cosgrave and O'Higgins and their department vigorously pursued the objective of local government economy and efficiency, aiming their fire particularly at such nests of jobbery as poor boards and road works. With regard to unemployed road workers in Laois, O'Higgins said that 'the Department's attitude is not that these men should be re-employed if at all possible', but should be re-employed only 'if the County Council is in a position to pay wages regularly'. The task undertaken by the Dáil Éireann Department of Local Government would have been extraordinary in normal times, never mind against the background of a revolutionary war in which officials of that department were in hiding from the authorities. A handful of inspectors made their rounds to the various local bodies, all of which had to submit regular reports in double envelopes to various mail drops in Dublin from where the inner envelope would be forwarded to the department at whatever location it would be operating at the time. The detailed intricacy of the administrative undertaking in such circumstances was striking. To that must be added the mission of achieving government reform, specifically the imposition of economy and efficiency against a tradition of jobbery and localism.[68]

An excellent summary of the achievement of the Department of Local Government was the report given to the Second Dáil Éireann after the truce of 1921 by Cosgrave. He noted the difficult situation caused by the withdrawal of £1,750,000 of grants usually received from the Local Government Board. 'On top of that came the opposition to the rate collectors which was practically universal throughout the country.' Only in a few areas were the collectors willing to lodge money in treasuries other than those designated by the British authorities. Furthermore, there was a popular inclination to avoid paying any rates, if possible, to anyone, even to the local bodies supportive of the popular national cause. 'In most places rate collection ceased altogether,' and at one point it came near to local councils having to close down. As for the problem of garnishee orders against local councils, Cathal Brugha, the Minister for Defence, had directed his office to threaten solicitors who had obtained such decrees, and all but three of the decrees were withdrawn. However, 'agitation against the payment of rates' remained a continuing problem, and had been intensified by increases in rates and by a slump in agricultural prices. Cosgrave argued that 'there was no extravagance' in local government, and 'a great tuning up had been done' bringing 'greater efficiency than since the Local Government Act [1898] was passed'. Believing that the Local Government Department had come out very well during 'the period of intensified terrorism [August 1920–July 1921]', he paid 'the highest tribute to his colleague, K. O'Higgins, and to the staff'.[69]

SOFTENING VIEWS AND THE TRUCE

During the War of Independence O'Higgins' public pronouncements, such as the previously quoted articles, and comments in private letters to his fiancée, Brigid Cole, make him appear a hardline republican separatist, almost a member of what Tom Garvin and other scholars have labelled 'The Public Band'. This term refers to revolutionaries of a Jacobin nature whose 'political mandate seemed to belong to their militant organization rather than to a parliamentary assembly'.[70] But that would change in time as Garvin noted that both Cosgrave and O'Higgins 'were acutely aware that Sinn Féin's psychological hold over the people was fragile and conditional: the victories of 1918 [general election] and 1920 [local government elections] were due to abnormal political conditions; come peacetime, Sinn Féin would have to deal with large numbers of people whose political sympathies were elsewhere, whether it be with Labour, farmers' interests, or unionist.'[71] The practical experience of directing a non-military government department, even if in unusual circumstances, and the day-to day encounters with ordinary routine questions tempered the zeal of young O'Higgins and readied him for the more pragmatic role he would play in the Irish Free State.[72]

Another factor was the mediating influence of O'Higgins' fiancée, Brigid Cole. None of her letters to him have survived, but there are four folders of his letters to her during this period, 1920 and 1921. While O'Higgins' letters display the revolutionary zeal, one can also detect in them, no doubt in response to her entreaties, an appreciation of other people to whom the situation was not all black and white, but who were bearing a good deal of the discomfort that had been brought about by the combatants. In the same letter written before he proposed, in which he advised her not to be troubled by her earlier suitor, O'Sullivan, he commented philosophically:

> It's a queer complex kind of old world, and just at present this particular clod of ours is about the most complex of the whole darned lump with the juggernaut of politics butting into every phase of our existence. It's different for us, we have the fun of the fight, but it's bad to think of the old wheel catching little people who didn't go looking for trouble – at least from that quarter.[73]

His letters in May 1921 indicate optimism about the political situation. That was the month in which elections were called, in accord with the Government of Ireland Act, 1920, for two separate parliaments, one for Northern Ireland and one for Southern Ireland. Unionists won 40 of the 52 seats in the northern parliament, whereas all candidates for the 128 seats in the southern parliament were unopposed. All but four of the latter refused to recognize the Parliament for Southern Ireland and instead assembled as a second Dáil Éireann. Peace manoeuvres had already begun, including a 5 May meeting between James Craig, the Northern Irish Unionist leader, and Eamon de Valera. On 17 May, O'Higgins was confident that 'despite all appearances to the contrary "things" are tending very well and any week now might bring momentous changes'.[74] In a subsequent letter he told his fiancée that she was 'really privileged to live in the most absorbingly interesting time in the history of this little clod of ours'.[75] By the end of May he was convinced that they had the British 'fought to a standstill quite apart from the recent debacle [Customs House assault]'.[76] On July 9 his perception that the struggle had reached a standstill was borne out when a truce was signed that went into effect two days later. But ahead lay extensive diplomatic manoeuvring about the credentials of the negotiators and the agenda of the meetings, which would determine the relationship between Ireland and Britain.

## NOTES

1. Senia Paseta, *Before the Revolution: Nationalism, Social Change and Ireland's Catholic Elite, 1879–1922* (Cork: Cork University Press, 1999), pp. 1–3, 153.
2. By the nineteenth century the family name, O hUiginn, had been anglicized to Higgins, with the 'O' being reattached only with Kevin's involvement in the Sinn Féin cause.
3. Thomas F. O'Higgins, *A Double Life* (Dublin: Town House, 1996), pp. 3–6.
4. Healy was T.D.'s nephew by marriage and later became his son-in-law. Healy's brother, Maurice, married a daughter of A.M.
5. Conor Cruise O'Brien, *Parnell and His Party, 1880–1890* (Oxford: Clarendon Press, 1957), chapter I and II.
6. Frank Callanan, *T. M. Healy* (Cork: Cork University Press, 1996), pp. 159, 225–6, and 441.
7. Three of the children died in infancy.
8. O'Higgins, *A Double Life*, pp. 9–10.
9. Patrick Hogan, 'Kevin O'Higgins. An appreciation', *an t-Oglach*, October 1917, pp. 12–13.
10. Terence de Vere White, *Kevin O'Higgins* (Dublin: Anvil Books, 1986 edn; first published, London: Methuen, 1948), pp. 6–9.
11. Robert Kee, *The Green Flag* (first published London: Weidenfield and Nicolson, 1972; London: Penguin Books, 2000 edition), p. 534.
12. Kathleen O'Higgins to Brigid O'Higgins, 5 April 1928, *O'Higgins Papers*, Book 5.

13. Paseta, *Before the Revolution*, pp. 151–3.
14. de Vere White, *Kevin O'Higgins*, p. 13.
15. Richard Egan, 'Kevin O'Higgins, the Tullamore Realm Trial and the ideas of a complex revolutionary', *Offaly Historical and Archaeological Society Annual Journal* (2004).
16. Kevin O'Higgins, 'To P.H. Pearse', Belfast Prison, 5 September 1918, *O'Higgins Papers*, Book 6.
17. Kevin O'Higgins, 'Easter Week, 1916', *O'Higgins Papers*, Book 6.
18. Kevin O'Higgins, 'February 1917', *O'Higgins Papers*, Book 6.
19. Brian M. Walker, ed. *Parliamentary Election Results in Ireland, 1918–1992* (Dublin: Royal Irish Academy, 1992), pp. 4–9.
20. Charles Townshend, *The British Campaign in Ireland, 1919–1921* (London: Oxford University Press, 1975), pp. 8–12.
21. Only in August 1919 did the Irish Volunteers, who would be called the Irish Republican Army, take an oath to the Irish Republic (or Dáil Éireann) and only in March 1921 did the Dáil take full responsibility for the IRA. D.G. Boyce, *Englishmen and Irish Troubles: British Public Opinion and the Making of Irish Policy, 1918–22* (Cambridge, MA: MIT Press, 1972), pp. 43–4.
22. Kevin O'Higgins, 'The Disloyal Irish', *The Nationalist and Leinster Times*, 31 April 1919. However, it is hard to imagine how Henry Grattan, whose celebrated achievement of Irish parliamentary independence in 1782 had been far short of what the Home Rule Act provided, would have interpreted this definition of national degeneracy.
23. Kevin O'Higgins, 'Still Conquered', *The Nationalist and Leinster Times*, 7 June 1919. John Dillon attributed the Parliamentary Party's collapse to 'blunders in not realising what was going on, digging a gulf between the party and the younger generation', and 'Redmond's persistence in what had been called his imperialist policy long after it had become apparent to me that such a course would inevitably throw the country into the hands of S.F.' [John Dillon to T.P. O'Connor, 25, 28, and 29 December 1918, F.S.L. Lyons, *John Dillon* (London: Routledge & Kegan Paul, 1968), pp. 454–5.] The attitude of young talent like O'Higgins proved the accuracy of Dillon's analysis of the Parliamentary Party's failures.
24. T.D. Sullivan, *Recollections of Troubled Times in Irish Politics* (Dublin: Sealy, Brynes & Walker, 1905), p. 14, UCDA, *Healy Papers*, P6/E/19.
25. Paseta, *Before the* Revolution, pp. 151–3.
26. Kevin O'Higgins, 'Abstention', *The Nationalist and Leinster Times*, 14 June 1919.
27. Kevin O'Higgins, 'Unionism', *The Nationalist and Leinster Times*, 28 June 1919.
28. Kevin O'Higgins, 'Sinn Féin and Ulster,' *The Nationalist and Leinster Times*, 12 July 1919.
29. Townshend, *The British Campaign in Ireland*, p. 24.
30. *Ibid.*, pp. 33–6.
31. *Ibid.*, p. 21.
32. *Ibid.*, pp. 47–9.
33. *Ibid.*, pp. 92–5; Martin Gilbert, *Winston Churchill: 1916–1922, The Stricken World* (Boston: Houghton Mifflin, 1975), IV, pp. 450–4.
34. Townshend, *The British Campaign in Ireland*, pp. 101–2. Thomas Jones, *Whitehall Diary* (London: Oxford University Press, 1971), III, pp. 25–31.
35. National Library, *Rev. Patrick J. Doyle Papers*, MS 13561 (12).
36. Kevin O' Higgins to Brigid Cole, 29 May, 28 June 1920, *O'Higgins Papers*, Book 1.

37. Kevin O'Higgins to Brigid Cole, n.d., *O'Higgins Papers*, Book 1.
38. Kevin O'Higgins to Brigid Cole, 24 June 1920, *O'Higgins Papers*, Book 1.
39. Townshend, *The British Campaign in Ireland*, pp. 119–24.
40. Kevin O'Higgins to Brigid Cole, 5 October 1920, *O'Higgins Papers*, Book 2.
41. Kevin O'Higgins to Brigid Cole, 22 November 1920, *O'Higgins Papers*, Book 2.
42. Arthur Mitchell, *Revolutionary Government in Ireland* (Dublin: Gill and Macmillan, 1995), pp. 220–1.
43. KOH to Brigid Cole, n.d., *O'Higgins Papers*, Book 2.
44. *Sunday Independent*, 17 July 1927.
45. Kevin O'Higgins to Brigid Cole, n.d., *O'Higgins Papers*, Book 3.
46. Kevin O'Higgins to Brigid cole, n.d., *O'Higgins Papers*, Book 3.
47. Kevin O'Higgins to Brigid Cole, n.d, *O'Higgins Papers*, Book 4.
48. Mitchell, *Revolutionary Government in Ireland*, pp. 173–4.
49. Kevin O'Higgins to Bridget Cole, n.d., *O'Higgins Papers*, Book 3.
50. Townshend, *The British Campaign in Ireland*, pp. 133-5.
51. Mary A. Daly, 'Local Government and the First Dáil,' *The Creation of the Dáil*, ed. Brian Farrell (Belfast: Blackwater, 1994), 123-36; Garvin, *1922, The Birth of Irish Democracy* (Dublin: Gill and Macmillan, 1996), pp. 62–91.
52. Mitchell, *Revolutionary Government in Ireland*, pp. 122–6.
53. Report to An Dail, 19 June 1920, *Local Government Department*, NA, DE 2/243.
54. *Ibid.*
55. *Ibid.*
56. Report No. 2, 2 June 1920, *Department of Local Government*, NA, DE 2/243.
57. C. Ó'hUiginn to County Councils, Rural District Courts, Boards of Guardians, 21 June 1920, *Department of Local Government*, NA, DE 2/243.
58. *Dáil Éireann Debates*, 29 June 1920, 169–72,185.
59. Interim Report, 6 August 1920, *Commission of Enquiry into Local Government*, NA, DE 2/243.
60. Tom Garvin, *1922*, p. 85.
61. Final Report, *Commission of Enquiry Into Local Government*, NA, DE 2/243.
62. *Dáil Éireann Debates*, 25 January 1921, 245, 259.
63. See his different attitude toward the rate collectors after the War of Independence. Chapter 4.
64. *Dáil Éireann Debates*, 11 March 1921, 268–9.
65. In later years O'Higgins would again display an aptitude for drastic action that would contrast with the more conciliatory Cosgrave, but then O'Higgins would be acting from a conservative perspective. See Chapter 5 on the Army Crisis.
66. Kevin O'Higgins to Brigid Cole, n.d., *O'Higgins Papers*, Book 1.
67. *Cabinet Minutes*, 27 August 1920, NA, DE 1/2.
68. Daly, p. 133. No doubt such conservatism would meet with present-day disapproval, as for example, in an exhibit, 'A Nation and Not a Rabble – Ireland in the Year July 1921–June 1922', arranged by the National Archives and originally hosted by the Ministry for Arts, Culture and the Gaeltacht in February 1997. Paul Gallagher, 'Other lives, glimpsed', *The Irish Times*, 8 February 1997.
69. *Dáil Éireann, Private Session*, 22 August 1921, 35–8.
70. Tom Garvin, *1922*, p. 40.
71. *Ibid.*, p. 73.
72. *Ibid.*, p. 73.
73. Kevin O'Higgins to Brigid Cole, 29 May 1920, *O'Higgins Papers*, Book 1.

74. Kevin O'Higgins to Brigid Cole, 17 May 1921, *O'Higgins Papers*, Book 4.
75. Kevin O'Higgins to Brigid Cole, n.d., *O'Higgins Papers*, Book 4.
76. Kevin O'Higgins to Brigid Cole, 31 May 1921, *O'Higgins Papers,* Book 4. The debacle was the 25 May assault on the Customs House prompted by the more militant republicans like Cathal Brugha, and concurred in by de Valera, but opposed by the more astute realpoliticians Collins and Richard Mulcahy, the Commander-in-Chief of the IRA. It saw the destruction of the Customs House and irreplaceable government records, as well as the loss of several lives and the capture of over 100 IRA members.

# 2

# From Truce to Civil War

THE NEXT YEAR would see a dramatic change in O'Higgins' role in the Irish independence movement. From having been a relatively hardline and uncompromising separatist, as demonstrated by his attitude toward timid rate collectors, his willingness to employ the IRA against persons securing garnishee orders, his condemnation of late 1920 advocates of peace, and his annoyance at the moderation of the Church, he became a leading champion of a treaty that would fall far short of Irish independence and he increasingly cooperated with British representatives in implementing that treaty.

## TRUCE AND TREATY PLENIPOTENTIARIES

Peace often follows the most intensive period of a war. Such was the case in the Irish War of Independence. The employment of the Black and Tans and Auxiliaries, the Restoration of Order in Ireland Act, and the application of martial law were accompanied in December 1920 by the Government of Ireland Act, which called for the election of two home rule parliaments, one for Northern Ireland and the other for Southern Ireland. The measure also called for a 'Council of Ireland', at which representatives from the two parliaments would meet to deal with certain matters of common concern, specifically railroads, fisheries, and animal diseases, but which some, like the former Foreign Minister, Lord Grey, saw as an instrument that ultimately might enable the now formally separate parts of Ireland to unite.[1] However, the measure also allowed the government to transform that area into a Crown colony with even more intense martial law should those elected to the parliaments refuse to act as such, as would the probable Sinn Féin victors in the election to the Southern parliament.[2]

When Sinn Féin did win 124 of the 128 uncontested seats in the

Parliament of Southern Ireland, the government agreed on the combined Crown colony–military coercion approach. However, General Macready, the Commander in Ireland, and Field Marshall Henry Wilson, the Chief of the Imperial General Staff, advised against taking drastic action unless the country was clearly behind such. In the House of Lords, the Earl of Donoughmore, a southern Unionist long identified with reform and conciliation efforts, particularly with regard to land, moved that the government 'authorize negotiations to be opened'. His motion failed by only nine votes, but within a few days the government came to realize the absence of broad popular support for an intensification of the military effort and used the speech by King George V at the inauguration of the Parliament of Northern Ireland on 23 June 1921 to signal the desire of the British for a truce.[3] In his remarks, the king expressed his hope that his coming to Ireland might 'prove to be the first step toward an end of strife' and he appealed to all Irishmen 'to join in making for the land which they love a new era of peace, contentment, and good will'.[4]

The inability of the government to be able to rally popular support for an intensification of a military solution can in part be attributed to the widespread condemnation of policies like the reprisal campaign of the Black and Tans and the Auxiliaries that came from such varied groups as the Labour Party and the Trade Union Council on one side and the Peace with Ireland Council on the other. The later group included prominent academics like Basil Williams, and L.T. Hobhouse, clergymen like Bishop Charles Gore of Oxford, and even the then still-Conservative politician, Oswald Mosley. Other condemnations of policy in Ireland came from men of letters like G.K. Chesterton, Hilaire Belloc, Bertrand Russell, and Sidney and Beatrice Webb, as well as the Oxford and Cambridge Unions, and even the Archbishop of Canterbury, Randall Davidson, whose protest was joined by a substantial number of other Church of England bishops, various Methodist, Presbyterian and Congregational clergy, and other religious figures.[5] Lloyd George followed up the King's speech with letters to James Craig, now the Prime Minister of Northern Ireland, and Éamon de Valera, the President of Dáil Éireann, asking them to confer with him. After de Valera met with Jan Christaan Smuts, the South African Prime Minister who was acting as intermediary, the British cabinet agreed that representatives should meet Dáil Éireann leaders to work out a truce, which came about on July 11.[6]

It would be several months before the formal negotiations between the British government and Dáil Éireann would commence. Any ultimate settlement would revolve around two questions: the relationship of Northern Ireland with the rest of the island and the relationship of Ireland with the British Empire. The Unionists insisted that Ulster (more specifically the six counties of Northern Ireland) remain an integral part of the United Kingdom, while the Conservatives were anxious that the rest of Ireland remain part of the empire. The acceptance of Ireland's becoming a dominion was a significant advance in position on the part of a government that less then a year before had dismissed such suggestions by Liberals like H.H. Asquith.[7] However, the Sinn Féin (and Dáil Éireann) position was that the entire island of Ireland should be an independent republic. David Lloyd George sought to resolve these seemingly opposite aspirations by suggesting a united Ireland as a dominion within the empire. Ultimately dominion status for the south came about, but not the unification of the island.[8]

The British refused to accept the Irish insistence that Dáil Éireann was a sovereign power, as they saw the question as an internal constitutional readjustment within the empire. Nonetheless, the truce held, though not without occasional violent incidents. Preliminary exchanges took place between de Valera and Lloyd George seeking a formula whereby Dáil Éireann would not have to abandon its assertion of independent sovereignty nor Britain have to formally acknowledge the same. They ultimately agreed on negotiations, in diplomatically refined phraseology, to 'ascertain how the association of Ireland with the community of nations known as the British Empire can best be reconciled with Irish national aspirations'.[9] De Valera would name a number of plenipotentiaries to take part in the negotiations.

All of those elected to the Parliament of Southern Ireland except the four elected for Trinity College assembled as the second Dáil Éireann in Mansion House and re-elected de Valera as its president. O'Higgins was made Assistant Minister for Local Government, and, on de Valera's insistence, was invited to attend cabinet meetings.[10] He was among the many Dáil members who insisted that those attending the impending peace conference settle for nothing less than an independent republic, that the plenipotentiaries not go 'on any other than a Republic basis', and that the 'Dáil should go back to war if Lloyd George stood on his present terms and said he would not confer with us except on an Imperial basis'.[11]

The plenipotentiaries nominated by de Valera and approved by the Dáil included three cabinet members, Arthur Griffith, the Minister for External Affairs who had been the original leader of Sinn Féin, Michael Collins, the Minister for Finance, but more importantly, the real director of the guerilla war campaign that was the War of Independence, and Robert Barton, the Minister for Economic Affairs, a substantial landowner who had joined Sinn Féin and, along with his cousin, Erskine Childers, sat for Kildare–Wicklow, and two other TDs, Eamon Duggan, an Easter Week veteran who had been director of intelligence for the Irish Volunteers and sat for Louth–Meath, and George Gavan Duffy, the son of the Young Ireland writer, a successful attorney in London, who returned to Ireland to join Sinn Féin, and sat for Dublin.

Cosgrave moved that de Valera should chair the delegation since he was already experienced in negotiating with Lloyd George, the British Prime Minister, as otherwise 'they were leaving their ablest player in reserve'. De Valera argued against his own participation:

> it was vital at this stage that the symbol of the Republic should be kept untouched and that it should not be compromised in any sense by any arrangements which it might be necessary for our plenipotentiaries to make. He was sure the Dáil realised the task they were giving to them – to win for them what a mighty army and navy might not be able to win for them.

In retrospect these remarks suggest that de Valera himself was apprehensive that they would have to settle for something far short of a republic. Significantly, O'Higgins spoke in opposition to Cosgrave's motion and reiterated de Valera's point: 'They had to safeguard the Republic and the symbol of the Republic and to face the unpleasant fact that the plenipotentiaries might have to discuss other proposals than the sovereign independence of Ireland and it was not right the President should discuss such proposals.'

De Valera further explained to the Dáil that he had made the delegates plenipotentiaries so that they 'had the power to deal with a question subject to ratification'. Naturally 'they would go first with a Cabinet policy and on the understanding that any big question should be referred home before being decided by them'. He added that he believed 'his oath of allegiance was to do the best he could for the Irish nation. The plenipotentiaries would go over to do the best thing they could for the Irish nation and the Irish people.' Reiterating his warning about the immense task asked of them, he advised: 'They had got to face facts no matter how high their ideals were and to deal with a practical solution as they found it.' Cosgrave's motion was defeated and the Dáil subsequently approved the delegation.

De Valera then asked the Dáil to approve as secretaries to the delegation three of their members: Erskine Childers, who came from an English political family, was a Boer War veteran, a novelist and military writer, had used his yacht to bring weapons to the Irish Volunteers in 1914, served in the British Navy in the world war, but who joined the republican cause in 1919 and sat for Kildare–Wicklow Harry Boland, an IRB figure who sat for Roscommon, and was a close associate of Michael Collins, but who had accompanied de Valera on his American travels during the War of Independence; and Kevin O'Higgins. J.J. Walsh, a member for Cork Borough and later Minister for Posts and Telegraphs in the Irish Free State asked that a secretary be appointed with knowledge of Irish, such as Piaras Beaslaí, a member for Kerry who edited the Gaelic League journal, *An tÓglach*. O'Higgins agreed with Walsh's point, but also asked that his own name be withdrawn as 'it would be a matter of considerable personal inconvenience to himself if he had to go'. (The inconvenience was his forthcoming marriage, which had been delayed pending peace.) When Beaslaí suggested that the secretarial nominations did not need Dáil approval, de Valera withdrew them.[12] The ultimate designees were Erskine Childers and John Chartres, a barrister who had served in the intelligence branch of the Ministry of Munitions and who had expertise in constitutional law.

Later in October, O'Higgins and Brigid Cole were married. Father Patrick Doyle, the president of Knockbeg College, officiated. Occupying important places in the group wedding photo were his assistant at Local Government and best man, Rory O'Connor, TD, and Éamon de Valera – two men who would be enemies of O'Higgins within a year. The couple honeymooned in London while the negotiations were going on. Collins sent presents to the bride and arranged a box for the couple at the theatre. A dinner was given to them by the Irish delegation.[13]

O'HIGGINS: CHAMPION OF THE TREATY

The negotiations and the treaty have been explored extensively and will not be done so here, other than to note that the Irish delegation accepted terms far short of an independent republic. The Irish delegation returned to Dublin to present a proposed treaty to the Dáil cabinet on December 3. That treaty included dominion status, an opt-out option for Northern Ireland, and British retention of naval facilities in Ireland. The cabinet instructed the plenipotentiaries to return and attempt to get the British to accept an alternative treaty entailing a de Valera authored concept of 'external association' rather than dominion status. However, de Valera's proposal was unacceptable to the British.

On December 4 and 5, Arthur Griffith raised the issue of the exclusion of Ulster. Lloyd George had originally gotten him to accept dominion status in return for a promise that weight would be placed against Unionist opposition to Irish unification.[14] Now Lloyd George confronted Griffith with a promise he had signed on November 12 to not break on the issue of Ulster.[15] Griffith acquiesced when promised a boundary commission should the Northern parliament opt out of inclusion in the Irish Free State. He assumed such a commission would so reduce the size of Northern Ireland as to make unity of the island inevitable. When confronted on late Monday evening, December 5, with Lloyd George's stern threat of resumption of war within three days, the Irish delegation accepted the treaty without seeking further instructions from Dublin.

De Valera was outraged. When he met with those of the cabinet who were not plenipotentiaries – Cosgrave, Brugha, and Stack, as well as the non-voting O'Higgins – he expressed a desire to dismiss those who had signed the treaty from their ministries. With great difficulty, O'Higgins and Cosgrave were able to dissuade him from such a step as they argued that the signatories should first be heard before he would split the Sinn Féin movement.[16] When the full cabinet met the next day for five hours, with O'Higgins, Duggan, Gavan Duffy and Childers also present, there was a four to three vote, with Cosgrave joining Collins, Griffith, and Barton in accepting the treaty and de Valera being supported only by Stack and Brugha in opposition. It was decided to present the treaty to the Dáil, but with the president, de Valera, also issuing a statement of opposition in which he categorized the treaty as being 'in conflict with the wishes of the majority of the nation as expressed freely in the successive elections during the past three years'.[17]

His outrage at de Valera's formal dissent from the cabinet majority galvanized the articulate O'Higgins, who assumed a senior role in the defence of the treaty in the subsequent Dáil deliberations that began on December 14 with Eoin MacNeill, who was a member for Derry, acting as Ceann Comhairle. De Valera indicated his objection to the delegation having failed to comply with instructions to not sign a treaty before coming back again to the cabinet for instructions.[18] After a bitter argument about the credentials of the plenipotentiaries and their responsibilities, it was decided to have the Dáil meet in private sessions starting the next day, where de Valera explained his alternative to the treaty, a system of external association with the British Empire that the British negotiators had rejected.[19]

Treaty proponents like O'Higgins attacked the concept of external association because it differed very little from the treaty other than in the concept of dominion status and the required oath and they challenged the idea of returning to warfare because of the minimal difference. A recent rationalization of de Valera's position was a suggestion that he was aware of the unlikelihood of attaining a republic, but sought to maintain Sinn Féin unity, that is, the support of the die-hard republicans like Cathal Brugha, a member for Tipperary–Waterford and Minister for Defence, and Austin Stack, a member for Kerry and Minister for Home Affairs. He thought he could do so by rejecting the British offer and allowing negotiations to break down, with the expectation that at the last minute, prior to any resumption of hostilities, his alternative proposal of external association would gain British acceptance. That apparent victory would not bring a republic, but would appease the hardliners.[20] On the other hand, as the treaty champions would assert, was the slight difference worth the risk of resumed warfare – even if not likely – since the treaty had brought substantial advances in the Irish position?

O'Higgins emerged as one of the more articulate spokesmen for the treaty. He argued that those who criticized the signing of the treaty because it did not bring an Irish Republic ought to similarly object to de Valera's external association concept. He played upon an apparent contradiction in the position of the treaty's opponents: Erskine Childers, who viewed external association as 'a very considerable improvement upon the treaty', and saw 'very great and fundamental differences' between both, and de Valera, who claimed external association 'differed so little from the treaty that rather than make war the English government would give way' and spoke of the differences 'as one merely of shadows'. If de Valera's assumption that the differences were minimal was true, then it would have been a grave risk, and an insult to the 'five men of judgment, five men of outstanding worth' that had been sent to London and who believed 'they were getting the last ounce that could be got from the British', to have asked them to risk the alternative of 'terrible and immediate war' for so little. As it was, on the last day of negotiations, they had been able to secure further favourable terms on a number of issues like trade, full fiscal autonomy, having a military force proportionate to that of Britain on the basis of population, and a shortening of Northern Ireland's opportunity to opt out of the Free State to just one month. At that point their only alternatives were either to sign or to return with no treaty for the cabinet and Dáil to consider and run the risk of resumed warfare. Had they not signed at that point they would have 'shirked their responsibility, they would have failed in their duty to the Dáil and the people of Ireland'.

O'Higgins admitted that two months earlier his own position had been very hardline. He would 'not recommend any settlement involving allegiance to the King of England', and he 'would have gone back to war rather than recommend a settlement involving allegiance if the treaty had not been signed'. However, since then he deferred to 'some of the biggest personalities in our movement – men who did more for the country than any other men – that they considered this is the last ounce could be got from England'. The country should not be asked to resume war in face of the consequent disunity. Nor should it be asked of an army that said: 'What was good enough for Arthur Griffith and Michael Collins is good enough for us. Why should we be hurled back to war again on a whim.'[21]

Two days later O'Higgins admitted that 'ratification of the treaty is technically a break of the mandate of this Dáil and is technically *ultra vires*', but given that the alternative was 'war on a scale on which we are scarcely in a position to stand up against', he argued that: 'It is better we should commit a technical breach of our mandate than to commit the people.' Furthermore, if the issue of the treaty's acceptance was put to the people he had 'personally very little doubt that the country will accept it'. In this way he was beginning to draw a distinction between the mandate of the republican movement and the will of the populace at large.[22]

When the Dáil returned to public session on December 19, de Valera did not deal with his external association alternative, but more with the flaws of the treaty, which did not 'reconcile Irish national aspirations with association with the British government', nor 'end the centuries of conflict between the two nations of Great Britain and Ireland', and would end up with the same fruitless results as Pitt's labours in imposing the Act of Union. He was particularly opposed to the oath which would make the Irish ministers the king's ministers and the Irish Army the king's army. In essence, the treaty 'gives away Irish independence; it brings us back into the British Empire; it acknowledges the head of the British Empire not merely as the head of an association, but as the direct monarch of Ireland, as the source of executive authority in Ireland'.[23]

Erskine Childers opposed the treaty as 'not being honourable to the Irish nation' and giving much less autonomy than Canada had because it had ceded naval ports on the island to Britain and accepted continued British naval defence of Irish coasts. These points and Ireland's proximity to Britain, which denied her 'effective power to implement' foreign policy decisions and placed her 'remained immovably under the shadow of Britain', made useless the talk of 'equality, ... of a share in foreign policy, ... of responsibility for making treaties and alliances with foreign nations'.[24]

In defending the treaty at the same public session, O'Higgins repeated his insistence that the Dáil ought to defer to the perspective of the plenipotentiaries. Arguing that they were 'within their rights in signing' since they had been given no terms of reference, he reminded his colleagues that the five were 'men of sound judgment, conspicuous ability; men whose worth had been tested in four strenuous years. They were men capable of sizing up the situation ... who knew our strength and where and how we were not strong.' They brought back 'a document which they believe represents the utmost that can be got for the country short of the resumption of war against fearful odds'.

O'Higgins noted, as he had earlier in a private session, how nominal was the difference between the treaty and de Valera's proposal for external association. When de Valera objected to the raising of the issue of external association, which he regarded as a private cabinet matter, in a public session O'Higgins replied that the President and 'the two ministers [Austin Stack, the Minister for Home Affairs, and Cathal Brugha, the Minster for Defence] who stand with him for rejection of the treaty' should let the Irish nation know that they are taking their stand not on the differences between the terms of the treaty and a sovereign Irish Republic, 'but on the very much narrower ground' between the treaty and external association. Invoking the concerns of the general public, rather than just the committed republicans, he told the Dáil to ask 'to what extent it affected the lives and fortunes of the plain people of Ireland'. While he would not praise the treaty in the same adulatory terms with which Redmond had greeted the 1914 Home Rule Act, that is, 'as a full, complete and final settlement of Ireland's claim', he said it 'represents such a broad measure of liberty for the Irish people and it acknowledges such a large proportion of its rights', that the Dáil members were 'not entitled to reject it without being able to show then you have a reasonable prospect of achieving more'. He went on more positively about the treaty:

> Neither honour nor principle can make you plunge your people into war again. What remains between the treaty and the fullness of your rights? It gives to Ireland complete control over her internal affairs. It removes all English control or interference within the shores of Ireland. Ireland is liable to no taxation from England, and has the fullest fiscal freedom. She has the right to maintain an army and defend her coasts. When England is at war, Ireland need not send one man nor contribute a penny.

O'Higgins agreed that 'the most objectionable aspect of the treaty is that the threat of force has been used to influence' the Irish to remain in the empire. But he took a more positive view of membership in an empire that was 'a league of free nations' in which it would be 'unwise and unstatesmanlike' for the British to attempt to bind members 'by any ties other than pure voluntary ties'. In a prediction he himself would help fulfil, he expressed his belief that 'the evolution of the group must be towards a condition, not merely of individual freedom, but also of equality of status'.[25] In the meantime, the involuntary and still unequal status of Ireland in the Empire, were 'not defects which press so grievously on our citizens that we are entitled to invite war because of them'. He reminded his colleagues in the Dáil: 'They sit and act here today as the representatives of all our people and not merely as the representatives of a particular political party within the nation (hear, hear). I acknowledge as great a responsibility to the 6,000 people who voted against me in 1918 as to the 13,000 who voted for me.'

On the matter of the treaty being a betrayal of those 'who died for Irish independence in the past', he asserted that the principle of Irish nationhood was immortal; otherwise it would have died many deaths since the time when 'chieftains of the Irish clans swore allegiance to Henry VIII. The members of Grattan's Parliament were pledged in allegiance to the King of England. From 1800 to 1918 we have been sending Irishmen to Westminster pledged in the allegiance.' When 1916 took place, the rebels were not seen as acting dishonourably because of the earlier pledges of allegiance. He regretted that 'there has been too much talk of what the dead men would do if they were here'. He insisted: 'The men who died for Ireland never intended that the country should be sentenced to destruction in a hopeless war if all its rights were not conceded.'

While he acknowledged that he hardly hoped 'that within the terms of the treaty lies the fulfilment of Ireland's destiny', he did 'hope and believe that with the disappearance of old passions and distrusts, fastened by centuries of persecution and desperate resistance, what remains may be won by agreement and by peaceful political evolution. In that spirit I stand for the ratification of the treaty.'[26]

Dáil Éireann approved the treaty on Saturday, 7 January 1922 by a vote of sixty-four to fifty-seven. At the next meeting on Monday, de Valera resigned as President and a motion for his re-election was defeated sixty to fifty-eight. The following day, Arthur Griffith was selected to succeed him as President of Dáil Éireann, and George Gavan Duffy, Cosgrave, O'Higgins, Duggan, and Richard Mulcahy, a member for Dublin who was Chief of Staff of the IRA, became his ministerial colleagues.

The treaty required approval on the Irish side by the members elected to the Parliament of Southern Ireland, which body formed a Provisional Government to which the British would transfer the powers and machinery of government. The members elected to that parliament were virtually identical to the members of the second Dáil, except that it did not include a republican who had been elected to the Parliament of Northern Ireland but who attended the Dáil and did include the four independents elected for Trinity College who had not attended the Dáil. The Parliament of Southern Ireland met on the following Saturday, January 14. Because he had given assurances to the anti-treaty deputies upon his election to succeed de Valera that he would not use his office as President to destroy the republic, Griffith felt bound to absent himself from office in the Provisional Government that would be formed and which, in reality, was an alternative to the republic. Michael Collins was selected as its chairman. While this Provisional Government for all intents and purposes became the *de facto* as well as *de jure* government of Ireland, regard for republican mythology necessitated the continuation of Dáil Éireann and its cabinet, both of which continued to have meetings up until a summons was issued for an election to a new parliament that would be both the constituent assembly of the Irish Free State and the third Dáil Éireann.

O'HIGGINS IN THE PROVISIONAL GOVERNMENT

One of the most remarkable aspects of the attainment of self-government in Ireland was the continuity of the public bureaucracy or administrative officialdom. While such may have been disappointing to many revolutionaries who anticipated public positions in return for their involvement in the uprising – and this would include many supporters of the treaty who would become disappointed within a couple of years[27] – it was one of the things that spared Ireland the turmoil and tendency to slip into military dictatorship that accompanied the attainment of political independence by so many newly independent nations of the twentieth century. Contributing to the continuity was the increasing presence of Catholics and nationalists in the administrative and judicial positions of Ireland for thirty years, and particularly since the Liberal government formed in 1906, which pattern one historian has labelled 'The Greening of Dublin Castle'. In 1892, Protestant unionists held forty-five of the top forty-eight administrative positions, but by 1914 twenty of the forty-eight were Catholics. In the judiciary a comparable change took place, as the composition of the supreme court bench changed from overwhelming unionist presence to almost equal division by 1914. Catholics formed the overwhelming majority of county court judges in 1914, and on the local bench, a Protestant domination in 1892 of four to one had shrunk by 1914 to three to two. Accordingly, had the Home Rule Act came into effect in 1914 an Irish government controlled by the Irish Parliamentary Party would have taken charge of a greatly changed officialdom.[28] Eight years later, when the transfer to the Free State occurred, the top forty-nine officials were almost evenly divided religiously, as were the 1,600 professional staff, and Catholics occupied nearly all the rank and file positions.[29]

Although it was the consequence of an armed uprising rather than the legislative triumph of home rule, the transfer of administration was exactly what had been anticipated long before the ascendancy of Sinn Féin by those involved in the transfer and most of the educated Catholic population. The role O'Higgins would play in the negotiations implementing the transfer would solidify his support for the treaty and his hostility to the more romantic revolutionaries and make him disposed to use the administrative, judicial and law-enforcement mechanisms of the old regime now that they were in the hands of a government responsible to the people of Ireland. As a prelude to the transfer, on January 17, the day after the British army had withdrawn from Dublin Castle, its new inhabitants, the Provisional Government issued a proclamation directing all public functionaries, 'hitherto acting under the authority of the British government', to 'continue to carry out the functions unless and until otherwise ordered by us'. Collins, while retaining Finance himself, named various ministers and departments for the Provisional Government to which the various sectors within the existing administration were allocated. Several of the new ministers, like Collins, Duggan at Home Affairs, O'Higgins at Economic Affairs, Cosgrave at Local Government, and Mulcahy at Defence, were also members of the nominal Dáil cabinet. Others, like P.J. Hogan, a member for Galway and a close associate of O'Higgins, Fionán Lynch, a member for Kerry, and Joseph McGrath, a member for Dublin, became respectively Ministers for Agriculture, Education, and Labour. J.J. Walsh was made Postmaster General but not included in the cabinet. None of the ministers, other than Cosgrave, had experience in normal civil administration, which resulted in a disposition to leave most of the day-to-day administration in the hands of the existing civil servants.[30]

At the first meeting of the Cabinet on January 17, O'Higgins and Eamon Duggan were directed to go to London to meet with a British Cabinet committee, formally called the 'Provisional Government of Ireland Committee', but better known, because of its chairman, as the 'Churchill Committee',[31] to discuss the general questions of handing over the functions of the different departments of state to the Irish Provisional Government. These were the type of administrative details, much like the direction of the department for Local Government, in which O'Higgins excelled, but which lacked the excitement and glamour of revolutionary warfare. They were also instructed to press for the immediate release of Irish prisoners arrested and sentenced in England and Scotland, as well as the Irish members of the Connaught Rangers who had been sentenced for mutiny. Another matter, close to O'Higgins' earlier role in Local Government, was to recapture the money seized by the British government from the various local taxation accounts in Ireland to meet criminal and malicious injury awards, and to gain immediate access to grants withheld by the Local Government Board from the local bodies. The Irish delegates were to inquire about the British attitude regarding the position of the judiciary, as the existing court system had in many areas ceased to function with legal issues being resolved by the revolutionary Dáil Éireann Courts. Lastly, they were to press for British payment of compensation for damage done by the British government forces. Patrick McGilligan, who had served as secretary to O'Higgins in Local Government, was named as the secretary to O'Higgins and Duggan.[32]

The following day Duggan reported that Churchill thought that the issue of prisoners, including the Connaught Rangers, could be arranged satisfactorily and that the moneys required for local government grants would be made available, although he was not sufficiently conversant with the details. Churchill requested that Michael Collins himself come over to meet with James Craig, the Prime Minister of Northern Ireland, to resolve difficulties connected with Ulster.[33]

O'Higgins wrote to his new bride of his expectation that the delegation would not 'be here a second longer than is *absolutely* necessary as it is bad business to have so many of us away at the moment'.[34] Their work the next few days was intense, especially after Collins joined them on Saturday, January 21, and they and the Churchill Committee were able to arrive at an agreement implementing the treaty. Among the items settled was to allow existing malicious injury awards to stand, but to have the respective governments, the British and the Provisional Government, give the damages from the recent troubles to their respective supporters, that is, unionist victims would be compensated by the British and nationalist victims by the Irish. Duggan and Sir John Anderson, the Undersecretary of State for Ireland, were to determine the motive of prisoners, whether political or non-political, as a basis for awarding amnesty. The Provisional Government would assume both the liabilities and the assets of each of the departments it would take over. The Royal Irish Constabulary was to be demobilized as soon as possible and the Dublin Metropolitan Police (which had never incurred the same public and nationalist distrust as had the RIC) was to come under the authority of the Provisional Government. Significantly, the existing judges would continue to have their tenure of office, a consideration that would inhibit the Dáil Éireann Courts becoming permanent.[35] Governmental duties to be performed were those that had been stipulated by existing legislation and, at least in theory, the expenditure of money was to be in accord with the existing budget and drawn from taxes already collected or in the process of being collected. An indication that the transfer of civil servants was successful was that of the 21,000 transferred to the new government, less than 1,000 resigned in the first few years, in addition to a few hundred personnel being exchanged between English and Free State departments and 300 officials transferring to Northern Ireland.[36]

O'Higgins wrote to his wife on Saturday, January 21, that 'as to results up to date E.J. [Duggan] and I are well pleased as was MC [Michael Collins] when he heard our account'. Two days later he wrote to her giving his impressions of the British with whom he was dealing:

> I only straighten up when Dublin Castle – represented by Hamar [Hamar Greenwood, Chief Secretary for Ireland] and Sir John Anderson [Undersecretary for Ireland] – is falling across the green table. Hamar is – and looks – the complete charlatan, full up of loud-mouthed insincerities – crossing his hands over his stomach and turning his eyes to heaven at any suggestion that he has any motive other than effervescing affection and good will towards ourselves personally and the new order generally. The other fellow is a more dangerous type – the well trained civil service sneak – plausible, vigilant, malevolent, and false as hell. Churchill is not a bad fellow – emotional and enthusiastic – he's like a child with a new toy about this New Departure, and would be utterly inconsolable if there was any hitch or calamity – a boy of sixty, but a clever boy [actually Churchill was only 48 at the time]. Montague, Secretary of State for India, is a thoroughly decent type, he is an extremely able chap and never raises a point against us. Whenever there is a hitch or a deadlock he comes limbering in, puts *our* proposition into a different form of words and stands four squares for its acceptance. He always introduces his remarks by emphasizing how little he knows about our affairs, but it seems to me he knows more than most of them. We met the P.M. on Sunday afternoon, we were almost an hour with him – he is certainly a remarkable devil – he flirted with his eye glass and faced us now with the beaming ingenuous face of a boy and now like an old fox.[37]

That Saturday night, January 21, O'Higgins got his introduction to London high society when he, Duggan, and Collins (who had responded to Churchill's invitation to come over to meet with Craig) had dinner at the home of Sir John and Lady Hazel Lavery. He innocently reassured his wife that he was getting 'all brushed up – yes me tie is middlin straight and I'll try to put me hat and coat on right'. He found that the 'evening passed pleasantly enough', with Churchill, his brother, their wives, 'another Lady whose name I missed [Juliet Duff] and the Lavery pair – who are awfully fine folk'.

John Lavery was a Belfast-born Catholic and artist, painting society portraits in particular. His younger, American, and originally Protestant wife had developed an extraordinary sympathy for the Irish nationalist cause out of character with her social background and milieu, although she did have some degree of Irish ancestry. The couple served as a gate of entry into London society for the young and provincial Irish revolutionaries turning into statesmen. She acted as a go-between, advisor, and source of introductions. Despite these social pleasantries and real diplomatic accomplishments, O'Higgins was anxious to leave London as soon as possible, hopefully by Tuesday, January 24. His homesickness was reflected in his message to his wife: 'I want to get home to you away from the artificial atmosphere of wooden men and painted women – this place quite fails to grow on me – I want to go hoam [*sic*].'[38] The innocence of his account of these social encounters would stand in stark contrast to the unrestrained infatuation he would later develop for Lady Lavery.

The agreement with the Churchill Committee on terms for implementing the treaty did not remove other matters of contention. A major question was what actions legitimized the Provisional Government and authorized the transfer of powers. Irish nationalist ideology liked to assume that Dáil Éireann's approval of the treaty was sufficient. From the British perspective, Irish approval had come not from a revolutionary body, Dáil Éireann, but from a meeting of the members elected to the Parliament of Southern Ireland that had been called into being by the 1920 legislation. These same members then established the Provisional Government. The Irish did not want to regard the Provisional Government as having been a creature of British legislation. Yet, the Parliament of Southern Ireland had been created by an act of the Westminster parliament. Hence the play on words in the treaty that it was the members elected to that parliament, rather than the parliament itself, that approved the treaty. But the treaty also had to be approved by the Westminster parliament. There was uncertainty if that act of recognition would be sufficient to complete the recognition of the Provisional Government and authorize the transfer of power to it.

Nothing was said in the treaty about a constitution for the Free State other than to require the members of its parliament to 'swear true faith and allegiance to H.M. King George V... in virtue of the common citizenship of Ireland with Great Britain', and membership in the Commonwealth. The Irish would have preferred that they be left to their own devices in writing a constitution, which presumably would be drafted by the existing Dáil and/or Parliament of Southern Ireland, or better still by a third Dáil Éireann to be elected in the near future. No one doubted that the constitution had to be in conformity to the treaty, but the British believed that the dominion status bestowed on the Free State meant that its constitution, like that of other dominions, would have to be ratified by the Westminster parliament. Members of the Provisional Government, especially Collins, would have preferred that such not be necessary, hoping to draft a constitution that would be as republican as possible, and thereby gain acceptance by the opponents of the treaty. If the constitution did not need Westminster sanction, it would also remove the implication that it was a British-imposed or authorized document.

The meetings on 21 January had left the Irish delegation with the impression that the single act of ratification of the treaty by the Westminster parliament (which took place on 31 March 1922) would imply the acceptance of whatever constitution would be developed for the Free State. However, a specially appointed legal committee reported to the British cabinet that the ratification legislation would have to include the agreed heads of matters to be covered in the prospective constitution so as to ensure its conformity with the treaty. Lionel Curtis, the second secretary to the British delegation at the treaty negotiations and the Colonial Office advisor on Irish affairs, raised these concerns.

O'Higgins and Duggan met with Curtis in Dublin on Wednesday, February 1 to promote the passage of a one clause act of ratification by the British parliament as soon as possible without any reference to the constitution. They were instructed by the Provisional Government to make no statement that 'might compromise the ratification of the constitution being subsequently allowed to go by default', which is what they assumed and hoped would ensue from the act of ratification. However, Curtis insisted that the act of ratification would have to contain both the treaty and agreed heads of matters to be covered in the constitution, such as the position of the Governor General. When reporting this to the Provisional Government O'Higgins and Duggan were told that such was unacceptable and that they should tell Curtis that an election within Ireland on the treaty was essential as a preliminary. He was to be given every assurance that the constitution would be drafted within the terms of the treaty, but that 'the inclusion of the schedule contemplated in a ratification act would jeopardize the political situation'. The next day, February 2, O'Higgins was sent to London to continue 'to press for immediate ratification of the treaty', and instructed to 'give assurances that the constitution will be shown to the British authorities before publication, and that it will not be objectionable in any of the points raised'.[39]

When O'Higgins had returned on Saturday, February 4, the Provisional Government decided that he, Duggan, and Collins should return to London that evening, with Griffith to follow later if necessary. Difficulties had developed with regard to the ratification question. The British continued to regard the prospective Free State constitution as something subject to Westminster parliamentary ratification. The Irish delegation returned early the next week and reported on a tentative timetable. The British parliament would ratify the treaty later that month (in fact it would be late the following month), to be followed by the dissolution of Dáil Éireann and the calling of an election for the twenty-six counties (and, if possible, a simultaneous dissolution and election in Northern Ireland). The Provisional Government would meet in April and a constitution would be framed and passed by the newly elected parliament (or Dáil) in early May. The British parliament would register the adoption of the constitution the following month.

The negotiations should be seen as a victory for the British position, since there was nothing explicit in the treaty about the ratification of the constitution of the Free State. The way in which the parliamentary ratification became necessary was by the interpretation of what was to be the 'Ulster month', that is, the month in which Northern Ireland could opt out of the Free State. The treaty had stated it was to be the month after Westminster ratification of the treaty. But at these early February negotiations it was decided that 'the Ulster month' would run from the date of the British parliament's registering of the Free State constitution, which implied that Westminster parliamentary ratification of the constitution was comparable to the other dominions.[40] The Irish were able to convince themselves that the legitimacy of the Free State constitution came from the international treaty of 6 December 1921, ratified by Dáil Éireann on January 7, by the members elected to the parliament of Southern Ireland on January 14, and by the British parliament on March 31. But because the treaty imposed certain obligations on the Irish government, the constitution would explicitly state that nothing in it or any law passed under it could be repugnant to the treaty. Therefore, both sides emerged satisfied: the

British would regard themselves as ratifying the constitution of a new dominion, while the Irish would regard themselves as having exercised sovereign power in writing a constitution limited only by an international treaty to which they had assented.[41]

The Provisional Government had to tread a very fine line in complying with the treaty and satisfying the British, from whom they received the instruments, money, and indeed, weapons of governance, and calming the minority in Ireland who had not accepted the treaty and who looked upon Dáil Éireann, not the Provisional Government, as the only government in Ireland. Meetings of the increasingly symbolic Dáil Éireann and its cabinet were held with some regularity until late May in a quest for solidarity with old allies who might yet be won over by slight nuances of phrase or definition. A further gesture toward building bridges to the anti-treatyites was an attempt to preserve the unity of the political organization, Sinn Féin. At its Árd Fheis on February 22 and 23, the pro-treaty Minister for Defence, Richard Mulcahy, moved for an adjournment rather than have a vote on the treaty that would split the organization. The motion was accepted in return for an agreement that any election to a new Dáil or Irish parliament would be delayed for three months – to June rather than in March – and that the prospective constitution, which would be republican in character, would be published before the elections.[42]

In addition to his being one of the central figures in frequent contact with the British government, O'Higgins had assumed important domestic responsibilities as Economics Minister, both in the figurative Dáil Éireann Government and in the Provisional Government. Tasks he had to undertake included the recruitment of a trade advisor and securing a loan for the Provisional Government from the National Bank. He was able to obtain the latter without really being able to claim approval from the still to be elected Free State parliament. All he could promise the bank was that 'in the last resort...that the members of the Provisional Government would favour the taking up of the loan by the Free State Parliament' (January 28). He also formed a committee to deal with profiteering (February 18), and directed efforts to prevent the exportation of scrap metal (February 13). He and Collins discussed with Cosgrave, the Minister for Local Government, his desire to use £256,000 of grant money to provide relief from rates rather than for housing and road works (February 13). O'Higgins organized a committee to determine the future management of the Haulbowline Naval

Dockyards in Cork that were being turned over by the British. The recommendation of the committee, that the Provisional Government take over and maintain the dockyards as a national shipyard, was accepted (April 5).[43] He and Duggan agreed with the British to establish a war losses commission to recommend the proportion of the total compensation that would be borne by each government. No agreement was reached about damage that came under the headings of loot, confiscation and commandeering, nor was responsibility settled for the burning of the General Post Office during the 1916 rising.[44]

O'Higgins' deep involvement with these very practical administrative considerations, as well as his frequent dealings with the British in the process of achieving the transfer of power, made him impatient with the republican posturing in Dáil Éireann by the minority who recognized neither the treaty nor the Provisional Government. De Valera, for instance, asserted in the Dáil on February 28 that 'the supreme authority of this nation is this Dáil, that any Executive Acts that are performed in this country derive any authority they have in virtue of the fact that the majority of this Parliament assents to it'. O'Higgins was irked as he noted: 'this brings us right up against an issue that has been raised, off and on, for the last three weeks or a month', that of the executive authority of the Provisional Government. He noted that the anti-treaty Lord Mayor of Cork, Daniel O'Callaghan, had addressed a letter requesting £2 million for the rebuilding of Cork to Collins as Minister for Finance, Dáil Éireann. The liability for the damage done to Cork was Britain's and if the money became available it would be 'only by way of payment in advance of the British government's liability'. But 'Mr. Collins, Minister for Finance, Dáil Éireann, is not in a position – and the Lord Mayor of Cork knows it – to put £2 million... but Mr. Collins, Chairman of the Provisional Government, is in a position to secure from the British government payment in advance on the liability which will be settled by an inter-governmental commission'. He added that since it was not this body (Dáil Éireann) 'that appointed the Provisional Government... as one member of the Provisional Government, I will not answer questions here regarding actions I take as a member of the Provisional Government'.

Anti-treatyite Seán MacEntee, a member for Monaghan who later would be a senior figure in all Fianna Fáil governments until 1965, protested strongly against the impression O'Higgins 'wishes to create in this House and outside – that the only body competent to do anything in this country is the Provisional Government. Before the Provisional Government was established we had succeeded in making this the *de facto* government of this country.' De Valera also objected, insisting that it was only because of the approval of the majority in Dáil Éireann 'that there is any such thing permitted in Ireland as the Provisional Government, and that any functioning of that Provisional Government is permitted in virtue of the fact that you have a majority here'. But O'Higgins persisted in his refusal to cater to the minority's efforts to condition the Provisional Government's legitimacy by bluntly stating:

> ...in my capacity as a member of the Provisional Government I am engaged in taking over certain departments of the British government – the Ministry of Transport, Mercantile Marine Department of the Board of Trade, and so on. When I am doing these things certain people – a minority in this house – say I am a national apostate. Now in my capacity as a national apostate I will not answer questions to the minority of this house.[45]

The next day, when told by de Valera: 'You are in your position by virtue of the majority you secured here', O'Higgins replied:

> in my capacity as a member of the Provisional Government I will give fullest account at any time to the body that appointed the Provisional Government. But what is being attempted here to-day in various ways and by various resolutions is to establish the principle that the people whose policy is to put the treaty in the fire are going to dictate to the Provisional Government as to their attitude consequential on the treaty. That is a position which I cannot accept; it is a practice which I definitely, as a member of the Provisional Government, will not accept.[46]

### CRITIC OF TREATY OPPONENTS

Although the Provisional Government was avoiding confrontation with the anti-treaty party, O'Higgins was not inhibited from attacking them. He wrote a series of articles for the weekly, *Free State*, analyzing their position. In the first article, which appeared on February 18, a week before the agreement at the Sinn Féin Ard Fheis to postpone elections for three months, he criticized an anti-treaty deputy for having insisted that 'there must be no election until the last British soldier has left Ireland', arguing instead that 'the people have a right to decide the issue in a constitutional and democratic way'.

Calling for the popular acceptance of a treaty even if it did not bring a 'Republic', O'Higgins recognized that the 1918 electoral mandate had been 'to secure the independence of Ireland' which goal was best expressed by the word 'Republic'. This had been 'not so much because of any special preference for that form of government, but because it seemed the word which best emphasized the completeness of the independence we desired, and the completeness of the separation from England we aimed at achieving'. Unfortunately, recognition had come neither from the Paris Peace Conference, from the United States, nor from Britain. A combination of 'passive resistance to British rule by the civilian population with an active guerilla defensive warfare by the IRA' after three years brought 'an armed truce, then formal negotiations', and finally 'the terms now before you in the treaty'. The Irish plenipotentiaries, on the basis of their understanding of the military, political and economic situation, urged its acceptance. The majority of the Dáil, 'believing the alternative to be a resumption of war or political chaos, which would leave you further than ever from the realisation of your hopes', approved the treaty and asked for public acceptance.

O'Higgins went on to argue that the opponents of the treaty were trying to have the people think that 'their objective is the Sovereign Independent Republic'. In fact 'De Valera, as President, did not instruct the plenipotentiaries to seek recognition of the Irish Republic', but to do the best for the Irish nation 'in any circumstances that might arise', and not consider the republican oath as binding them 'irrevocably to any particular form of settlement'. Instead, de Valera's alternative Document No. 2 should be seen as 'the official statement of the political objections of the anti-treaty minority', and for which the Irish people 'are asked to tear up the treaty, and to chance the fortunes of war against the forces and resources of a great empire'. He indicated that Document No. 2 continued to associate Ireland with the British Empire 'for such matters of common concern' as 'defence, peace and war, political treaties and all matters now treated as of common concern amongst the states of the British Commonwealth', recognized the King as 'Head of the Associated States' and would authorize the voting of a yearly sum 'to the King of England's personal income as outward and visible sign of that recognition'.[47]

In a subsequent article O'Higgins challenged the anti-treaty argument of Erskine Childers that even though the treaty said the Irish Free State was to have the same constitutional relationship to the Crown as Canada, Ireland's close 'geographic propinquity' to England left her bound to the Crown and Parliament.[48] O'Higgins, however, indicated that the Irish plenipotentiaries had insisted on including the terms 'practice and constitutional usage', in addition to the 'law', in the treaty description of the relationship of the Irish Free State to the Crown and Parliament precisely because of a memo written for them by Childers. In it he had argued that practice and usage had made Canada virtually independent and had outgrown the limitations of the British North America Act of 1867, the legal constitution. But now, after the treaty, Childers, who had approved a constitutional status for Ireland comparable to that which had developed in Canada, where 'the Crown has no authority', and 'Canada alone can legislate for Canada', argued that such a status made the Irish 'bound slaves to the British Crown'. To the contrary, O'Higgins argued: 'under the treaty British troops evacuate, leaving the country in complete control of the Free State Army; English government in Ireland disappears, and the administration of the country passes into the hands of the Free State government. England's footing in Ireland consists of one man and a clause in an oath taken by about a hundred Irish citizens.'[49]

In a later article O'Higgins discussed the disregard for majority feeling by the anti-treatyites. He noted that Liam Mellowes, a more socialist-minded republican who had travelled with de Valera in America and sat for Galway, had dismissed reports that the popular majority were supportive of the treaty with a remark: 'That is not the will of the people; that is the fear of the people.' Such a remark would imply that the people's will can only be ascertained when you 'first attain to a condition of things when all external pressure will be removed'. Until that 'kind of national vacuum' is achieved, then 'any attempts on the part of the people in the meantime to influence decisions gravely affecting their lives and fortunes must be waved aside'. Mellowes and those holding such views were like philosopher-kings or Rousseauist magistrates interpreting the General Will: 'They claim the right to take as the national will what they conceive that will would be if functioning in absolute freedom, and thus, paradoxically enough, they claim to have a mandate from the people to deny to the people the right to have any will at all.' He saw such attempts as 'a declaration of the right of certain gentlemen, claiming almost a monopoly of spiritual and intellectual capacity to override the wishes of their less exalted and less enlightened fellow-citizens until such time as their country will have won complete...military victory over a neighboring country with ten times our population and material resources'. Accordingly, while the treaty terms did not give the Irish the desired 'unfettered self-determination', he insisted: 'It is untrue to say that acceptance of the treaty is not the "will of the people".'[50]

O'Higgins saw three distinct groupings within the anti-treaty party. A few believed 'in the possibility of winning out to the Sovereign Independent Republic and would be prepared to fight on at all costs to themselves or to the country'. Another group, the 'Document Two-ites', who would still leave Ireland associated with the British Commonwealth and 'recognize His Britannic Majesty as Head of the Associated States, voting him a yearly sum in token of that recognition', included de Valera, Childers, the previously more doctrinaire Austin Stack and Cathal Brugha, and the treaty signatory, Robert Barton, who had changed sides. The third group was personified by Countess Markiewicz, a lady of Anglo-Irish parentage, married to a Polish noble, who had been transformed into a rebellious champion of feminism, Irish republicanism, and socialism, was associated with James Connolly, sat for Dublin South, and had been Minister for Labour. Although committed to a 'Workers' Republic', she seemed 'strangely blind to what, after all, is the dominating factor in the whole situation – the economic condition of the country', which included, according to the estimation of the Labour Party leader, 130,000 unemployed. He thought those concerned about the working class should regard 'our economic condition' as 'a very relevant factor' before 'contemplating a course which points directly to a resumption of hostilities'.[51]

Unfortunately, despite the Sinn Féin Ard Fheis compromise setting back an election for three months, the prospects for accord between the pro and anti-treaty factions worsened on the military front. The IRA had a highly decentralized structure and the majority of the local division officers were anti-treaty. They took the position that the Army's allegiance to Dáil Éireann was conditional on the republic being upheld. The acceptance by the Dáil majority of the treaty and the Provisional Government was seen as 'a subversion of the Republic and relieved the Army from its allegiance to An Dáil'. Accordingly they demanded a meeting of an Army Convention, in a situation remarkably parallel to the Cromwellian Army Convention that forced a more radical political agenda on what was left of the British parliament in 1648–9.

Richard Mulcahy, the Minister for Defence, sought to hold off a split within the military since he was just beginning to consolidate the pro-treaty military forces. He suggested that an Army Convention be delayed for two months, but allowed the formation of a watchdog committee to ensure that the interests of a republican IRA not be departed from. He even allowed local units to take over barracks being evacuated by the British military without testing their commitment to the treaty. At the same time he began organizing a Provisional Government army consisting of IRA units loyal to the treaty, primarily from areas outside of Munster and the West, and new recruits. Unfortunately, in an effort to win over members of the IRA to the government, many were made officers undeservedly. In addition, great autonomy continued to be left to individual units, resulting in an often uncontrolled, badly officered, and poorly trained army. A major confrontation between pro and anti-treaty forces almost broke out in Limerick subsequent to British withdrawal. Both sides were ready to employ substantial numbers from outside the area to force their point. However, a compromise was reached whereby the local city corporation took control of the police barracks, and purely local forces, admittedly under the command of the anti-treaty commander, Liam Lynch, a Brigade Commander of the IRA during the War of Independence, took over two military barracks. Again it was an example of delaying tactics by Mulcahy, who reasoned: 'The pro-treaty forces were not yet ready from the point of view either of psychology or even of military training to carry out satisfactorily the suggested operation.'[52]

After the incident O'Higgins lamented the drift toward anarchy that would impede the treaty issue being decided by the people. He argued that 'political parties must be content to work constitutionally as political parties', and regarded 'mutinies and incitements to mutiny' as 'attempts by intimidation to prevent the free exercise or expression of individual opinion'. Such were 'deadly poison in the body politic', and 'those who have recourse to them are criminals' who 'violate a natural right and sin against the commonwealth'. He said, 'the Limerick incident should give people pause', as it was 'significant in its implications'. He noted that the only guarantee Mulcahy had asked of the troops occupying the former British positions was 'an undertaking that they will not use their power to prevent free expression of the people's will at a

General Election, nor turn their arms against any government that may be returned as a result of such election'. However, it was questionable whether the anti-treaty commanders would provide such a guarantee.[53]

TOWARD CIVIL WAR

On March 16 Arthur Griffith as President of Dáil Éireann issued an order prohibiting a convention of the IRA scheduled for early April. Richard Mulcahy got IRA leaders, like Liam Lynch, who would become its Chief-of-Staff, to agree to postpone the convention if the Provisional Government would discontinue the recruitment of a police force, the civic guard, and leave such under IRA control. Not surprisingly the Dáil cabinet rejected the compromise. Although prohibited, the Army Convention met without interference on March 26 and 27 in Dublin. About two-thirds of the 223 delegates in attendance were from the south and the west of the country. The convention reasserted the republican status of the IRA, and insisted it should be under the complete control of its own executive selected at the convention. Furthermore, the IRA was going to resume the Belfast Boycott, would claim for itself revenues from dog licences, and would subject the Provisional Government's civic guard or police to the same boycott encountered by the RIC. The Executive Committee of the Army would determine if steps should be taken to prevent a general election.[54]

The action of the IRA in asserting its independence from a Dáil that it saw as having sold out the republic put the political leader of the anti-treatyites, de Valera, in a quandary. The pro-treatyites had deliberately kept the Dáil and the Dáil government in existence in order to satisfy the ideological scruples of the anti-treaty party. However, the anti-treatyites in the military had now rejected that very Dáil. In an effort to keep ahead of his own movement, de Valera had begun to lapse into provocative oratory that would plague him for the rest of his days. Admittedly, his oratory had a conditional character, which would enable apologists to argue that he was drawing hypothetical situations rather than urging specific actions. At Carrick-on-Suir on March 17 he told a crowd, many of whom were in the anti-treaty IRA, that 'If the treaty was accepted the fight for freedom would still go on; and the Irish people, instead of fighting foreign soldiers, would have to fight the Irish soldiers of an

Irish government set up by Irishmen.' The same day, at Thurles, he told another group, many of whom were gun carrying IRA members, that their work, should the treaty be accepted, would have to be completed 'not over the bodies of foreign soldiers, but over the dead bodies of their own countrymen', and that 'They would have to wade through Irish blood, through the blood of soldiers of the Irish government, and through, perhaps, the blood of some of the members of the government in order to get Irish freedom.' The next day, at Killarney, he said that in the case of electoral acceptance of the treaty, the IRA 'will have to march over the dead bodies of their own brothers. They will have to wade through Irish blood.'[55]

O'Higgins said such utterances by de Valera 'surprised and saddened those who knew him well in the past, and particularly those who knew him in the intimacy of the secret councils of Dáil Éireann, and of the cabinet of Dáil Éireann'. He had abandoned the qualities 'which characterize the head of the State', and had taken the very easy course of being a wrecker seeking 'by force of fiery rhetoric to rouse high-spirited and patriotic young men to a pitch of frenzy in which they are ready to believe that a section of their own countrymen are the only barrier between them and the realisation of an ideal on which they have concentrated for years'. In doing so, 'De Valera has travelled far from his first pronouncement', made when he had come out against the treaty, that 'there is a constitutional method of settling these differences that must not be departed from'. O'Higgins feared de Valera had shirked the 'definite and grave responsibility – the responsibility of seeing that the armed split which he thus invited and precipitated did not degenerate into fratricidal strife and anarchy'.[56]

The situation continued to deteriorate on several fronts. One was Northern Ireland. A second pact reached between Collins and Craig in London on March 29 and 30 was stillborn like the earlier agreement of late January that had called for the replacement of the Boundary Commission with representatives named by both men, the discontinuance of the boycott of Belfast goods in the south, the return of displaced Belfast Catholic shipyard workers, and a large-scale relief system for the Belfast unemployed. On the eve of the second pact and during its actual signing O'Higgins played very much the role of the irreconcilable. Two days before, he suggested to Tom Jones, the British Cabinet Secretary, that the placement of British troops on the border would 'draw a ring fence round our people and leave them to be murdered in Belfast'. As for the difficulties of apportioning blame between the two communities in Northern Ireland, he remarked: 'The Orange Lodges can call off or turn on the outrages as they like.' He himself did 'not believe in the appeal to force' but 'would put the boycott on all trade between the North and South and see that not a single parcel of goods crossed'. When Jones suggested a boycott would only incense opinion and inhibit amity, and suggested instead a conference on economic development, O'Higgins replied that the British had 'created their Ulster situation by giving Ulster a Parliament...[and] it was impossible for him to promote publicly such a conference at the present moment'. Even at the signing of the pact two days later, Jones noted: 'O'Higgins, however, raised difficulties at once and continued to do so throughout.'[57]

The pact had ambitiously sought to reform the Special Constabulary in Belfast by recruiting Catholics, to establish an advisory committee for the group, to use Specials from both communities for arms searches, and to require members to place their arms in the control of an officer when they were not on duty. The Northern Irish government again promised to restore to employment Catholics displaced from the shipyards. The British government was expected to provide a grant of half a million pounds for relief to be distributed proportionately to the respective communities, Protestant and Catholic. IRA activities were to cease in Northern Ireland and the reforms being made in the Belfast Special Constabulary were to be extended to the rest of the province. However, the IRA's Northern campaign continued and both pro and anti-treaty units collaborated on it. The police and Special Constabulary reforms never took place, as loyalists regarded 'Catholic' Specials as a contradiction in terms and the Catholic community itself would have frowned on Catholic recruits.[58]

On April 14 anti-treaty units of the IRA, led by Rory O'Connor (O'Higgins' assistant in Local Government and best man at his wedding, who had stated, when asked at a press conference if the IRA would prevent an election: 'it will be in its power to do so', and, when asked if his movement was becoming a military dictatorship, said: 'you can take it that way if you like'), Ernie O'Malley (who had joined the Easter Rising while a medical student and had become Commander of the Second Southern Division during the War of Independence), and Liam Mellowes, acting under orders of the IRA Executive, took over a number of public buildings, including the Four Courts in Dublin which they made the republican military headquarters. The Secretary of State for the Colonies and Chairman of the Ireland Committee, Winston Churchill, found this blatant challenge to the authority of the Provisional Government discouraging. While understanding that Collins and Griffith had to play for time, he feared 'a process of degeneration is going forward' in which there would be capitulation to the republicans and postponement of elections. His fears were partly assuaged by Alfred Cope, the Assistant Undersecretary for Ireland, who was acting as liaison with the Provisional Government, and by General Neville Macready, the last British commander in Ireland. They reassured Churchill that Collins and Griffith would act effectively at the right time.[59]

Within the next month British confidence in the Irish signatories to the treaty was disturbed by two other matters: the shape being taken by the prospective Free State Constitution and an electoral pact between the rival wings of Sinn Féin. In both, Collins and the Provisional Government appeared to be appeasing the republicans in order to avoid a Civil War. On the matter of the constitution, Collins had told the chairman of its drafting committee, James Douglas, a Dublin businessman, a Quaker, and a humanitarian activist, that he wanted 'a constitution that would be short, simple, and easy to alter as the final stages of complete freedom were achieved'. He added that 'the committee should omit in the constitution everything that was already covered in the treaty concerning the relations between Great Britain and Ireland', that it concern itself 'only with what was necessary to establish constitutional machinery to govern Ireland', and that 'the constitution should rest solely upon authority derived from the Irish people'. He felt there was no need for the oath, and did not see how members elected to an Irish parliament after the passage of the constitution could be removed for not taking the oath.[60] In other words, Collins was hoping to fit the square peg of republicanism into the round hole of dominion status as a means of reconciling the anti-treatyites.

Then, on May 20, there appeared an electoral pact between Collins and de Valera with the hope of further avoiding division within Sinn Féin and Ireland. The terms of the pact called for a single panel of Sinn Féin candidates in the forthcoming election to the third Dáil, which would be the constituent assembly of the Free State. The panel was to be divided between pro and anti-treaty candidates in exactly the same proportion as in the existing Dáil. Presumably the electorate would obligingly elect a Dáil comparable to the incumbent Dáil. The subsequent cabinet would consist of a coalition of five pro and four anti-treatyites. It was agreed to hold the elections in June.

The pact confirmed the worst fears of the British about the weaknesses and/or untrustworthiness of the Provisional Government. Churchill had been insistent for some time that Collins move against the IRA takeover of the Four Courts. When reports of the electoral pact with de Valera reached him, he wrote: 'We will have nothing to do with such a farce, nor will we pass any act of Parliament creating the Free State or according a permanent status to the Irish government on such a basis.' Insisting that the fulfillment of the treaty required free elections, he saw 'the Irish terrorists' as 'naturally drawn to imitate Lenin and Trotsky'. He insisted: 'We should take our stand on the will of the people freely expressed.' His aides expressed alarm about his anger, which found vent in a letter he sent to Collins on May 16:

> I think I had better let you know at once that any such arrangement would be received with worldwide ridicule and reprobation. It would not be an election in any sense of the word, but simply a farce, were a handful of men who possess lethal weapons deliberately to dispose of the political rights of the electors by a deal across the table. Such an arrangement would not strengthen your own position in the slightest degree. It would not invest the Provisional Government with any title to sit in the name of the Irish nation. It would be an outrage upon democratic principles and would be universally so denounced.[61]

When the pact was signed on May 20, Alfred Cope tried to give a more reassuring interpretation of the action as being a means of getting 'the country out of the state of anarchy which exists at present' since de Valera 'only wanted a face saving and the agreement gave it to him'. However Lionel Curtis, the Colonial Office's advisor on Irish affairs, was not as sanguine, asserting that the pact 'provides for the perpetuation of the present Dáil. It is obviously designed to prevent the transfer of political power from the Sinn Féin and IRA organization to the Irish electorate, by healing the split in the organization. The two parties agree simply to monopolize power.'[62]

The British summoned the leaders of the Provisional Government to a conference on the pact. The Cabinet decided that Griffith, Duggan, and Hugh Kennedy, the Provisional Government's legal advisor, should go to London on Thursday, May 25, with Collins to follow over the next day. Before the group departed, it was agreed that Kevin O'Higgins should also join them. The rationale they agreed to use in justifying the pact was that it was necessary 'in order to enable the Provisional Government to carry out the terms of the treaty and to restore order', and that 'it was essential that there should be unity of the political forces in the country to cope with disorder'. To confirm the impression that they saw a difference between the political de Valera and the military Four Courts occupiers, they boasted that 'as a result of the agreement, election registers for certain areas which had been seized have been returned, with the result that the elections could now be held in these districts'. Finally, those going to London were instructed to make clear 'that the Provisional Government are determined to stand by the treaty'.[63]

At the conference Churchill raised several objections to the pact. The election would not be a free expression of the will of the people, since there was no contest, but only candidates reflecting the incumbent membership of the Dáil. The parliament elected would therefore be just an *ad hoc* body, not a parliament referred to in the Free State Agreement Act of March 31. Lastly, if any members of a coalition government would not signify their acceptance of the treaty in writing, then the British Government would regard such as a violation of the treaty.

The Irish delegation did not challenge the British premises, but defended the pact on utilitarian grounds. Griffith argued that it was done to prevent turmoil and bloodshed. O'Higgins argued that de Valera's followers 'believed they were going to follow constitutional courses', but had gotten themselves into a wrong position. 'But if we had forced the issue; we would have had disastrous consequences. Red flag elements were taking advantage of the situation. The feeling among two-thirds of the de Valeraites is that they are well out of a damned mess. We have to get a compromise, for without it they would have gone through with their opposition.' Duggan added that had they gone to the election without the pact 'the treaty would have been smashed'. O'Higgins also reminded the British that other parties besides the pro and anti-treaty wings of Sinn Féin would be contesting the elections: 'The Labour Party will contest seventeen or eighteen seats. This will compel the Farmers' Union to run candidates in opposition. By June 6 there will be a great many independents in the field.' Essentially, the results would guarantee a pro-treaty majority, but a majority that would not be as big as under normal circumstances.

In response to Churchill's objection about potential Irish govern-ment members not declaring their acceptance of the treaty, Griffith and Duggan argued that they would be only external ministers, not members of the cabinet. O'Higgins asked on practical terms if they were 'to be debarred from doing our best for the treaty'. He asked further: 'Does it matter if de Valera is in charge of education? Are we bound to take steps which would wreck the treaty?' But Churchill remained unconvinced, arguing: 'We made a big concession to you in the shape of the Free State, disbanded the army, handed over the revenues, placed you in a position of authority.' The British had insisted there be no republic, 'but you have made one surrender after another to the republicans and have not obtained the free opinion of the Irish people'. He recognized their difficulties, but noted: 'You will find that we are just as tenacious on essential points – the Crown, the British Commonwealth, no republic – as de Valera and O'Connor, and we intend to fight our points.'[64]

Collins arrived Saturday, May 27, to join the discussions. During the deliberations, he played the harder role of irreconcilable, while Griffith, Duggan, and O'Higgins seemed more appreciative of the British anxieties. Thomas Jones, the British cabinet secretary, noted on June 1 how 'Griffith, as usual, had been quiet and reasonable but Collins seemed in a more militant mood, obsessed with the Ulster situation, thoroughly distrustful of our Cabinet and even of the P.M.' He noted how Duggan tried to be reassuring, 'reiterating that his desire was to conform to the treaty', and reminded Jones of 'the life Collins had led during the last three years. He was very highly strung and overwrought, and sometimes left their own meeting in a rage with his colleagues.' Duggan also agreed 'it had been a serious blunder to have failed to hold the election immediately after the signing of the treaty as the situation had deteriorated since and their difficulties had vastly increased'.[65]

Churchill, a political realist, eventually accepted the Provisional Government's explanation for the pact with de Valera, especially if it would result in a pro-treaty majority and enable Labour and other independent members to be elected, after which a constitution could be drawn up that would formally link Ireland with the empire and the Crown.[66] However, within the British Cabinet there was some contention between Churchill, who was increasingly sensitive to the restiveness of the Conservative–Unionist supporters of the government, and the Prime Minister, Lloyd George, an outsider in the eyes of the Conservative–Unionists and whose Irish policy was

sure of support from only a handful of his personal Liberal
followers.[67] While they acquiesced to the pact, the British Cabinet
confronted the Irish delegation with a series of questions relating to
the prospective Free State constitution:

1. Would the Free State be within the empire?

2. Was the position of the Crown to be the same as in Canada?

3. Was the treaty-making power of the Irish Free State to be the
same as that of Canada?

4. Were the courts of the Irish Free State to stand in the same
relation to the King in Council as the Canadian courts?

5. Was the oath set forth in the treaty to be incorporated in the
constitution as the oath required of members of the Free State
Parliament?

6. Would members of the Irish Provisional Government be
required to sign the declaration required under article XVII that
they accepted the treaty?[68]

The Irish delegation reported to their own Cabinet on June 2 that
the British government had rejected the proposed constitution
because it was 'that of an independent Republic rather than that of
a state such as was provided for in the treaty'. They also noted that
the Collins–de Valera pact and recent shootings of soldiers and ex-
policemen in Ireland had made 'the attitude of the British
government toward the Provisional Government...one of
suspicion', and they interpreted the proposed Free State constitution
from that point of view. The Cabinet continued to discuss how to
respond to the six questions the next day. They decided to use the
British insistence on the use of the letter of Canadian law relating to
dominion and Crown relations to their own advantage by insisting
'that the practice obtaining in Canada be also explicitly embodied in
the Constitution', which would obviously imply a degree of
autonomy or independence comparable to that of Canada.[69]

Griffith, accompanied by O'Higgins and Hugh Kennedy, returned
to London on June 6 to work on the modification of the constitution.
An important part of the modification entailed negotiations between
Griffith, O'Higgins and Eamon Duggan, and Southern Unionists
represented by Andrew Jameson, a Director of the Bank of Ireland, a
distiller, a member of the Irish Privy Council, and President of the
Dublin Chamber of Commerce; Dr John Henry Bernard, who had

been the Church of Ireland Archbishop of Dublin and was the Provost of Trinity College; the Earl of Midleton, a landowner and former Secretary of State for War; and the Earl of Donoghmore, the Deputy Speaker of the House of Lords, on the question of minority representation in the parliament of the Free State. The institution that would afford such was a Senate indirectly elected by a limited electorate and having delaying powers over legislation. This agreement would also be part of the constitutional revision.[70]

The revised constitution was published on June 16, the very day of the election, giving republican opponents no opportunity to criticize it. Two days before, on June 14, Collins told a gathering of potential voters in Cork that he was 'not hampered now by being on a platform where there are coalitionists'. Therefore he could 'make a straight appeal to you – to the citizens of Cork – to vote for the candidate you think best of'. This was a remarkable contrast to the joint appeal Collins and de Valera had made as late as June 5 for voters to support the pact and reduce electoral contests, as 'many of the dangers that threaten us can be met only by keeping intact the forces which constituted the national resistance in recent years'. Both had also spoken at an opening meeting of the election campaign at the Mansion House on June 9.[71] All of this leaves some uncertainty as to what were Collins' real aims: appease, but ultimately dupe de Valera, or court him as an ally in a subsequent effort to force a further constitutional modification that would be more appealing to the anti-treatyites.[72]

The results of the election were fifty-eight pro-treatyites, thirty-six anti-treatyites, seventeen Labour, seven farmers, and ten Independents. This represented a clear defeat for the anti-treatyites, especially since they received only 134,000 first preference votes out of an electorate of 620,000. Interestingly, non-pact candidates (Labour, etc.) surpassed the pro-treaty panel by 247,000 to 239,000. The conclusion to be drawn from this election was that it was a clear mandate for governmental stability and the getting on with the regular cares of life. When IRA members assassinated Field Marshall Sir Henry Wilson, the retired Chief of Staff of the British Army who had been elected MP for County Down and had become security advisor to Northern Irish Prime Minister, James Craig, in London on June 22, the British demanded immediate action against the republicans, specifically the occupants of the Four Courts.[73] The kidnapping of General J.J. 'Ginger' O'Connell, the Deputy Chief of Staff of the Free State Army, and his imprisonment in the Four Courts on June 27, provided the Provisional Government with an excuse to attack the place the next day. This was the beginning of the Civil War.

O'Higgins wrote to his wife that: 'The general situation is very serious at the moment – the results of the elections and the publication of the Constitution has driven the "proud fellow" into a very ugly mood.' An indication of his own growing prudence on issues was the comment: 'A married man has not the right to cast his bread on the water as recklessly as a juvenile.' He also noted that Wilson's assassination was 'another barrel of oil to the conflagration'. When the attack on the Four Courts began he wrote to her: 'As you probably have heard by this time we moved against the Four Courts.' He told her that as a result 'the movement of ministers will be somewhat restricted' and that he and colleagues 'may have to sleep here [Dublin Castle] or together somewhere – under guard'. But he reassured her there was 'no need for anxiety', and saw the 'situation clearer in a few days'.[74]

Alas, the die had been cast that would divide the Irish body politic for at least half a century, and in the struggle significant leaders on both sides would be lost, including, although a few years after the actual war, O'Higgins himself.

NOTES

1. John McColgan, *British Policy and the Irish Administration, 1920–22* (London: George Allen and Unwin, 1983), pp. 47–9; Boyce, *Englishmen and Irish Troubles*, pp. 111–12.
2. Boyce, *Englishmen and Irish Troubles*, pp. 132–4.
3. Thomas Jones, *Whitehall Diary* (London: Oxford University Press, 1971), III, pp. 78–9.
4. Boyce, *Englishmen and Irish Troubles*, pp. 135–8.
5. Jones, *Whitehall Diary*, pp. 61–81.
6. *Ibid.*, III, pp. 82–5.
7. Boyce, *Englishmen and Irish Troubles*, pp. 22–3.
8. Paul Canning, *British Policy Towards Ireland, 1921–1941* (Oxford: Clarendon Press, 1985), pp. 5–7.
9. Dorothy Macardle, *The Irish Republic* (Dublin: Irish Press Edition, 1951, first pub., London: Victor Gollancz, 1937), p. 513.
10. C. Ó Conaill to K. O'Higgins (9 September 1921), NA, D 388.
11. *Dáil Éireann, Private Session* (14 September 1921), 93.
12. *Ibid.*, 96–7.
13. de Vere White, *Kevin O'Higgins*, p. 60.
14. Lloyd George may have sensed that Griffith was a 'soft republican', since his original aim in starting Sinn Féin was to achieve a dual monarchy, not a republic.
15. Lloyd George had requested that of him to calm a possible rebellion at a

Conservative Party conference. That rebellion threatened to replace Lloyd George with Andrew Bonar Law, who was unsympathetic to Irish interests and very supportive of the Unionists.

16. *Dáil Éireann, Private Session* (15 December 1921), 173.
17. Joseph M. Curran, *The Birth of the Irish Free State 1921–1923* (Alabama: University of Alabama Press, 1980), pp. 141–2; The Earl of Longford and Thomas P. O'Neill, *Eamon de Valera* (Boston: Houghton Mifflin, 1971), pp. 169–70.
18. Francis J. Costello, 'The Irish Representation to the London Anglo-Irish Conference in 1921: Violations of Their Authority or Victims of Contradictory Instructions?' *Éire–Ireland*, XXIV, 2 (1989), pp. 52–78.
19. Longford and O'Neill, *Eamon de Valera*, pp. 172–3; Carlton Younger, *Ireland's Civil War* (London: Fontana Books, 1970), pp. 210–11.
20. John M. Regan, *The Irish Counter-Revolution 1921–1936* (Dublin: Gill & Macmillan, 1999), pp. 29–31.
21. *Dáil Éireann, Private Session* (15 December 1921), 148, 172–5.
22. *Ibid.* (17 December 1921), 223.
23. *Dáil Éireann, Debate on Treaty* (19 December 1921), 24–7.
24. *Ibid.*, 36–42.
25. See Chapter 8 for more on O'Higgins' role at Imperial Conferences in advancing this concept of equality of status.
26. *Dáil Éireann, Debate on the Treaty* (19 December 1921), 43–7.
27. See Chapter 5.
28. Lawrence W. McBride, *The Greening of Dublin Castle: The Transformation of Bureaucratic and Judicial Personnel in Ireland, 1892–1922* (Washington, D.C.: Catholic University of America Press, 1991), pp. 190–1.
29. *Ibid.*, p. 310.
30. McColgan, *British Policy and the Irish Administration*, pp. 96–7.
31. McColgan, 'Lionel Curtis and Constitutional Procedure', *Irish Historical Studies*, XX, 79 (March 1977), 325.
32. *Meeting of the Provisional Government* (17 January 1922), NA, G 1/1.
33. See p. 58 on abortive Collins–Craig pacts.
34. Kevin O'Higgins to Brigid Cole O'Higgins (19 January 1922), *O'Higgins Papers*, Book 5.
35. *Implementing the Treaty Agreement* (23 January 1922), NA, G 1/1. See also Chapters 3 and 4.
36. McColgan, *British Policy and the Irish Administration*, p. 136.
37. Kevin O'Higgins to Brigid Cole O'Higgins (23 January 1922), *O'Higgins Papers*, Book 5.
38. Kevin O'Higgins to Brigid Cole O'Higgins (23 January 1922) *O'Higgins Papers*, Book 5.
39. *Meeting of Provisional Government* (31 January and 1/2 February 1922), NA, G 1/1.
40. *Ibid.* (7 February 1922), NA, G 1/1.
41. John McColgan, 'Implementing the 1921 Treaty: Lionel Curtis and constitutional procedures', *Irish Historical Studies*, XX, 79 (March 1977), pp. 329–33. The best theoretical pronouncement of the Free State rational was a memo drafted for the Provisional Government's Attorney General, Hugh Kennedy, by the Dublin solicitor, Arthur Cox, who became a close confidant and advisor to O'Higgins (in 1940 Cox married O'Higgins' widow), (20 May 1922), *Kennedy Papers*, UCDA, P4/236 (1).
42. Michael Hopkinson, *Green Against Green* (New York: St. Martin's Press, 1988), p. 56.

43. *Meeting of Provisional Government* (28 January, 13 and 18 February, and 5 April 1922), NA, G 1/1, 1/2.

44. *Report of the Cabinet Committee on War Losses Commission*, NA G 1/2.

45. *Dáil Éireann* (28 February 1922), 95–101.

46. *Ibid.* (1 March 1922), 156.

47. Kevin O'Higgins, *Civil War and the Events Which Led to It* (Dublin: Talbot Press, 1922), pp. 10–13.

48. Childers regarded the treaty's award of specific naval ports in Ireland as part of the reliance on Britain for defence by sea as 'allowing the permanent military occupation of Ireland'. F.M.A. Hawkins, 'Defence and the role of Erskine Childers in the treaty negotiations of 1921', *Irish Historical Studies*, xxii, 87 (March 1981), pp. 251–70.

49. O'Higgins, *Civil War*, pp. 16, 21.

50. *Ibid.*, pp. 22–4. O'Higgins' arguments have been reasserted by contemporary political scientist Tom Garvin, who discusses the clash between the 'public band' and the people at large. O'Higgins obviously broke with the 'public band' in abandoning pure revolutionary doctrine to become a democratic political leader. Garvin, *1922*, pp. 40–62.

51. O'Higgins, *Civil War*, pp. 31-3.

52. Hopkinson, *Green Against Green*, pp. 59–66.

53. O'Higgins, *Civil War*, pp. 33–4.

54. Hopkinson, *Green Against* Green, pp. 68–9.

55. Tim Pat Coogan, *De Valera: Long Fellow, Long Shadow* (London: Hutchinson, 1993), pp. 310–11; Curran, *Birth of the Irish Free State*, pp. 173–4; *Irish Independent* (18, 20 March 1922).

56. O'Higgins, *Civil War*, pp. 35, 46.

57. Jones, *Whitehall Diary*, III, pp. 195–7.

58. Michael Hopkinson, 'The Craig–Collins Pact of 1922', *Irish Historical Studies*, XXVII, 106 (Nov. 1990), pp. 151–4.

59. Canning, *British Policy Toward Ireland*, p. 37; Gilbert, *Winston Churchill*, IV, p. 709.

60. D.H. Akenson and J.F. Fallon, 'The Irish Civil War and the Drafting of the Free State Constitution', *Eire–Ireland*, V, 1 (Spring, 1970), pp. 23–4.

61. Gilbert, *Winston Churchill*, IV, pp. 714–15.

62. Thomas Towey, 'The Reaction of the British Government to the 1922 Collins–de Valera Pact', *Irish Historical Studies*, XXII, 85 (March 1980), p. 69.

63. *Provisional Government Meeting* (23 and 25 May 1922), NA/G 1/2.

64. Towney, 'Reaction of British Government to Collins–de Valera Pact', pp. 71–4.

65. Jones, *Whitehall Diary*, III, pp. 203–4.

66. Gilbert, *Winston Churchill*, IV, pp. 718–20.

67. Canning, *British Policy Toward Ireland*, pp. 42–3.

68. Jones, *Whitehall Diary*, III, p. 205.

69. *Provisional Government Meeting* (5 and 6 June 1922), NA G 1/2.

70. D.H. Akenson and J.F. Fallon, 'The Irish Civil War and Free State Constitution', *Eire–Ireland*, V, 4 (Winter 1970), pp. 61–2.

71. Macardle, *Irish Republic*, pp. 719–21.

72. Akenson and Fallon, 'The Irish Civil War and Free State Constitution', V, 4, p. 66.

73. Serious consideration has been given to the suggestion that the assassination had in fact been ordered by Michael Collins. He never shed his IRB conspiratorial instincts, remained dedicated to aiding the nationalists in Northern Ireland, and might have seen the killing of Wilson, the most renowned and outspoken proponent of the unionist position at that time,

apart from James Craig, as a stroke that might rally anti-treatyites to the Provisional Government. It would confirm the impression that he had signed the treaty for tactical reasons. If so, he would have been alone among the Provisional Government cabinet. Hopkinson, *Green Against Green*, pp. 109–14. Another historian refuses to implicate Collins and argues that the killers acted on their own. Peter Hart, 'Michael Collins and the assassination of Sir Henry Wilson', *Irish Historical Studies*, XXVIII, No. 110 (November 1992), pp. 150–70.

74.  Kevin O'Higgins to Brigid Cole O'Higgins (22 and 27 June 1922), *O'Higgins Papers*, Book 5.

# 3

# The Civil War and Constitution

D URING THE CIVIL WAR O'Higgins was responsible for drastic actions and severe policies designed to guarantee the survival of the new state. Those actions and policies solidified an enduring animosity toward him. His strong measures toward the irregulars were prompted by the conviction that he was acting in defence of a state responsible to the Irish people and in opposition to self-appointed champions of a revolutionary ideal. He believed their assault on legal institutions had opened the door for general lawlessness and anarchy in a society on the edge of general economic breakdown.

## O'HIGGINS: FROM CABINET TO GENERAL STAFF TO VICE-PRESIDENCY

Some argue that the failure to call the newly elected Dáil into session for almost three months after it was elected weakened the democratic credentials of the Provisional Government. It is suggested that the commencement of the Civil War – the assault on the Four Courts held by republicans – soon after the elections did not have parliamentary sanction, nor would have had it from either the second or the still unassembled third Dáil. But to expect a parliament to be called into session by a 'provisional government', which was confronted with the existence of a substantial armed force that challenged its authenticity, seems to reflect an unwarranted preoccupation with democratic niceties.[1]

This was especially the case since it was not obvious at the start of the Civil War that the Provisional Government would prevail. A substantial portion of the IRA remained anti-treaty and controlled many weapons. The newly formed 'National Army', which consisted of pro-treaty IRA members and hastily enlisted recruits, many of whom responded to the July 7 call to arms by the government, remained untested and untrained. Furthermore, many of its members did not have the ideological fervour of the anti-treatyites.[2] But despite earlier ominous prognostications, the Provisional Government gained control over most of the country within a few weeks. The insurrection in Dublin was suppressed in the first week of July. Offensive action by the government forces during July and August included the capturing of cities like Limerick, Waterford and Cork and, subsequently, towns like Westport, Tralee, Youghal and Fermoy.

During the first weeks of July, as Economics Minister, O'Higgins concerned himself with transportation problems, both rail and automotive, caused by the extensive irregular ambushes and disruptions. On July 3, for instance, he reported that 'all the railways are now interrupted', although he hoped the Midland Great Western would be able to run trains by the evening and that the position of the Dublin–South Eastern was fair. The next day he and Patrick Hogan, a TD for Galway, the Minister for Agriculture, and O'Higgins' closest friend among the ministers, were given authority to issue permits for travellers whose reliability could be satisfactorily guaranteed. Within Dublin, carters had been able to resume their work. But fear of all railroads being put out of action prompted the formation of a committee to work out a scheme of road transportation. On July 10 the railroad situation was regarded as having worsened and a need was noted for 'suitable propaganda to rouse public feeling against interference with railway communications', and a coordinating committee of railway corporation general managers and military and public authorities was to be set up. All this indicates an uncertain prognosis for the government that with hindsight might appear to have been unwarranted.[3]

On July 12 Collins withdrew from the civilian arena and appointed himself the Commander-in-Chief of an undefined War Council. Cosgrave became temporary Chairman of the Provisional Government, O'Higgins, Joseph McGrath, and Fionán Lynch were relieved of their civilian ministerial posts and given military staff positions.[4] O'Higgins became Assistant Adjutant General. According to a report by their sister Kathleen, the imprisoned Gerry Boland, later a minister in several de Valera governments, was refused parole by O'Higgins in his military position to visit his grieviously wounded and soon-to-die brother Harry, a close associate of Michael Collins, who had travelled with de Valera to America and had taken the anti-treaty side. The sister who made the request claimed O'Higgins had a cold and hostile attitude.[5]

On August 12 Arthur Griffith died from a cerebral haemorrhage, and ten days later, on August 22, Michael Collins was fatally ambushed at Béal na mBláth, not far from his 'place of origin' in County Cork.[6] Three days later, on August 25, Cosgrave, the temporary Chairman, became President of the Executive Council, as the Cabinet would be called. O'Higgins was released from his military duties on August 26 and appointed Minister for Home Affairs and Vice President of the Executive Council on August 30 as part of a Cabinet reorganization subject to approval by the Third Dáil, which finally came into session on 9 September 1922.[7]

The ascendancy of Cosgrave and O'Higgins guaranteed that the government would no longer be an appendage to a military establishment, as it of necessity had to be during the first months of the Civil War and under the dominance of Collins. The same historian who suggested the 'undemocratic' character of the pro-treaty commencement of the Civil War, the suspension of the Second Dáil, and the delay in calling the Third Dáil into session, commented on Collins' premature death: 'It momentarily speeded up the process of democratisation within the regime and the movement toward government by an executive council rather than by a single executive mind.'[8]

But too sharp a contrast should not be drawn between Collins and Cosgrave and/or O'Higgins. In a eulogistic message upon Collins' death, O'Higgins described Collins as 'a great bulwark', who protected the Irish people from 'the fanatics and doctrinaires and pseudo-intellectuals who he knew were menacing the life of the nation by setting it an impossible task'. In contrast to the mixed ancestry, as well as the more intellectual and/or socially elitist background of some of the anti-treatyites, (e.g. Childers, Barton, Countess Markiewicz, de Valera), Collins was as 'flesh of the people's flesh and bone of the people's bone, and his love for them was too real a thing to give place to an insistence on empty formulae'. Collins had acted in the spirit of the instructions given in 1921 by de Valera about the meaning of the Dáil oath: 'To do the best for the Irish people in any circumstances that may arise', and 'His conception of Irish nationalism was big and broad, not a thing of dry formula.' Shortly before his death Collins had told O'Higgins that he regarded the Civil War fight 'as a fight for the foundations of a state'. The people would 'mould its development and destinies, but we could never make a start unless we had recognition of the basic principle of representative government – majority rule'.[9]

Other members of the Executive Council besides Cosgrave and O'Higgins were Mulcahy as Minister for Defence, Joseph McGrath as Minister for Local Government, Desmond FitzGerald as Minister for External Affairs, Eoin MacNeill as Minister for Education, Patrick Hogan as Minister for Agriculture, and J.J. Walsh as Postmaster General, while Eamon Duggan and Fionán Lynch were ministers without portfolio. Of the group, O'Higgins was closest to Hogan, who had also been educated at University College Dublin, although a few years earlier, and had similarly deviated from a family pattern of being educated at Clongowes Wood, going instead to a college near Ballinasloe, Co. Galway. He was elected to the first Dáil largely because of his being imprisoned. Their friendship grew with their mutual hostility toward aggressive nationalism and militarism, their relative disinterest in cultural and linguistic separatism, their mutual legal training, with Hogan having actually practised as a solicitor, and their common wit and articulateness. Desmond FitzGerald, the London-born son of an Irish builder, whose wife Mabel was a Belfast-born Presbyterian, with whom he shared an enthusiasm for the Irish language and nationalist cause, who had been the director of Dáil Éireann's Department of Publicity that had played a significant role in discomforting the British authorities during the War of Independence, became another close associate of O'Higgins. No doubt the three shared an intellectuality and perspective that differed from the outlook of some colleagues, particularly the militarism and nationalism of Mulcahy, or the populism of McGrath, a trade union activist, and Walsh, a Gaelic Athletic Association organizer. Blythe, a Northern Irish Protestant and Irish language enthusiast, earlier had all the militancy of a convert, but as time went by was drawn more into the O'Higgins perspective, especially in espousing economic orthodoxy. Beyond a mutuality of shared views and intellectual camaraderie, it would be inappropriate to try to read much more into their alliance, or to suggest social and economic explanations, as, then as well as presently, such are inadequate explanations of human attitudes.[10]

## THE FREE STATE CONSTITUTION

O'Higgins played the primary role in steering the Free State's constitution through the constituent assembly, that is, the third Dáil Éireann. This was the constitution that had been modified from the earlier version objected to by the British. O'Higgins, Griffith, and Duggan had been the major figures in the Irish team that negotiated with the British over the constitutional revisions. Dáil approval of the constitution was a foregone conclusion in view of the rejection of the anti-treatyites in the June elections, and especially in view of their abstention from the Dáil. But an articulate and critical role was played by a few independents and Trinity College members as well as by the seventeen members of the Labour Party delegation, especially their leader, Thomas Johnson. He had been born in Liverpool, but had come to Ireland when he was twenty and worked as a commercial traveller. A trade union activist, he was a founder member and vice chairman of the party, which had abstained from contesting the 1918 and 1921 elections for the first two Dáils. However, he had helped draft the Democratic Programme of the first Dáil.

In his management of the case for the constitution, O'Higgins took on two distinct issues. The first was the fact that the constitution did not establish a republic, but rather a dominion with the appendage of monarchism, at least symbolically, and with some restraints on Irish sovereignty and independence. The second issue was the conservative or Whiggish flavour of the constitution that dealt with the specific powers and functions of government and the process of its selection rather than with various social ideals or ambitions common to many twentieth century constitutions, specifically matters of social entitlements and sexual equality.

The first issue arose in the discussion of the very Enabling Act of the constitution, which stated it had to be construed with reference to the treaty, whose terms were 'given the force of law'. Furthermore, 'if any provision of the constitution or of any amendment thereof or of any law made thereunder is in any respect repugnant to any of the provisions of the scheduled treaty, it shall, to the extent only of such repugnancy, be absolutely void and inoperative'. O'Higgins acknowledged the inadequacies of the constitution from the nationalist and republican perspective in his opening remarks in introducing the constitution to the Dáil, admitting that: 'Had the circumstances here been other than what they were, I do believe that we could have got a more pleasantly worded constitution.' However, the constitution was 'a strict but fair interpretation of the treaty', and he did not believe that 'in any important point of substance we could have gotten a better constitution than we in fact have got'.

As one of the group that had negotiated with the British about the constitution, he believed they had gotten the best they could 'within the limits of the treaty'. Realizing that some would say, 'we brought home a constitution dictated by the British', he reassured the Dáil that 'the men who went to England were not out to cheat their country out of one jot or title of her rights'. However, they had to work in a most unsavoury atmosphere, as 'every time we crossed to England to negotiate points consequential on the treaty, things happened here that were meant to be mines under our feet', such as British soldiers being shot in College Green or raids across the six-county border. Nonetheless, he had no apologies in introducing the constitution. Rather than have to apologize for the constitution, he regarded it as something that held 'great possibilities for our country'.

That first article, which in proclaiming the Irish Free State as 'a co-equal member of the British Commonwealth of Nations', meant 'that the administration of Ireland, the making and moulding and amending of its laws, the shaping of its destiny, is as much in the hands of the Irish people as those matters with regard to England are in the hands of the English people'. While there were 'things in the constitution which we would wish out of it, just as there were things in the treaty which we would have otherwise, if we had our way', he asked the Dáil to look beyond 'to the really precious thing that is embodied in the constitution, and that is the real freedom it contains; the real control it gives the Irish people to live their own lives and develop their own civilization'.[11]

During the debate on the second reading of the constitution, Bill O'Higgins admitted that the constitution was 'not a republican constitution', since it contained 'the trappings, the insignia, the fiction and the symbols of monarchical institutions'. But he reminded his listeners that under the constitution, as in Britain, 'the real power is in the hands of the people'. He noted that the Crown had lost the great constitutional struggles of the previous few centuries, which left the King 'a useful fiction, an imposing symbol', but 'the real power is in the hands of the people acting through their Parliament'. The monarchical features in the Irish constitution, such as summoning and dissolving of the Dáil and the appointment of the President of the Executive Council, were similarly figurative, leaving the real authority in the Dáil. The clash in the constitution between the monarchical wording and the democratic reality, which was comparable to that of the constitution of Canada, were 'some of the penalties we are paying for our inability to achieve all the things we wrote on our battle standards'. But when set against the alternative, that is, a resumption of war with minimal prospects of achieving more, he argued they should be accepted as the treaty was accepted.

O'Higgins dismissed a proposal to regard the taking of the oath by Dáil members to be faithful to the King, as required in the constitution and in the treaty, as a voluntary option. He reminded the Dáil that it would be ridiculous to regard as voluntary an oath that had been a matter of 'quite considerable tension' in the negotiations with the British ministers, who, while having 'racked their brains to devise some form or another that would be least objectionable to Irish sentiment', had remained adamant on safeguarding the monarchical principle.[12]

The following day, in response to the argument that the constitution was written under duress, he asked the Dáil to be realistic and realize that duress was 'always the position between two nations, one of which has the greatest navy, and perhaps also the greatest army in the world; that has a population of 40 millions, and the other an island country of 4 million inhabitants and no navy'. Suggesting that those who disliked the constitution also disliked the treaty, he asked those holding such views if they were ready to risk the hazard of putting 'back into the melting pot the destinies of the country, and, in view of the chaos and futility we have outside, to re-open the whole matter of the constitution'. He repeated his earlier description of the atmosphere under which the terms of the constitution had been negotiated the previous spring in London by asking the Dáil to:

> try to remember the British soldiers and British ex-policemen who were covered under the terms of the Amnesty that had been issued were being shot almost daily, almost as a matter of routine. Try to remember that certain people differing from the majority in religion, and perhaps also, and I am not so sure of that, even in political outlook, were driven from their homes and from their positions.

In that unpleasant atmosphere, 'in which any day or any week might have brought back the British power', they were still able to return a constitution which 'is a strict and fair interpretation of the treaty'.[13]

One feature of the constitution that O'Higgins had been instrumental in formulating was that part dealing with the second legislative chamber, Seanad Éireann or the Senate. He and Arthur Griffith had met in London in June, with representative Southern Unionists, Most Rev. Dr John Henry Bernard, Andrew Jameson, the Earl of Midleton and the Earl of Donoughmore, in an effort to include them in the new state.[14] O'Higgins argued that it had been appropriate to go 'a little beyond the line in meeting these people, when the thing they looked to and felt was a buttress and shelter for them is suddenly swept away and they find themselves in the awful position of being at the mercy of their fellow countrymen'. Because of that 'it comes well from us to make a generous adjustment' and show that these people are regarded 'as part and parcel of this nation, and that we wish them to take their share of its responsibilities'.[15]

To ensure that the upper house, which would have a suspensive veto power of delaying legislation for 270 days, did not duplicate the overwhelmingly nationalist majority in the Dáil, thirty of the sixty members of the first Seanad were to be named by the President of the Executive Council, which would allow a significant unionist presence, while the other thirty were to be selected by the Dáil. Every subsequent three years one fourth of the body was to be up for re-election for twelve-year terms, with one third of the candidates being nominated by the Seanad and two-thirds by the Dáil, with the total number being limited to three times the number of seats up for re-election. The electorate would be limited to those thirty years of age and over. The nominating role of the Seanad and the older electorate, it was thought, would also enhance unionist prospects.

O'Higgins hoped that, in accepting the Senate, the Dáil would 'work away from what some people call the narrow trade unionism of Sinn Féin'. He believed 'it is better to err on the side of an over-generous advance than on the side of what would appear to be a rebuff or slight to people who will gradually come around to what is the general view of the nation'.[16]

At the end of the debate on the second reading, the leader of the Labour Party, Thomas Johnson, asked O'Higgins to name the specific clauses the government believed ought not be amended if the constitution was to remain consistent with the treaty. O'Higgins listed fifteen specific articles of the constitution, such as the first and second which declared the Free State's membership in the Commonwealth and the principle of popular sovereignty and those articles designating the King as part of the legislature along with the Dáil and the Seanad, and the one in whom executive authority was vested. This authority meant the King, or his representative, summoned and dissolved the legislature and gave assent to legislation. Also, his Privy Council could hear final judicial appeals. Naturally, these royal powers were in fact symbolic and would be exercised only with the advice of the Executive Council. Other 'non-amendable' articles dealt with judicial tenure and technicalities related to the transfer of authority from the British government to the Provisional Government or the Free State.[17] This admission significantly narrowed the area in which there would be debate on the constitution, but could be seen as a consequence of the treaty without which there would have been no constitution in the first place.

Since the non-amendable articles foreclosed any serious challenge to the first issue – the sovereignty shortcomings of the constitution – consideration could still be given to what some saw as the document's inadequacies from a social and civil libertarian perspective, especially issues like socio-economic ideals, women's rights, and due process. In this phase of the debate, O'Higgins had occasional assistance from Eamon Duggan, who moved several refining amendments, and the Minister for Local Government, Ernest Blythe, an Antrim-born Protestant, an active Gaelic Leaguer, who had joined the Irish Volunteers, then Sinn Féin, and represented County Monaghan in the Dáil, whose view of what a constitution should be ran counter to the egalitarian and social democratic agenda of the Labour Party.

For instance, an article moved by Thomas Johnson would have required the Free State to:

> oblige economic undertakings and associations to combine, on a self-governing basis, for the purpose of ensuring the co-operation of all the productive factors of the Nation, associating employers and employees in the management and regulating the production, manufacture, distribution, consumption, prices, and the import and export of commodities upon principles determined by the economic interests of the community.

The wording was redolent of guild socialism, then much in vogue, and various forms of corporatist thinking. O'Higgins replied in classic Whig terms that the constitution should include 'only matters on which we will get the broadest possible measure of consent, and that we should aim at keeping out of our constitution matters which will stir up controversy, and which will stir up fears'.[18]

A follow-up motion by Johnson would have declared it the duty of every citizen 'to make such use of his mental and bodily powers as shall be necessary for the welfare of the community', and that 'provision should be made for his support' where there was no suitable employment for a citizen. Ernest Blythe viewed the motion as either calling for a compulsory system of state direction or simply stating an ideal. From his perspective, guaranteeing employment was 'a rather tall order' if it was 'meant to be mandatory upon the state'. If the word 'should' were substituted for 'shall', it would be a commendable, but pious, aspiration.[19]

The constitution proclaimed the right of all citizens 'to free elementary education'. A Labour colleague of Johnson, Thomas O'Connell, deputy for Galway and general secretary of the Irish National Teachers Organization, moved a detailed amendment proclaiming the 'right of the children to food, clothing, shelter', as well as state-controlled compulsory education where teaching was to be 'imbued with the spirit of Irish nationality and international goodwill'. O'Higgins disapproved, since he believed that a constitution should 'simply and boldly set out' fundamental rights, but that it was 'not necessary to set out in full detail all the most modern and up-to-date amplifications of those rights'.[20]

A motion by William O'Brien, Labour deputy for Dublin South and a founder member of the Irish Transport and General Workers Union, sought to replace Article 10, which proclaimed the state's unalienable right to natural resources by an assertion that all ownership of lands and waters were 'vested originally in the Nation, which has had and has the right to transmit title therein to private persons, thereby constituting private property', and that private property could also be expropriated for public utility, and the state could regulate natural resources 'in order to conserve them and equitably to distribute the national wealth'. O'Higgins feared O'Brien's amendment was likely 'to frighten timid people', and argued it was 'a very unwise thing at the embarking of a new state, where you must depend on the goodwill and hard work of all sections to make a success of that state, to embody in the constitution what certainly looks very much like a Communist doctrine'.[21]

Contemporary feminist historians have a very critical view of the Irish Free State and of O'Higgins in particular.[22] The beginning of feminist displeasure began with the absence of any clause in the constitution about equal rights for women. While the original constitution had read: 'men and women have equal rights as citizens', the government had changed the wording to read: 'men and women have equal political rights', in addition to retaining the guarantee that citizenship and the right to vote were 'without distinction of sex'. Feminists feared the change could imply limiting equality to political rights, while denying equality in other rights.

Blythe and O'Higgins justified the change out of their concern that the original wording might be construed to deprive women of certain distinct rights and privileges reserved for women. However, feminists regarded the distinctions less as protections and more as inequities.[23]

A few weeks later, in opposing an amendment that would restore the 'equal rights as citizens' terminology, O'Higgins argued such wording might endanger certain feminine 'privileges', such as the wife's ability to claim in court to have acted under duress of her husband, the civil service rule requiring married women to retire on gratuity, existing provisions regarding married women, settlements of marital family deductions, etc. He did admit that 'there is coming into existence a certain type of woman, an extremely able woman, an extremely strong-minded woman, a woman of highly developed public spirit and civic sense', but the Dáil should

> remember that there are still alive a great many women of a very, very different type, who certainly need the protection of these enactments and who certainly must not be deprived of that protection ... They do not protrude themselves perhaps, but we must realise that they are left and that a great many of these laws provide very necessary protection for them.

Johnson expressed disappointment at the government's legal advisors' inability to formulate an article that could assert both the principle of citizen equality without distinction of sex and still recognize sexual differentiation. Accordingly, he would be as happy if they dropped the article about men and women having equal political rights entirely. O'Higgins moved the same and it was deleted.[24]

Like many constitutions of the period, the Free State document included provisions for both referendum and initiative. The former, which ultimately would be Article 47, was a conservative or delaying concession to minority, and specifically Southern Unionist, positions. It enabled two-fifths of the Dáil, or a majority of the Senate, to delay the implementation of passed legislation for ninety days, during which period three-fifths of the Senate or a petition signed by one-twentieth of the registered electorate could compel a referendum on that measure. Article 48 allowed for the Oireachtas to establish popular initiative for laws and constitutional amendments. If such was not done within two years, a petition signed by 100,000 voters could require a referendum on whether or not such should be established. If initiative were to be established, any petition for a specific measure or amendment would require only 50,000 signatures.

Thomas Johnson did not oppose the referendum article, but he made clear that it should be seen not as a means whereby 'the people in the mass will have a right to put their veto on an Act', but as 'a brake upon the activities of reformist, radical, socialistic, or Bolshevistic Parliaments'.[25] On the question of initiative, he was upset that it was not mandatory, but was left to the option of the Oireachtas or to a petition requiring a very large number of signatures. He believed 'if the referendum is to be part of the constitution, the initiative is equally necessary'. O'Higgins was willing to consider requiring a lesser number of signatures on the petition for initiative. The number was reduced from 100,000 to 75,000.[26]

Many of the amendments to the constitution offered by the Labour Party, with which O'Higgins had to contend, have a striking resonance to contemporary Irish political debate, specifically on issues of Irish neutrality, freedom of the press and expression, and state provision of education. For instance, Thomas Johnson supported an effort by the independent Darrell Figgis, deputy for Dublin and a freelance journalist involved in gun running for the Irish Volunteers in 1914, to require the consent of the majority of registered voters in a referendum, rather than just that of the Oireachtas, for Irish involvement in any war other than actual invasion of the country. Johnson and allies were anxious that a future government and parliament might be so swept off its feet by Commonwealth pressure, aided especially by a potential increase in circulation in Ireland of the popular British press, as to be involved in some war.

O'Higgins, however, was confident that any government or parliament elected by the Irish people would not involve the country in war against the wishes of the people. Distinguishing the present Dáil from the Irish Parliamentary Party that had endorsed Irish involvement in the Great War, he noted that then there was not 'a Parliament at that time functioning in Ireland', and that Redmond and his party were 'divorced from the people', as 'not a single one of them stood in the peculiarly intimate relation to their constituents and people as a whole that they would have been in if there had been a Parliament in the country responsible to the people'. O'Higgins also said there were strategic considerations against having a referendum prior to entering war, which could necessitate that 'Parliament must act immediately upon its own judgment.'[27]

O'Higgins did not have civil libertarian concerns in his opposition to an amendment proposed by Thomas Johnson to guarantee 'the secrecy of correspondence and communication by post, telegraph, telephone or other common means'. O'Higgins warned against 'falling into the error that, because certain measures were taken against ourselves, in the past, consequently that particular precaution, for the preservation of the state and for the preservation of public morality, should be entirely abandoned'. Simply because certain measures were taken by the British should not mean that 'we will have to abandon very many useful precautions, and very many useful weapons for the preservation of the state'. The proposed amendment would prevent the use of measures to check 'very grave abuses that exist here'. He had in mind measures 'to check betting and lottery correspondence' and 'to check the spread of indecent and immoral circulars and advertisements'. The latter advertisements were for 'encouraging the limitation of childbirth', 'all kinds of immorality', and 'all kinds of indecent devices sent through the post'.[28]

Another instance where O'Higgins acted as the conservative naysayer to the social idealism of the Labour Party was in reaction to a proposed amendment guaranteeing free education for the young 'up to an age to be prescribed by law'. The constitution already contained a clause proclaiming the right of all citizens to free elementary education. He feared the proposed amendment was too loosely worded and could open the door for state provision of not just elementary education, 'but for secondary education, and possibly for a certain amount of university education'. While many would have liked to see provision of post-elementary education by the state, he thought such a burden to be 'something we ought to examine very carefully, and it must be taken relative to the resources of the state'.[29] Here again he was displaying a mindset unsympathetic to a common twentieth-century pattern of stating social aspirations in constitutions without heed to the material capacity of a state to provide the same.

Despite O'Higgins' earlier indication that certain clauses of the constitution were not subject to alteration in view of the terms of the Anglo-Irish Treaty and the negotiations with the British regarding the proposed drafts of the constitution, there were efforts, especially by George Gavan Duffy, who had resigned as Foreign Minister in the Provisional Government in protest at the closing of the Dáil Éireann Courts and who would later resign from the Dáil, to minimize the monarchist wording. For instance, he moved to delete all reference to the monarch in the article establishing the executive authority of the

Free State. He argued that it was 'a contradiction in terms to state that your Executive is vested in the King in one breath and in the other to say your Executive is responsible to Parliament'. O'Higgins replied that Gavan Duffy's motion would contradict the treaty clause that the relationship of the Crown to the Free State should be similar to its relationship to Canada, which made the royal authority almost entirely symbolic.[30]

During the debates on the constitution O'Higgins and colleagues in government were strongly influenced by the advice of Hugh Kennedy, the law officer of the Provisional Government and subsequently Attorney General of the Irish Free State, 1922–4, and first Chief Justice of the Irish Free State, 1924–36. Kennedy, the son of a surgeon and an Irish speaker from Donegal, was one of the few barristers who had identified with the Sinn Féin cause. He was committed to the maximizing of Irish sovereignty within the constraints of the treaty. The way he sought to do so was by emphasizing the Canadian parallel, as did the treaty. As often as possible in the constitution of the Free State, when the role of the King or his representative was mentioned, allusion was made to the Canadian situation. In his words, 'What we have done is to take the full length and breadth of the Canadian position in the widest terms.' He regarded as one of the outstanding features of the treaty the fact that the constitutional position of Canada was 'chosen as the type because of the great advance that had been made by that Dominion on the road to liberty in association'.[31]

Gavan Duffy also objected to wording in the transitory provisions of the constitution that stated 'the passing and adoption of this constitution by the Constituent Assembly and the British Parliament' would be announced not later than 6 December 1922 'by proclamation of His Majesty, and this constitution shall come into effect on the issue of such proclamation'. He wondered whether the Free State was also 'taking the position that the foundation of our authority lies in a British Act of Parliament?' O'Higgins replied that it was 'in the power of the British Parliament to refuse to adopt this constitution if it were not, in their opinion, within the four corners of the treaty'. Therefore, the adoption of the constitution by the British parliament 'marks the completion of the treaty negotiations, of the treaty bargain'. To try and assert that all the British parliament would do was to register the constitution was 'simply in a small way trailing your coat for trouble at a time when it is not advisable to have trouble'.[32]

Another issue disturbing to the more Nationalist-minded was the inclusion in the constitution of the title Governor-General, which Gavan Duffy regarded as 'objectionable to a great many of us, because it connotes the idea of domination'. O'Higgins insisted that the Provisional Government's negotiators had deliberately accepted the title of Governor-General 'because of its fixed meaning', as 'the moment that you accept that name you stamp the man's limitations in a way that people all over the British Commonwealth of Nations will understand'. Gavan Duffy moved an amendment specifically stipulating that the Governor-General would be appointed with the consent of the Irish Executive Council. The amendment failed. O'Higgins opposed it since the existing wording, that the appointment be 'in like manner as the Governor General of Canada', was sufficient to guarantee the Irish input into the nomination. He reminded the Dáil that the issue was 'one of the most touchy and thorny points with the British' and explained that 'all they had left here in this country was that link of the Crown and that it was important for them'.[33]

The final stage of the constitution debate was completed on October 25, leaving only the passage of the enabling legislation by the British parliament, and the Irish Free State came into being on 6 December 1922, a year after the treaty.

## EMERGENCY POWERS

Even while the Dáil was considering the constitution, the Provisional Government had to contend with the continued insurrection by the irregulars. The government had assumed authority over much of the country, but the irregular campaign continued in a new phase, that of guerilla warfare, in rural and mountainous areas of the country where they had the advantage of operating in their own locality with intimate knowledge of the terrain and acquaintance with the local population. They remained strong in the rural areas of South Tipperary, West Cork, Kerry, and Mayo. Their tactics consisted of ambushes and raids on the forces and agents of the Provisional Government, which found itself in the same awkward situation as had the British from 1919 through 1921. As has been inevitable in such situations in Ireland and elsewhere in the world, the responses of the forces of authority to guerilla attacks often assumed a 'terrorist' character themselves, especially in the matter of taking of prisoners.

Further complicating matters were the absence of any laws or regulations governing the military response to actions by the irregulars and a natural reluctance to invoke the powers of the British Martial Law Acts. To meet the dilemma, the government responded to the request of Mulcahy, the Minister for Defence and Commander in Chief of the Army, and formulated a resolution to be subject to Dáil approval giving certain requested extraordinary powers to the Army. Entitled the Army Emergency Powers Resolution, the measure was introduced on September 27 and passed the following day. However, it was only a resolution since the constitution empowering the Dáil to pass legislation had not yet been approved. Accordingly, it also did not need royal sanction, and could, in a way, be seen as simply Dáil approbation of an existing martial law regime.[34]

The measure was an attempt to legalize a situation in which several thousand had been imprisoned. O'Higgins called for the Dáil to approve 'a certain policy with regard to prisoners and to regularise their internment and the conditions of their internment'. He prefaced his request by calling to mind the difficulties which the Provisional Government had encountered, wondering 'if in the history of the world there was ever greater responsibility on nine very young and rather inexperienced men', than had been placed on the Executive Council. 'Between the dissolution of one Parliament and the assembling of another' they were faced with evidence 'that the majority will in this country was not accepted ... and that certain men, from whatever motives, had determined to take a step which we felt would once and for all dispose of this treaty on which so many people in Ireland have based their hopes for Ireland's future'. Not having at their disposal 'machinery so that all things could be done according to law' or 'according to precedent' he and his colleagues did what they 'considered was the best for the Irish Nation in the circumstances that had arisen'.[35]

The Emergency Resolution, introduced on 27 September was a response to a request from the Army Council for power to 'set up military courts or committees with full powers of inquiring into charges and inflicting punishment on persons found guilty of acts calculated to interfere with or delay the effective establishment of the authority of the government', to detain persons in military custody, and to control the dealing in and possession of firearms. The military courts were to include 'at least one person nominated by the Minister for Defence and certified by the Law Officer to be a person of legal knowledge and experience'. To be tried were those accused of 'taking part in or aiding or abetting any attack upon or using force against the National Forces', of 'looting, possession without proper authority of any bomb ... or other explosive substance or any revolver, rifle, gun or other firearm', or of 'the breach of any general order or regulation made by the Army authorities'. Those courts could inflict 'the punishment of death or of penal servitude for any period or of imprisonment for any period or of a fine of any amount with or without imprisonment on any person found guilty ... of any of the offences aforesaid'. The Army authorities could detain any prisoners within or without the jurisdiction of the government and regulate and control the sale, possession, transfer of and dealing in weapons.[36]

The measure met with understandable objections. Darrell Figgis asked that the powers be given to the Minister for Defence instead of the Army authorities, since he was 'a Minister of this Dáil, and is answerable to this Dáil'. He also asked that the person of legal knowledge who would be on the court be the person responsible for carrying out the charges and trusts committed by the resolution, that is, to be the presiding official. He would limit the powers of the courts to detention, rather than capital punishment, imprisonment, or fines, as he believed the power of such punishment ought not be exercised 'for crimes that are not specified'. Lastly, he argued for a time limitation on the powers of the army courts subject to periodic Dáil renewal.

O'Higgins assumed the burden of replying, since he, 'the minister who, if things were normal, would be solely responsible for order in the country, should speak to the motion'. He stressed the fact that 'we have not in the civil government at the moment the machinery to deal adequately with the situation with which we are presented, and we have not at our disposal the tribunals necessary to deal adequately with crimes that are so abundant throughout the country'. He also thought the concern over the taking of human life or the death penalty had to be balanced against 'the life of the nation' and 'a spectacle of a country bleeding to death, of a country steering straight for anarchy, futility and chaos'. As for the severity of the penalties he argued that the surest way of discouraging the irregulars is to 'not encourage them in the belief that they can continue to do these things with impunity' or 'that we are so soft, or so sentimental, that the penalty for these hammer blows to the country's life is only going to be internment under very comfortable conditions'. The employment of Army courts was necessary because of the peculiar situation of the civil tribunals at the time, where some courts were of the old regime, 'which so many are ready to call British Courts ... not deserving of the confidence of the people', and the popular Dáil Éireann Courts which sprung up simultaneously with the War of Independence, 'have been the subject of very severe criticism and condemnation'. Therefore, the Dáil was asked 'to trust the National Army to hold the gap until such time as civil machinery can be forged, and a civil police force sent out through the country that will be a protection and a service to the people'.[37] He would play a very important role in the establishment of that police force and in the assertion of the supremacy of civilian authority over the military. As expected, the measure passed the Dáil on September 28, but an amnesty was announced on 3 October for any irregulars willing to turn in their weapons and accept the authority of the government by October 15.

### RESTORATION OF REGULAR JUDICIARY AND CIVIL ADMINISTRATION

One of the more celebrated features in the War of Independence was the system of Dáil Éireann Courts. Their general public acceptance, even by people not sympathetic to the Sinn Féin cause, was as much, if not greater, an indication of the popular mandate for Dáil Éireann than its acceptance by most of the locally elected governmental bodies. The concept of an independent court system, as an alternative to the existing court system, had been raised as early as 1905 by Arthur Griffith, but was formally called to come into being by Dáil Éireann in August 1919, taking a cue from arbitration bodies that had sprung up impromptu in the west of Ireland amidst widespread agrarian violence. In June 1920 the Dáil initiated a regular hierarchy of civil and criminal courts, while courts hearing land disputes came under the authority of the Ministry for Agriculture. The shrinking of the RIC and its disinclination to involve itself in ordinary police matters, being more concerned with the campaign against the IRA, increased the readiness of people to resort to the rival courts system and its rival police force, IRA volunteers.

The basic court in the system was a Parish Court, but from mid-1920 on there were District Courts whose boundaries conformed to parliamentary constituencies, which could hear claims not exceeding £100 in value. In the districts there were also circuit sittings to hear appeals from the Parish Courts, to hear cases exceeding £100 in value, and to hear criminal proceedings. Finally there was a Supreme Court with unlimited jurisdiction and an appellate role. The parish justices were elected by a convention of representatives of Sinn Féin, the IRA, and other local bodies. Those elected would in turn elect district justices. In establishing a constitution for the courts, Austin Stack, the Minister for Home Affairs at the time, drew upon the advice of four barristers: Arthur B. Clery, Professor of Law at University College Dublin; Cahir Davitt, the son of Michael Davitt of the Land League; Diarmuid Crowley, a former Customs official; and James Creed Meredith, who had studied at Trinity, was a D. Litt and had written on philosophy, and had taken part in the Howth gun running. All four also served as Justices, Clery and Meredith on the Supreme Court and the other two on the Circuit Court. With the intensification of the British campaign against the uprising in 1920, the proceedings of the courts became riskier, and more difficult to take place. Nonetheless they continued and resumed with the truce.[38]

After the approval of the treaty and the establishment of the Provisional Government to take over the existing public institutions of the old regime or establish new bodies in their place (as the Garda Síochána replaced the RIC), a dilemma developed with regard to the existence of two judicial systems, the courts of the old order and the Dáil Éireann Courts. Naturally British opinion unjustifiably viewed the Dáil Courts as tribunals created to advance a revolution rather than act as judicial bodies. On the other hand, the other courts were linked to the old regime with all of its unpleasant connotations. The Ministry for Home Affairs, under Eamon Duggan and his legal adviser, Hugh Kennedy, later Attorney General and Chief Justice, increasingly preferred the continuation of the courts of the old system, the High Court, the County Court, and the petty sessions, but with the employment of legally qualified justices of the Dáil Éireann Courts. In a way parallel to the formation of a national Army to replace the IRA, the fate of the Dáil Éireann Courts became intertwined with the issue of acceptance or rejection of the treaty.[39]

The Provisional Government's uncertainty about the Dáil Éireann Courts was solidified in the early months of the Civil War when Diarmuid Crowley, as a Circuit Judge, granted an order of *habeas corpus* directing the governor of Mountjoy Jail and Mulcahy, the Minister for Defence, to show cause why George Oliver Plunkett, the brother of Joseph Mary Plunkett, the Easter Week martyr and Proclamation signatory and son of Papal Count George Plunkett, the first successful Sinn Féin candidate for parliament elected for Roscommon in a 1917 by-election, a prisoner apprehended at the Four Courts, was being detained. A few weeks later the same judge, at the behest of Mrs Tom Clarke, the widow of another Easter Week martyr and Proclamation signatory, issued an order of *mandamus* to Eoin MacNeill, the Speaker of the second Dáil, to convene that body. Both the *habeas corpus* and the *mandamus* were ignored. Instead, the Minister for Home Affairs, Eamon Duggan, on 25 July 1922 ordered the rescinding of the Dáil decree that had established the Dáil Courts, except insofar as it extended to Parish and District Courts outside Dublin.[40]

On 29 September 1922 O'Higgins who had now taken that ministry, asked the Dáil to state that the government should, when the military situation permits, move toward the re-establishment of Civil Administration, that is, the pre-War of Independence judicial system, and, 'rescind the Decree establishing [Dáil Éireann] District and Parish Courts, insofar as it has not already been rescinded'. In other words, he wanted to complete what Duggan's decree had started. Suggesting their temporary character, 'hastily conceived as they were in a time of stress', he acknowledged that the Dáil Éireann Courts did do the work that it was intended they should do and very largely 'achieved the object for which they were set up'. But they were 'not the kind that could remain permanent structures in the administration of justice in the country'. While the Dáil Courts had been able 'to exhibit to the world the spectacle of a whole people turning from the alien administration to even the rough and hasty administration set by parliament and by the government [Dáil Éireann] that was holding its own in the teeth of armed terror [Black and Tans, etc.]', now, 'when the entire administration of the country has passed into the hands of the people, and can be moulded by the representatives of the people', the government did not consider those courts 'as adequate to the needs of the time'.

Accordingly, as a temporary measure, the government would appoint district justices with summary magistrates to serve throughout the country in the wake of the arrival of the civil police where the campaign by the irregulars had been brought under control. In addition, a Judicial Committee would be appointed to recommend a national system of justice. But in the meantime, the ordinary County Courts, those courts of the old system, would continue to function. He believed the Irish people should grow out of the 'prejudiced criticism' of those courts as 'British Courts', as 'the authority for making, altering and rescinding of law in this country is now in the hands of the people'. As for the Dáil Courts, a commission would 'wind up and straighten out any tangles there may be in particular counties'. While all the judgments given by the Dáil Courts in the past should not stand, neither could it be argued 'all the judgments given by the Dáil Courts in the past should be reviewed'.[41] The task of that commission was much more formidable than straightening out tangles in view of the understandable anxiety of thousands who had cases either pending in or awaiting enforcement by the now suspended courts. Its success in several months of work was attributable to two men who had been justices in the Dáil Courts, James Meredith and Hugh O'Friel, who had become the secretary to the Department of Home Affairs.[42]

Gavan Duffy complained of the absence of reference to the Dáil Éireann Courts in the constitution. In a reply that may explain much of the rationale behind the government's actions, O'Higgins noted that the constitution had 'to be confirmed, registered, or ratified in the British Parliament', and since the 'British did not recognize the Dáil as such', they could not 'recognize the existence of those particular courts, which were the creatures of the Dáil'.[43]

The same motion dealing with the Dáil Éireann Courts also gave tentative approbation to the Civic Guards, the unarmed national police force that O'Higgins was placing in those parts of the country where the irregular campaign had been brought under control. Their original organization and recruitment had taken place in the spring before the Civil War when Eamon Duggan was the Minister for Home Affairs. Michael Collins recruited ex-RIC men who had been collaborators with his intelligence squads to help form the organization as few of its members had any real police experience.

The new force had not been drawn into the pro and anti-treaty split that divided Sinn Féin and the IRA, even though most of its recruits were active IRA volunteers. However, it was not without problems. The most serious was a mutiny among its 1,500 recruits at the Kildare barracks in May and June 1922. Their major demand was to replace the Commissioner, Michael Staines, a Collins-appointee who had been on the revolutionary Irish republican police, and his staff of several ex-RIC members, with leaders more clearly identifiable with the struggle for independence. Staines and staff discreetly exited and did not reappear in the camp, although he remained as the Commissioner. Collins accepted the leader of the mutineers, Deputy Patrick Brennan, to act as commander of the camp.

After the June election, O'Higgins visited the camp where he addressed the men and told them that the government was prepared to forget the events of the previous few weeks, would appoint a new Commissioner, and conduct an enquiry into the causes of the discontents, and reassured them that no member would be victimized as a result of the enquiry. Three days later, the siege of the Four Courts occurred and the Civil War began. When O'Higgins next visited the camp the following month he told the men that they would soon have to go out among a people divided by Civil War. But central to the police being able to gain popular confidence was their being able to remain above the Civil War conflict. Therefore, in the early months of the conflict, they were used primarily to protect railways and bridges and had only minimal gunfights with anti-treaty forces. The foremost gesture in the effort to gain public acceptance for the force was the decision that they not be armed. This was a great risk as some units of barely trained young men were sent to remote areas, where lawlessness had been rampant, and often housed in temporary or dilapidated quarters with minimal contact with other units or superiors. The first major uniformed appearance by the police was as part of the funeral cortege of Michael Collins.[44]

When the Third Dáil had come into session, O'Higgins gave reassurances that admission and promotion were based on tests, and that the growing pains of the first six months of the organization, including a mutiny at the Kildare training depot, were being overcome. Ex-RIC men, whose presence had caused difficulties would not be included in the future, although provision would be made for those RIC who had resigned from the force during the War of Independence, presumably out of sympathy with the nationalist struggle, and forfeited comfortable pensions. He also agreed that the Commissioner, Eoin O'Duffy, a Deputy for Monaghan, a trained engineer, who had been assistant Chief of Staff and then GOC South Western Command during the Civil War, would cease to be a politician, and his early resignation from the Dáil could be expected.[45]

IMPLEMENTATION OF EMERGENCY POWERS

On October 10, the Catholic hierarchy issued a pastoral condemning the campaign of the irregulars and confirming the authority of the government. The sacraments were to be denied to those who persisted in the irregular campaign, although a significant number of clergy turned a deaf ear to the directive. A government that was still wet behind the ears in the exercise of conventional authority appreciated clerical support. That appreciation would be manifested by an especially deferential attitude toward hierarchical opinion on various issues in the decade that followed. Indeed, when most of the irregulars had turned constitutional and ultimately came to power in 1932 they also persisted in that deference as a means of demonstrating their legitimacy.

On October 12 the government announced that the military courts would begin to function three days later. On the morning of November 17, the court ordered the first executions, which were of four rank and file irregulars charged with possession of revolvers without authority. The cold indirect announcement of the action, which Dáil members learned about in a newspaper, prompted expressions of outrage by Labour members. Johnson criticized the 'bald form' in which the announcement of the trial and executions had taken place and wanted more explanation of the circumstances, as he doubted anyone believed that 'the possession of a revolver warrants the execution of the man or the woman who possessed it'.

O'Higgins defended the executions as necessary for the life of the nation, and insisted the executions were not vindictive, but were for deterrence. He argued that the deterrent would be most effective on the irregulars if the first cases were from the rank and file, rather than of a well-known figure. Otherwise, some irregulars might argue that the one executed was killed not for what he had done, but 'because he was a leader' or 'because he was an Englishman'. The reference to 'Englishman', was understood by everyone to be Erskine Childers, who had been captured by the government forces in possession of a revolver (ironically, given to him by Michael Collins). The specific reference weakened O'Higgins' point about the deterent effectiveness of punishing rank and file figures. It caused many to assume he was personally anxious for the execution of Childers for whom he had a great dislike.[46] Earlier he had specifically named Childers as 'the able Englishman' who played a leading role in promoting the irregular objective of 'the complete breakdown of the economic and social fabric'.[47] The invalid significance he attached to Childers among the irregulars was prompted by ideological and personal hostility shared by Arthur Griffith and was partly a consequence, but scarcely justified by, Childers' own eccentricity and elitism.

The execution was delayed until November 24 because Childers had consented to a *habeas corpus* action being undertaken in his name on the grounds that it might benefit eight others charged with him. When it did take place his execution raised expected outrage in the Dáil. O'Higgins' defence of the execution suggested that his own nationalism was of a more ethnic and representative character than that of the republican ideologists. His rhetoric had the same tone as the O'Connellites' championing 'Old Ireland' against the Young Irelanders or the Bantry Band's criticism of the 'English Protestant' Parnell. He expounded on the problem of 'the people who came into this national struggle on the last emotional wave, who have not the tradition of Irish nationality, who have not the conception of the grim continuity of this struggle and the grim upward rise of a submerged race'. He insisted that 'this country is not a stage or a platform whereon certain neurotic women and a certain megalomaniac kind of men may cut their capers'. What was at stake was 'the ownership of this country by all the men and women and little children who inhabit it'. The loss of some lives was worthwhile 'to vindicate the principle which is the basis of democracy – the very basis of representative government'.[48]

### ASSASSINATION AND RETALIATION

On November 27, after five IRA prisoners had been tried and convicted by military court and executed, the IRA Army Council issued a retaliatory warning to the Speaker of the Dáil that 'every member of your body who voted for this resolution [the Public Safety Resolution] by which you pretend to make legal the murder of soldiers is equally guilty', and 'due notice' was given that unless IRA prisoners be treated according to the rules of war 'we shall adopt very drastic measures to protect our forces'.[49] On December 7, the day after King George V had proclaimed the constitution of the Irish Free State to come into operation, members of the Dublin Brigade of the IRA killed Seán Hales, a pro-treaty TD for Cork (and, ironically, the brother of one of the party that had ambushed Michael Collins), and seriously wounded Pádraic Ó'Máille, Deputy Speaker of the Dáil and Deputy for Galway, just outside Leinster House. That morning both had attended an organizational meeting of what was to become the pro-government political party, ultimately called Cumann na nGaedheal.[50]

Finding itself under serious assault, with the very members of its parliament under threat, the Executive Council responded in a most drastic and decisive manner and approved the retaliatory execution of four republican prisoners: Rory O'Connor, Liam Mellowes, Joseph McKelvey, and Richard Barrett, all of whom had been captured at the siege of the Four Courts. Their apprehension had preceded the establishment of the military courts by several months and they had never been tried. Accordingly, their executions were outside of any law, even the emergency military law.

The Minister for Defence, Richard Mulcahy, was the major advocate of the action, with Joseph McGrath and O'Higgins being the last to agree, but because O'Higgins was the Minister for Home Affairs (later renamed Justice) and was a strong law and order advocate, he became the cabinet member most clearly linked with the deed. The fact that one of those executed, Rory O'Connor, had been the best man at his wedding a year earlier and had been his assistant in the Department of Local Government during the War of Independence made O'Higgins appear particularly ruthless. While consenting to the 'extra-legal' execution of his own best man and close friend might consolidate a view of O'Higgins as tyrannical, what would be said if he had asked that his friend be exempted and the others executed? The only approach that would have spared him later criticism would be to have opposed the execution of all four. The fact that he had reluctantly accepted the retaliatory action, as noted in the diary of his close friend, Patrick Hogan, and his commitment to the unity of the beleaguered government can be seen as mitigating considerations.[51]

The announcement of the executions in the Dáil provoked almost universal condemnation that ranged from the charge 'murder' and 'foul, bloody and unnatural' made by Labour deputies through the muted criticism of the *Irish Independent*, which said 'we deprecate such a proceeding', and hoped that 'what happened yesterday morning may not occur again', to a private letter to Cosgrave from the Catholic Archbishop of Dublin, Edward Bryne, insisting that the action was 'not only unwise but entirely unjustifiable from the moral point of view. That one man should be punished for another's crime seems to me to be absolutely unjust.' He added the practical advice that the policy was 'bound to alienate many friends of the government, and it requires all the sympathy it can get'.[52]

Mulcahy, as Minister for Defence and Commander-in-Chief of the Army, was the major governmental spokesman on the matter, but O'Higgins also spoke to the Dáil, insisting that the action was not one of anger, but 'was done coldly; it was done deliberately – simply looking the whole situation in the eye and in the belief that only by that method would representative government or democratic institutions be preserved here'. The assault on the members of the Dáil the day before was the same as striking at the people who elected them, and 'therein lies the most criminal aspect of the wretched crime that was committed yesterday'. It was 'part and parcel of the continuing crime against the people and against the whole basis of democratic government and democratic thought that has been carried on in this country for a full twelve months now'. To those who appealed to the rules of war, O'Higgins said there was 'but one answer': that was 'that while the existence of this nation is at stake, there can be but one code – though it sounds a grim code – whereby to judge the actions of those who have been made responsible for the restoration of order here, and that is the code, "*Salus populi suprema lex*"'. There had developed 'a state of affairs which takes things out of the hands of the civil power and out of the hands of the ordinary constitutional machinery of the country, and it demands that large and far-reaching powers be delegated to your Army'. The Army Council carried out the executions after the fullest discussion with the government, and the government 'will stand with the Army Council when there is a question of indemnity for that act'.

Noting that the government consisted of young men with minimal experience, O'Higgins acknowledged that, 'if we had years of apprenticeship, if we could have foreseen in our youth that we would be in this particular capacity and in this particular position to-day, we would be wiser'. But 'fate, or the will of the people, call it what you wish, has placed us in this position that we are the custodians of the life of the nation . . . and we know no better means than the means we have been employing since last June.' While the government did not have 'the long tradition of government that families in other countries have – families from which rulers have been selected for generations', he reassured them that nothing had been done 'that was inspired by any other motive than the securing of the welfare and the safety and the freedom of the Irish people'. Nothing was done 'through personal vengeance' or 'through hot blood'. As for suggestions of personal spite or vindictiveness, he asserted, 'One of these men was a friend of mine', at which point he broke down in tears.[53]

Subsequent to the retaliatory executions, no further member of the Dáil was killed or wounded, although the homes of four members were torched soon after. A child was burned to death in one, that of Deputy Seán McGarry for Mid Dublin. There were no further official retaliatory executions, although executions authorized by the military tribunals continued. While fear of governmental retaliation might have inhibited further assassinations, republican reluctance to employ assassination, regardless of the formally proclaimed organizational policy, also might have been a reason for there not being any more.[54]

Although there were no further assassinations, republican outrages intensified and would be countered by outrages by some of the National Army forces, as the Civil War entered its most bitter period, December of 1922 and the early months of 1923. Members of the Seanad also were subject to intimidation. On December 6, the same day that Deputy Hales was killed, Senator Martin Fitzgerald, the proprietor of the *Freeman's Journal* (a pro-government paper), received a death threat if he did not leave Ireland within two days, although he ignored the threat. Four days later, the business premises of Senator Mrs Wyse Power, who had been in the Ladies' Land League, the Gaelic League, and was one of the founders of Sinn Féin, was bombed. The day after Christmas, Sir William Hutcheson Poe, an elderly senator, was kidnapped, threatened, and robbed. Although released, he shortly afterwards took up residence in England. At a cabinet meeting O'Higgins suggested providing protection for Hutcheson Poe's house, which would merit very high compensation for damages. He furthermore recommended that in retaliation for the destruction of the homes of members of the Dáil and Seanad, the military should order the closing of the homes of prominent irregular leaders or supporters for each time a home of a member of the Dáil or Seanad would be attacked.[55]

On January 9, the ancestral home of Senator John Bagwell, who had been a Justice of the Peace for County Tipperary and was the General Manager of the Great Northern Railway, was burned. It had contained valuable art works and a fine private library. On January 12, the surgeon and man of letters, Senator Oliver St John Gogarty, a champion swimmer, barely escaped republican captors by swimming the icy waters of the Liffey. On January 29, Palmerstown, the beautiful Kildare mansion of the Earl of Mayo, a member of the Seanad who had been a representative peer[56] from Ireland in the British House of Lords, was burned. Both the County Mayo home of Senator Maurice Moore, a veteran officer of the Connaught Rangers and an instructor with the Irish Volunteers, and the residence of Senator Thomas Linehan at White Church, County Cork, were burned on February 1. The attacks on senators and their property persisted until the end of March. There had been a total of thirty-seven senators' homes burned in January and February alone.[57] Even President Cosgrave's home was destroyed on January 14. On Sunday, February 11, three irregulars came to Woodlands, Stradbally, County Leix, the home of O'Higgins' father, determined on burning it. When the doctor tried to disarm one, the others shot and killed him. While they did not destroy the house, they did burn the hayrick. All the while O'Higgins' mother and two younger sisters were present. Significantly, O'Higgins' mother gave no evidence as to the identity of those involved, although she may well have recognized them as neighbours and possibly patients of her husband, and no one was ever charged with the deed.[58]

The actions of the Army of the Free State at times became unwarranted and illegitimate. One area in which its record was most deplorable was County Kerry, a stronghold of the irregular guerilla campaign. While most of the towns had been taken in Kerry, the irregulars were still very strong in the countryside. The Army units that were sent to Kerry included many of the Dublin fighters employed so effectively by Michael Collins in his murderous campaign against the authorities of Dublin Castle. Paddy Daly, who became the commander of the Free State forces in Kerry in January, was reported to have said 'Nobody asked me to take my kid gloves to Kerry and I didn't take them.'[59] It was reported that the Kerry Command executed nineteen people, even before the Army Emergency Powers Resolution, which authorized the military courts with power of execution, had gone into effect.[60] When five Free State soldiers had been killed by a mine on 6 March, Daly ordered that irregular prisoners be employed in any further clearances of mines. Within the next five days, in three separate and highly suspicious incidents, twenty-two prisoners were killed while engaged in clearing mines. In one incident, at Ballyseedy, it was charged that the Free State soldiers had in fact detonated the mine after the prisoners had been tied together. The only inquiry about the incidents, which exonerated the Army, was conducted by Daly and other officers of the Kerry Command.[61] When Thomas Johnson asked about them in the Dáil, Mulcahy, the Minister for Defence, replied that the commanding officers in question 'have my fullest confidence', that he had 'the fullest confidence that the honour of the Army is as deeply rooted in them as in any of us here at Headquarters or in any member of the government', and that he was 'convinced that there is no foundation in fact' for the charges about the incidents. But O'Higgins, when asked if he would consider an inquest in view of the circumstances that had been made known, replied he certainly would.[62]

O'Higgins' reaction contrasted with Mulcahy's vigorous confidence in the military. This was symptomatic of differences between the two men, which would magnify over the next year culminating in the Army Mutiny crisis of March 1924. Mulcahy's defence of the Kerry Command was unjustified, although understandable given his efforts to put a military force together under most difficult circumstances. The great expansion of the size of the army was not accompanied by well-trained ranks, as was borne out by internal army reports of the same period. The Dublin Guards and other units serving in the South West of the country were described as 'very badly disciplined, frequently mutinous, very inefficient from a military point of view, sometimes treacherous, and, except in certain barracks, dirty and slovenly'. The report went on to state that: 'the inefficiency of the officers is amazing. Large numbers cannot read a map. They know nothing of fighting beyond the limited tactics of ambushing, street fighting, car bombing, and private assassinations. They have no control over the men, and while mixing among them in a manner fatal to discipline, do not look after the health, sanitation or comfort of the men.'[63]

In addition to the weaknesses in terms of discipline and military competence, the crossing of lines of command and authority created tension within the government. The Executive Council recommended that Cosgrave, Joseph McGrath, the Minister for Industry and Commerce, O'Higgins, and Mulcahy should make recommendations about a tentative 'Council of Defence' to supervise the military. Three days later, on 9 April 1923, Mulcahy submitted a letter to the Executive Council tendering the resignation of the Army Council in response to the implication of criticism in the very creation of that Council of Defence. However, the resignations were not accepted. Eight days later the Council of Defence was set up, consisting of Cosgrave, McGrath, O'Higgins, and Mulcahy, with the power of inquiring into the administration of the military, of recommending the removal of any officer above the rank of Major General as well as vetoing the nomination of his successor, and 'to exercise a general supervision and direction over strategy'.[64]

O'Higgins was not blind to deficiencies within agencies that were his responsibility. One in particular was the Criminal Invesigations Department. Operating out of Oriel House as a counter-intelligence agency, it had been recruited from the same circles of hardened Collins men as the Dublin Guard that performed so outrageously in Kerry. O'Higgins summarized the character of the CID in a report to the Cabinet: 'out of a total of eighty-six men, twenty-five were of a good type and could possibly be absorbed into the present "G" Division of the DMP [Dublin Metropolitan Police], thirty-one were "hopeless" and would have to be got rid of, while the remaining thirty constituted a middle group whose case would probably be met by disbandment, with perhaps payment of a bonus by way of compensation'.[65]

HUNGER STRIKE PROTESTS AND THE END OF THE CIVIL WAR

Although critical of Army shortcomings, O'Higgins was uncompromising in his response to any threat from the irregulars and their sympathizers to the authority of the Free State, especially anything bordering on intimidation. One area where the irregular cause tried to gain mileage was in the matter of prisoners, of whom the government had interned nearly 10,000 by the spring of 1923. When an irregular threat forced the managers of Dublin theatres to close on March 15 as a gesture of solidarity with prisoner grievances, O'Higgins urged the government to be uncompromising and order the theatres to reopen the next day under threat of fine and to continue their advertisements without reference to the enforced closing. Ten days later he reported the theatres had agreed to remain open. At the same time, privileges such as letters, parcels, and fresh tobacco were withdrawn from the prisons until further notice.[66]

Another issue confronting the government was hunger striking by prisoners as a means of securing release. In the autumn of 1922 Mary MacSwiney, the sister of the Cork Lord Mayor who had died on hunger strike during the War of Independence, was released when she undertook a protest fast upon arrest. When compassion was sought for two more hunger-striking women during the following spring by alluding to the MacSwiney case, O'Higgins acknowledged that the concession to her 'was due to her family'. But since her release she continued 'to exhort young people of both sexes throughout the country to continue to fling themselves down at the new born state, to drag it down, and to continue to wage a campaign of criminal methods', which had resulted in her re-imprisonment. [67]

He had no doubt that MacSwiney's earlier release had inspired the action of the current hunger strikes, and if they were released it would influence 'future hunger strikers and it will become more and more difficult for the government to take a stand on any future case'. However, he ultimately conceded to the release of the hunger-striking women when his colleague for Leix–Offaly, Dr Patrick McCartan, moved that, in the opinion of the Dáil, in the future 'prisoners who decide to go on hunger strike to secure release should be allowed to take the full consequence of their act'. In his statement seconding the motion, O'Higgins reiterated his conviction that if the state was to be saved, 'if it is to live and flourish in present circumstances', they must assert 'our right to arrest and detain its citizens and citizenesses'. He added that if the state's right to arrest and detain citizens participating in a conspiracy against the state is 'challenged in the future by this women's weapon of the hunger strike', then, thanks to the resolution, the state had 'the moral support of the Dáil, in allowing a person who does that to reap all the consequences of that course'. [68]

On the question of the internees in general, he admitted the impossibility of any legal system being able to try the 10,000 or 12,000 prisoners 'that as a matter of necessity we arrested and detained within the last ten months'. But the internment was required by the wartime conditions, and even with the increased talk of peace towards the end of April, he sensed from the perspective of his department 'that we are not out of the wood'. He noted how in many areas 'you have conditions bordering on anarchy'. Property is 'in possession of people who have not a scrap or vestige of legal title to it'. In what might be a prophetic indication of his own subsequent career, he noted the grave legal problems any executive in the country would have to face, problems which would 'make it utterly out of the question for any Executive to be over worried about the popularity of this or unpopularity of that course'. If the government has 'to do their real honest duty by the people they will frequently have to take courses that irresponsible people will not consider popular'. [69]

The Civil War ground to a halt in April. A peace resolution presented by de Valera to the members of the IRA Executive at a series of secret meetings in County Waterford in the last week of March was narrowly rejected by a vote of six to five. De Valera had proposed to end the armed campaign if abstentionist TDs were allowed to take their seats without having to take the oath to the King and if republicans would not be obstructed in the peaceful pursuit of full national independence. Liam Lynch, however, was convinced that it was not yet time to give up the military struggle. Within a couple of weeks, on April 10, he himself was mortally wounded. A few days later six more IRA commandants, including Austin Stack and Tom Deerig, an abstentionist TD for South Mayo, would lead a hunger strike by interned prisoners in the autumn of 1923, and served as a minister in all de Valera governments until 1954, were captured. The Army Council, at the behest of the newly appointed commander, Frank Aiken, a Commandant of the Northern Division of the IRA during the War of Independence and an abstentionist TD for Louth, and later the holder of major ministerial positions in Fianna Fáil governments until 1968, agreed to give up the armed struggle. Four of them on April 26 met with de Valera and the rump of his 'republican' cabinet and it was unanimously agreed to suspend hostilities.

The next day de Valera issued on behalf of the 'Government of the Republic of Ireland' his peace proclamation. It reiterated republican doctrine about the indefeasible and inalienable sovereign rights of the nation and about legitimate authority deriving from the people of Ireland, and accepted as the ultimate court of appeal 'the people of Ireland, the judgment being by the majority vote of the adult citizenry'. The decision of the people had to be followed, 'not because the decision is necessary, right or just or permanent', but its acceptance is necessary for peace, order, and unity and 'is the democratic alternative to arbitrament by force'. The IRA Command simultaneously issued orders to suspend 'all offensive operations' as of noon, April 30, but to 'ensure that – while remaining on the defensive – all units take adequate measures to protect themselves and their munitions'.[70]

De Valera sought through Senators Jameson and Douglas to get Cosgrave and his government to accept a peace agreement. Under the agreement the republican forces would be allowed to keep in each province an arsenal of weapons under their own supervision, republican supporters would not be discriminated against in the awarding of compensation for losses incurred in the conflict with England, a general amnesty would proclaim that 'all political prisoners of war shall be released', and 'further military or civil action' against supporters of the republican cause would cease, and the funds of the republic 'subscribed in the U.S. and elsewhere, and at present sealed up by injunction', would be immediately available 'for peaceful efforts in support of the republican party'. In his conversations with Douglas and Jameson, de Valera indicated a wish to meet with Cosgrave and other members of the government, but not with O'Higgins. When Jameson reported on the meetings to Cosgrave and other ministers, O'Higgins was the most suspicious of de Valera's desire for peace, and, indeed, had been opposed to any meeting with de Valera.[71]

Understandably, the government rejected the proposal, as the cabinet was convinced that 'the interests of the country would not be served by the government's entering into peace negotiations with the irregulars whose power was now definitely broken'.[72] Then, on May 24, de Valera issued his celebrated message to the 'Legion of the Rearguard'. He announced that 'the Republic can no longer be defended successfully by your arms and the military victory must be allowed to rest for the moment with those who have destroyed the Republic'.[73]

At the same Cabinet meeting at which the government had rejected the peace overtures by the republicans O'Higgins alerted his colleagues to the fact that 'as soon as a state of war was definitely ended the special powers enjoyed by the military with regard to search, arrest, trial and detention of civilians would have to be replaced by somewhat similar powers exercised for a limited period by the civil authorities,[74] for which the necessary sanction would have to be sought from the Oireachtas'. Accordingly, he and other relevant ministers were directed to submit memoranda to the Attorney General who would prepare legislation for the new situation.[75] The new legislation, a Public Safety Bill, would be attended to in the closing sessions of the Third Dáil. O'Higgins' energies for the next several months would be taken up with that legislation and its enforcement, specifically the matter of prisoner release.

### NOTES

1. John M. Regan, *The Irish Counter-Revolution*, pp. 67–74.
2. Hopkinson, *Green Against Green*, pp. 109–14.
3. *Provisional Government Meetings* (30 June, 3, 4, 5, 6, 7, 8, and 10 July 1922), NA, G 1/2.
4. *Ibid.* (12 July 1922), NA, G 1/2.
5. Jim Maher, *Harry Boland* (Dublin: Mercier Press, 1996), p. 243.
6. The later incident leaves open to this day grounds for conspiratorial speculation as to why and how it happened. Probably Collins' own bravado in

ordering his cortege to stand and fight a small ambushing party and his reckless exposure of himself were as much to blame as anything. Possibly the ambushers themselves were unaware at the time that the one casualty in the fracas was Collins himself. A more substantial question is why was Collins in such an irregular infested area? No doubt he was trying to make contact with some of his old comrades-in-arms, now on the other side, with the hope of winning them over. Would he have been ready to offer terms that would undo the electoral results of June, further revise the proposed constitution, and, possibly, endanger the treaty? Whatever might have been his inclinations, his successors in government would not be of such a disposition.

7. *Provisional Government Meetings* (26, 30 August 1922), NA, G 1/3.
8. Regan, *Irish Counter-Revolution*, p. 81.
9. Kevin O'Higgins, 'The Quenching of Our Shining Light', *Arthur Griffith: Michael Collins* (Dublin: Martin Lester, n.d.), pp. 42–3.
10. De Vere White, *Kevin O'Higgins*, p. 105; Regan, *Irish Counter-Revolution*, pp. 83–95.
11. *Dáil Éireann*, I (18 September 1922), 357–61.
12. *Ibid.*, (20 September 1922), 476–81.
13. *Ibid.*, (21 September 1922), 572–3.
14. Donal O'Sullivan, *The Irish Free State and its Senate* (London: Faber and Faber, 1940), pp. 76–81.
15. *Dáil Éireann*, I (20 September 1922), 481–2.
16. *Ibid.*, 483-5.
17. *Ibid.*, 578.
18. *Ibid.* (26 September 1922), 753–5.
19. *Ibid.*, 756–8.
20. *Ibid.* (25 September 1922), 696–8.
21. *Ibid.*, 706–7, 710–11.
22. Maryann Valiulis, 'Power, Gender and Identity in the Irish Free State', *Journal of Women's History* 6, 4; 7,1 (1995).
23. *Dáil Éireann*, I (25 September 1922), 670–2.
24. *Ibid.* (18 October 1922), 1,671–84.
25. *Ibid.* (5 October 1922), 1,211–2.
26. *Ibid.*, 1,214–19.
27. *Ibid.*, 1,225–6, 1233–4.
28. *Ibid.* (10 October 1922) 1,429–34.
29. *Ibid.* (18 October 1922), 1,701–2.
30. *Ibid.* (5 October 1922), 1,240–53.
31. Thomas Towey, 'Hugh Kennedy and the Constitutional Development of the Irish Free State', *The Irish Jurist*, XII (1977), pp. 359–60; Ronan Keane, 'The Voice of the Gael: Chief Justice Kennedy and the Emergence of the New Irish Court System', *Ibid.*, XXXI (1996), p. 210. *Kennedy Papers*, UCDA, P4/301. Memo by Hugh Kennedy on implementation of treaty.
32. *Dáil Éireann* (11 October 1922), 1,458–65.
33. *Ibid.* (19 October 1922), 1,768–78.
34. Colm Campbell, *Emergency Law in Ireland, 1918–1925* (Oxford: Clarendon Press, 1994), pp. 163–4, 246–7.
35. *Dáil Éireann* (14 September 1922), 275–8.
36. *Ibid.* (28 September 1922), 892–5.
37. *Ibid.* (27 September 1922), 857–62.
38. Mary Kotsonouris, *The Winding-up of the Dáil Courts, 1922–1925: an obvious duty* (Dublin: Four Courts, 2004), pp. 6–13.
39. *Ibid.*, pp. 17–18.

40. Ronan Keane, *The Irish Jurist*, XXXI (1996), pp. 210–11.
41. *Dáil Éireann*, I (29 September 1922), 953–5, 958, 984–5.
42. Kotsonouris, *Winding-up of the Dáil Courts*, p. 49.
43. *Dáil Éireann* (10 October 1922), 1436–7.
44. Conor Brady, *Guardians of the Peace* (Dublin: Gill and Macmillan, 1974), 40–6, 57–70.
45. *Dáil Éireann* (29 September 1922), 985–9.
46. *Ibid.* (17 November 1922), 2,262–68.
47. *Ibid.* (27 September 1923), 857–62.
48. *Ibid.* (29 November 1922), 2,404–5.
49. *Ibid.*, 975.
50. John M. Regan, *Irish Counter-Revolution*, p. 115.
51. De Vere White, *Kevin O'Higgins*, pp. 256–7.
52. *Dáil Éireann*, II (8 December 1922), 49; *Irish Independent* (11 December 1922); Dermot Keogh, *The Vatican, the Bishops and Irish Politics 1919–1939* (Cambridge: Cambridge University Press, 1986), p. 98.
53. *Dáil Éireann* (8 December 1922), 67–73.
54. Hopkinson, *Green Against Green*, pp. 191–2; Regan, *Irish Counter-Revolution*, pp. 119–20.
55. *Cabinet Minutes* (10 January 1923), C 1/27, NA.
56. Following the Act of Union of 1800 and the ending of both houses of the Irish Parliament, members of the Irish House of Lords elected representative members to sit in the British House of Lords.
57. Donal O'Sullivan, *The Irish Free State and its Senate*, pp. 102–8, Hopkinson, *Green Against Green*, p. 195.
58. De Vere White, *Kevin O'Higgins*, pp. 145–6; Una O'Higgins O'Malley, *From Pardon and Protest* (Galway: Arlen House, 2001), p. 20.
59. Hopkinson, *Green Against Green*, p. 205.
60. James Eoin Lynch, 'Operations and Conduct of the Free State Army Command during the Irish Civil War', (UCD: MA thesis, 1996), p. 40.
61. *Ibid.*, pp. 54–5.
62. *Dáil Éireann*, II (17 April 1923), 185–90.
63. *Mulcahy Papers*, UCDA, P7A /141.
64. *Cabinet Minutes* (30 March, 9, 17 April 1923), NA, C 1/78, 81, 85.
65. *Ibid.* (25 May 1923), NA, C 1/111.
66. *Ibid.* (16, 26 March 1923), NA, C 1/64, 74.
67. *Dáil Éireann*, III (25 April 1923), 439.
68. *Ibid.* (2 May 1923), 522–6.
69. *Ibid.* (20 April 1923), 355–6.
70. Macardle, *Irish Republic*, pp. 843–8.
71. J. Anthony Gaughan, ed., *Memoirs of Senator James G. Douglas, Concerned Citizen* (Dublin: University College Dublin Press, 1998), pp. 101–2.
72. *Cabinet Minutes* (16 April 1923), NA, C 1/84.
73. Macardle, *Irish Republic*, pp. 851–8.
74. O'Higgins' desire to replace the military with a civilian authority, including the police force, in the effort to contain the irregulars was suggestive of the growing differences between himself and Mulcahy. See Gillian McGoey, 'The assassination of Kevin O'Higgins and its implications for law and order policy in the Irish Free State', UCD: MA thesis, 1996.
75. *Cabinet Minutes* (16 April 1923), NA, C 1/84.

# 4

# The Free State Triumphs

O'HIGGINS' ROLE in the closing days of the Third Dáil and in the opening months of the Fourth Dáil was to assert the ascendancy of the new government against a substantial movement that challenged its legitimacy and some who violently opposed it. He saw tolerance for such opponents as an opening of the door for illegality and anarchy. Accordingly, while he sought to re-establish a regular judicial system and a police force, he thought it necessary to renew, this time in the hands of civilian rather than military authorities, the power of detention. He also accepted the need for the extraordinary punishment of flogging for certain types of crime that had become rampant and sought to strengthen the ability of sheriffs and bailiffs to seize property from debtors. He did not accept the view of some Dáil and Seanad members that the absence of war ought to have allowed concessions to the irregulars, whether through release from internment or admission of those elected to the Dáil. He did not share the civil liberties concerns about severe penalties and arbitrary apprehensions or seizures or the notion that 'law and order' policies were only serving propertied interests.

O'Higgins' position on these issues was in accord with his conservatism on a variety of other matters. For instance, during the debate on the Governor General's address to the Oireachtas, he noted the relationship between security – that is – law and order, and business enterprise. Decidedly appreciative of the entrepreneurial spirit and distrustful of socialistic rhetoric, he asserted that

> A man will not sow unless he has reasonable prospect of reaping. It is only natural to expect that, and a man will not put money into a

> commercial enterprise unless he has a reasonable prospect of getting
> his return...Men do not go into business enterprises from any other
> motives than the motives of the man who works...lack of security
> kills enterprise, kills development, creates an unhealthy atmosphere in
> which development and enterprise die, and then you have
> unemployment.

Furthermore, 'the general tone and outlook of organized labour in
the country' would make him, if he was a farmer, sceptical to 'break
the field', as he 'would consider it questionable whether I would reap
what I had sowed or not, whether I would have a disastrous strike
that would leave my produce caught by the weather'.[1]

When he was with local government during the War of
Independence he was sceptical about the jobbery and incompetence
of many local authorities. That distrust persisted into the Free State
era, when he advocated greater power over them by ministers,
including that of dismissal. Darrell Figgis suggested that Dáil
approval should be required for the specific dismissal of a local
authority by a minister. O'Higgins replied that he did not expect it
would be an ordinary thing that local authorities 'should prove
themselves so utterly false to their trust, or so utterly incompetent to
perform the duties attaching to their representative positions', that
they would have to be dismissed and replaced with a Commissioner.
But if it did happen, then the procedure of being closed down and
replaced should be 'quite an ordinary or natural or routine thing',
and 'a proper thing'. It was 'the barest justice to the ratepayers,
whose money these people are handling under a stewardship or
trusteeship, that such action should be taken, and taken promptly,
by the responsible central authority'.[2] In these remarks, as in his
subsequent career, O'Higgins demonstrated a patrician sense of duty
and public rectitude quite out of tune with the more populist
tolerance for human weakness and political jobbery often connected
with Irish political figures, both at home and abroad.

One of the clearest expressions of O'Higgins' conservatism
occurred in a debate concerning the Free State Army's seizure of
trespassing cattle on land in Galway belonging to a landlord who
refused to sell land or even give conacre facilities to his tenants. His
home had been taken over by the irregulars, who burned it the night
they evacuated it. Some property was taken and fences were broken
to use as roadblocks. Cattle belonging to tenants strayed onto the
now derelict farm. These cattle were seized by the military and sold.

The issue was raised by Thomas O'Connell, Labour deputy for Galway and general secretary of the Irish National Teachers Organization, who regarded the seizures as arbitrary. He thought they punished people who were not the real culprits, who were the irregulars. Accordingly, trespassing should be dealt with by civil action. But O'Higgins replied that the situation was one of 'anarchy', preached by voice and pen and 'sent out in documents from philosophers in jail'. He argued that 'such things as have happened in Galway are done under cover of an irregular campaign and are, in fact, merely an acute manifestation of irregular mentality'. The Army, the armed servants of the government, has a mandate 'to restore order and to uphold and maintain the legal rights of all the citizens'. Furthermore, 'it is right that we should use these armed servants in the way that we think best calculated to restore in the shortest possible space of time normal conditions'. Like a doctor who comes on a serious case, we 'will treat the cause. And the cause is greed; the desire to get rich quick regardless of law human or divine; to get something for nothing; to get the fruits of work without work'.

To the suggestion that the outrage was not so severe since the victim was a landlord, he answered that 'for many a long day we have been seeking in this country a time when one man would be as good as another'. Accordingly, the owner's 'home and property will be defended as sternly and as rigidly as the home and property of any poor man, or tenant or labourer in the country'. The government was seeking to 'restore conditions in which people will, if charity is not sufficient, if neighbourly spirit is not sufficient, respect the legal rights of their neighbours'. Unfortunately, 'the bonds of religion and human respect have broken down, and people are running amok in riot and plunder'. Because the cause was greed, it had to be made clear to them that robbery was not going to be profitable. 'We cannot make omelettes without breaking eggs. We cannot build up a disciplined and self-respecting decent country without hitting pretty hard a head here and there to encourage the rest.' He insisted the revolution against the British should not be interpreted as the advocacy of 'the non-payment of particular things' or that people 'ought not to meet their liabilities'. Dáil Éireann had sought, 'with a clear mandate from the people...to make British administration impossible here', but they had done so 'with all due respect for the rights of all our citizens, and we never declared war on a particular class or section of our fellow-citizens'. He boasted that 'we were probably the most conservative-minded revolution-aries that ever put through a successful revolution'.[3]

The few remaining years of his life were dedicated to ensuring the permanence of that conservative self-government that he had helped to achieve. As Minister for Justice (earlier called Home Affairs), he advanced a substantial legislative agenda to enhance the enforce-ment of law and order during the Civil War and immediately after. Those measures helped earn for him the reputation of, in the eyes of some, a repressive tyrant or, others, the saviour of the state. Central to his approach was a willingness to employ the instruments of the old regime, including its judges and judicial system, since they had become responsible to a democratic government.

### NORMALIZING LEGISLATION

Among the earliest measures introduced soon after the establishment of the Irish Free State were a British Enactments Bill and an Expiring Laws Continuance Bill, which gave force to existing British legislation having effect in Ireland, allowed existing statutory boards to continue, and renewed certain British pieces of legislation applicable to Ireland of a non-controversial and routine nature, such as game and traffic laws.[4] Another earlier measure of significance was an Amnesty Bill, which indemnified 'persons who supported the British Government for the last few years, by carrying out orders, or being in any way responsible for acts, which would be or might be the subject of legal proceedings'. To soften possible misgivings about the measure, 'the release of the Connaught Rangers' was announced as 'a further proof of the British Government's desire to efface bitter memories of the more recent trouble'. Those being released were Irishmen in the Connaught Rangers who had mutinied while serving in India, but who had not been released as had been other republican prisoners upon the treaty settlement because their imprisonment had been 'under separate military jurisdiction'.[5]

Two weeks later O'Higgins introduced the first of a series of law and order measures. It was the Enforcement of Law (Occasional Powers) Bill. The measure granted power to the Minister for Home Affairs to appoint sub-sheriffs to assist sheriffs and to allow them to sell goods seized by judicial decree 'at any time and in any place, whether inside or outside the bailiwick of the sub-sheriff making the particular seizure, and, if necessary, outside Saorstát Éireann'. The measure was justified because of the development in the country since the treaty, if not since the truce, of 'a certain amount of static illegality', that is, 'people taking advantage of the political and national situation, withholding payment to their neighbour for value received, withholding money due in various forms, whether through debts, rents, Land Commission annuities'. The legislation sought to deal with 'passive irregulars'. Unlike the active irregulars who are 'out with rifle or bomb or torch' and could be dealt with by the military, the passive irregular is like 'the jackal that prowls near the fighting line, never going into the line of fire, but always ready to pick up the garbage of war'. He can be dealt with by 'the civil machinery', but with the necessary protection and cooperation of the Army.[6]

He argued that the under-sheriffs needed the ability to sell seized goods anywhere, without giving notice that they were seized goods, because they had been subject to intimidation and had seized material stolen back with popular approbation. Turning to his frequent theme of 'the failure of the bailiff as a factor in our civilization', he acknowledged the bailiff had 'a certain amount of odium in this country', but still served a most useful public function in guaranteeing the payment of debt, without which credit would collapse within the country and internationally. 'Nothing will make so speedily for the intensification of the already intense and acute unemployment in the country' than the serious impairment of credit. If he doesn't have the means of recovery, the shopkeeper closes down on credit. 'When credit is stopped there will be less purchasing.' Purchasing power is reduced, orders to the factory will be diminished, and unemployment will spread. He emphasized that 'the disappearance of credit reacts firstly and most strongly on the weakest' in spite of incidents of popular jubilation over failures by bailiffs. They did not realize the 'profound truth...that when commercial enterprise or commercial security in this country disappears the first to be hit is not the person whom someone would call a bloated capitalist, and others an enterprising business man, but the poor man who is laid off from his factory because the orders from the shop are not as great as they were a month or two months ago'.[7] While he accepted that some debtors were 'in genuine financial embarrassment' and unable to pay, 'the great bulk of the cases are simply people who have given way to the human tendency to avoid payment as long as possible'.[8]

Another concern of O'Higgins' was the restoration of a normal judicial system and the removal of the military from a judicial role. To that end on 29 January 1923 the Executive Council had appointed a judiciary committee chaired by James Campbell, Lord Glenavy, the first chairman of the Seanad, who had been a Unionist MP for Dublin and then Dublin University, Solicitor General, Attorney General, Lord Chief Justice, and Lord Chancellor for Ireland, to propose a judicial system for the Free State. For the interim, O'Higgins introduced a District Justices (Temporary Provisions) Bill, which called for the appointment of District Justices to conduct a civilian court system for matters not under the authority of the army courts. The measure also called for the appointment of Parish Commissioners to perform the duties of the old Justices of the Peace, such as signing summons, warrants, administering oaths, committing lunatics, and remanding arrested persons on bail or in custody, and for the appointment of court clerks.

Labour Party leader Thomas Johnson criticized the appointment and removal power it gave to the Executive Council, feared the Parish Commissioners might be selected, as had been the old Justices of the Peace, on the basis of social standing, and that political influence would effect the appointment of clerks. Professor William Magennis, Belfast-born Professor of Philosophy at University College Dublin, and an independent deputy for the National University, sarcastically described the replacement of the JPs with the Parish Commissioners as removing the 'plumaging of the old order', by substituting a new one, since the new District Justices were as removable as the stipendiary magistrates of the old order, who were nicknamed 'Removable Magistrates', because of the uncertainty of their tenure. O'Higgins, however, defended the removing power of a democratically responsible government, arguing there was 'no analogy between the Removable of the past and the District Justice of to-day' as there is 'no analogy between the Executive of to-day and the Castle of the past'. He also gave reassurances that the Parish Commissioners would not be appointed on the basis of social status or wealth. He also understood the wishes of many that those who served on the Dáil Éireann Courts be considered for appointment. But he sought to diminish the renown of those bodies, asking that those courts not be idealized. He even asked that there be consideration in making appointments of court clerks of people who had served in that capacity as long as fifteen to twenty five years in the old courts.

These remarks further indicated his increasing separation from purist revolutionary nationalism and his growing appreciation that the nation of Ireland consisted of more than Sinn Féin supporters. He insisted that: 'It is not in itself a stigma to call a man an ex-Head Constable of the RIC', recalling that 'there was a time when there was very, very little stigma indeed attaching to the man who went into that force. Let us not forget that it was the height of ambition of most young fellows who happened to be five feet nine inches or thereabouts.' Accordingly, having been an old Petty Sessions Clerk or Head Constable of the RIC should not be a barrier to consideration for the new clerkships.[9]

### TEMPORARY PUBLIC SAFETY LEGISLATION

Upon the end of the Civil War (and before the national election required by the constitution within a year of the establishment of the Free State) O'Higgins introduced public safety legislation of six months duration that gave the Minister for Home Affairs the power granted to the military by the Emergency Resolution of the previous autumn. While the new measure did not take the powers away from the military and allowed the continued detention of those presently interned, it was introduced 'in the hope that within a period a situation may arise in which the powers vested at the moment in the military authorities might pass gradually and easily to be exercised by a civil department, and some to cease entirely'.

Gerald Fitzgibbon, an independent TD for Trinity College, who was also a King's Counsellor, applauded the measure because it was 'a step back towards the normal process of law' in contrast to the military tribunals. But Thomas Johnson challenged the need for legislation, which duplicated the existing resolution. Gavan Duffy correctly sensed that O'Higgins' real motive was to offset a pending court ruling that would suspend the emergency resolution on the end of the Civil War, as did Cathal O'Shannon, Deputy Leader of the Labour Party and TD for Louth–Meath, who was born in Antrim, educated at St Columb's College, Derry, a member of the Gaelic League, the IRB, and the Irish Volunteers, an advocate of Labour contesting the 1918 election, a delegate to the Socialist International in Berne, and an advocate of neutrality on the treaty issue. O'Higgins confirmed their suspicions, as he acknowledged that the Bill was designed to meet a likely court decree that there was no longer a state of war to justify the continued internment of 12,000 people under the existing military powers resolution (which the Court of Appeals did on July 31), and the government was 'not prepared to consider the wholesale indiscriminate release on this country, which is barely beginning to settle down to normal conditions, of these twelve thousand'.[10]

In the debate on the second reading of the Bill, O'Higgins repeated the alternative:

> to release upon the country, which is barely finding its feet, barely passing out from a stage of national hysteria to conditions of peace and order, and to some kind of appreciation of civic responsibility, thirteen thousand men – or the great majority of them at any rate – who throughout the last year have been engaged in the most heinous and disgraceful campaign of crime that ever disfigured the pages of this country's history, turn them out to man the hidden guns again, if the people's vote in the coming election fails to coincide with their particular fancy.

He continued his graphic depiction of the state of affairs throughout the country:

> the moral standard has been lowered, and there has been such a wave of degradation that many people have lost all rudder and compass to guide them in matters of right and wrong; they have thrown the moral law to the winds, the law of God as well as the law of man.[11]

The measure stipulated the penalties for certain specific crimes that would be tried in civilian courts. One called for whipping as a penalty for the crimes of armed robbery and arson, both of which had become common during the previous ten months. In response to another problem – cattle trespassing, that is, the use of the land of others for grazing without their permission – the measure would allow the seizure and sale of such stock with the receipts going as compensation to the owner of the land and the rest to the state. Such provisions prompted Johnson to draw parallels between the Bill and a comparable measure passed by the Northern Irish Parliament. He regarded the Minister for Home Affairs as having 'a most extraordinary state of mind' in asking the Dáil for 'powers to co-operate with the military defence forces, and to have handed over to them the power to govern every individual of the state, to intern, as they wish, every person'. Gavan Duffy said he had 'been brought up to believe that the Star Chamber disappeared with the Stuarts, that *lettres-de-cachet* were never to be heard of after the fall of the Bastille', but that now we were going back to 'the same methods that ancient history found so futile'. Instead of the proposed legislation he would 'prefer open and naked government by authority and no Dáil at all. At least we should know where we were and would not pretend to be acting constitutionally'. The proposed legislation was 'a flat, a direct negation of the constitution that the Dáil passed'.[12]

Replying the following week, O'Higgins dismissed as 'extravagant language' the critics' depiction of the measure and repeated that the primary aim of the measure was to detain for six months those of the interned whose release was 'considered prejudicial to the public safety'. He explained that 'to detain any it is necessary to get power to detain all', but having once gotten it, 'you can proceed to use your discretion and to sift fairly harmless and fairly decent men amongst them and give them an opportunity of taking up the broken threads of their lives'. The proposed measure, he insisted, was 'not harsh', and those in the government 'would be false to our trust and to our responsibility to the people' if they would 'turn loose upon them twelve or thirteen thousand men' who have been challenging them and their fundamental rights during the past year. He read from documents containing a statement by prominent irregulars which suggested a readiness to take up arms again upon release and another by an irregular supporter outside the jurisdiction of the state insisting that the republican army was not beaten, had retained its arms, and was intent on going on the offensive in the winter. He depicted the situation as 'a loosening of bonds throughout the last year, a breakdown of moral restraints, a breaking down of the restraint of human respect'. Robbery, which ten to fifteen years ago was 'happily a rare crime in this country, and one of which people stood ashamed, has become rather a routine'. In addition to the momentary 'wave of demoralization', there was 'a supply of arms and explosives secreted throughout the country and available to many'.

A more appropriate parallel was not in the similarity of the terms of the measures with those of the Northern Irish Government, but the employment of arson by both the irregulars and by Black and Tans. Regarding arson and robbery under arms as 'crimes of terrorism', he knew of 'no means of meeting those crimes of terror save by something that will be to the perpetrators a greater terror'. He knew this would seem 'a very crude thing to say' to 'deputies who preen themselves and strut before us as liberals'. Being liberal 'is a delightful *role* to play, but one may not be liberal of one's country's honour and one may not be liberal of the fundamental rights of one's fellow-citizens'. However, while he was not ready to jeopardize the country by the immediate release of up to thirteen thousand prisoners, he envisioned, were the state of the country improved, the possible release of 'prisoners at a very much quicker rate than' the current rate of 200 to 300 a month.[13]

During the committee stage of the debate opponents were concerned about appellate rights for those interned, visiting committees for the detention centres, judicial discretion on penalties, and the specific penalty of flogging. O'Higgins opposed allowing an appellant to receive copies of the reports that justified his detention to the Appeals Council, for that would make of the council a court, when the very fact of detention meant imprisonment without trial, that is, detention of citizens short of legal proof. He doubted the wisdom of another amendment to give the local government bodies the duty to establish committees for the purpose of visiting detention centres to 'hear any complaints' and with 'free access to every part of the place of detention', and 'to every person detained', and 'to all the books of every such place of detention', as he wondered if the local bodies were appropriate 'to entrust this function to', since, for example, 'five-sixths of the County Council of Kerry have been out in arms against the executive government of the state'. He also opposed amendments giving judges discretion on penalties, such as the inclusion of hard labour with imprisonment, insisting that 'there ought to be for these offences a mandatory penalty that would be the minimum'.[14]

Johnson moved to delete the article calling for the whipping of those guilty of armed robbery or of arson. He doubted its effect as a deterrent, since if a person was so brutal that the only way to deter him was physical punishment, it would be 'better to impose a long period of imprisonment', than 'to allow that brutalized person to be free after a period of imprisonment, and to allow his brutalized nature to have full fling upon the body politic'. But O'Higgins defended the penalty, recalling what had happened in the previous ten months, when

> all sense of appreciation of the sanctity of the home, all restraints of human respect, restraints of respect for the moral law, restraints of respect for the law of man, have gone whistling down the wind, because the worst instincts of man have been summoned up, deliberately summoned up in this country, because that criminality

which is latent in man everywhere, which is part of his baser nature, has been called up here.

He continued that men who 'never felt themselves called upon to face the British administration, who never felt themselves called upon to make any particular sacrifice to achieve the object of getting the British out of Ireland', and who waited until the British were out of Ireland, have turned 'on the first native administration here with a ferocity and wantonness that was surprising'. Two kinds of their activity stood out: 'the crime of arson and the crime of robbery, the robbery of the unarmed man with the gun'. The severe penalty was necessary 'to strip the thin little rag of idealism from these two crimes'. As to the suggestion that the use of flogging was not Christian, he alluded to Christ's whipping the moneychangers at the temple. He concluded saying that to meet 'a retrogression from the standards to which civilisation and society had attained' it was necessary to 'step back also in your penalty'.[15]

O'Higgins also opposed a motion by Cathal O'Shannon that notice be given before seizure to enable the owner to discontinue the trespass as some people might not be 'quite aware' they were committing an offence since certain irregular habits had developed during the War of Independence when 'force was used on the national side for the purpose of seizing...certain lands in the possession of people belonging to certain orders, and for the driving of cattle on certain lands which locally were considered as not being put to the best use in the national interest'. An unreceptive O'Higgins, however, was aware that 'a regular traffic and vested interests grew up around this kind of thing', arguing 'the passage of the Bill must be taken as notice by all' and that 'people will have to learn to keep their stock on their own land'.[16]

O'Higgins had to test his wits in defending the measure in the upper house as well. Colonel Maurice Moore, for instance, saw the measure as being 'in direct opposition to the constitution', and while admitting there was some 'sporadic crime throughout the country', believed the emergency powers were unnecessary since the Civil War was over. Senator James Douglas appreciated the position of the government in view of the refusal of de Valera and his followers to 'recognize this government as the lawful government', and 'hand up their arms to it', but found himself in 'very considerable difficulty with regard to the Bill' in view of its reaffirmation of capital punishment, its introduction of flogging, and the removal, for six months, of the discretionary power of the judiciary in sentencing. Mrs Stopford Greene, an historian, a home-rule supporter, and a fundraiser for the Irish Volunteers, feared the alienation of the middle of the road people, the pursuit of whose consent the government might endanger by its preoccupation with crime and its employment of flogging.

O'Higgins replied to the Seanad along the same lines as he did in the Dáil. He recalled that they had 'been through a year of hell, a year of anarchy, crude, naked, and unashamed, in which men robbed with the strong hand that which they could lay hold of'. While there was 'criminality latent in men everywhere', and 'the savage is more or less dormant in most men', the existing situation in Ireland was one 'in which the worst passions and the basest instincts of the people had free play'. Although appreciating 'the fine susceptibilities of the senators and teachtai who deplore the flogging clause', he asked the senators who lived in the orderly and well-guarded capital to consider 'the plain people of this country'. They 'have had no guards, and will have no guards unless the law and the sanctions of the law are adequate for their protection'.[17]

The government did accept some Senate amendments such as one which placed the responsibility for detention for reasons of public safety on a minister rather than on a Garda or Army officer, and another which required the Executive to grant a release of an internee if recommended by the Appeals Council, refer the question back to the Council, or formally charge the prisoner. Another, which gave discretion in sentencing to the summary court judges, was opposed by O'Higgins, who asked if it was too much 'to say that we here, the Parliament, the highest court in the land, should decide the penalties for particular offences' for the next six months? The Seanad vote was a tie and the Speaker cast the deciding vote in favor of the amendment. O'Higgins also accepted an amendment establishing unremunerated inspection committees for the internment camps to be appointed by the minister.[18]

Because Article 47 of the Free State constitution delayed the implementation of legislation for seven days to enable either two-fifths of the Dáil or a majority of the Seanad to petition that it be submitted to a referendum, the possibility existed that a judicial ruling overturning the existing emergency resolution would allow the immediate release of the 12,000 prisoners detained. To prevent that and secure the immediate implementation of the law, the government asked for and received Dáil and Seanad consent, as also allowed in Article 47, to a declaration that the legislation was 'necessary for the immediate preservation of the public peace, health or safety'. Accordingly the Act became capable of immediate implementation upon the signature of the Governor General,[19] which offset the possible effect of a court ruling that the state of war was over and the internment powers of the military were invalid.

### DÁIL ÉIREANN COURTS

Even before the constitution was passed, O'Higgins had secured from the Dáil approval to replace the Dáil Éireann Courts with a combination of temporary justices and the re-employment of the older courts pending the establishment of a permanent court system. Now at the end of the Dáil, a measure was introduced to formally end the revolutionary courts. O'Higgins complained of the difficulties in winding down the business of those courts since the October resolution because of the uncooperative attitude of many of the officials in those courts, who had a hostile attitude toward the government. For instance, only half of the district registrars and only a quarter of the parish clerks had lodged final accounts and statements. Therefore, the new legislation would appoint a Judicial Commission to enforce delivery of these accounts and deal with pending cases in and appeals from enforcement of decrees given by the Dáil Courts. A registry of still unenforced Dáil Court decrees would be set up; and, if no appeal were made, these decrees would be 'binding on the under-sheriff in the same way as decrees given by the ordinary state courts'.[20]

Gavan Duffy, who had dissented from the original decision to end the Dáil Éireann Courts, repeated his dissension and regretted the courts would not 'be continued and perpetuated for certain purposes'. He disagreed with the view 'that we have anything to be ashamed of in the Dáil Courts...that they were incompetent, and ...that they ought to be buried'. He considered the setting up of the courts as having been 'a great tribute to the common sense of the people'. The courts had 'effectively smashed the British machinery' and had been one of the things 'which did most outside Ireland to make our name respected and to show up the fact that the English occupation was usurpation'.[21] Johnson also noted: 'No other activity had anything like the same effect on the minds of the people of other countries, as the institution of the Dáil Courts, their successful work, the courage of the people who instituted them, and the popularity and confidence that attended them.'[22]

Possibly in reaction to Gavan Duffy's idealization of the courts, O'Higgins took the opposite line and went far beyond his primary objective to regularize a national judicial system and to conform to a treaty that did not give formal legitimacy to 'revolutionary institutions' until they had been recreated, like the Army and the police, by the parliament of Southern Ireland and its successor, the Third Dáil. Instead, he stressed the flaws of the Dáil Éireann Courts. He considered it a mistake for 'having delayed overlong in abolishing them', as it had 'allowed the country and the commercial interests of the country to plunge about for many months in the chaos that was created by the dual jurisdiction, or the dual lack of jurisdiction, of two sets of courts and two systems of justice'. He acknowledged that the Dáil Courts, which 'were, of their nature, occasional and provisional', were forged to meet the popular needs upon the collapse of the British Petty Sessions Courts and their executive arm, the RIC. This was 'a period of great restraint on the part of the people, of great selflessness, of great exaltation, and crime and minor abuses were at a minimum through the country'.[23] He described the Dáil Courts as 'rough and ready tribunals where people could get the minor disputes that are inevitable from every day life settled in a spirit of neighbourliness and equity, rather than a spirit of strict law', and the summer of 1920 was their high point, but regardless of 'what may have been heard by our representatives abroad', at home 'from September, 1920, we heard little of these courts until after the truce'.

He would have preferred not to hear many things he heard about them after the truce. While the courts 'had certainly a useful record when they appeared first and had won a good name', after they reappeared following the truce, they seemed 'only to be made the channels and the vehicles of corruption and abuse, and only to be used by people not in search of justice, but as an obstruction to justice', as litigants jumped from one court to another 'seeking injunctions according as one thought the case was going to go'. It was evident that 'if there was to be security for business enterprise in this country, if there was to be security for debt collection, and for these things on which all trade and commerce are based, that the period of dual jurisdiction would have to come to an end soon'. The Dáil Courts had a hold on the communities when they 'were knit together by the bond of common resistance to British administration', but when the movement, which inspired these courts, was split, 'you had the poison and the bitterness of that split circulated into every hamlet and into every home in the country'. Accordingly, it was better in the circumstances to abandon 'these rough and ready, improvised, tribunals' and 'face the fact that they had not within themselves the elements of a useful future for the country.'[24]

A recent historian of the Dáil Courts, Mary Kotsonouris, has called O'Higgins' attack 'extraordinary', and has said that when challenged on the facts he became 'irrational and vindictive'. In her history, *The Winding Up of the Dáil Courts*, she suggests that O'Higgins' remarks contrasted with the careful work of his own officials in the commission, and might well have been prompted less by the question of the courts themselves than by his own annoyance at Gavan Duffy. However, his depreciatory characterization of the courts contributed to a perception that they were highly irregular, even though many of their judges went on to splendid judicial careers in the new court system.[25]

## TEMPORARY CIVIC GUARD ACT

The Third Dáil passed a Temporary Civic Guard Act, which gave statutory power to the raising and maintaining of the national police force that had already been organized. The only objection raised to the measure was by Labour Party leader Thomas Johnson, who did not think it fair or reasonable to be asked in the last two or three days of a session 'to consider a detailed scheme for the organization of a police force for the future'. Cathal O'Shannon, his Labour colleague, made much the same objection and wondered why the Civic Guard Bill could not be made a temporary measure. O'Higgins accepted this request, but asked that it be for twelve rather than six months, since at least a month would be wasted between the dissolution of the present Dáil and the assembly of the next. The only debate on the measure was over the question of prohibiting the membership of police in political or secret societies, which Johnson opposed. Johnson did not believe in 'the attempt to prevent a Civic Guard having an opinion on public matters and of approving of the action of other people in public matters'. He thought the clause was framed in a way that it could prevent a policeman from supporting or belonging to societies dealing with causes, sometimes single causes, which might be construed as political. O'Shannon agreed and added that 'it does not require any great stretch of imagination at all' to describe associations like the Gaelic League and the Gaelic Athletic Association 'as in some measure political in their object'. O'Higgins justified the ban on membership in political societies in order to preserve the neutrality of the police who had to serve 'succeeding governments', and had a duty to see that the law is obeyed, 'whether they like it or not, whether they think that a particular law ought to be repealed or not'. He believed that 'the mass sense of the citizens would heartily endorse that provision' which sought 'to exclude members of the police force from joining political organizations or secret societies'. The Dáil rejected the effort to remove the oath and the measure passed, but only after O'Shannon had successfully moved that the words Civic Guard in the title of the measure be replaced with 'Garda Síochána', the Irish equivalent for Guardians of the Peace.[26]

## FOURTH DÁIL ÉIREANN

The Fourth Dáil Éireann, elected on 27 August 1923, was the first parliament elected by an independent Ireland. The first two Dáils had been revolutionary bodies whose members had been elected to other institutions, the British Parliament and the Parliament of Southern Ireland, but assembled instead as Dáil Éireann. In addition, those elected to the Second Dáil were unopposed. The Third Dáil was a constituent assembly of the Irish Free State. In accord with Article 81 of the constitution it had approved, that Dáil could not last for more than a year after the date, 6 December 1922, when the constitution went into effect. In the contest for the Fourth Dáil the rival wings of the old Sinn Féin Party ran substantial numbers of candidates in opposition to each other. Significantly, the anti-treatyites, led by de Valera, kept for themselves the name of Sinn Féin. The government, in an effort to appeal to many voters who had either opposed or been indifferent to Sinn Féin, but who accepted the new order of things, formed a new party, which they called Cumann na nGaedheal. That party won sixty-three seats, while Sinn Féin won forty-four. Labour won fourteen, the Farmers Union fifteen, and seventeen independents were elected. Sinn Féin abstained from attending what the party doctrine regarded as an illegitimate Dáil, which enabled the government to turn a plurality into an absolute majority. After the election there were slight changes in the government as Ernest Blythe became Minister for Finance, which post Cosgrave had held along with the Presidency, and James A. Burke, a deputy for Tipperary, replaced Blythe as the External Minister for Local Government.

An interesting incident occurred in the earlier months of the Fourth Dáil that was illustrative of O'Higgins' perception of Irish citizenry as extending beyond those who supported Sinn Féin and the War of Independence. A Local Authorities Indemnity Bill sought to protect local governments from claims against them for certain illegal actions, such as hiding funds from criminal injury suits and striking rates without legal sanction, which they had undertaken at the behest of Dáil Éireann during the War of Independence, or, more specifically, at the request of O'Higgins as assistant to the Minister for Local Government. Richard Corish, a Labour deputy for County Wexford feared the Bill might allow four Wexford rate collectors, who had been dismissed by the local body for not having performed these illegalities, to now apply for compensation for their ouster. If such was to be awarded, he asked that it not be a burden of the local county council.

In an eloquent statement of political ecumenism, O'Higgins indicated that he 'had considerable sympathy' with the extremely difficult 'position of rate collectors throughout the country, after the break with the British Local Government Board'. He admitted 'in the position I occupied at the time, I could not give rein to that sympathy' as it was his order from the Ministry for Local Government that the four in question had refused to obey. But he was broadminded enough to acknowledge that these men 'were invited by their local authorities to act in a manner contrary to the bonds into which they had entered, and contrary to the law as it stood, without any real confidence that that law and the authority behind it would ultimately be upset and overwhelmed'. He added 'Naturally we fulminated against them, against their treachery and disloyalty, and against their unpatriotic conduct, and so on. But all the time anyone with a real grasp of the situation knew that from the human point of view these men were in a serious predicament.' They were not thinking just of themselves, but 'of those who had been so good to them as to become their sureties. And while a man might be willing to incur considerable loss himself, he is less willing to involve in loss people who had befriended him.' He asserted that

> it does not become us, who, after all, won that struggle, to try and go

back now and in any way victimise or in any way lean against the people with whom we had differences. And now at any rate, if not then when the strife was on, we should realise that these men were placed in a very difficult position indeed, and we should realise that not all the country was Sinn Féin, not all the country approved of the course that we were taking, and that the rate collector as much as anybody else was entitled to his individual views.

He appreciated Corish's anxiety about the added burden for the Wexford County Council and suggested it could be taken up with the Minister for Local Government, but insisted that 'either by the Local Authority or the Central Authority those men should be compensated'.[27]

Even before the election, O'Higgins threatened Cosgrave that he 'could not agree to join a future government' if the alleged assault on the daughters of a Doctor Randall McCarthy of Kenmare by Free State Army officers was not handled in a 'perfectly clear straight way'. One of the officers was the commanding officer of the Kerry Command, Major General Paddy O'Daly. Officers who had given evidence against him at a preliminary inquiry were themselves arrested on a six month old charge that they were implicated in the burning of an irregular house and were to face a courts martial trial. The revival of this second case after so many months made O'Higgins conclude that it was 'intended to discount their evidence in the other case'. As for the former case, he could not accept any political exigencies that could condone 'an outrage of that kind, if it be shown that officers of our Army were implicated'. He added that people inside and outside the Army regarded it as a test case, and that even Lady Lavery, with whom he was becoming increasingly familiar since his apprehensive first encounter (See Chapter 2, pp. 46–7), had spoken to him about it, 'having heard of it in London from Lord and Lady Kenmare', adding that 'you can imagine the use that will be made of it there'. He appreciated 'that there are many things wrong in the Army, as elsewhere which it will take time and patience to set right', but this particular case he saw 'as in a class to itself' in which they should 'apply ample disciplinary measures to whomsoever is found guilty'. The case was being watched by both the 'decent disciplined officers' and 'those who are neither decent nor disciplined', as they realize that 'it is going to ring the death knell of either discipline or banditry'.[28]

The matter came before the Executive Council on September 17 when it considered a letter from Dr McCarthy. It decided to have the Attorney General, Hugh Kennedy, take possession of all the documents relating to the case, including the burning of the irregular house, and for him to advise the Executive Council as to appropriate action. O'Higgins was a solitary dissenter in the Executive Council, wanting it to order a courts martial trial since the Advocate General believed a *prima facie* case had been made. On September 28 the Executive Council received the Attorney General's report, which expressed reservations, 'assuming the outrage to have been committed', about the existence of 'prima facie evidence as to the identity of the perpetrators' and how they 'should be proceeded against'. Accordingly, he recommended, if the McCarthy sisters were confident of their story, they should 'institute proceedings for assault'. He thought it 'very remarkable' their not having done so.[29] The Executive Council then directed the Attorney General to draft a letter, which Cosgrave would send to Dr McCarthy informing him that, if his daughters were willing to testify against those whom they charged with the crime, the case would be prosecuted by the ordinary machinery of criminal law. This was a far cry from the more certain conviction and punishment that O'Higgins anticipated a court martial would render.[30] The case was symptomatic of the mounting disparity between O'Higgins and Mulcahy over the character of the Army and its relationship with the civil administration. In this case, O'Higgins preferred that a court martial, rather than an ordinary court, try the alleged offenders, which contrasted with his commitment to restoring the regular instruments of justice. Obviously, he expected that a court martial, which would be faster and less taken with procedural niceties, would reverse the military enquiry cover-up he had criticized and reach the verdict he expected.

At any rate the McCarthys never pursued the option, although three and a half years later their father sent an angry letter to O'Higgins demanding compensation for expenses incurred in bringing five witnesses and himself to Dublin in June of 1923 soon after the incident to give testimony on it to a State Solicitor and a Garda Superintendent. O'Higgins replied that he could not consider the request nor hold out 'any hope of payment of compensation' in view of the McCarthys' failure to act on the suggestions of the Executive Council in September 1923.[31]

Although having occupied a central role in the debates on the Public Safety, Arrest and Detention, and Enforcement of Law Acts, as well as the winding up of the Dáil Courts, O'Higgins paradoxically played virtually no role a half year later in piloting the Courts of Justice Bill through the Oireachtas. That measure implemented the recommendations of the Judicature Committee formed the previous year and established a permanent court system for the Irish Free State to replace the temporary District Justices authorized by the late 1922 Temporary Provisions (District Justices) Act, which provided a system of civilian justice in those areas where the Civil War disorder had receded and military tribunals were unnecessary and which was a substitute to the suspended revolutionary Dáil Éireann Courts. The new measure retained the District Justices that O'Higgins had appointed as a temporary measure, but dropped the Justices of the Peace and the Grand Jury. The next level of justice was to be the Circuit Court that replaced the old County Courts and had wider common law and equity jurisdiction. Then there was to be a High Court with unlimited original jurisdiction. It acted as the Central Criminal Court and would try all capital cases and the Attorney General could apply to have any pending Circuit Court prosecution transferred to it. In addition there would be a Court of Criminal Appeal and a Supreme Court as a final court of appeal. President Cosgrave and Attorney General Kennedy directed the measure through the Dáil and the Seanad. It passed its final stage in the Seanad on 14 March 1924 without any major alterations. It remains obscure why O'Higgins did not take part in these debates, other than possibly a desire to divide tasks with colleagues and devote his energies at this point more to law enforcement than to legislation.[32] At any rate it was in that same month, March, that he was to play one of the more decisive roles in his career in directing the government's response to the Army mutiny.[33]

### HUNGER STRIKE

In the fall of 1923 thousands of Civil War prisoners remained detained under emergency legislation, although several hundred, who in the judgment of the authorities were not a threat to the state and were unlikely to take up arms, were released weekly. But on October 12, the prisoners at Mountjoy Jail called a hunger strike demanding unconditional release. Soon thousands in the other detention centres at the Curragh, Newbridge and North Dublin Union joined them. The strikers also protested against alleged maltreatment. Edward J. Byrne, the Archbishop of Dublin, appealed to Cosgrave, the President of the Executive Council, on their behalf, regarding it as 'a downright calamity for the country if any of these hunger strikers were allowed to die'. Since the political leaders of the strikers had declared 'the reign of violence is over and that they will seek henceforward to spread their views only by the constitutional way of educating the public', he asked the government to weigh in the balance 'whether the release of these people would be a greater danger to the state than allowing them to die of hunger strike'. The Archbishop himself thought that, 'the latter course would be fraught with far greater danger to the state'.[34] In addition to the plea by the Archbishop, various local government bodies, such as the Macroom and Westmeath Rural Distict Councils, voted to not conduct business until the prisoners were released.[35]

In his reply to the Archbishop, Cosgrave said he was yet to be convinced 'that there had been a change of heart as well as label in this matter of armed versus constitutional agitation'. He asserted that documents in the government's possession demonstrated opposition by the prisoners and their supporters not just to the government, but also 'to the Free State itself'. While he was sorry if there were any deaths from the hunger strike, he had the responsibility to say 'on no account should a single man be released save when the ordinary machinery of the state operates to secure it'. He reminded the Archbishop that three to four thousand had been released, and that some of those on hunger strike would also have been released but for their having undertaken the strike. The government hoped to get the total number of prisoners down to 4,000 by Christmas and was considering a general release by spring. He added that his most recent information was that the end of the strike was in prospect. There might be casualties, but that would accelerate the end of the strike rather than bring about the more disastrous effects the Archbishop had foreseen.[36]

O'Higgins gave a similar analysis a few weeks later before the Dáil. He recalled that when the hunger strike started, the Minister for Defence had been signing release orders 'at the rate of about 100 per day'. He wondered if the hunger strike might not have been in response to the judicious selection of which ones were being released. The more militant prisoners and leaders were finding themselves isolated and still imprisoned. Accordingly, the hardliners called the strike because they became aware 'there might be some delay before those on whom the real responsibility lies [themselves] would return home'.[37]

On 19 November, Michael Cardinal Logue, the Archbishop of Armagh and Primate of Ireland, issued a statement read at all Masses. He indicated his anxiety, 'owing to the danger to the health or life, even to the salvation of those concerned'. He called the hunger strike 'foolish, ineffective and of very doubtful morality' as it was 'unlawful for us to deliberately sacrifice our lives, or even to expose them to immediate danger, except for causes universally and unanimously acknowledged as sufficient to justify the sacrifice'. He considered it 'very doubtful whether the desire of liberation from even a severe and harassing imprisonment is a sufficient cause', and appealed to the strikers 'to abandon this dangerous and unlawful expedient, and to seek in future some more reasonable, natural and lawful means of enforcing their liberation'. But he also appealed to the Free State Government, which had declared 'their readiness to liberate untried and unreconciled prisoners, not to do things by halves and by driblets'. In view of the republican party having 'declared that they are prepared to abstain from violence and seek to secure their political aims by constitutional means', and despite the reluctance of many of the interned 'merely from pride or sentimentality' to give to the government an undertaking to that effect, 'the best policy of the Free State Government would be to clear the prisons and camps as quickly as it could be effected of all internees, except those convicted of crime, or liable to be tried of crime'.[38]

The tactic of a mass hunger strike did fail, and the government's position of no release of strikers, never mind an unconditional release of all, succeeded. Of the 8,024 prisoners in custody at the beginning of the strike, 7,604 had joined the strike. But by early November the number of hunger strikers was down to about 2,500, and by the middle of November it was down to a few hundred, with the release of non-striking prisoners continuing at a regular pattern. Two strikers died: Denis Barry in Newbridge Camp on November 20, and Andrew Sullivan in Mountjoy on November 22.[39] On the next day, strike leaders, Tom Derrig and D.L. Robinson were allowed to visit the various other prisons and subsequently called off the strike. They presented the decision to call off the strike as having been prompted by the appeal of Cardinal Logue, the Archbishop of Armagh, and an appeal by Professor Alfred O'Rahilly of UCC, a TD for Cork, an advisor on the drafting of the Free State Constitution, later President of UCC, and, upon retirement, a priest.

O'Higgins had been against any concessions to the hunger strikers. He issued a memorandum to colleagues on the Executive

Council on November 15 opposing a more general release programme suggested the day before by Minister for Defence Mulcahy. O'Higgins based his attitude on the 'far from encouraging reports' from certain counties received at a conference of Garda Síochána officers. In the light of such he felt that 'anything in the nature of a wholesale release of prisoners would be highly impolitic'. Before granting such he wanted 'a detailed report from military intelligence as to the general attitude and activities of released prisoners'. He was also concerned as to 'the question of whether there is employment available for these men on their release', for 'if they are idle they will probably be mischievous, and if they are both idle and hungry the probability becomes a certainty'. He was also apprehensive that 'if releases on a large scale synchronize with the hunger strike or follow too closely after it, the public mind and the minds of the prisoners themselves will associate the two and the general feeling will prevail that the policy of the hunger strike was justified and vindicated'. His alternative was to make Christmas 'the occasion for getting the numbers of internees down to about 2,500'. At that point large numbers could be released and, if the conduct of those released warranted such, further releases would continue at about 500 to 700 a month. But he thought the situation was 'not so stable that we can afford to throw bread upon the waters to the extent of a general release within the present year'. He did not regard it wise in particular areas 'to make a bad situation worse by unloading prisoners into them'.[40]

Later that month O'Higgins submitted to the Executive Council reports showing the state of law and order in each county. Conditions in thirteen counties were reported as 'normal'. In six other counties the Civic Guards could accept responsibility of the maintenance of order 'provided they had the moral support of military garrisons'. But in all or portions of seven counties, Cork, Leitrim, Clare, Galway, Tipperary, Offaly, and Roscommon, 'the presence of bands of armed men' meant that 'the Civic Guards could not take responsibility for the prevention of crime'.[41] In the memo of the Department of Home Affairs that accompanied the extracts from the report of the Commissioner of the Garda Síochána, it was stated that the suppression of the irregular revolt 'cannot be said to be complete whilst so many armed irregulars roam about the country, some of whom are even banded together in "columns" quite definitely under the standard of irregularism', and under the leadership of men elected to Dáil Éireann.[42]

PUBLIC SAFETY BILL

In December 1923, in view of the situation described by monthly Garda reports, O'Higgins, as Minister for Home Affairs, sought renewal of the six-month or temporary public safety legislation passed by the last Dáil on the eve of its adjournment. In contrast to the earlier legislation, the new measure dealt only with internment, that is, imprisonment without trial, for both future internees and those already detained. A separate Bill, a Punishment of Offences Bill, was introduced dealing with punishment for fifteen specified crimes subject to ordinary trials. Both pieces of legislation were to be temporary, that is, of twelve months' duration.

Referring to Garda reports, O'Higgins noted that the unsatisfactory conditions that continued in several counties necessitated the renewal of the emergency legislation and the continued detention of internees. He was reluctant to grant a general amnesty to those still interned under the previous law because of the bad experience on the eve of the Civil War when anti-treatyites were allowed to hold their weapons 'in the hope and confidence that they were really of too fine a mould to turn those arms against their fellow citizens, or use their power to prevent the majority will prevailing in the country'. However, they would release the prisoner whom he called 'the ordinary poor "mug"... stampeded into this thing, when crime was presented to him, wrapped around with the picturesque tricolour', but not those for whom proof could be produced of serious crime.[43]

Thomas Johnson challenged the continued detention of current prisoners that were held from before the current crime wave, which was used to justify the Bill. He thought that 'the offences of these men' should be considered 'in a different category from that of ordinary crime'. Since, 'they are not guilty of crime in the ordinary sense', and the 'occasion for which they have been arrested and detained is past', then they should be released. He opposed the minister's request for power 'to detain such prisoners for another twelve months', while refraining from bringing them to court. The absence of armed activity in the previous few months gave him reasonable ground to assume 'that the release of those who are still in custody would not be followed by any further armed activity'. Denis Gorey, Farmers' Union TD for Carlow–Kilkenny, supported the measure in the present situation where intimidation had made jurors unable 'to function honestly and fearlessly as citizens'. But Patrick Baxter, also Farmers' Union and TD for Cavan, however, objected to the departure from the constitution that the suspension of trial by jury and internment would entail. He believed too much was made of proclamations issued by the supposed rival republican government to which the interned adhered. He doubted if O'Higgins really feared these were 'going to seriously affect the state'.[44]

The Attorney General, Hugh Kennedy, intervened in the debate to emphasize the difficulty of getting juries to convict in parts of the country. He was confident that when the new judiciary would be established and groups of counties would be drawn into the ambit of particular circuits, that they would 'be able to get much more efficient trial by jury', and ultimately, when each of these courts would be established, they will 'arrive at a situation in which all crime can be dealt with within its own circuit'. In the meantime, there was no choice but the 'simple expedient of deterrent detention'. O'Higgins insisted the case for the Bill, in a nutshell, was that in areas of the country armed men were 'enforcing their will on the people, billeting themselves on the people', and 'creating conditions of terror'. The result was that 'you will not get evidence of crime, and that if you are so fortunate as to get evidence of crime, it is almost asking too much from juries to convict'.[45]

After the holiday break, Dáil members made extensive efforts at amending. They sought to tighten the powers of arrest for internment purposes, to require warrants and court approbation for detention, to inhibit the use of the military or the delegating of arresting powers, and to make public and final the decisions of an appeals court to which the interned could challenge their detention. Farmers' Union deputy Baxter unsuccessfully argued against the ability of the military to act as arresting and detaining officers: 'It is not good for the army itself; it is not good for the state; it is bad for the citizens, and it is bad for the peace of the state.' O'Higgins justified the use as necessity for such, since 'the police force of the country is not an armed force', and that in certain areas of the country armed men were 'preying on their neighbours'. The alternative was: 'Either the police force should be armed, or these powers of arrest should be given to military officers.' The amendment failed.[46]

O'Higgins accepted amendments by Labour deputies Johnson and O'Connell that changed the wording in defining certain offences. 'A revolt against the government' was replaced by 'an attempt to overthrow by violence the established form of government', and threatening any person 'to abandon his allegiance to the Government of

Saorstát Éireann' was replaced with inducing 'any officer of the Government of Saorstát Éireann to refuse, neglect or omit to discharge his duty as such officer'. The new language emphasized obedience to the laws of the Free State more than philosophical loyalty. O'Higgins also accepted substituting 'unlawfully' for 'without lawful authority' so as not to revoke immunity granted to labour unions' actions by existing trades dispute legislation.[47]

Later, during the Seanad debate, O'Higgins even accepted the principle behind an amendment proposed by Senator John T. O'Farrell, secretary of the Railway Clerks' Association, and member of the executive of the Irish Labour Party and the Trade Union Congress, requiring the presence of a police officer at any entry of a dwelling house by the military to effect an arrest as being 'in line absolutely with the whole trend of government policy and outlook, and that is to bring the country back gradually to absolutely normal conditions'. But, he argued the patchwork condition of the country was such that it would be impractical to insist on a military force having a Civic Guard to accompany them in making an apprehension in all areas. Accordingly, the words 'wherever reasonable practical', were added to the amendment at a later stage.[48]

The Seanad debate focused on the continued detention of those interned under the previous act. O'Farrell, for instance, argued that any good results that might have accrued from a general amnesty when the reign of violence had ceased, 'when the military power of the irregulars had been definitely smashed', and 'their unpopularity was at a height', was lost by the manner in which the government was slowly releasing prisoners and continuing to detain others. He saw no reason for detaining the remainder, unless there were intentions of trying them. Col. Maurice Moore saw the motive in the retention of some not as 'an attempt to keep in prison ruffians who break into houses, but to keep a number of political prisoners in jail because they are political prisoners and because they are opposed to the present government and the present state of affairs'. He also argued that since some of those detained had been elected to the Dáil the measure was unconstitutional because 'every member of the Oireachtas shall, except in cases of treason, felony, and breaches of the peace be privileged from arrest in going to or returning from or while within the precincts of either House'. Senator James G. Douglas remained of the opinion that 'once you had got to the state of an established peace, it would be better frankly to face the situation and try your prisoners or release them'. He hoped at the end of the twelve months, when the bill would expire, the government would see 'that there will be no need for it, because they will gradually have evolved to a state in which ordinary law can operate'.

In rebuttal O'Higgins noted that those in custody had been reduced in seven months from 12,000 to 1,500, 'a programme of releases which might be described as generous to the point of rashness'. However, that course could not have been taken without 'the confidence that both Houses of the Oireachtas would appreciate the necessity of arming the Executive throughout the next year with very special and very exceptional powers'. The releases would continue 'until it will boil down perhaps to 200, 300, or 500 of those chiefly responsible for the situation of the last two years. Then, when our responsibilities to the people for the safety of their persons, the safety of their property, the freedom of their lives, seem to permit it, those persons will be released.'[49]

The measure passed, as did an emergency resolution allowing its immediate implementation in view of the imminent expiration of the existing six month Public Safety Act.[50]

## PUNISHMENT OF OFFENCES ACT: THE FLOGGING BILL

Since the special powers legislation dealt only with internment, O'Higgins introduced a separate bill in February, also of twelve months' duration, which stipulated the punishment for specified offences such as arson and armed robbery subject to formal trial. Punishments ranged from life imprisonment through to five years' imprisonment with hard labour and a fine. Offences tried in a summary court could be punished to a maximum of twelve months' hard labour and a fine. In addition, any male convicted of robbery under arms or arson would be subject to flogging. Exceptions could be made by the judge for reasons of health or age of the convicted. Thomas Johnson argued the legislation was superfluous since 'the ordinary law is quite capable of dealing with most of the offences which are dealt with in this Bill'. He was particularly opposed to the flogging provision, which he did not regard as a deterrent since the real deterrent in these matters is not the weight of the punishment, 'but the certainty of arrest'. Furthermore, this particular punishment, flogging, was placing the state in ignominy.[51] A week later he would argue that flogging did 'not deter', or 'make a good citizen out of a bad citizen' and that all it did was 'satisfy the elemental passion of man called vengeance'.[52] But O'Higgins insisted that when 'the ordinary law is not considered adequate to check and deal with' the intensity of crime prevalent in the country, then there is 'good and sufficient cause for altering the ordinary law'. He refused to 'accept the view that it is arrest that criminals are afraid of, and not punishment', as he 'always thought they were afraid of arrest because of the punishment'.[53]

During Seanad consideration of the measure, Senator Thomas Farren, Secretary of the Dublin Workers Council and a member of the National Executive of the Irish Labour Party and the Trades Union Congress, supported by Senators Gavan Duffy, Douglas, and Colonel Moore, moved to delete the flogging section. Senator O'Farrell opposed flogging less out of concern for the criminal than for the nation, and believed they should move along lines other than 'mere corporal punishment', as 'You cannot make a nation by flogging; you cannot civilise a people by merely punishing them.' Even Senator Sir Thomas Esmonde, a Papal Chamberlain, a member of Parliament from 1885 to 1918, who appreciated the difficult situation in which the Minister for Home Affairs found himself and acknowledged 'the extraordinary courage, firmness and ability with which he has dealt with the difficult situation so far', did not think 'we are improving our position in any way by condoning barbarism ourselves'. O'Higgins argued that such punishments were defensible if necessary, when 'the other normal sanctions of the law are inadequate', as was the situation in the country 'at this time'. Senator Thomas Westropp Bennett, a prominent Limerick land-owner and farmer, supported the government, as did Senator Mrs Wyse Power, who had been a Sinn Féin activist and later a Cumann na nGaedheal official. She felt her original vote in favour of flogging had been justified when she realized that the first person on whom it had been afflicted was one who had broken into a house and beaten the housekeeper into unconsciousness for four days. The Seanad rejected the anti-flogging amendment by a vote of twenty two to thirteen and approved the bill.[54]

### ENFORCEMENT OF LAW BILL

Another temporary measure of one year's duration, which O'Higgins introduced in early 1924 was an Enforcement of Law (Occasional Powers) Bill, which was comparable to a measure of six months' duration of the previous spring. The Bill was designed to facilitate the enforcement of judicial decrees against debtors. It was the measure on behalf of which O'Higgins made his celebrated remark about 'the ceasing of the bailiff to function is the first sign of a crumbling civilization'. He pictured that function, the execution of court decrees, as 'the ultimate act of government. It is the vindication of the legal right of the individual citizen as against his neighbour.' He feared that: 'If law and the machinery of law break down, then we are back to the stone axe or some other suitable instrument by which one man can enforce his right, real or imaginary, against his neighbour.'

He reported that there were 2,000 decrees outstanding for public debts, 746 of which were for rates, and 5,100 decrees for private debts. While there had been some recent improvement, it was 'nothing very striking', and it was hoped the new measure would 'mark a definite turning point'. The measure sought temporarily to increase the number of sheriffs and to allow undersheriffs to employ additional bailiffs; to remove checks on the ordinary operations of the undersheriff; to allow District Court inquiry about the means of debtors who were without chattels that could be seized, 'but who are believed to have assets or sources of income which an undersheriff cannot seize'; and to provide 'a speedier inquiry into the merits of claims made by third parties, that is a debtor's wife, parents, or children, to goods seized on the debtor's premises', which claims were used to prevent seizures.

The success of the earlier Bill was proven by reports 'that the mere fact that the additional powers were in existence was usually sufficient to induce judgment debtors to pay'. Furthermore, 'no single instance of abuse or hardship was brought' to his notice during the enforcement of the previous act 'in spite of the dismal prophesies of its opponents'. Without the measure he feared the undersheriff would have to face 'unscrupulous and determined resistance', and would be 'hedged round by so many rules and regulations' that he would frequently feel 'the contest is hopeless'. Under the existing rules the seizure had to take place in daylight; the sheriff had to keep the seized goods for three days, not take them out of the county to sell, and advertise their sale as a sheriff's sale; money could not be seized regardless of how much the debtor may have in hard cash; the sheriff could not enter a house unless peaceably admitted; they were not allowed to have more than two bailiffs as assistants; and it was virtually impossible to disprove claims by members of a debtor's family that they were the owners of specific items that were about to be seized. All this was 'in districts where even the Garda Síochána stations are in danger of armed raids and where the debtor's premises are situated fifteen miles from a town or a railway station and are approachable only by rough mountain roads'. The ultimate justification for the measure was the existence of thousands of outstanding decrees. Insisting that 'there will be no real progress, no real credit, no commercial atmosphere until the situation represented by these figures is dealt with, and dealt with thoroughly', he thought that the Labour deputies would be the last to oppose a measure that would help to correct the economic depression in the country.[55]

Thomas Johnson sought to minimize the debt situation, arguing that the private debts averaged £30 per decree, that is, were 'in the main, for small amounts'. Insisting the deputies had 'a duty not merely to the creditors but to the debtors', he thought the proposed Bill would work 'to encourage the *gombeen* man in giving credit, to encourage the moneylender to lend small sums and to encourage that class of person who is going through the country pressing people to buy on credit', and its supporters assumed 'that every debtor is criminally minded, that every decree obtained against a man ought to be enforced, because he could pay but would not'. But O'Higgins saw the question at issue not as one of sympathy for the creditor as opposed to the debtor, but whether the laws of the courts should be enforced or not. The responsible court officer 'must have his hands strengthened, and must have his powers considerably widened' if there would be any inroads on the arrears. 'The alternative is a breakdown of law and the idea of law, and a return to the stone axe, or something equivalent to the stone axe, as the medium by which men may settle their conflicting claims.'[56]

During the committee stage, Farmers' Union deputy Michael Heffernan for Tipperary sought to limit the ability of the under-sheriff to seize property that might have belonged to the spouse, parent or child residing in the same home as the debtor. O'Higgins said this also worked to inhibit the undersheriff, as such claims of ownership were 'quite an easy thing to say to the undersheriff coming to a home', and it would be 'beyond the wit of the average under-sheriff to disprove it'. Johnson accepted that O'Higgins' point might apply to ninety seven per cent of the cases, but he asked: 'Are you going to risk very grave injustice upon the other three per cent for the sake of a problematic securing of the running of the writs, even for ninety-seven per cent of the cases?' Johnson added that, in urban areas where 'the domestic property is the only property available for seizure', 'every member' of two or three families of the same name living in the same house might be 'liable for the debts incurred by any one of them'. He described a university student living with his parents, but 'not in close touch with his parents' financial affairs'. Bailiffs might enter his room and take possibly valuable paintings in the course of debt recovery from the parents.

O'Higgins acknowledged that 'there may be situations in which it is impossible to have cast-iron safeguards against possible injustice', but noted, with regard to the hypothetical university student whose paintings were seized in lieu of the father's debts, that Johnson did not say who was paying the university fees. If the fees were being paid by the parents, then 'it would not be such an outlandish thing, or such a hardship, that the property of the son should be seized in respect of debts contracted possibly by the parent in his attempt to pay the son's university fees'.[57]

The measure passed both Dáil and Seanad later that spring.

## NOTES

1. *Dáil Éireann*, II (4 January 1923), 510–11.
2. *Ibid.* (2 March 1923), 1,949–50.
3. *Ibid.* (1 March 1923), 1,909–14.
4. *Ibid.*, II (14 December 1922), 224–7, (18 December 1922), 367-80.
5. *Ibid.* (4 January 1923), 487–93.
6. *Ibid.* (19 January 1923), 968–73.
7. *Ibid.* (24 January 1923), 1,033–9.
8. *Ibid.*, 1,064–6.
9. *Ibid.* (2 February 1923), 1,276–98.
10. *Ibid.*, III (15 June 1923), 1,987–8, 1,993–4, and 2,003–4.
11. *Ibid.* (26 June 1923), 2,501–5.
12. *Ibid.* (27 June 1923), 2,514–31.
13. *Ibid.* (2 July 1923), 2,598–604.
14. *Ibid.*, IV (12 July 1923), 605, 610–11, 660, 685–6, 723–30.
15. *Ibid.*, 739–46.
16. *Ibid.*, 801–3, 811–12.
17. *Seanad Éireann*, I (26 July 1923), 1,421–6, 1,428–9, 1,431–7, 1,437–40, and 1,455–64.
18. *Ibid.* (30 July 1923), 1 576–81, 1,629–32, 1,660–8, and 1,723–4.
19. *Dáil Éireann*, IV (2 August 1923), 1,853–8.
20. *Ibid.* (24 July 1923), 1,305–10.
21. *Ibid.*, 1,310–13.
22. *Ibid.*, 1,321–12.
23. Unionists and parliamentary nationalists might dissent from his idealization of the Irish population at the time of the War of Independence.

24. *Dáil Éireann*, IV (23 July 1923), 1,325–8.
25. Mary Kotsonouris, *Retreat from Revolution, The Dáil Courts, 1920–24* (Dublin: Irish Academic Press, 1994), pp. 99–100; Kotsonouris, *Winding Up of the Dáil Courts*, pp. 65–70.
26. *Dáil Éireann*, IV (31 July 1923), 1,688–1709.
27. *Ibid.*, V (23 November 1923), 1,209–13.
28. Kevin O'Higgins to William T. Cosgrave (17 August 1923), *Mulcahy Papers*, UCDA, P7a/133.
29. Hugh Kennedy to William T. Cosgrave (27 September 1923), NA, S 3341.
30. *Cabinet Minutes* (17, 28, and 29 September 1923), NA, C 1/147,8,9, C 2/5,6.
31. Randal McCarthy to Kevin O'Higgins (27 January 1927); Kevin O'Higgins to Randall McCarthy (28 January 1927), NA, S 3341.
32. Keane, *The Irish Jurist*, 31 (1996), 215–17.
33. See Chapter 5.
34. Edward J. Byrne, Archbishop of Dublin, to William T. Cosgrave (28 October 1923), NA, S 1369/10.
35. NA, S 1369/13.
36. William T. Cosgrave to Edward J. Byrne, Archbishop of Dublin (28 October 1923), NA, S 1369/10.
37. *Dáil Éireann*, V (22 November 1923), 1,104.
38. *Irish Times* (19 November 1923), *Mulcahy Papers*, UCDA, P7/B/423.
39. NA, S 1369/10. Bishop Cohalan of Cork refused to allow Christian burial to one of the strikers, Denis Barry, stating that the republican leaders had directed 'an unscrupulous campaign against the souls of the prisoners for the purpose of forwarding a political campaign', and insisted that 'By the law of the Church anyone who deliberately takes his own life is deprived of a Christian burial.'
40. Kevin O'Higgins to members of Executive Council (15 November 1923), *Blythe Papers*, UCDA, P24/193.
41. *Extract from Minutes of Meeting of Executive Council* (30 November 1923), NA, S 3435.
42. Ministry of Home Affairs to members of the Executive Council (28 November 1923), *Blythe Papers*, UCDA, P24/323.
43. *Dáil Éireann*, V (14 December 1923), 1,939–47.
44. *Ibid.*, 1,947–51, 1,957–60, and 1,970–3.
45. *Ibid.*, 1,974–8.
46. *Ibid.*, VI (10 January 1924), 23–6.
47. *Ibid.*, 73–82.
48. *Ibid.*, 552–7, 583.
49. *Seanad Éireann*, II (23 January 1924), 481–98.
50. *Ibid.*, 710.
51. *Ibid.* (20 February 1924), 1,221–7.
52. *Ibid.* (28 February 1924), 1,557–9.
53. *Ibid.* (21 February 1924), 1,255–8.
54. *Ibid.* (26 March 1924), 1,175–86.
55. *Dáil Éireann*, VI (11 March 1924), 1,925–38.
56. *Ibid.* (12 March 1924), 1,947–54.
57. *Ibid.* (1 April 1924), 2,697–700.

# 5

# O'Higgins, the Army Crisis, and Division within Cumann na nGaedheal

A CONSISTENT AIM of O'Higgins' was to restore normal legal institutions, even if operating under emergency procedures and applying extraordinary penalties, and to reduce the role of the Army in judicial and law enforcement matters. The persistence in the Army of private organizations, especially the Irish Republican Brotherhood, intensified his determination. Their existence seemed to him a contradiction to the ascendancy of the democratic process. His concern about indiscipline in the Army during the Civil War (see Chapters 3 and 4) aroused great distrust between himself and Richard Mulcahy, the Minister for Defence, who was closely identified with the IRB. Events in March 1924, provoked by a group that was a rival to the IRB within the Army, brought the animosity to a head. O'Higgins would prevail, as both Mulcahy and Joe McGrath, the Minister for Industry and Commerce and a champion of the rival group, would leave the Cabinet. In his analysis of the crisis, F.S.L. Lyons described O'Higgins as acting 'with characteristic incisiveness' in answering the question – 'could a civilian government impose its authority on those who, in effect, had brought it to power'? Having no doubt but that those who wear the uniform of the state 'must be non-political servants of the state', his firm stand 'ended an affair which, if O'Higgins had not shown his quality at the critical moment, might well have resulted in the fall of the regime'.[1] J.J. Lee is less appreciative of O'Higgins, who in his clash with Mulcahy turned 'an issue of tactics' into 'an issue of principle'. He even suggests that O'Higgins' actions 'would have been criminally reckless but for the fact that...Mulcahy was as devoted a democrat as O'Higgins himself'.[2] Let us recount the course of events.

THE ORIGINAL MUTINY

On Thursday, 6 March 1924, President Cosgrave received an ultimatum from Major General Liam Tobin and Colonel Charles Dalton, both members of Michael Collins' squad, acting on behalf of the IRA organization in the Free State Army. They said they had accepted the treaty and the Free State Government, but only 'as a means of achieving its [the IRA's] objectives, namely, to secure and maintain a republican form of government', but now concluded that Cosgrave's government 'has not those objects in view', and its policy was 'not reconcilable' with the reason for 'the Irish people's acceptance of the treaty'. Claiming to be acting in accord with the aims of Michael Collins, they demanded a conference with the government to discuss 'our interpretation of the treaty', the removal of the Army Council, and the suspension of Army demobilization and reorganization. Failing such, they threatened to take 'such action that will make clear to the Irish people that we are not renegades to the ideals that induced them to accept the treaty'.[3] At the time, the Army Council, that is, Chief of Staff Seán MacMahon, Adjutant General Gearoid O'Sullivan, Quartermaster General Seán Ó'Muirthúile, and Minister for Defence Richard Mulcahy, were implementing a policy of demobilization and organization. The Army had being reduced from the fiscally impossible size of 52,000 men and 3,000 officers at the end of the Civil War to 30,000 by the end of 1923, with further projected reductions to 13,000. More immediately, 1,000 officers were to be selected for demobilization on March 7.[4]

The motive of the mutinous officers remains uncertain. Were they upset by the perception that the Free State government was abandoning the pursuit of national unity and republicanism, which would include armed action toward that end? Or might the major impulse behind their action have been the prospect of being demobilized into an economy heavily hit by unemployment and stagnation, consequent of the Civil War? No doubt, both motives existed. The relative ease with which the mutiny was brought under control suggests the economic consideration was the strongest. On the other hand, the fact that their numbers were relatively few would suggest the ideological motive.

The government had not been without warning. The IRA within the Army, who were called the Old IRA to distinguish them from the irregulars or anti-treaty forces in the Civil War, had been formally organized in January 1923, at the height of the Civil War. The leaders, Tobin, Dalton, Frank Thornton, and Tom Cullen, all members of Michael Collins' Intelligence Unit, had missed the camaraderie and intimate contact with the commander during the War of Independence and were uncomfortable with the more professional administrative character brought to the Army by Mulcahy. The membership was limited to officers with a proper 'past and present outlook from a national point of view'. They sought a 'strong voice in Army policy, with a view of securing complete independence when a suitable occasion arose', and urged members to 'take control of the vital sections of the Army and oust those undesirable persons who were and are holding those positions'.[5]

Paradoxically, a comparable group, the Irish Republican Brotherhood, was revitalized to counteract these ideological soldiers. Historically, the IRB had regarded itself as the remnant that could bestow republican legitimacy on an Irish government. Collins' importance in the War of Independence had largely come from his presidency of the IRB and many argued that the acceptance of the treaty by the Second Dáil was because of the personal loyalty to him from some deputies who were also in the IRB. More zealous republicans and treaty opponents like Cathal Brugha and Austin Stack were not linked to the IRB. After Collins' death, pro-treaty IRA members, lead by Seán Ó'Muirthûile, reorganized the group to ensure that anti-treatyites did not take it over. The organization continued after the end of the Civil War. A new constitution completed in June 1923 reaffirmed the organization's intention 'to establish a free and independent republican government in Ireland' and 'arranged for the reorganization of part of the IRB within the national army in the form of clubs and divisions corresponding exactly to the Army's formations'.[6] The exclusion of Old IRA officers from the leadership of the reconstituted IRB implied the same men would be subject to demobilization. Old IRA complaints during the summer of 1923 had prompted a series of meetings of their leaders and an ally, Joe McGrath, the Minister for Industry and Commerce, with Cosgrave and, reluctantly, Mulcahy. Just as he attempted to appease the hardliners in the IRA in the months before the Civil War while constructing the new national Army, Mulcahy, in the autumn of 1923, held meetings with Old IRA figures, while persisting in his plans for demobilization. A Cabinet committee, formed to examine disturbances at the Curragh in November 1923 over the matter of demobilization, failed to find fault with his dismissal of some officers. However, he interpreted the very existence of the committee as political interference in the work of the Army.[7]

When the mutiny occurred in March, the government immediately condemned it and ordered the arrest of the officers involved. Cosgrave called their action 'a challenge to the democratic foundations of the state, to the very basis of parliamentary representation and of responsible government'.[8] In fact, the mutiny had not amounted to much: forty nine officers had resigned from the Army in sympathy with it and fifty had absconded with less than fifty weapons, but with 35,000 rounds of ammunition.[9] During the weekend of March 8 and 9 several houses were searched for Dalton and Tobin, including that of McGrath, the Minister for Industry and Commerce. The Cabinet also agreed to appoint Eoin O'Duffy, the Commissioner of the Police, to a newly created post, that of General Officer Commanding the Defence Forces of Saorstát Éireann.[10] On March 11, McGrath told the Dáil that he had resigned from the Executive Council because of the 'absolute muddling, mishandling and incompetency' by the Minister for Defence, which he saw as the cause of the mutiny, and promised to make a statement to the Dáil the next day explaining his resignation.[11]

## SOFTENING ON BOTH SIDES

That evening, a five-hour meeting of the Cumann na nGaedheal parliamentary party resulted in an agreement whereby McGrath withdrew from making his promised statement to the Dáil and the government would have an inquiry 'into the administration of the Army', and consult with McGrath about the same. Opposition spokesmen were disturbed by the lessened sense of urgency and by the impression that what had been described as a challenge to the democratic foundation of the state was dealt with by a party caucus and regarded by the Executive only as an internal government matter. Thomas Johnson argued that 'a matter of urgency and of such sufficient public importance' warranted discussion by the Dáil, and Independent deputy Bryan Cooper agreed, asserting that 'you cannot settle matters of vital importance to the state in a party conclave behind closed doors', for 'once that begins, you get a distrust of the Dáil and of the whole system of parliamentary government'. In contrast to Cosgrave's expectation that Dáil discussion on the matter would be foreclosed by McGrath not giving his statement, Johnson demanded a discussion of this suddenly changed focus.[12]

To contend with the opposition outrage, Cosgrave then had the Dáil adjourned for an hour and fifty minutes, and then a further adjournment until the following day. But he also read a statement from the mutiny leaders, Tobin and Dalton, in which they sought to mitigate the implications of their earlier letter. They claimed it had been sent 'with the sole object of exposing to the government and the representatives of the people what we consider to be a serious menace to the proper administration of the Army', and they 'fully recognize that the Army, just as the Police, must be subject to the absolute control of the civil authority, and further, that the Army should not have within its ranks any sections or organizations tending to sap allegiance from the only and proper constitutional authority, viz., the government of the people'. But Johnson refused to accept as satisfactory either the letter or Cosgrave's statement about the Executive Council's decision to have an inquiry in cooperation with McGrath into the administration of the Army. He was disturbed that a changed approach to the mutiny with a lessened sense of urgency and even apparent capitulation was in response to a party meeting rather than 'to the Dáil and the country'.[13]

O'Higgins more articulately explained the seeming change of face by the government. He acknowledged the seriousness of the March 6 ultimatum, which, 'in its terms', was 'a challenge to the Parliament of the country', and to which 'there was no alternative' other than 'regarding this matter as constituting mutiny', but added the qualifying and mitigating phrases, 'if it was taken on its face value, if it was taken literally'. The Executive Council had been told that the authors of the mutiny statement were incensed at 'the military authorities' and at 'abuses, irregularities and so on, within the Army', and 'while they might have written a foolish, an almost criminally foolish document', they 'were not really taking up the position of challenging the fundamental right of the people to decide political issues'. While 'disciplinary measures will undoubtedly be taken' against the officers, O'Higgins implied that they would not be too severe since 'there are situations in which even a government or even a parliament cannot afford to be doctrinaire'. He noted that thousands of interned republicans had been released, even though against many of them 'proofs could have been produced of a crime which could be called no other name than treason', because 'it was not considered politic in the interests of the state that these men should be tried'. Admitting it was opportunistic, he said 'in the handling of national affairs and in the handling of very delicate situations, there must need be opportunism'.

O'Higgins said inquiries had to be made into the 'allegation that this situation need not have arisen, that it should not have arisen, that it is the fault of a particular minister', which was the complaint of the mutineers and of McGrath. But 'the safety of the state and the welfare of the people' would not have been 'served by anything in the nature of the wrangle which seemed imminent when we adjourned yesterday evening', when McGrath was threatening to deliver a speech on the issue in the Dáil. While Cosgrave, 'could have talked more, could have made a longer statement', and 'could have used more words', what mattered was not the words, but the action he announced, and the determination to discover the real facts about 'this conflict of opinion that has arisen between two members' of the Executive Council.[14]

Darrell Figgis complained that the Dáil itself, not just a Cumann na nGaedheal caucus, should be aware of the maladministration in the Ministry of Defence of which McGrath complained. Differing with O'Higgins' view that 'these matters should not be mentioned and debated publicly', he thought otherwise as 'they will become more magnified because they have not been mentioned'.[15] Deputy Bryan Cooper wondered if the proposed inquiry was necessary, or if it was just in response to the letter of retraction from the mutineers. He wondered about its effect 'on the Army, on the Army Council, and the Minister for Defence', and the maintenance of their authority. He had reservations about the Executive Council being the appropriate judges since 'they are inquiring into the results of their own actions' and asked for a date when it would be held.[16]

Cosgrave answered that the inquiry would be held 'immediately', and that he had 'to consult with the Minister for Industry and Commerce', McGrath, about its members. Continuing in the softer tone toward the mutineers, he stated: 'I take it that it is generally admitted that soldiers are not good politicians, and that when they enter into the political arena they are not remarkable for any great success.'[17]

## NEW CRISIS

The following week the Army crisis took on a new dimension in which the IRB-linked Army Council replaced the mutineers of the Old IRA as objects of condemnation. O'Higgins, acting as chair of the Executive Council in view of Cosgrave having taken ill, reported on the events to the Dáil on Wednesday, 19 March. The night before there had been an Army raid of Devlin's Hotel on Parnell Street in search of a group of the mutinous officers who were meeting there. Eleven officers were arrested and eight weapons and ninety rounds of ammunition were surrendered. He regarded the Army action as inconsistent with the implications of a letter of 17 March from the President to McGrath, as well as an order of the Minister for Defence on 18 March to the Army Council, which was read and approved by the Executive Council, giving the terms of surrender to the mutineers. Both documents ordered 'all arms and equipment removed from barracks to be returned', and all persons 'concerned in the removal of such material' were to surrender 'by Thursday, March 20, at 6 pm', in return for which parole would be granted and 'the persons concerned allowed out under open arrest'. But the Parnell Street raid contradicted the promised 20 March surrender deadline. Also, it was taken without consulting General Eoin O'Duffy, whose powers had been expanded the afternoon before by the Executive Council when he was made Inspector General of the Defence Forces of Saorstát Éireann in addition to being Officer Commanding the Forces. The increase in power gave him authority over the Army Council itself, that is the Chief of Staff, the Quartermaster General, and the Adjutant General, staff officers responsible to the Minister for Defence.

At a meeting of the Executive Council on the morning of 19 March, chaired by O'Higgins because of Cosgrave's illness, the majority regarded the action of the evening before as having 'cut across government policy'. At that point Mulcahy withdrew from the meeting. The Council requested and received President Cosgrave's approval of the demand for the resignations of the three members of the Army or Defence Council, McMahon, O'Sullivan, and Ó'Muirthûile. It was also suggested that Cosgrave ought to ask for Mulcahy's resignation. When Mulcahy was told by O'Higgins of the request for the resignation of the three generals, he said such 'would involve his resignation also'.

In explaining the changing and somewhat contradictory developments since the original mutiny, O'Higgins said that the Executive Council had agreed to hold the inquiry in return for McGrath's withholding his statement from the Dáil to avoid having to deal with 'every charge and counter-charge' in public debate. The board of inquiry would not necessarily include the Cabinet, but 'would be constituted by the Cabinet' and 'report to the Cabinet'. The second letter from the mutinous officers, 'explicitly withdrawing and repudiating the original document', suggested that the original letter should not be taken at face value. Consequently, the Executive Council, including the Minister for Defence, had agreed to give those mutinous officers the option to surrender and return arms, which would be followed by parole. But the action against them on the night of 18–19 March contradicted that option.[18]

While the mutiny might not have been as dangerous as first appeared, it should be noted, in partial defence of the Army Council, that the Old IRA had enquired about political support for a *coup d'etat* from non-commissioned officers and from ex-officers serving in the Garda Síochána, and had meetings with anti-treaty irregulars. Furthermore, the purpose of the meeting in Devlin's was purportedly 'to stage a *coup* or formulate plans to kidnap the entire Cabinet'.[19]

But O'Higgins insisted it was not 'simply and solely as a result of last night's activities' that 'the resignation of certain high Army officers was demanded by the government'. Rather it was because the ousted Army Council members were 'not the personnel to deal with a mutinous revolt', as 'these men had been too long in their positions, that something of a proprietorship was springing up'. He added that it would have been wiser to have removed the Army Council earlier, but it could not be considered 'in the face of the mutiny' which had called for their removal. But the government had to require their resignations when, without consultation with the government, or with O'Duffy, they took action 'calculated to have, possibly, grave reactions within the Army and throughout the country, calculated to set the heather on fire, the heather we have been so assiduously attempting to quench and damp down'.

O'Higgins noted that the existence in the Army of 'factions, organizations, societies' was something that should not exist in normal, disciplined armies, and that the personnel factor 'was too much in the forefront', so as to override discipline, which 'must be impersonal'. Acknowledging the 'great service to this country' that had been done by those being asked to resign, O'Higgins impersonally insisted 'in national affairs it is not by the water that has passed that the mill is turned, and . . . it is impossible to carry on administration on the basis of swooping records'. National and political affairs, and the role of specific individuals in particular positions, had to be viewed much like the coral island 'that is built up by the insects coming along and doing their particular little bit of

1. Young Kevin O'Higgins surrounded by brothers Jack, Tom and Michael.

2. Brigid and Kevin O'Higgins.

3. Kevin O'Higgins at his desk.

4. Diarmuid O'Hegarty, secretary of the Executive Council; Kevin O'Higgins; Desmond FitzGerald, Minister for External Affairs; Joseph Walshe, secretary, Department of External Affairs; and Michael McWhite, official, Department of External Affairs.

5. Treaty supporters including O'Higgins (seated left), Arthur Griffith, President of Dáil Éireann (seated second left); and Sean MacEoin, a War of Independence IRA commander and general in the Free State Army (seated right).

6. Group photo at wedding of Kevin O'Higgins and Brigid Cole in October 1921. Among those in the group, besides the wedding party, were the bride's mother, the groom's parents, many of his siblings, his maternal aunts, William T. Cosgrave, and Eamon de Valera.

7. Free State cabinet (1923): Joe McGrath, Minister for Economic Affairs; Diarmuid O'Hegarty, Secretary of the Executive Council; Hugh Kennedy, Attorney General; Desmond FitzGerald, Minister for External Affairs; William T. Cosgrave, President of the Executive Council; Ernest Blythe, Minister for Finance; Kevin O'Higgins, Vice President and Minister for Justice.

8. Mr and Mrs Kevin O'Higgins at the RDS.

9. Wedding picture of Kevin O'Higgins and Brigid Cole in October 1921. On O'Higgins right is Eamon de Valera and on his left is Rory O'Connor, his best man, who would be executed fourteen months later by the Free State Government. The bridesmaids are the bride's sister, Molly Cole, and the groom's sister, Irene Higgins.

work, and some other insects coming along and building on top of them'. He seemed to suggest that it was not so much because of specific deeds or actions that the Army leaders had to step down, but because of the enmities they had caused: 'in a particular set of circumstances these three officers had reached the limit of their utility'. Situations arise where, regardless of the merits, 'Men may sometimes be rendered inoperative, their future utility may be prejudiced beyond hope of recovery by what is known as incurable unpopularity.'[20]

Historian John M. Regan states that O'Higgins had been briefly in the IRB and was confident in taking the risky action of ousting the Army Council because he assumed those officials, as IRB members, would not challenge the civilian government in view of the IRB's acceptance of the treaty of 1921. This reasoning implied that O'Higgins did not really consider the IRB a threat to the government, but was more anxious to remove more nationalist-minded figures like Mulcahy from the government. However, even if O'Higgins assumed the IRB would not act illegally, his anxiety about private factions within the army was not unwarranted, nor was his desire to steer the government away from a revolutionary flavour to one more comprehensive in its political perspective.[21]

Mulcahy, in reply, argued that the action of the night of 18–19 March was consistent with the letter sent by himself to his officers, as that letter should not have been interpreted to 'allow officers who had committed offences, either by deserting their posts, or by taking away material belonging to the Army, or by engaging in a conspiracy that might have had disastrous results, to walk and meet openly and publicly in the streets or in the country'. Giving the mutineers until the 20th to surrender, as O'Higgins suggested, would have seemed to imply that their walking about and meeting openly would be tolerated and that the attitude of the Executive Council was 'condoning mutiny' and 'prejudicial to the discipline of the Army'. While he had misgivings about the appointment of O'Duffy, 'who had not been in touch with the work of the Army, or the development of the Army for many months past', he was confident that O'Duffy would 'get absolute and scrupulous service from every officer in the Army who is untouched by the mutiny', for which they could 'thank the men who have been turned down so ungraciously as they have been in the speech of the Minister for Home Affairs'.[22] To their credit, Mulcahy and his dismissed colleagues in the Army Council indicated to potentially rebellious supporters in the forces their disapproval of anything other than obedience to the government.[23]

DEBATE ON THE MILITARY SITUATION

Before the Dáil began to debate the military situation the next day, O'Higgins announced that Cosgrave would assume the Ministry for Defence, but pending his recovery from illness, he would act for him in that office.[24] In the subsequent debate, Labour Party leader Thomas Johnson attacked Mulcahy for supporting the premature arrest of the mutineers on March 18–19 when he, as a member of the Executive Council, had 'accepted part of the responsibility' for the more generous surrender terms offered to the same officers. He also criticized the Executive Council for demanding that the members of the Army Council resign just their positions and not their commissions as well. That leniency was 'a kind of admission that these officers were in a position of independence – or semi-independence – of the Executive Council'. That mild discipline implied that the Army Council 'did actually occupy a place which many of us feared they would, and uttered warnings about... a position of autonomy and independence'. In view of the impending inquiry with regard to the Army, he insisted: 'the Dáil has a right to be told why that searching inquiry was not ordered long ago'.[25]

Independent deputy Major Bryan Cooper abandoned his first earlier instinct to support the Minister for Defence 'in dealing with the matter drastically,' and concluded from the action of 18–19 March that 'the Army Council have put themselves, in my opinion, utterly and indefensibly in the wrong. They have tried to be an *imperium in imperio*, and to a certain extent a law unto themselves.' Regardless of whether the policy in the letter of the Executive Council to McGrath 'may have been right or may have been wrong', the fact that it was accepted as the act of the government meant 'it was not for any Army officer – the Adjutant-General or whoever it was – to depart from that policy'.[26] Denis Gorey, Farmers' Union deputy for Carlow–Kilkenny, said of secret societies in the Army that there was 'no room... in the Ireland of to-day', and saw them 'all equally undesirable' and 'equally objectionable'. He believed the only purpose served by such societies was 'to subordinate the civil authority to the authority of the society and to subordinate democratic rule to the rule of the gun', which remark prompted O'Higgins to interject 'Hear, hear'.[27] O'Higgins even received accolades from a frequent critic, independent deputy Darrell Figgis, for 'the candour, tact, and discretion with which a very difficult and unpleasant mission was discharged'. He believed the steps that O'Higgins had taken would lead to what the people desired: 'a small army – the smaller the better, the less costly the better; but an army that shall, in all points, be subject to the civil power'.[28]

At that point, Mulcahy insisted that he had not thought to call O'Duffy on the night of the Parnell Street action because the expansion of his powers had occurred only shortly before. As for Deputy Gorey's strictures against brotherhoods and secret societies, Mulcahy hoped he would realize 'that they have had their uses and that things cannot be to-day and be absolutely non-existent tomorrow'. He also hoped that the people 'not get too tired' of arms, as it appears unfortunate when a public representative appears 'to shut his eyes to what has been the necessity for arms in the past...simply because of the difficulty of demobilisation'. If the people forgot the necessity for arms, they might allow themselves to get into 'a wrong and dangerous frame of mind'. Nothing had been said of the dismissed officers of the Military Council about 'their unsuitability for their offices' at the Executive Council meeting of the previous month 'when nominations to every position in the Army were being considered', and 'neither the Chief of Staff nor the Quartermaster General could have had anything to do with the events' at Parnell Street. Therefore, he suggested that they were dismissed because 'the mentality of the Executive Council to them for some time past was a mentality that was shaped by complaint, rumour and story of varying kinds'.[29]

O'Higgins challenged Mulcahy's attempt to present himself as 'the strong man, the stern disciplinarian, the upholder of law', and as one who 'felt his arm paralyzed by a weak and pusillanimous government' by hinting that cases could be cited, 'which would blow that interesting fiction sky-high'. When Mulcahy said he was perfectly willing to have all this made public, O'Higgins answered that the cases in question would be raised before the Committee of Inquiry. As for Mulcahy's downplay of his responsibility to O'Duffy on Tuesday night, O'Higgins reminded him how he and O'Duffy had met Cosgrave from which meeting Cosgrave drafted the letter to McGrath and Mulcahy drafted his comparably worded instructions to the Army Council about 'the action that would have to be taken with regard to mutinous officers'. He insisted that it was 'a clear implication' from that letter and the instructions that the action that was taken on Tuesday night 'cut straight across the policy outlined'. He added that 'the antics in Parnell Street' were 'deliberately calculated to set the heather on fire and create a war situation in a greater or lesser degree throughout the city, and possibly throughout the country'.[30]

MCGRATH'S DISSATISFACTION

The crisis turned in another direction on Monday, 24 March, focusing on the original mutineers again, when McGrath issued a statement to the press suggesting that the government had not lived up to commitments made in the agreement with the mutinous officers on March 11. He had assumed that the agreement meant the mutineers, upon return to barracks and the giving up of arms, would be restored to their positions. Instead, there had been the arrests on March 19 and the paroling of those who had subsequently returned to barracks.[31]

McGrath's statement prompted Thomas Johnson to ask if the government still adhered to the memorandum announced by O'Higgins the week before according to which the mutineers were required to surrender and return arms, after which they would be paroled, which differed from McGrath's claim that upon their surrender the *status quo* would be reinstated and 'the incident regarded as closed'.[32] O'Higgins explained that the agreement gave an undertaking that 'when and if officers, who in varying degrees were implicated in the mutiny, did all in their power to undo the harm which they had done the incident would be regarded as closed'. Also, 'no vindictive action would be taken against them', that is, they would not be charged or punished; but this did not imply their retaining their Army positions. He agreed that in retrospect the governmental undertaking 'might have been more explicit'. If it had been, there would have been no chance that the concept of no victimization, that is, a return to the status quo, and not just an absence of vindictive action or punishment, would have been 'read into the undertaking'.

He continued that there was no way that harm done by these officers 'could be entirely undone', but it could be 'partially undone' by 'a formal submission, a full and unequivocal unreserved submission to that authority which had been flouted'. The procedure to achieve such had been detailed in the letter to McGrath on March 17 and in the memorandum of the Minister for Defence the following day. As for the events of the night of 18–19 March, the fact that the apprehension of the officers was 'a breach of the clear and necessary implication of the memorandum of the Minister for Defence', did not mean that it would be proper to release 'unconditionally, the officers who came into custody' as a result of the Parnell Street operations. While O'Higgins disagreed with how 'these men came into custody', he did not think it was 'inconsistent' or a 'breach of faith' to insist on 'at least some undertaking and some assurance being given' that they would not lead 'a mutinous revolt'. For the mutinous officers who presented themselves and restored any arms, there would be 'no question of arrests' or 'of court-martial', but 'only a question of accepting these officers' resignations'. The sane course would be to say to each of them 'Go in peace, friend, as civilian.' To reinstate them 'would put an undue strain on the officers who stood loyal throughout the last fortnight of crisis'. He would not support such 'for one moment' and he 'did not read into any understanding or any agreement come to with Deputy McGrath at a party meeting that anything of that kind would take place'.[33]

McGrath, however, claimed that after the meeting he had asked how could he approach the officers unless he would be 'in a position to say there is no victimization', and insisted that he 'would not have left the room that night, nor have undertaken to go and see these men on any other conditions but that there should be no victimization'.[34] Several deputies who later seceded from Cumann na nGaedheal spoke in agreement with McGrath, confirming the growing distance between O'Higgins as a champion of constitutional normalcy and their continued adherence to the revolutionary fervour of the War of Independence. Typical was deputy Seán Milroy, Deputy for Cavan, a journalist who had escaped from Lincoln Jail with de Valera in 1919 and who had been a close friend of Arthur Griffith, who hoped no one was under the illusion 'that I am going to try and stand by the Minister for Home Affairs [O'Higgins] in this matter'. He said the way in which ministers spoke 'in that tone of inflexible determination, to see that the law is carried out', would suggest that 'this state was an old-established one, with traditions of established authority behind it', when 'it was but yesterday it was considered a virtue and a criterion of patriotism to be able to defy every authority that claimed to be instituted in the country'. He asked: 'Is the temperament that grew out of resistance to law to simply disappear by the wave of the hand of the Minister for Home Affairs?' As for the understanding that had been arranged at the Cumann na nGaedheal

Party meeting, he challenged the notion that the agreement 'was capable of any interpretation other than that which Deputy McGrath would point out'.[35]

But a different interpretation of the 11 March meeting was presented by the Minister for Foreign Affairs, Desmond FitzGerald, who denied that there had been any suggestion at the meeting of 'restoring these men to their ranks' or 'the no victimization theory'.[36] Also, Peter Hughes, Cumann na nGaedheal deputy for Louth, soon after to be named Minister for Defence, who had chaired that party meeting and had been the author of the document 'accepted by the party, and handed it to Deputy McGrath for the purpose of guiding him in whatever conversations he might have with the people he was going to see', said that McGrath 'was not told that there was to be no victimization', but only that 'there was to be no raising of bad blood or anything else as a result of the matter'.[37] Similarly, the Minster for Finance, Ernest Blythe, also insisted that the government had made no guarantees to the officers and that 'it was not at all the intention of the Executive Council that these men should be promised reinstatement in the Army'.[38]

Cosgrave described the party meeting as a means of allowing McGrath to present his complaints against the Ministry for Defence without their being aired in public, adding that the Dáil members 'lost, in my opinion, very little' in being deprived of listening to them. He told McGrath at that meeting specifically that 'I am making no agreement with the officers, no agreement whatever with the officers; my agreement is with you, absolutely with you'. He had told McGrath that 'we were impressed with the necessity for having an inquiry', and that 'he was at liberty to tell the officers what the government's intentions were', but 'he was not appointed as a plenipotentiary'.[39]

ARMY INQUIRY

The following week, on April 3, Cosgrave appointed the Army Inquiry Committee. The Chairman was James C. Meredith, a judge who had been associated with John Redmond in the pre-1916 Irish Volunteers and who in 1923 had served on the committee recommending the permanent reorganization of the Irish judiciary. Other members of the committee included Patrick McGilligan, who the same day was appointed Minister for Industry and Commerce to replace McGrath, the independent Bryan Cooper, Denis J. Gorey of the Farmers' Union, and Gerald FitzGibbon, a barrister who had sat for Trinity College in the Third Dáil Éireann. The terms of reference were: 'To enquire into the facts and matters which caused or led up to the indiscipline and mutinous or insubordinate conduct lately manifested in the Army.' Specific subjects to be examined were 'the existence of factions, conspiracies, secret societies, or political organizations, or groups amongst the officers and men, the considerations determining and making promotions or appointments', and 'whether the discontent amongst certain officers and men shown in the recent threat of mutiny and insubordination is justly and fairly attributed to muddling, mismanagement, and incompetence in the administration of the Army'.[40]

Despite a request made by Mulcahy on March 28,[41] the dismissal of the Army Council on March 19 was not included as part of the scope of the inquiry. However, he and officers did testify before the committee. The mutineers, on the other hand, refused to testify before the committee, which did not have subpoena powers to compel them to do so. McGrath also refused, as he would have needed their evidence to substantiate his charges.[42]

After holding forty-one meetings and examining twenty-seven witnesses, the committee issued its report two months later. It dealt with three specific matters: the cause of the mutiny, discipline within the military, and whether the discontent shown by the mutiny was 'justly attributed to muddling, mismanagement and incompetence in the administration of the Army'. It was noted that the mutinous organization 'had become a problem to General Collins before his death in August, 1922', after which its members drew more closely together to further objects, 'which were partly personal and partly political'. Their organization 'did not regard the Army as a non-political servant of the state, but as an engine to be used if necessary, and to be kept in a condition to be used, for the purpose of obtaining personal and political objectives', including 'imposing their views upon the civil government'. The group, which 'acted more or less in concert', was 'not in general amenable to discipline', included some who 'were not qualified for the positions which they considered they should receive', and 'attempted to dictate to the GHQ and to the government'. The committee concluded that their objects and their methods 'were wholly incompatible with discipline and the obedience which an Army must render to the government of any constitutional state', and 'that there would have been no mutiny but for the existence of this organization'.[43]

But besides this unambiguous condemnation of the Old IRA, the committee was equally convinced 'that its activities were intensified by the revival or reorganization of the IRB with the encouragement of certain members of the Army Council, the lack of confidence and want of intercourse between these two sections of Army officers, and the failure of both to appreciate their position as servants of the state'. General Ó'Muirthúile had testified that the IRB had been 'reorganized to prevent the irregulars from getting control of it' and 'using its name to stir up disaffection against the state'. However, the Old IRA group had regarded that reorganization 'as directed against them', especially since 'none of them were allowed to share in the control of the reorganised IRB'. The committee concluded that 'the reorganization of the IRB, carried out as it appears to have been by the actual heads of the Army, was a disastrous error of judgment and accentuated a mutiny which might not have occurred at all, and which could have been more firmly suppressed if those in authority had not weakened their position by leaving themselves open to the charge of acting in the interest of a hostile secret society'.[44]

It had not been proven to the committee that any appointments or promotions had been made for reasons of IRB membership or 'influence corruptly exercised by the IRB', although there was 'a natural suspicion' by non-members 'which undermined confidence in the impartiality of the Army Council and the higher command'. The committee report further noted how the leaders of the Old IRA thought they had been tricked by Mulcahy when, after entering into negotiations with them in July 1923, he had given written assurances that he was prepared to deal directly with them on 'matters which are considered vital to the progress of the Army on national lines with a view to the complete independence of Ireland', but then held no further communication with them.[45]

The general state of discipline in the Army was found to be 'fairly satisfactory' and 'a steady improvement both in discipline and efficiency' was noted, although 'there was a feeling in some quarters that efficiency was not a predominant factor in deciding questions of promotion or retention, while others considered that sufficient weight was not given to pre-truce service'. The secret societies, factions and political organizations 'did affect discipline among officers' and undermined 'the confidence of Army officers in the impartiality of their superiors'. They had received no evidence 'to justify a charge of muddling, mismanagement or incompetence on the part of the late Chief-of-Staff [MacMahon] in carrying out his duties', and, aside from the remarks about the inappropriateness of the reorganization of the IRB, no other charges 'were made against the Quartermaster General [Ó'Muirthûile].' Mulcahy was criticized for not having 'at the earliest opportunity' informed the Executive Council 'of the proposed reorganization of the IRB' and 'of the course of his negotiations with the Tobin group [the Old IRA]', which omission 'increased the difficulty in dealing with the mutiny'.[46]

While vindicating the dismissal of the Army Council, the report did not endorse O'Higgins' claims in his testimony about discipline in the Army, which he had based on information given to him by a Colonel Jephson O'Connell. He also criticized Mulcahy for attempting to buy off the mutineers and for even having conferred with them (although the original meetings had been prompted by Cosgrave). Much of his critique of Mulcahy dated back to the Kenmare case, when court martial proceedings were not instituted against three officers accused of assaulting the daughters of a Dr McCarthy (see Chapter 4, pp. 122–3).[47] With regard to that case the committee exempted the Adjutant General, O'Sullivan, from blame as he had 'strictly followed the advice of his legal adviser, the Judge Advocate General', who 'had put the case in train for a court-martial, and was not party to dropping the proceedings'. The inquiry regarded Mulcahy's dropping the case, for which he had 'accepted full responsibility', as 'a grave error of judgment on his part. 'It did not contribute to the mutiny, but it did militate against discipline generally by encouraging suspicion in the minds of officers and others that the Army authorities were disposed to hush up charges against persons high in authority'.[48]

## MULCAHY'S RESOLUTION

After the report of the committee had been issued, Mulcahy moved a motion of censure of the Executive for its 'ill-considered action' in removing the Army Council, an issue the committee had not considered. He argued that the officers had been

> swept away to satisfy the personal wishes of certain members of the
> Executive Council and to satisfy the demand of certain mutinous
> officers for their removal, and that the result of sweeping these officers

away was to impair the proper sense of military authority in the Army, to discredit the authority of the Executive Council, to drag the Army into politics, to hearten the mutiny and to make, what the Inquiry Committee will tell was an exaggerated affair, a movement that some day might very well be a serious menace to the state.

He challenged the suggestion that the Army Council had been 'justly dismissed because of anything in connection with that incident [the Parnell Street incident of March 19]'. Instead, 'the charge against the three officers was that they were connected with a secret society, and that secret society was the IRB'.

He spoke in defence of the IRB. It had 'stirred up forces scattered throughout the country' subsequent to 1916, and 'controlled them, moulded them, and directed them to the achievement of freeing the nation'. Then 'they utilized those forces as the backbone on which to build up a required and a bigger organization to deal with the irregular revolt'. It would be a disastrous error of judgment to have tried to say at the end of 1922 and in 1923 that 'these forces should not be there'. In explaining its revival he recounted how in June 1923 irregular leader Tom Barry had appealed for the formation of an organization to which irregulars could switch their allegiance from the de Valera-led movement, 'a body to whose wishes the leaders of the irregular side could acquiesce in matters of disbandment and arms without feeling humiliated'. In response, he envisioned a 'second organization', with which members of the government 'should not be associated', but over which 'it was essential that they should control its moulding and development'. He, MacMahon and Ó'Muirthûile, had met on 10 June 1923 with Cosgrave, O'Higgins, and MacNeill, and 'discussed matters arising out of these points and discussed our general action with regard to the organization'.[49]

O'Higgins interrupted and asked 'whether it was discussed as a project or an accomplished fact, and whether there was any acquiescence or approval on the part of the ministers whom he saw, and also whether he saw those ministers in their official capacity as members of the Executive Council or in a purely personal way'? Mulcahy could not answer the later question, and as for the former he answered 'the fact that the organization existed and had been brought into alignment with the present constitutional position was put before them as an accomplished fact'. He added that it was 'not a fact that there was … an emphatic repudiation of the position'.

O'Higgins insisted that there was 'the strongest and most emphatic dissent', which Mulcahy disputed.[50]

The former Minister for Defence continued his historical presentation stating that since the three ministers had undertaken not 'to give any definite advice' nor 'any definite instructions', he assumed 'they were satisfied' that any Army officer having responsibility with regard to the IRB was doing 'what appeared to him to be the best and the most wise thing in all our circumstances here'. He emphasized that the policy of the IRB would be 'securing that the discipline of the Army and its allegiance to the government would be absolute and unequivocal'. He had reported that to the Army Inquiry Committee, but the Committee had not acknowledged that 'the attitude of the IRB was in these matters generally...distinct from the IRA group'.[51]

O'Higgins then spoke, to 'take my place in the dock', as he had 'primary responsibility for the action that was taken' for which Mulcahy asked a Dáil condemnation. Taking no pleasure in speaking about the matter, and having neither personal venom nor vindictiveness toward the dismissed officers, he insisted: 'The substantial, broad fact is that the Executive Council had lost confidence in these men as a group.' He went on: 'There was a lack of confidence; there was a certain distrust; and that distrust was due to the uneasy feeling that there was going on, and had been going on for a considerable time, within the Army, things that ought not to be going on.' Acknowledging that 'it was something more than suspicion and something less than knowledge, something regarding which not a title of evidence or proof could be produced', he insisted 'there are times when governments have to take action on something that is more than suspicion, and falls short of knowledge'. The suspicion was that you had 'lining up within the Army, two groups, or factions, or secret or semi-secret societies'. The Dáil was now being asked to censure the government 'because we did not allow the national position to be bedevilled by a faction fight between two letters of the alphabet'.

As for Mulcahy's suggestion that there was 'knowledge with assent, with approval' by members of the Executive Council of the existence within the Army of the IRB, he insisted: 'There was no such thing.' He repeated the testimony he had given to the committee that he had told Mulcahy in February, 1923 that officers were being summoned from around the country to meet under the chairmanship of Ó'Muirthúile 'for the purpose of reorganizing the

Irish Republican Brotherhood within the Army, resurrecting and reorganizing it', which Mulcahy had denied. He had made these charges at a meeting of the Executive Council. The following June, Mulcahy came to him in a personal way to discuss the IRB. O'Higgins made clear his view that 'in the altered condition of things within the country' he 'believed that that organization, or any other secret organization, would be bad for the country and particularly bad for the Army'. Nothing was presented to him and two other ministers when they met with Mulcahy, MacMahon, and Ó'Muirthúile 'as an accomplished fact', but rather as 'a tentative proposal for the future'. He denied the suggestion that 'there was knowledge, and almost something more than knowledge, assent or approval, on the part of the ministers'. He himself had 'denounced the project as one that would inevitably react on the Army, one that would tend to sterilise the Army, to rot discipline and efficiency'. At the meeting 'there was no assent, there was no approval', and the participants could not have concluded but that 'there was a complete and profound disapproval in the minds of the ministers'.

As to whether it was the existence of the IRB within the Army or the Parnell Street incident which prompted the dismissals, O'Higgins insisted: 'It was both. It was a lack of confidence, and that lack of confidence was proved and justified by the Parnell Street incident.' He described the action that night as 'taken directly and flatly contrary to government policy'. He added that

> a faction struck venomously and bitterly at another faction behind the back of the government and behind the back of the people, and we had to act and act promptly to show to the people and anyone concerned that we were not willing to allow this country's interests to go back into the melting pot so that there might be an interesting dog fight between any two groups.[52]

Mulcahy's position has been favourably summarized by his biographer, Maryann Gialanella Valiulis, as being motivated by a desire 'to preserve Army unity and prevent the outbreak of another Civil War'. His 'ambiguous and, to a degree, inconsistent' dealing with the Old IRA and his desire to not challenge them in a 'direct and straightforward manner' was based on an attempt 'to stall for time' so that possible recruits to that movement could instead be drawn 'into a disciplined routine', an approach that was prompted in part by pressure from Cosgrave and McGrath.[53] She noted Mulcahy's separation 'both physically and mentally' from ministerial colleagues during the Civil War, when he was at the Army headquarters attempting to 'forge a professional army', while they were developing civilian institutions. The distance dimmed his understanding of 'the fears and frustrations of his colleagues *vis a vis* the Army', and their 'appreciation of the obstacles the Army was facing', and put 'Mulcahy on edge' and likely 'to act as if he were holding "a working brief" for the Army'.[54]

O'Higgins acknowledged in his testimony to the Army Inquiry Committee that Mulcahy and his Army Council colleagues had the best of intentions in using the IRB as a means of guaranteeing that the Army remain subordinate to civil power when he said he didn't believe 'that there were any sinister motives' in their exercise of poor judgment in reviving the IRB.[55] Their acceptance of their dismissal confirms that. Significantly, Seán MacMahon, whose commission was removed upon his refusal to resign his post, was re-commissioned as a major general three months later. Mulcahy himself would be welcomed back into a Cumann na nGaedheal government following the 9 June 1927 election, although he would not be a colleague of O'Higgins' for long as the latter would be assassinated a month later.

On the other hand, the very use of a private faction to combat other factions was contradictory to the ideal of civilian ascendancy, and was more likely to encourage rival groups. What validated O'Higgins' fears was the persistence of Old IRA elements within and without the Army for sometime after, necessitating a further demobilization of 'certain officers, NCOs and men' in December 1924, as well as 'reports of negotiations between Tobinites and "prominent irregulars"' toward the end of 1925. Along those lines, it was not remarkable that in the de Valera era Joseph McGrath and Liam Tobin, both linked with Oriel House, an instrument of questionable Free State actions during the Civil War, could make fast friends with old antagonists: McGrath developed an excellent relationship with Seán Lemass, whose brother was murdered by Oriel House men, and Tobin in 1940, at the height of Fianna Fáil ascendancy, became the superintendent of the Oireachtas, responsible for its security.[56]

DIVISION WITHIN CUMANN NA NGAEDHEAL

The Army crisis had brought to a head tensions that had been building within the Cumann na nGaedheal Party. On one side were those who could be considered a wing of Sinn Féin, but who supported the treaty out of loyalty to Michael Collins and as a tactical step toward an economically self-sufficient and united Irish Republic. They assumed that supporters of the revolutionary War of Independence would receive first preference for government positions and existing large landholdings would continue to be rapidly transferred to landless elements of the population. Others in the party viewed the government as responsible to the entire population, including former unionists, held it should be staffed with personnel qualified in accord with civil service principles, and supported policies based on standard thinking on economic matters, which at that time was hostile to deficit financing. Central to the division was the relationship between the party organization, the parliamentary party, and the Executive Council or the government itself.

The preliminary meeting of the party was on 7 December 1922, the same day in which the irregulars had assassinated Deputy Seán Hales and wounded Deputy Pádraic Ó'Máille. The first general convention, held in the Mansion House on 27 April 1923, elected Eoin MacNeill as the President of the organization. A General Council (Ard Comhairle) and a Standing Committee (Coiste Gnotha) were also formed, with the latter being named by the former and holding more frequent meetings. The minutes of the latter, even from before the 27 August 1923 election, reflected internal party dissatisfaction with governmental unresponsiveness to the rank and file, particularly on populist and nationalist issues.

For instance, a report from Kerry noted general apathy caused by the Army having 'given contracts to people who, while the British were here, were our opponents'. A report from Wexford complained of the same, as well as 'promotions and dismissals in the Army' making 'the work of organization almost impossible'. From Offaly came a complaint about court decrees won by landlords against tenants and a fear that the military would be employed to enforce them by seizing cattle, which would 'have a very bad effect in this county and will turn thousands of votes against our candidates at the election'.[57] At a meeting of the Standing Committee with the Executive Council on 3 December 1923, Eoin MacNeill warned of the party organization being regarded as simply an instrument to support the government. While 'the responsibility of legislation and administration lay on the ministers', he said, 'the organization could, and should, do much to shape public opinion'. A real question was 'what we should put before the people as an inducement to join', as 'the treaty issue was worn out'. But O'Higgins, who had 'serious objection' to ministers giving out advance knowledge of legislation', said policy should 'crystalize round legislation initiated by the government', and admitted that 'old friends would be lost' and that 'new ones would arise'.[58]

In a meeting of the General Council later that month, member C. Crowley from County Cork asserted the need to 'concentrate on winning back the men who made the Irish Ireland movement'.[59] The next month, at the annual convention of the party, resolutions were approved which called for 'immediately putting the boundary clause of the treaty into effect', for setting aside in the distribution of untenanted lands and ranches a 'portion for eligible IRA men and men who had fought in the national Army', for 'immediately acquiring the grazing ranches for the purpose of re-distribution', and for having a government policy of 'making the country self-sufficient and self-supporting'.[60] At a meeting of the General Council in May, after the Army Crisis but before the Army Inquiry Committee had issued its report, a resolution was approved calling for the government to take soundings through the party organization as to public views on contemplated controversial legislation and to provide TDs with adequate explanation for such legislation. Rather than directly challenge the motion, O'Higgins described it as positive and agreed that 'nothing could be more disastrous than the virtual isolation of the government'.[61]

The Standing Committee even invited the nine TDs, led by Joseph McGrath, who resigned from the party and began calling themselves the 'National Group', to meet on 30 June to discuss differences. However, McGrath rejected the invitation as he thought the Standing Committee appeared 'merely to acquiesce' in and had 'neither inclination nor power to influence' the policies of the government.[62]

In October the Standing Committee sought to disprove McGrath's allegation about their being supine towards the Executive Council by issuing a statement of its views on the present political situation. That statement reiterated certain populist complaints about the Cumann na nGaedheal Party organization, such as negligible 'influence on government policy' and 'power to affect patronage' and the impression 'in parts of the country' that 'connection with Cumann na nGaedheal is in most cases a handicap and in many cases a complete bar to appointments, preferments or even a fair deal in land or compensation'. Disappointment was expressed at the administration of the Land Act of 1923, which sought to complete the land purchase legislation of the old regime. The government was seen as regarding the Irish Farmers' Union, an independent political party whose members were stronger farmers, 'as representing farming opinion in the country', when 'the vast bulk of the real farmers', presumably smallholders, were supporters of Cumann na nGaedheal or of the new Sinn Féin'. But 'the sorest question of all' was the matter of public appointments: 'those who won the fight have not done well out of the victory, whereas the pro-British ascendancy who lost the fight have done disproportionately well and got a new lease of life from the Free State. *The civil servants are the government* and there is... fear that vital Irish interests are in the hands of men whose allegiance does not lie in Ireland.' That fear was 'increased by the belief that there is a constant reference to London officials for decisions of all sorts of concrete administrative issues'. Finally, the 'insulation of the Executive Council from the currents of thought of its supporters is perhaps the most dangerous of the conditions that menace the state'.[63]

In an actual meeting with the Executive Council, Standing Committee members reiterated the complaints of that statement. Seán Collins, the brother of Michael Collins, thought the people 'lacked confidence and felt no improvement with the new regime', land divisions were moving too slowly, and that the officials in the Treasury 'were all-powerful and dictated policy'. Michael Tierney, a Professor of Classics at University College Dublin and TD for the National University, said: 'Retrenchment and collection of debts at the point of the bayonet were the features by which the government was best known to a large portion of the electorate.' Denis McCullough, a Belfast-born former president of the IRB who would be elected to the Dáil for Donegal the following month, thought 'it was impossible to keep life in the organization if the present discontent were not met. The budget was being balanced in the interest of future generations at the expense of the people of today.'

Both Blythe and O'Higgins sought to respond to these criticisms as Blythe expressed regret that the Executive Council was not in closer touch with the Standing Committee. He reassured them that he had no objection to borrowing, but 'current expenditure must be paid out of revenue', but that revenue might not be adequate since the country was poor. O'Higgins noted that the treaty obligation to pay pensions to any officials discharged because of the change of regime inhibited any massive displacement of personnel, and reminded them that 'the Free State was unfortunate in being born when prices were at a peak and the main producers had been working since on a falling market. It was hard luck that a period of unprecedented depression had set in with the evacuation of the British.' However, he was confident that the work of the government 'could bear the closest examination and its effect would tell increasingly in the future'.[64]

Later that month on 29 October, McGrath and his eight followers resigned from Dáil Éireann, which necessitated by-elections the following March. Five by-elections were already scheduled for November because of a death, a disqualification, and three resignations. One of those who had resigned, Alfred O'Rahilly, did so because of dissatisfaction with the government. Accordingly, fourteen seats, originally held by government supporters, would be on the line. In this atmosphere the Standing Committee met with the Cumann na nGaedheal TDs on 29 October to report on their meeting with the Executive Council. The general sentiment was that there should be greater communication between the Executive and TDs and the organization, but that there should be no private negotiations between any Cabinet member and the National Group.[65] The latter concern emerged following unsuccessful negotiations between McGrath and Cosgrave, with Irish-American activists Daniel Cohalan and John Devoy as intermediaries, about possible re-instatement of officers who had mutinied and an appointment of a Defence Minister suitable to both the government and the National Group.[66]

In the November by-elections, abstentionist Sinn Féin won two of the five seats formerly held by government supporters.[67] Later that month the General Council convened a special meeting with O'Higgins, Blythe, and J.J. Walsh, the Minister for Posts and Telegraphs. At the meeting O'Higgins reported on the dire financial position of the party, in response to which a general appeal was to be sent out to 'peace commissioners, district justices, state solicitors, barristers and medical men and a judicious selection of the clergy' for support. In view of the impending March by-elections, he announced the formation of an Organizing Committee, to be selected from the present Standing Committee, from ministers, and from some others not presently connected with the party or the organization. Walsh was to be the Chairman and a major task would be fund raising. The party headquarters was changed from Parnell

Square, near Devlin's Hotel and other IRB centres, to the south side of the city, with a place on Dawson Street ultimately being purchased, which some might interpret as symbolic of the downplaying of the nationalist and populist elements within the party. While O'Higgins insisted the new committee would not exist apart from Cumann na nGaedheal and that its powers were 'delegated to it by the Cumann na nGaedheal executive', he asserted, significantly, that 'the assets of the Organizing Committee would be the assets of the organization, but handled by the committee'. This implied the new committee would be the *de facto*, if not *de jure*, master. These developments received general approval from such varied figures as Richard Mulcahy, Senator Mrs Wyse-Power, and even Denis McCullough. The following were to be the members of the Organizing Committee: O'Higgins, Blythe, Patrick Hogan, Eoin MacNeill, Patrick McGilligan, Fionán Lynch, J.J. Walsh, Senator John McLoughlin (of the Donegal shirt manufacturing family), Michael Tierney, P.J. Egan, (a TD for Leix–Offaly and a close O'Higgins supporter), H.B. O'Hanlon (a Dublin solicitor), Mulcahy, T. Montgomery, and Senator Mrs Wyse-Power.[68] The Organizing Committee directed specific members to use their contacts to draw financial support; for instance, H.B. O'Hanlon was to approach the legal profession and P.J. Egan was to approach the Licensed Vintners Association.[69]

The formation of the new committee was a victory for O'Higgins and colleagues like FitzGerald, Hogan, Blythe, and McGilligan, who were unresponsive to the Irish–Ireland and nationalist–populist agenda of rewarding the faithful with positions and pursuing a policy of economic self-sufficiency, and more concerned with making the new state work, even if it meant employing the old civil service and listening to the advice of former Unionists. O'Higgins' attitude is best reflected in a letter he wrote shortly after the Army crisis and the appointment of his friend Patrick McGilligan to replace McGrath as Minister for Industry and Commerce. Commenting on the more vehemently nationalist elements either within or about to leave the party, he noted:

> None of those fellows care a curse about the country or the people in the country. McGilligan, who wasn't 'out in 16' has no particular 'record' and no 'Gaelic soul', has done more in two weeks than his predecessor in two years ... I have come to the conclusion that men like Hogan, McGilligan ... could do more for the country in a year

(even for the realisation of all its ideals) than all the Clans and Brotherhoods could effect in a generation.[70]

A further indication of an aim to appeal to non-party members, whether former Unionists, former Irish Parliamentary Party supporters, or the many indifferent to nationalist ideals, was the decision that Cumann na nGaedheal not nominate their own candidates for local public bodies except in instances where there might be no other pro-treaty candidate going forward. Similarly, the party endorsed the entire panel of seventy-six candidates for the senatorial election in 1925.[71] A week later the committee advocated 'legislation by which the abstentionists would be penalized financially and their seats handed over to the runners-up',[72] a policy that would ultimately force de Valera and his followers into Dáil Éireann in 1927.

O'Higgins' attitude toward the dissenters in the party was reflected in his response to a complaining memorandum from the Roscommon Cumann na nGaedheal about matters like the reduction in old-age pensions, a step taken by the government in accord with its orthodox economic approach to fiscal difficulties. He insisted that the system could not be financed by borrowing 'without serious damage to the national credit and consequent economic damage to the people and especially to the poorer classes', and that to use taxation would require a great increase in a burden 'which every interest in the country is anxious to have reduced'. An increase in money spent on pensions would 'diminish the funds available for economic relief and development'. He stated that those using the pension issue as 'a reason for withdrawing support from the government and thereby strengthening those whose policy is to break the treaty should be asked to say what prospect the pensioners would have if the treaty was broken'. As for abandoning Irish ideals and pursuing a business policy, he insisted '…the government will endeavour to place the country in a sound position economically, and that it does not believe that this involves any sacrifice of National ideals'.[73]

The government was successful in seven of the nine by-elections occasioned by the resignations of the members of the National Group. Significantly, only one of the National Group TDs who had resigned, Seán Milroy himself, stood (and came in last of five candidates in Dublin North). However, two abstentionist republicans gained seats and republican votes in all constituencies exceeded their returns in the 1923 general election, which suggests a significant move by many nationalist–populist Cumann na nGaedheal members toward Sinn Féin.[74]

NOTES

1.  F.S. Lyons, *Ireland Since the Famine* (London: Weidenfeld and Nicolson, 1971), p. 490.
2.  J.J. Lee, *Ireland 1912–1985* (Cambridge: Cambridge University Press, 1989), p. 103.
3.  *Dáil Éireann*, VI (11 March 1924), 1,894–5.
4.  Maryann Gialanella Valiulis, 'The "army mutiny" of 1924 and the assertion of civilian authority in independent Ireland', *Irish Historical Studies*, XXIII, No. 92 (Nov. 1983), p. 358; M.G. Valiulis, *Portrait of a Revolutionary: General Richard Mulcahy and the founding of the Irish Free State* (Dublin: Irish Academic Press, 1992), p. 202; J.J. Lee, *Ireland; 1912–1985*, p. 99.
5.  Valiulis, *Mulcahy*, p. 202.
6.  IRB constitution, 1923, clause 13b, quoted in John O'Bierne-Ranelegh, 'The I.R.B. from the treaty to 1924', *Irish Historical Studies*, XX, No. 70 (March 1976), pp. 34–5.
7.  Valiulis, *Mulcahy*, pp. 203–7.
8.  *Dáil Éireann*, VI (11 March 1924), 1896.
9.  Valiulis, *Mulcahy*, p. 272; 'Army Mutiny', *IHS*, p. 360.
10. *Chronological Statement of Events Connected With the Army Mutiny*, NA, S 3678A.
11. *Dáil Éireann*, VI (11 March 1924), 1894–8.
12. *Ibid.* (12 March 1924), 1971–84.
13. *Ibid.*, 1,984–88.
14. *Ibid.*, 1,995–2002.
15. *Ibid.*, 2,003–7.
16. *Ibid.*, 2,007–11.
17. *Ibid.*, 2,019–24.
18. *Ibid.* (19 March 1924), 2,204–5.
19. Valuilis, *Mulcahy*, p. 214.
20. *Dáil Éireann*, Vol VI (19 March 1924), 2,204–25.
21. John M. Regan, 'Kevin O'Higgins, Irish Republicanism and the Conservative Counter-Revolution', *Laois History and Society*, ed. Pádraic Lane and William Nolan (Dublin: Geography Publications, 1999).
22. *Dáil Éireann*, Vol VI (19 March 1924), 2,226–30.
23. Valiulis, *Mulcahy*, p. 216.
24. *Dáil Éireann*, Vol VI (20 March 1924), 2,242–3.
25. *Ibid.*, 2,245–8.
26. *Ibid.*, 2,251–2.
27. *Ibid.*, 2,255–7.
28. *Ibid.*, 2,260–5.
29. *Ibid.*, 2,275–84.
30. *Ibid.*, 2,284–8.
31. *The Irish Times* (24 March 1924), p. 5.
32. *Dáil Éireann*, VI (26 March 1924), 2,354–8.
33. *Ibid.*, 2,359–65.

34. *Ibid.*, 2,366–71.
35. *Ibid.*, 2,379–86.
36. *Ibid.*, 2,394.
37. *Ibid.*, 2,396.
38. *Ibid.*, 2,406–10.
39. *Ibid.*, 2,421–2.
40. *Report of the Army Inquiry Committee* (7 June 1924), pp. 3–4, NA, S 3678C.
41. Dáil Éireann, VI (28 March 1924), 2,663–7.
42. *Ibid.* (3 April 1924), 2,669; Valiulis, *Mulcahy*, p. 222; *Army Mutiny File*, NA, S 3678B.
43. *Report of the Army Inquiry Committee*, pp. 4–6.
44. *Ibid.*, p. 6.
45. *Ibid.*, pp. 7–8.
46. *Ibid.*, pp. 8–9.
47. Valiulis, *Mulcahy*, pp. 230–31. O'Higgins' Testimony to the Army Inquiry Committee (22 April 1924), UCDA, *Mulcahy Papers*, P7/C/21–23.
48. *Report of the Army Inquiry Committee*, p. 9.
49. *Dáil Éireann*, VII (26 June 1924), 3,110–24.
50. *Ibid.*, 3,124–5.
51. *Ibid.*, 3,125–7.
52. *Ibid.*, 3,155–60.
53. Valiulis, *Mulcahy*, p. 224.
54. *Ibid.*, p. 232.
55. O'Higgins' Testimony to the Army Inquiry Committee (22 April 1924), UCDA, *Mulcahy Papers*, P/7/C 22.
56. Eunan O'Halpin, *Defending Ireland. The Irish State and Its Enemies Since 1922* (Oxford: Oxford University Press, 1999), pp. 52–3.
57. Standing Committee (13 July 1923), UCDA, *Cumann na nGaedheal/Fine Gael Minute Books*, UCDA, P 39/Min/ 1, p. 334.
58. Conference of Standing Committee with Executive Council (3 December 1923), *Ibid.*, p. 376.
59. Meeting of General Council (14 December 1923), *Ibid.*, p. 377.
60. Annual Convention (29 January 1924), *Ibid.*, pp. 466–7.
61. Meeting of Ard Chomhairle (13 May 1924), *Ibid.*, pp. 415–17.
62. Seamus ÓhAodha to each member of the National Group (24 June 1924), and Joseph McGrath to Seamus ÓhAodha (25 June 1924), UCDA, *FitzGerald Papers*, P 80/1100 (1).
63. Statement of Views of Coiste Gnotha Relative to the Political Aspect of the Present Situation (10 October 1924), *Ibid.*, P 80/1101 (1–4).
64. Meeting of Standing Committee (10 October 1924), UCDA, *Cumann na nGaedheal/Fine Gael Papers*, P39/ Min/ 1, pp. 439–41.
65. Meeting of Coiste Gnotha with Cumann na nGaedheal TDs (29 October 1924), *Ibid.*
66. John M. Regan, 'The Politics of Utopia: Party Organization, Executive Autonomy and the New Administration', *Ireland: The Politics of Independence, 1922–49*, ed. Mike Cronin and John M. Regan (London: Macmillan, 2000), pp. 56–8.
67. One of the victors, from Dublin South, was the future Taoiseach, Seán Lemass.
68. Special Meeting of the Standing Committee (27 November 1924), UCDA, *Cumann na nGaedheal/Fine Gael Papers*, P39/ Min/ 1, pp. 449–51, and Regan, *Irish Counter-Revolution*, pp. 227–30.
69. Executive Organising Committee (16 December 1924), UCDA, *Cumann na nGaedheal/Fine Gael Papers*, P39/Min/ 1.

70. O'Higgins to Mrs Powell (19 May 1924), cited in Valiulis, *Portrait*, pp. 233–4 (also in Regan, *Irish Counter-Revolution*, p. 245).
71. In that election, which was the first of the triennial elections of one-fourth of the Seanad, the entire State was regarded as a single constituency and voting was done by the same proportional representation as other elected offices. As might be expected, so large a number of candidates for so many offices discouraged sizeable turnout by voters. The constitution was changed before further Seanad elections in 1928, 1931, and 1934.
72. Executive Organising Committee (16 December 1924, 13 and 25 January 1925), UCDA, *Cumann na nGaedheal/Fine Gael Papers*, P 39/Min/ 1; Regan, *Irish Counter-Revolution*, pp. 249–50.
73. Kevin O'Higgins to Rev. M. Brennan (8 January 1925), UCDA, *FitzGerald Papers*, P80/1065 (1–3).
74. Walker, *Parliamentary Election Results*, pp. 116–17.

# 6

# The Police and a Treason Act

IN MAY 1924, in the wake of the Army crisis, O'Higgins introduced legislation giving permanency to the Garda Síochána that had only the July 1923 Temporary Civic Guard Act as its legal foundation. The force was to be national rather than local; its officers would be appointed by and subject to dismissal or removal from rank by the Executive Council; and it would have from 5,300 to 6,300 members in 837 stations, with their distribution to be determined by the Minister for Justice. Members of the force would be required to declare that they did not and would not 'belong to any political society or secret society'.[1] The legislation passed the Dáil and the Seanad with minimal objection.

A month later, in June, comparable legislation was passed giving the Executive Council power to appoint, regulate, and direct the Dublin Metropolitan Police. The DMP, which had existed in the old regime, was allowed to continue in the Free State because it had not been employed against the revolutionary forces and did not have the opprobrium attached to the RIC. When Thomas Johnson questioned the necessity for two forces, O'Higgins said he would favour ultimate unification when it would be 'administratively more convenient'. As he had earlier with the Temporary Civic Guard Act, Johnson objected to the requirement that members of the Dublin Metropolitan Force declare that they did not belong to any political society or secret society, as he saw such as 'very little value' and easy to evade, and could easily be applied to all types of societies, including the Gaelic Athletic Association and the Ancient Order of Hibernians. Furthermore, 'a political society may have for its purpose the good government of a locality', and such 'a political society might be a most admirable organization for a policeman to belong to'.[2] O'Higgins insisted that it was important to ask of 'any and every person joining the force, and every person at present a member of the force' that 'he will not take an active partisan part in politics, and that he will not enter into commitments unknown to the people at large which might possibly affect the impartial discharge of his duties'. He added that it was 'not something devised *ad hoc* or in any panic', but was a condition attached to police forces in the past 'which we see no sufficient reason for departing from'.[3]

Shortly after the passage of the Garda and the DMP Acts, the Dáil considered estimates for both bodies. The Garda had grown to over 5,000 in barely a year since the Civil War and Garda stations had increased to 756, almost 500 more than in the closing days of the war. But fiscal difficulties and the poor state of the national economy, both a consequence of the destruction during the War of Independence and the Civil War, made a reduction in Garda pay necessary. More gratifying was a report of 'a downward tendency in the number of reported offences and a somewhat upward tendency in the number of arrests made'. O'Higgins had 'a certain quiet satisfaction as regards the manner in which the Guards are doing their duty'. Even though they had gone out 'in a very difficult period', there was not much evidence of an expected obvious 'rawness and inexperience'. Throughout the country the men 'had won the respect and confidence of the people', and 'friendly co-operation' received from the people was on the increase. He hoped to see the feeling grow among the people that the Garda were 'their officials and their servants, out simply to uphold the laws'.[4]

O'Higgins' report was generally well received and the Garda appreciated. Darrell Figgis, for instance, acknowledged that the praise given to the Garda 'by the Minister for Justice, is a praise that has been more than well deserved'. Noting the friendly co-operation received in practically all parts of the country from the people, he regarded such as a credit to the rank and file, as much as those in command, who, 'in carrying out their duties', having shown 'a very considerable sense of discretion, coupled with discipline'.[5] Osmond Grattan Esmonde, a Cumann na nGaedheal deputy for Wexford, added that 'the minister himself cannot escape from a very considerable share of the praise which all sections of the Dáil give most willingly with reference to the outstanding success of the establishment and working of the Garda Síochána'.[6] But concern had been raised that some ex-RIC members in the Garda, who had remained in that force until it was disbanded after the treaty, and drew RIC pensions as well as their Garda salaries, were better off than other ex-RIC members in the Garda, who had not qualified for an RIC pension because they had retired during the War of Independence for nationalist reasons.[7] O'Higgins assured the Dáil that RIC pensions were suspended for any recipient who joined the Garda. He regarded the playing off of the disbanded RIC members against the resigned RIC members as 'thoroughly mischievous', and insisted that it was 'not safe or right or proper simply to take it as a general assumption that the men who remained on in the RIC until such time as that force was disbanded were, from the national point of view, any less worthy than the others who quitted it at an earlier stage'.[8]

O'Higgins reported the disappointing news of a great number of applications for retirement – 613 of 1,124 – among the DMP. Generous retirement terms had been offered, not so much to encourage a lot of retirements, but to induce the retirement of men 'who would be utterly obnoxious to a new government, or to whom a new government would be utterly obnoxious'. However, they were taken advantage of by many others, most of them 'probably sons of the small farmers of the country', whose continued service would have been more than desired. He announced a reduction in the pay rate for the DMP, as well as for the Garda Síochána, 'on exactly the same basis as was adopted in adjusting the pay of all other government servants'. An increase in one year in summons from 11,000 to 17,251 and in arrests from 3,925 to 5,288 he saw as an improvement in the force's efficiency. Lastly, he reported that the detective branch of the DMP had absorbed twenty-eight of the seventy-two members of Oriel House, the notorious intelligence service formulated by Collins for the Provisional Government that had been disbanded in November 1923.[9]

Toward the end of the year O'Higgins introduced a measure calling for the amalgamation of the two forces. What contributed to his decision was the tardiness in the apprehension of two bank robbers who had killed a Garda in Baltinglass, Co. Wicklow in late January, 1924. Inadequate communications between the Baltinglass station and Garda stations on the escape route back to Dublin inhibited their capture. The detective force of the DMP determined the identities of the culprits, discovered that they had fled to Monaghan, and sent detectives in pursuit of them, but they had only reluctant co-operation from the local Gardai.[10] He believed the armed detective branch of the DMP would be the appropriate reinforcement for the unarmed and uniformed Garda in cases of the more serious forms of crime, especially armed criminality, rather than the Army, as it was 'wrong that the military machine would be called upon to move every time some thug holds up a bank or post office, or perpetrates some robbery with arms in a rural area'. Under the amalgamation of the forces the Commissioner of the Garda would become Commissioner of the unified force and the Commissioner of the DMP would become a second Deputy Commissioner of the Garda. Existing DMP pay rates were maintained and no present member of the DMP would have to serve outside the Dublin metropolitan area without his consent.[11]

Bryan Cooper was concerned about Dublin losing out as a consequence of the amalgamation and introduced an amendment calling for the appointment of a Deputy or Assistant Commissioner specifically charged with the supervision of the police officers serving the Dublin metropolitan area. O'Higgins saw the amendment as 'inconsistent with the whole object the Bill seeks to achieve – the unity of control and responsibility of the police force'.[12] When the amendment failed Cooper introduced another which called for a consultative council whose members would be nominated by the Corporation of the City of Dublin, the various urban councils of the county, the Dublin Chamber of Commerce, and the Dublin Workers' Council, to advise and assist the Police Commissioner on matters relating to the public order and security of the metropolitan area. But O'Higgins thought police problems and responsibilities could not 'be shared between the police officer and a body of thirteen laymen – thirteen civilians – elected haphazardly by a half-dozen local authorities'. It was one thing for letters to be sent to the papers or to his department regarding police matters, but 'quite another thing . . . that the officer responsible for the police administration of Dublin must take counsel from time to time with a body of thirteen laymen', especially when the advice was advanced on the initiative of the lay board rather than in response to a request by the Commissioner of the Garda Síochána.[13]

Thomas Johnson questioned the idea of a centralized or national police force. He depicted O'Higgins' state of mind as adhering to 'the very essence of the idea of centralized control of any public service', which was 'centralized control in the hands of one man not subject to criticism', and argued that O'Higgins had 'imbibed the RIC spirit', with preference for 'a militarized police force in Ireland, and centralized control, not having any intervention or interference from any public authority of any kind'. Johnson looked forward to that time when the police forces 'will not be centrally controlled' and 'be, in fact, controlled locally, with whatever national co-ordinating authority there may be'.[14] Darrell Figgis also espoused the role of councils with which 'the Commissioner of the Garda Síochána' should 'under law be compelled to enter into consultation'. He considered 'the administration of a centralized force of this kind existing throughout the entire territory of the Free State, gathered entirely into the hands of one man', as 'a dangerous principle' unless that administration be 'brought into contact with local bodies', which would allow some contact 'between the administration of a force of this kind and the popular will'.[15]

O'Higgins answered that there were two alternatives for placing responsibility over the police: either 'to lie here in the Dáil, through a minister, or to dissipate it over the country to this local authority and that local authority'. The government thought, 'in the interests of the country' and 'in the best interests of efficient police administration', that the line of responsibility should be through the Dáil and regarded it as 'unwise to take a step that would tend in any way to weaken that line'.[16] Johnson was less confident that the Dáil could be responsible for administration in view of it being in session for only four to six months a year and able to comment on administration only during the debates on the Estimates.[17]

## PERMANENT PUBLIC SAFETY BILL

In early 1925 O'Higgins believed that 'such conditions of comparative peace' and 'security' had come to prevail that it was not necessary to renew such exceptional legislation as the Arrest and Detention Act and Punishment of Offences Act that were due to expire respectively in January and April 1925. In their place he advanced permanent legislation designed to outline the general powers of the state for dealing with 'any possible trouble or any possible challenge' in the future rather than to meet a specific and current situation.

The measure, the Treasonable and Seditious Offences Bill, listed certain actions, such as levying, or encouraging or conspiring with others to levy, war against the Free State, and attempting, or conspiring with or encouraging others, to overthrow by force the government of the Free State, as treasonous and liable to capital punishment. The accused would be indicted, arraigned, and tried in the same manner as would anyone charged with murder. Less severe punishments were prescribed for a variety of other offences. Failure to disclose knowledge of an intended or proposed treasonous act could subject a person to the charge of 'misprison of treason' with a possible penalty of ten years' hard labour. Other offences against the state, such as attempting, or encouraging, assisting, conspiring with, or harbouring others, to intimidate the Governor General, the Executive Council, other ministers, members of the Dáil or Seanad, or any judge, in order to influence their actions; setting up or being involved with a pretended court; and inciting any of the military or the police to mutiny, to desert, or refuse to perform duties, or incite any civil servant to perform his duty could merit twenty years' imprisonment. Falsely purporting to be the President, Vice-President, or other officer of the state, or a member of the military or the police, as did the irregulars and their continuing organizations, both political and military, could incur five years' imprisonment. 'Seditious libel', such as declaring that the constitution was not lawful, challenging the lawfulness of the Executive Council, the Oireachtas, or any of the courts, and 'seditious intention', that is, intending to 'excite disaffection against the constitution, or the Oireachtas', inciting attempts at altering the constitution (otherwise than in accordance with the law), and fomenting 'discontent or disaffection amongst the citizens…or hostility between different classes, or to incite breaches of the peace' could receive twenty years imprisonment with hard labour. Meetings within the vicinity of the Oireachtas, unauthorized military exercises, the promotion of any secret societies in the military or the police, and the administration of unlawful oaths were forbidden and searching for documents of a treasonable or seditious nature was authorized.[18]

The admittedly severe measure must be compared with other emergency measures passed in Ireland during and immediately after the troubles and the Civil War. In his book, *Emergency Legislation in Ireland, 1918–1925*, Colin Campbell listed seven different types of emergency legislation, and categorized them according to their departure from ordinary law. Ranked in order from that most compatible with ordinary law to that most deviant, the seven types were: 1. the utilization of ordinary law to respond to politically motivated crime; 2. the definition of certain types of political activity as illegal, but subjecting them to ordinary court procedure; 3. the use of special trial procedures for politically motivated crimes; 4. the administrative detention of subjects; 5. the use of a parallel legal system, like martial courts, for specific offences; 6. a pseudo-legal system operating without statutory powers; and 7. the absence of legal procedures as in conventional warfare. Among the various measures undertaken by the Free State, the Emergency Powers Resolution of October 1922, which had allowed martial court trials and executions during the Civil War, was seen by Campbell as the one departing the most from ordinary law and he placed it in the sixth category. The Public Safety Act of 1923 and its renewal of 1924, which allowed detention, were put in the slightly milder fourth category. The Punishment of Offences Act of 1924, with its special court procedures for politically motivated crime, was placed in the third category, while the Treasonous Offences measure was placed in the relatively liberal second category.[19] In other words, the difference between it and ordinary law was that it defined certain ordinarily innocent actions as political crimes, but allowed them to be tried in the ordinary courts and under ordinary procedure. To oppose the legislation, the position would have to be taken that politically motivated actions should be subject to apprehension, trial, and punishment only if those actions broke the existing ordinary law, not exceptional law that specifically defined these ordinary actions as illegal.

A central concern was O'Higgins' desire to have legal instruments to contend with a restrained but continuing illegal army within the state. Others were inclined to minimize the need for such powers in view of the relative calm that had set in and seeming restraint by the republican movement. Opponents feared the measure might provoke a return to violence by the republicans. Other criticisms were that it was unnecessary in view of existing legislation inherited from the British and that it was repressive of civil liberties, including the right of political agitation and organization. Its inclusion of capital punishment for certain offences was criticized as was the Bill's potential impact on the labour organization of civil servants.

Thomas Johnson led the criticism, arguing that existing and still-standing British legislation served the purpose of the proposed law, but claimed that the government wanted a new Bill as a substitute for 'a compilation of Bills passed one hundred years ago', so that deeds subject to prosecution under the old law would not have 'to be announced as treason against the King'. He was not troubled by anti-treaty republicans calling themselves to be the government or officers of the state, and thought it was sufficient to make it an offence 'to attempt to enforce the powers of government'. He feared that limiting challenges to the constitution to actions within the law could be interpreted to make even the advocacy of changing the treaty illegal since the constitution itself was bound by the treaty. He also depicted the Bill's prohibiting the administration of unlawful oaths as being 'within the spirit of the anti-combination laws', that is, those late eighteenth century laws designed to inhibit the organization of labour unions.[20] The next day he argued that the legislation was unnecessary since the ministry had succeeded 'in persuading the republican party to cease its militancy'. Now, he feared, it was trying 'to stir up those dying embers of passion and hate'. Instead of the proposed legislation, he thought 'a little patience would have brought the great majority of the people who had hitherto been opponents of the Saorstát into a state of mind in which they would say: "Well, we bow to the inevitable – we will do as better men have done in many countries – accept the situation not from choice, but from necessity."'[21]

Bryan Cooper, on the other hand, regarded O'Higgins' speech championing the Bill as 'very exhaustive and moderate'. He was very supportive of the sections dealing with mutiny and incitement to mutiny. But he thought more care should be applied in formulating the law of treason, as he noted that even the Tudor law against treason was more solicitous for the accused, requiring two witnesses. Like Johnson, he thought too much was made of pretensions by the republicans to be the government, and the section about these pretences was 'like taking a howitzer to kill a butterfly'. He would be happier if 'a lesser punishment...than the punishment of death' would apply to the crime of harbouring or comforting a rebel against the state and he had a civil libertarian apprehension about labelling as seditious intention the inciting of 'disaffection against the constitution or the Oireachtas', or raising 'disaffection amongst the citizens...or feelings of ill-will or hostility between different classes'.[22]

The independent Darrell Figgis accepted O'Higgins' premises about the necessity 'to have laid down exactly what we regard as offences against the state, and to mete out for each offence its requisite punishment'. He could not accept Johnson's argument that existing legislation from the old regime provided more than enough for the minister, as he thought it 'necessary for this state to lay down for itself what it regards as offences, to show that they are definite acts or definite incitement to acts, not the expression of opinion'. But he would have been happier had the words 'treason' and 'sedition' been dispensed with, for they were 'words of no happy history in this country', and were words 'that carry no meaning'. He agreed with Johnson that the anti-republican sections would serve the republicans by creating a backlash. The proposed legislation would give them 'exactly the resuscitation that they were looking for', and could 'create a new flock of martyrs in the land'.[23]

Former Minister for Defence Richard Mulcahy demonstrated his loyalty to the government as he supported the Bill because it defined treasonous acts, excluded secret societies from the uniformed forces, prohibited unlawful oaths, and asserted the right to search for seditious documents. However, he had reservations about the severity of some of its penalties such as 'ten years' penal servitude or two years' imprisonment' for harbouring treasonous or seditious persons. Like Johnson and Bryan Cooper, he saw no need for the clauses against the republicans claiming to be the Government of Ireland as those very speeches and printed statements by the irregulars made them appear irrelevant to most of the public.[24] Others less concerned about the irregulars were Farmers' Union deputies, Richard Wilson for Wicklow, Patrick Baxter for Cavan, and Patrick McKenna for Longford–Westmeath, who thought the existing relative peace made the Bill unnecessary and feared that it was likely to stir up trouble that had died down. William Hewat, Businessmen's Party deputy for Dublin North, regarded the Bill in its existing form as like 'throwing a bombshell into a situation which we were all hoping was working on the lines of a great improvement in the position of the country as a whole'.[25]

O'Higgins replied that without the legislation the state would be forced by the expiration of the existing Arrest and Detention and Punishment of Offences Acts 'to rely on the legislation passed in earlier times by the British Parliament'. While Johnson and others had asserted that those laws were sufficient, he was certain Johnson would be the 'first and most eloquent accuser and denouncer' were the government to employ them. While others might prefer to continue the temporary powers of detention, he preferred 'a proper and reasonable treason and sedition code for the country'. While critics in the Dáil seemed to believe the state 'requires no code of treason, no code of sedition for its defence, for its protection', and 'offences of a treasonable or seditious nature are unlikely to arise', he hoped they had not passed through the recent period 'in an unthinking, unlearning way drawing no moral from it, drawing no lesson from it' nor were 'prepared to walk blindly into a future that may be as unpleasant as that past'. Regardless of idealistic hopes for the future, the Bill was necessary to make sure 'that the nightmares of yesterday do not become the realities of tomorrow' and to equip the state 'with the ordinary proper powers to guard against any repetition of such a situation as that through which we have passed'. The present quieted situation should not be regarded as grounds not to make provision against sedition. Rather than take action only when the challenge comes, a wise state 'would endeavour to check and deal with the factors that were leading towards the challenge'. He would have been challenged had he asked for a renewal of the expiring temporary powers on the grounds that the abnormal situation justifying them had changed. Instead, in the 'comparatively normal and peaceful situation that now exists', he asked if the 'permanent powers the Executive ought to possess to deal with offences directed against the state and the welfare of the state'.[26]

### EFFORTS AT AMENDMENTS IN DÁIL AND SEANAD

The government agreed to a number of amendments significantly modifying the severity of the legislation. For instance, the penalty for the offence of assisting, encouraging, harbouring or comforting anyone levying war against the state or engaged in a forceful or violent attempt at overthrowing the government was reduced from capital punishment to imprisonment up to two years or to a fine up to five hundred pounds and/or penal servitude up to five years. In response to the point made by Deputy Cooper, a section was added requiring that conviction for treason not be 'on the uncorroborated evidence of one witness'.[27] Items central to republican symbolism, but not inherently dangerous, such as being a pretender or rival claimant to the offices of the state, assembling a rival Dáil or Seanad, and asserting that the constitution and the existing state were illegitimate were dropped as offences.[28]

In addition to government-endorsed changes, individual TDs offered a number of other amendments, especially ones to lessen the number of offences subject to capital punishment and to give discretion to the judiciary as to its application. Richard Mulcahy moved to not treat conspiring with or encouraging others to levy war against the state or attempt to overthrow the government by force or violence as capital offences. He believed that the wording cast too broad a net and could subject too many people to the death sentence. He wondered whether there was a need, even in the more severe cases, for the state, especially when it 'is not hampered by anything like Civil War or anything like any serious disturbance in it ... to inflict the penalty of death'. However, he realized 'that there might be circumstances in which it might be very necessary' for the minister 'to have this power'. Accordingly he was willing to withdraw his amendments, unless some deputies wanted them to be pressed to a division.[29] Johnson wanted a division as he was disturbed that the power to determine with which capital offence a prisoner would be charged would be left to the Minister for Justice or the Attorney General. Those officials could be subject to momentary agitation and popular pressure, as within the past century in Europe, 'Political excitement brings feelings to the front which lead to acts that in calmer moments are recognised to be unjust and unreasonable.' Mulcahy's amendments failed.[30]

Professor William Thrift, independent deputy for Trinity College, moved to allow judges the discretion to impose a lesser penalty than capital punishment. He criticized a legislative trend 'to fix the maximum penalty as the actual penalty and not allow the possibility of a lesser penalty'. O'Higgins thought it 'undesirable' to put 'the judge in the position of deciding whether, in a given case, the death penalty should or should not be imposed'. If treason was an offence warranting the death penalty, then the decision to impose the penalty should not be left to the judge, who was 'not responsible to the people', and 'not open to representation from the people', but to those who had 'political responsibility', and were 'available to receive and consider any representations that may be made from the general public'. Thrift said he wanted to assure that the judge believed that the criminal was deserving of the death penalty. O'Higgins responded that if the possibility of a lesser penalty was included in the legislation, a feeling would develop 'that a judge, confronted with the alternatives of passing the death sentence or imposing a lesser sentence, will invariably or almost invariably take the latter course', and the result would be, 'in practice, that the death penalty for treason disappears, or at any rate, that in the public mind, and in the mind of potential treasonable offenders, that belief will grow and harden'.[31]

Johnson opposed making 'failure to inform of treason and sedition' a crime. He thought that was the obverse of offering a reward for informers. He did not think it would 'add to the respect the public will have for the informant'. A good citizen, who 'considers that the offence he is aware is about to be committed should be informed of...will inform'. But to make not informing punishable would be 'simply inviting contempt of the law'. He reminded the Dáil that most of them during the War of Independence had 'been aware...of treason' and did not inform. O'Higgins thought that on some occasions Johnson 'wraps the green flag round him, and talks a kind of hybrid stuff between anaemic liberalism and what his conception is of advanced nationalism'. On other occasions he advocates 'the solidarity of the community' and the responsibilities of the individual 'beyond himself and beyond his family', while the principle behind the section requiring informing was 'merely the corollary to the individual's rights as against the state' as it embodied 'the state's rights in regard to the individual'. O'Higgins gave what was probably the real reason for the section: that it would be very useful in prosecuting cases where it might be difficult to prove participation in 'the overt act' of treason, but where it could be possible to prove that these persons 'had informa- tion in regard to the treason'. He added that the charge of failure to inform was often 'the only charge you can bring and prove against the person concerning whom there is no real doubt that he was in fact guilty of treasonable practices and treasonable intentions'.[32]

A clause making the inciting of 'any person in the civil service (other than the police force) of the government of Saorstát Éireann to refuse, neglect, or omit to perform his duty or to commit any other act in dereliction of his duty' a felony was seen by William Davin, Labour deputy for Leix–Offaly, as designed 'to preclude civil servants or state employees from membership of trade union organizations'. But O'Higgins insisted the motive was to prevent the state from being 'injured, undermined', and 'reduced to impotence', as without the clause there would be no restraint on the freedom of people 'to approach public servants, to approach state employees and urge upon them that they should refuse to perform their duties'. When Johnson appealed to the writings of the conservative Cardinal O'Connell of Boston[33] about 'a natural right of man to give or withhold his labour', even if a civil servant, Minister for Finance Ernest Blythe admitted that the legislation would 'prevent any person coming along and definitely organizing a strike of civil servants', and insisted that if they 'were to recognize the right to strike in the civil service you might easily have a Praetorian Guard of the pen which would be as potent to make or unmake a government as an armed body'.[34] William Hewat, Businessmen's Party deputy for Dublin North, expressed his surprise at the line Blythe had taken: 'A Bill brought in to prevent an organized attempt to overthrow the state...included within its scope trade disputes between the employer – the state – on one hand, and the employee on the other.' While he did not regard a strike as 'the best way of remedying grievances', he believed that 'if the government take up the position that no man has a right to strike', it would 'probably lead to a worse state of affairs than anything we have had to face in the past'.[35] O'Higgins made the government's position quite clear on the matter of striking by civil servants: 'the civil service, which is the executive arm of the state, cannot be paralysed from time to time by the temporary cessation of work on the part of any individual. The right of resignation is there, and no other right.' He reasoned that 'one of the means by which this state can be attacked and reduced to impotence and paralysed in the discharge of its proper function' was by 'suborning civil servants, undermining them from their allegiance, and undermining them from the due discharge of their duties'. Accordingly, 'part of the proper functions of this Bill' was 'to guard against that'. While insisting that 'the Executive has never recognized the right to strike' by civil servants, he thought the raising of the issue was a pure accident as the article being challenged had scarcely been prompted by concern over strikes. Rather it was proposed with the wish 'of protecting the state against all possible lines of attack', one of which was 'suborning of civil servants and inciting or inducing civil servants from performing their duties'.[36]

On the issue of prohibiting the recruitment of military and police to secret societies, Labour TD William Davin sought to extend the prohibition on such recruitment to the civil service and the judiciary as well. The secret societies that troubled some were not just the now-defunct IRB or the Old IRA, but also the Freemasons and the Ancient Order of Hibernians. Anxiety about the latter two was grounded in sectarian and class resentments.[37] Denis Gorey, Farmers' Union deputy for Carlow–Kilkenny, wanted the legislation to specifically name the Freemasons and the Ancient Order of Hibernians. Osmond Esmonde, Cumann na nGaedheal deputy for Wexford, charged that the government feared that such a prohibition on secret societies in the civil service and the judiciary might 'lead to sensational resignations from high positions in the service of the government if it was to become law'. He then alluded to 'the great and enduring benefits which that distinguished statesman, Signor Benito

Mussolini, conferred on the Italian people . . . by his recent action in suppressing and prohibiting secret societies in the Italian civil service', even if it was followed by an inevitable number of resignations. But he doubted if the Irish Free State government had 'the same degree of courage as Signor Mussolini'.[38]

Davin observed how 'the governments of Europe have changed very quickly, and that the forces behind these great and sudden changes of government in continental countries have been due to the agency and influence of secret societies'.[39] But O'Higgins argued that it would make no sense to prohibit inviting civil servants and judges to join secret societies since there was no legislation barring their membership, as was the case with the police and the army.[40] He reiterated the special circumstances and reasons for the prohibitions with regard to the army and the police, which were 'two very special bodies. Thousands of young men banded together in a disciplined organization, living a kind of communal life . . . in a different position from the ordinary citizen', and even civil servants were 'not grouped together in the same intensive organized way'. He dismissed the conspiracy theories which suggested that because of 'some secret or sinister influence' in the courts or the civil service, offenders were escaping and prosecutions were not being pursued. The amendment failed.[41]

In the final Dáil debate on the measure, Johnson bore down on O'Higgins. He doubted that 'anyone will accuse the Minister of being possessed of liberal ideas in respect to legislation affecting personal liberty'. He saw 'the minister leading a body of public opinion back to pre-Victorian years, or at least back into the Bismarckian era', and as 'a budding Bismarck, with his views as to the relations of the state and the individual – that loyalty to the state and good citizenship are going to be induced by repressive legislation'. While not doubting his sincerity, he was persuaded 'that the direction of the minister's mind, and the minds of those who were content to support him, is to produce a kind of Tory Junkerism, a kind of Prussianism, Bismarckianism in this country which conceives that the state is something above, beyond, and inde-pendent of the citizens, and that loyalty to that state is going to be induced by repression and the fear of punishment'.

O'Higgins replied that Johnson's protest was 'like a man talking in his sleep or a gramophone record turned on' with its mechanical denunciations. What had been passed was 'legislation that is necessary, sound and advisable in the interests of the state, and the people of the state'. While the ministry had borne 'all the taunts, all the jibes of Prussianism and Junkerdom', Johnson, Gorey, Figgis and others 'will come along and will rule in peace, piously, justly and freely without doing anything so terrible as introducing a Bill declaring certain offences treasonable'. He was confident of one thing these deputies would not do if and when they would come into office: 'They will not repeal this Bill and trust simply to the goodwill of the citizens to avoid bashing the state.'[42]

The measure passed the Seanad, but not without similar opposition argument such as that of Senator John T. O'Farrell, who was from County Roscommon, an active trade unionist, and the leader of the Labour Party in the Seanad, who argued that, rather than bring security, the measure would provoke 'a recurrence of all those things that make for destruction and insecurity'. He read the remarks of Minister for Finance, Ernest Blythe, on the illegality of inciting civil servants to not work as meaning 'that a strike was prohibited', which he called 'a direct interference with trade union rights of civil servants'. He suggested that the time had come 'to adopt towards our own countrymen with whom we do not agree the policy of forgiveness and forgetfulness that we have adopted towards our late foreign enemies'. He added that the citizenry would be grateful if the Minister for Justice 'did not stir up these smouldering fires which have been settling down because of the fact that no wind has fanned their business'. He feared the Bill, on the other hand, was 'a godsend to certain people, because it holds out the prospect of future martyrs'.[43] Senator Benjamin Haughton, a Peace Commissioner for the City of Cork and a timber importer and a sawmill proprietor, argued that 'opinion is rife in this country...that capital punishment should be abolished for all crime'.[44] Colonel Moore argued that the die-hard republicans who would not enter the Oireachtas were 'not likely to be induced to come in by threatening measures', like the legislation in question, but also, that 'the last thing' the ministers would wish, 'for their own political reasons', was 'that these people should come into the Dáil', implying that attendence by the absentees would give opposition a majority that could vote no confidence in the government.[45]

A NEW EMERGENCY

On 14 November 1926, the IRA attacked twelve police barracks in different parts of Ireland resulting in the deaths of two unarmed

Gardai, which prompted the passage of emergency legislation allowing detention on suspicion and the withholding of *Habeas Corpus* when an emergency was proclaimed. O'Higgins, in a letter to his wife from London, where he was attending the Imperial Conference at which leaders of the dominions in the British Commonwealth had assembled, was not too apprehensive about the situation: 'I hope you are not worried about last Sunday's happenings. I am not. It is unfortunate, of course, but it is just a kind of stunt flash in the pan and need not be taken seriously.'[46] A few weeks later he felt confident enough to announce the release of the fifty people interned under the Act and reported that the Executive Council had determined that a situation did not exist in the country 'which would warrant the continued detention of persons against whom it has not been found possible to formulate any charge'. He realized there existed in the country an 'unlawful subterranean organization' with which many have retained a connection. But their connection 'differed very much in degree and in reality in many cases'. Some 'have retained a nominal connection...but have been tending more and more to become entirely inactive and to accept the duties of citizenship, to obey the laws of the state'. But there was a new vintage of members, often 'boys of fourteen, fifteen, sixteen and seventeen yeas of age, seized on by propagandists, mostly feminine propagandists', who were 'inspired to commit utterly ruthless, desperate, irresponsible actions'. However, very few of those interned were likely 'to have been privy to these occurrences'. Their releases were granted with the hope that those maintaining 'an unlawful military organization will realize that the continued existence of such an organization, while it can achieve no good and no useful thing for this country and its people, can do, and is doing, serious harm'. He saw public acceptance and Dáil and Seanad approval of the emergency legislation as good and as 'an index and a reflection of the state of public opinion throughout the country'.

O'Higgins acknowledged an investigation he had authorized had confirmed that an assault by Gardai in Waterford on republican prisoners arrested before the 14 November attacks 'did undoubtedly take place'. He insisted that there was no disposition on the part of the Executive Council to 'approve methods of this kind'. As the minister responsible for the police, he wished to 'apologise through the Dáil to the people, as well as to the individuals who suffered injury', and proposed 'to set up a committee to hold an inquiry into these occurrences, to fix responsibility and to make compensation', which compensation would be borne by those responsible. Thomas Johnson asked if the assumption of compensation burdens by those responsible might mean that they would continue in the police. O'Higgins replied that, if the inquiry committee recommended their dismissal the state would then assume the compensation burden. But if any of them remained on the force 'it will be on the basis of themselves shouldering such compensation burden as may arise from their action'. He did not have any doubt that 'this marks the end of conduct of this kind on the part of members of the Garda Síochána', and he did not believe 'that there will be a case of this kind again'.[47]

O'Higgins had asked Police Commissioner Eoin O'Duffy for the dismissal of the accused officers, which O'Duffy resisted, threatening to resign himself. O'Higgins indicated that he could if he wished. O'Duffy's bluff was called. He did not resign and an inquiry suggested that officers be retained but bear the cost of compensation.[48] O'Higgins' principled opposition to any cover up was praised years later in the Dáil by Seán Moylan of Fianna Fáil, a leading irregular republican during the Civil War who served as Minister for Education and then Minister for Agriculture in later de Valera governments. On 7 February 1934 he noted:

> Some years ago in Waterford a number of men were very cruelly beaten. I know that, to the honour of the late Kevin O'Higgins, the matter was investigated and the officer who carried out the investigation reported that these beatings were carried out by official orders. Kevin O'Higgins, like the man he was, immediately suspended the man who gave the order. General O'Duffy threatened to resign. Kevin O'Higgins, again like the man he was, told him to do it. General O'Duffy went back to his headquarters and gathered around him all the senior officers of the Garda and got them to sign a statement offering their resignations to Kevin O'Higgins unless the suspensions of the men found guilty were removed. Kevin O'Higgins accepted those resignations on Friday evening, and on Sunday morning, he was dead.[49]

Moylan's account of the incident seems to have gotten the dates of the O'Higgins–O'Duffy confrontation off by several months, but he confirms O'Higgins' principled opposition to police abuse.

NOTES

1.  *Dáil Éireann*, VII (7 May 1924), 378–80.
2.  *Ibid.* (4 June 1924), 1,825–33.
3.  *Ibid.* (12 June 1924), 2,271–6.
4.  *Ibid.*, VIII (3 July 1924), 374–82.
5.  *Ibid.*, 386.
6.  *Ibid.*, 391–3.
7.  *Ibid.*, 384–5.
8.  *Ibid.*, 398–9.
9.  *Ibid.* (8 July 1924), 742–52. Joseph McGrath, the former Minister for Industry, had also been the political head of Oriel House, the CID, which had developed a reputation for ruthlessness during the Civil War. McGrath had hoped to continue the agency as an anti-subversive instrument in peacetime, but his proposal was rejected by the Cabinet as Mulcahy wished to reserve such functions for the Army while O'Higgins, whose views prevailed, preferred that such responsibilities be assumed by the police force. O'Halpin, *Defending Ireland*, pp. 53–5. Memo by McGrath (9 May 1923), NA, DT, S 583.
10. Conor Brady, *Guardians of the Peace*, pp. 131–2.
11. *Dáil Éireann*, IX (12 December 1924), 2,677–94; O'Halpin, *Defending Ireland*, p. 64.
12. *Dáil Éireann*, X (3 February 1925), 43–6.
13. *Ibid.*, 48–52.
14. *Ibid.*, 53–4.
15. *Ibid.*, 59–60.
16. *Ibid.*, 63–4.
17. *Ibid.*, 69–70.
18. *Ibid.* (18 February 1925), 272–91.
19. Campbell, *Emergency Law in Ireland*, pp. 338–42.
20. *Dáil Éireann*, X (18 February 1925), 292–301.
21. *Ibid.* (19 February 1925), 338–46.
22. *Ibid.*, 346–54.
23. *Ibid.*, 355–62.
24. *Ibid.*, 365–71.
25. *Ibid.*, 386–92.
26. *Ibid.*, 405–14.
27. *Ibid.* (12 March 1925), 1,024, 1,042, and 1,059–62.
28. *Ibid.*, 1,255–65.
29. *Ibid.*, 1,024–32.
30. *Ibid.*, 1,032–42.
31. *Ibid.*, 1,043–50.
32. *Ibid.* (19 March 1925), 1,226–32.
33. William Henry Cardinal O'Connell, the Archbishop of Boston from 1907–44, was a strong administrator and an ecclesiastical conservative. He was the eleventh child of Irish immigrant parents.
34. *Dáil Éireann*, X (19 March 1925), 1,233–8.
35. *Ibid.*, 1,240–2.
36. *Ibid.*, 1,247–54.
37. *Ibid.*, 1,279–80.
38. *Ibid.*, 1,294–6.
39. *Ibid.*, 1,296–8.
40. *Ibid.*, 1,279–89.
41. *Ibid.*, 1,301–8.

42. *Ibid.* (26 March 1925), 1,521–4.
43. *Seanad Éireann*, V (30 April 1925), 4–8.
44. *Ibid.*, 9–10.
45. *Ibid.*, 16–17.
46. O'Higgins to Brigid O'Higgins (17 November 1926), de Vere White, *Kevin O'Higgins*, p. 229.
47. *Dáil Éireann*, XVII (15 December 1926), 692–701.
48. de Vere White, *Kevin O'Higgins*, p. 231; O'Halpin, *Defending Ireland*, pp. 65–6.
49. *Dáil Éireann*, L (7 February 1934), 1,195–6.

# 7

# O'Higgins and the Boundary Commission

IN ADDITION TO the setting in place of the mechanisms of government, particularly the court system and the police, a major preoccupation of O'Higgins and his colleagues in the Executive Council was the realignment of the boundary with Northern Ireland and possible unification of the island of Ireland. Article 12 of the Anglo-Irish Treaty of 1921 had called for the establishment of a Boundary Commission to 'determine in accordance with the wishes of the inhabitants, so far as may be compatible with the economic and geographic conditions, the boundaries between Northern Ireland and the rest of Ireland'. The painful and drawn out process of establishing that commission and its disappointing outcome would contribute to developing in O'Higgins a more realistic perspective on how Irish unity might be achieved.

## LIMITED MANDATE FOR COMMISSION

When signing the treaty, both Collins and Griffith had assumed that the Boundary Commission would rule favourably for the nationalist territorial claim. They assumed that the continuation of the fiscal obligations imposed by the Government of Ireland Act of 1920 (which had originally partitioned Ireland) on Northern Ireland – in contrast to the near fiscal autonomy of the Free State – would overwhelm the Northern Irish government and induce gradual acceptance of unification. However, the British insistence on delaying the 'Ulster month' – during which the Northern Ireland parliament would be able to exercise the option of exclusion from the Irish Free State – to after the Westminster Parliament ratification of the Irish Free State Constitution, rather than after the parliamentary approval of the treaty, ought to have created some apprehensions about the inevitability of Irish unity. Very possibly Collins' signing futile pacts with Craig in 1922 (see Chapter 2, pp. 58–9) was based on a suspicion that a British appointed chairman of the potential commission might be unappreciative of the nationalist case and on a confidence that it was better to exclude the English altogether from whatever settlement would be realized by Irish nationalists and unionists. The breakdown of the pacts and Collins' willingness to encourage anti-treaty IRA elements in actions in Northern Ireland made the authorities in London even less sympathetic to the nationalist position.[1]

Further indications that nationalist confidence was unwarranted were the veiled reassurances that Northern Ireland would be protected as a separate 'economic entity' that were given by Winston Churchill, the Colonial Secretary and minister with primary responsibility for Irish policy, during the parliamentary debate on the approval of the treaty. Sympathy with Northern Ireland was further evidenced by a subsidy of £600,000 to meet a £530,000 shortfall in the Northern Irish unemployment fund and the immediate Westminster funding of the Northern Irish Special Police Forces, both steps questionable as to conformity to either the 1920 Act or the treaty. Later, coincidental with the Irish Civil War, was a further grant of £2,000,000 to the Special Forces, to whom active military officers had been temporarily assigned and to whom munitions that included 23,000 rifles had been supplied.[2] To offset suspicions on the part of the 'die-hards' in the Conservative Party of a betrayal of Ulster, Churchill expressed his general warm feelings toward the North and his private reassurance to James Craig of his opposition to any changes more than simple rectifications of boundaries.[3] Craig also won the coalition government's acceptance, despite earlier protests by Collins days before his death, of the abolition of proportional representation in local government elections in Northern Ireland.[4]

Perhaps the most significant confirmation of the inappropriateness of nationalist expectations or of unionist fears about the future of Northern Ireland was a letter sent on 2 March 1922 by F.E. Smith, Lord Birkenhead, a signatory to the treaty, to Arthur Balfour, the former Conservative Prime Minister and earlier Chief Secretary for Ireland. In it he insisted that the treaty 'contemplates the maintenance of Northern Ireland as an entity already existing – not as a new state to be brought into existence' upon ratification of the treaty. He asserted that the boundaries of Northern Ireland were 'defined by the Act of 1920', although the treaty called for them to be 'subject to determination by a commission. Accordingly, the Government of Ireland Act, to which express reference is made in the treaty, and the treaty itself, must be read together.' If it were otherwise the treaty should have specifically stated that the commission should 'determine in accordance with the wishes of the inhabitants, etc., what portions of Ireland should be included in the Irish Free State and what portions shall be included in Northern Ireland'. Therefore, he was confident that the commission, 'not being presided over by a lunatic, will take a rational view of the limits of its own jurisdiction,' and that Craig's apprehensions were unwarranted and that Collins' territorial expectations were the consequence of 'his over heated imagination' fuelled by pressure from his own people.[5]

The consideration of boundary revision was further delayed by the Civil War in Ireland, in which primary if not exclusive attention was given by the Irish Free State government to maintaining its own authority within the twenty-six counties. Then, in October 1922 the Lloyd George coalition was replaced by a Conservative government headed by Andrew Bonar Law, who during the pre-war confrontation over the Home Rule Bill had virtually encouraged unconstitutional action by its Unionist opponents. This made the prospects of immediate or substantial boundary revision less likely. While Bonar Law did not accede to the hopes of the 'die-hards' who wished to reject the treaty, the British figures who had signed the treaty were out of office and the members of the new government would have a different perspective on the implications of the treaty than the nationalists.[6]

EFFORTS TO START THE COMMISSION

The Provisional Government, on 2 October 1922, established a North-Eastern Boundary Bureau under the direction of Kevin O'Shiel, a barrister born in Tyrone who had been a judge in the Dáil Éireann Courts, to collect and compile data to present to the anticipated Boundary Commission, to act 'as a channel of communication between the government and Northern nationalists', and to conduct 'a publicity campaign' to inform the public 'as to the true implications of Article 12 of the treaty'. It was decided that since 'the government were trustees for persons unascertained, no specific claim should be made for a definite area'. Rather 'the area to be assigned to the Free State should be regarded as a matter for the commission to decide on evidence provided by the people themselves'. The latter view suggests an innocent expectation that the commission would act as a judicial body, rather than as a conference at which states could bargain over territorial claims.[7]

In January 1923 Kevin O'Higgins presented to his cabinet colleagues a letter from J.H. Collins, a Newry solicitor who was one of the North-Eastern Boundary Bureau's legal advisors, urging 'that steps be taken for the immediate setting up of the Boundary Commission'.[8] By May 12, the Cabinet decided 'to request the British government' to do just that and instructed Hugh Kennedy, the Attorney General, in consultation with O'Shiel, to draft a letter to Victor Cavendish, the Duke of Devonshire and Secretary of State for the Colonies, requesting such.[9] Devonshire, unlike his predecessor, Churchill, was unlikely to be an initiator of policies, but was dependent on permanent officials, the foremost of whom was Lionel Curtis, whose primary goal was to 'anchor the Free State firmly with the British Commonwealth' and to whom 'Irish unity' and 'the rights of northern nationalists' were 'secondary concerns'.[10] About this time there was yet another governmental change in Britain as Stanley Baldwin succeeded the cancer-stricken Bonar Law on 20 May 1923. Baldwin had been Chancellor of the Exchequer in the coalition, but desirous of preserving the unity of the Conservative Party, including the 'die-hards', he did not bring Austen Chamberlain or Birkenhead, treaty signatories, into the government, and in his heart of hearts hoped the boundary question could be indefinitely delayed.[11] However, Cosgrave sent a personal letter to the new Prime Minister advising him that 'a formal request that the commission proceed' was about to be made.[12]

Also to maintain pressure for the establishment of the commission, the Free State government nominated its representative for it. Cosgrave selected Eoin MacNeill, the Minister for Education, a northern Catholic, over whose selection O'Higgins had reservations. The selection of a minister implied that the appointment was political, which contradicted the government's instructions to the North-Eastern Boundary Bureau to view the commission as a judicial body, as well as MacNeill's own view of his position. In his fifties and almost a generation older than many of his colleagues, MacNeill seemed sceptical about the ultimate success of the commission and accepted the nomination with a sense of self-sacrifice and hope that younger colleagues not have to bear the onus of its possible failure. He aptly remarked about the prognosis of his political career: 'The ripest fruit first falls.'[13]

The Free State move did not, however, prompt action on the part of the British. Although Devonshire had explained to his Prime Minister that he was anxious to answer the appointment of MacNeill as soon as possible 'so as to avoid any appearance of hesitation', which would be exploited in the press by the 'extremists in Ireland', he hoped to bring Cosgrave and Craig to a conference in London to 'see whether a settlement cannot be reached which would avoid the necessity of appointing the Boundary Commission'. He delayed the establishment of the commission by insisting that the Free State had to meet the constitutionally required general election within the first year of its existence before the British government would take 'the further steps necessary to give effect to the provisions of Article 12'. Significantly, the retired and ailing Bonar Law, in a conversation with Tom Jones, the secretary to the Prime Minister, about the problems meeting his successor, Baldwin, expected 'that the real trouble would be over the Boundary Commission – it was a very dangerous topic'. Jones agreed that they 'ought to play for its indefinite postponement'.[14]

Along those lines, two months later, after the completion of the Free State's general election, Devonshire wrote to Tim Healy, the Free State Governor General, that, in lieu of establishing the commission, the British government thought 'it would be expedient for the matters in question to be made the subject of discussion between the three governments' and he invited each government to send up to three representatives to a meeting to be held in London.[15] The Irish Free State, through the Governor General, accepted the invitation for a conference, but prefaced the acceptance with an assertion that they had 'faithfully and scrupulously fulfilled their obligations' under the treaty regarding the 'procedure for determining the boundary between Northern Ireland and the rest of Ireland'.[16] A few days later, James MacNeill, Eoin's brother and the Free State's High Commissioner in London, wrote to O'Higgins that Devonshire 'seemed to think that some delay might be needed' in settling the boundary question.[17] The Free State accepted the conference because of their awareness of the lack of sympathy for the nationalist claim in British governing circles, of Craig's unwillingness to nominate a member to the commission, and of a view that it might be to their advantage as well to play for time.[18] But the conference itself was delayed when a British general election was called for 6 December 1923. The Conservatives remained the largest party, but dropped in numbers in the House of Commons from 344 to 258. Accordingly, Labour, with 191 members in the Commons, was able to form a government. Its leader, Ramsay MacDonald became Prime Minister with the endorsement of the Liberal Party which had 159 members in the house.

Finally on 24 January 1924, J.H. Thomas, a Labour politician and general secretary of the National Union of Railwaymen, who had succeeded Devonshire at the Colonial Office, invited the Free State and Northern Irish governments to send representatives to a February 1 conference (that some hoped could obviate the Boundary Commission). In preparation for attending that conference, Cosgrave, O'Higgins, and the Attorney General, Hugh Kennedy, held a meeting with O'Shiel and his successor as secretary to the North-Eastern Boundary Bureau, E.M. Stephens, an Irish civil servant; Ernest Blythe, the Finance Minister; and J.J. McElligott, the secretary in that department; Eoin MacNeill; and the cabinet secretary, Diarmuid O'Hegarty. At the meeting, O'Higgins insisted that no Irish government 'could waive the Boundary Commission' and replace it with a conference unless Northern Ireland would agree to recant its withdrawal from the Free State, which was unlikely. He asserted that in negotiating they had to be like granite.[19]

Two days later, Cosgrave, O'Higgins, Kennedy, and O'Shiel met with Tim Healy, the Governor General, who told them that 'Ramsay MacDonald and his ministers would be inclined to deal fairly and justly with us', particularly Arthur Henderson, the Home Secretary. However, 'in spite of its undoubted friendliness toward Ireland', the Labour government 'was absolutely ignorant about Irish affairs'. Accordingly, he advised them to be unhesitant about explaining the whole situation and to emphasize that the 1920 Act had partitioned Ireland 'at a time when the greater part of Ireland was subject to a tyranny' and that no member of an Irish constituency, unionist or nationalist, had voted for it. They should stress the 'treatment of the Catholic minority in the six counties', particularly 'the pogroms, the imprisonment of large numbers of Catholics without trial, the absolute immunity extended to criminals who were not Catholics, the driving out of their homes of Catholic men for no conceivable reason'. Also they should not neglect the historical argument 'that Ireland was always one compact unit, economically, geographically and historically'. Lastly, he told them to 'preserve a very stiff and unbending attitude, being careful never to yield an inch'. They should be like Craig who was 'a piece of iron', who never yielded. Also, the Northern Irish government was 'exceptionally intimate with very influential British political and social circles' and was 'informed through these quarters of exactly what they are to expect'.[20]

At the conference, which met on 1 and 2 February 1924, Thomas proposed the provisional suspension of the formation of the commission for one year and the activation of the heretofore primarily nominal Council of Ireland.[21] The Council would be made up of Free State and Northern Irish ministers and would administer certain mutual services for all of Ireland legislatively approved at joint sessions of the Free State and Northern Irish parliaments. That approval would require a 'double majority', that is, a majority of members in each parliament. The joint sittings were to be held alternatively in Dublin and Belfast with the local speaker presiding. For the duration of the provisional period the Free State government, 'while not abrogating in any degree their rights under Article 12 of the treaty', would not demand 'the appointment of the Boundary Commission', and the Northern government would keep for its parliamentary elections the single transferable vote proportional representation system that had been abolished in its local government elections in 1922.[22]

Significantly, the British civil servants with the most experience of Ireland, like the cabinet secretary Tom Jones, the Colonial Office advisor Lionel Curtis, and the former Assistant Undersecretary for Ireland, Alfred Cope, were pessimistic and doubted if 'Ulster would yield a fraction of an inch'. They understood the challenges faced by Cosgrave in the Free State from republicans. They also knew that many who supported the Free State and the treaty would, if the British were to break the treaty on the boundary matter, feel free to push for a republic. Accordingly, the civil servants advised their government that it was 'of supreme importance that we should keep strictly to our pledge, as Cosgrave and his colleagues are doing'.[23]

O'Higgins was sceptical of Thomas' proposal. He thought the one-year period of experiment too short, the services to be administered by the Council of Ireland too limited, and joint administration by ministers responsible to different governments 'likely to resolve itself into a tug-of-war'. He preferred equal delegations selected by proportional representation to joint meetings of both parliaments. For him the 'most fatal criticism of the proposals' was the fact 'that the country would not touch them'. He suggested challenging Craig 'to state definitely his objections' to the united Ireland envisioned by the treaty, but from which the North had exercised the privilege of withdrawal. He feared the Free State might 'be appearing to the British to allow this aspect [the idea of a united Ireland] to go by default'. Therefore, he insisted, Craig 'should be asked to state a logical case for opting out and wishing to remain out'. Ernest Blythe, the Minister for Finance, was as critical, seeing the proposal as impractical and not likely to 'provide an opportunity for the growth of a spirit of goodwill or a habit of co-operation'. Even if more promising, it was impossible for the Free State to accept 'any postponement of the Boundary Commission unless the government of Northern Ireland agreed to suspend the operation of recent local government legislation as well as to refrain from any interference with the present system of parliamentary elections'. He had in mind that the Northern parliament had ended local government proportional representation in 1922 and there was a threat to abolish it in Northern Irish parliamentary elections (which in fact, came about in 1929). Cosgrave was also dismissive, considering the proposal 'relatively and substantially inferior to the proposals of a kindred character in the Act of 1920 [the Government of Ireland Act]', which had been repudiated by the Irish people. They did not provide any reason 'for non-fulfillment or delay in carrying out the provisions of the treaty' for a Boundary Commission.[24]

Although scheduled to reassemble not later than March 2, the conference was delayed because James Craig had taken ill and had to travel abroad until April 24 as part of his recuperation. The Northern Irish government held it would be inappropriate to have a conference on so important a manner in the absence of its Prime Minister. Not surprisingly, Tim Healy, the Governor General, was directed to send a stern message expressing the Free State's annoyance at the Northern government's request 'for a further delay of a few weeks', since 'the questions being dealt with at the Conference' had been 'awaiting a decision for over two years'. He noted that large sections of the nationalist population had been practically disenfranchised in border areas (referring specifically to the suspension of nationalist controlled local authorities that had refused to recognize the Northern government), and that further postponement would be 'to deprive of the benefits of the treaty those persons whose interests Clause 12, without which the treaty would never have been accepted, was specially designed to protect'. Healy asked that the necessary steps be taken 'to complete the constitution of the Boundary Commission without further delay'.[25]

The Free State displeasure prompted Thomas to request Jones to go to Ireland to survey the situation. While there, he met individually with Cosgrave, O'Higgins, MacNeill, Blythe, Duggan, and Kennedy. He sought to persuade the Free State ministers to agree to resume negotiations upon Craig's return from his convalescence. He realized their anxiety about domestic opposition, especially if Article 12 was not put into operation, and, because of that, warned his government to offset the suspicion in the Free State that they were seeking 'to delay Article 12 indefinitely, while allowing Ulster to gerrymander constituencies in anticipation of any commission that may come along'. He suggested that they appeal to the Free State not to withdraw from the conference, to allow a few weeks' delay in view of Craig's illness, and to reaffirm their determination to stand by all their pledges.[26]

Thomas then wrote to Healy requesting the Free State not to ask for the appointment of the commission until the conference had been resumed after Craig's imminent return, since 'the appointment of the Boundary Commission in the meantime would seriously prejudice the value of our discussions'. Healy's reply noted that the Free State would not have allowed its President's indisposition (Cosgrave had been ill the previous month while the Army crisis was at its high point) to cause any delay, as a substitute representative would have taken his place. Nonetheless, they would meet in a conference on the day after Craig's scheduled return, which was April 24, on the condition that the British government would begin to constitute the commission by the beginning of the next month if 'the resumed conference does not result in, or give promise of, a more satisfactory solution of the boundary question than that provided for in Article 12 of the treaty'. Thomas replied that he was willing 'on any day upon which your ministers may intimate that in their view the conference has finally failed', to constitute the Boundary Commission called for in Article 12 of the treaty. A few days later Craig returned earlier than had been anticipated and, accordingly, a resumed conference was scheduled for April 24.[27]

The conference assembled with the same participants as in February. In the morning session things appeared to go smoothly towards a voluntary commission that would be set up by Craig and Cosgrave, consisting of local experts. But by the afternoon, when Craig insisted as the price of agreeing to a voluntary commission that Cosgrave surrender the legal claim to the Boundary Commission called for by the treaty, things broke down, and a communiqué was issued that it was not possible to find an agreement. Jones and Curtis visited Cosgrave that evening and agreed that he could not possibly agree to give up the right to assert Article 12, for had he done so 'it would be open to the North, unobtrusively but effectively, to block any agreement by the voluntary commission'.[28]

STARTING A COMMISSION

When the Free State declared that the conference had failed, the British government, as promised, started the process of establishing the Boundary Commission. The Northern Irish government was asked to name its member and the British set out to recruit a chairman. At the time O'Higgins was outraged at the suggestions of some British newspapers such as the *Daily Mail*, that the treaty requirement for the Boundary Commission be disregarded. In a speech at Howth on May 6, he noted that *The Times* of London had made a subtle suggestion that the Northern Irish government, in return for appointing a member to the commission, be given 'a hard and fast assurance that the commission would confine itself to making a dinge here and a bulge there along the existing line and would have no power whatever to draw a new boundary "in accordance with the wishes of the inhabitants"'. He noted the same paper had argued that the treaty only 'intended to provide merely for certain minor rectifications of the existing line'. He was also annoyed that one of the treaty signatories, Lord Birkenhead, in a speech in late April to the Liverpool Conservative Club,[29] had begun to throw his 'great legal and political prestige into balance in favour of this view'.

Noting Craig's description of the Free State as 'Shylock grasping for the last square yard of territory' because 'it is in the bond', he made clear that the bond was Article 12, half of which, the northern withdrawal from the Free State, had been adopted, while the other half, a Northern Irish appointment to the commission, had not been fulfilled. He reminded Craig that had Northern Ireland not exercised the Article 12 option of exclusion, Article 14 would have allowed him to 'retain his Parliament with the substantial powers assigned to it by the Act of 1920', and 'his present six county area of jurisdiction', but in a united Ireland. In return for 'recognition of the economic and geographic fact of Ireland's unity', the Free State would 'have asked the substantial nationalist minority in that six-county area to remain under the jurisdiction of the local Parliament'. In other words, Northern Ireland would have had home rule within a united Ireland (which, in turn, was a dominion in the Commonwealth). But Craig wanted an agreement in which, 'in the event of disagreement his view will prevail without any court of appeal'. Ireland had 'made great sacrifices for that treaty', was 'standing by that treaty in full confidence that it will be honoured in all its clauses', while the Northern position was 'no longer one of defence against the subversion of their civil and religious liberties but an arrogant claim to be entitled to subvert the civil and religious liberties of large nationalist majorities in areas contiguous to a boundary arbitrarily drawn in 1920 without the vote or approval of a single Irish representative North or South'.[30]

The next day O'Higgins sent a memorandum to Cosgrave warning against being 'manoeuvred into a position in which an alleged ambiguity in Article 12 of the treaty' would 'be left to the decision of the Boundary Commission, which, in effect, means to the decision of a chairman appointed by the British government'. The ambiguity was whether, in determining the boundary, the wishes of the people should prevail over economic and geographic considerations. In other words, should there be major changes conforming to plebiscite mandates, or just minor boundary adjustments? The Free State denied the existence of the ambiguity, but O'Higgins, as he had in his remarks at Howth, expressed concern because Birkenhead, as well as *The Times*, *The Observer*, and the *Daily Chronicle*, had raised the ambiguity and had suggested that 'the narrower construction' was 'the correct one'. He insisted the British government should be asked, 'to declare plainly whether it is their opinion that any ambiguity of the kind exists in this particular Article of, what is after all, an international document'. If the British thought it was ambiguous, 'then obviously we must have the ambiguity cleared up before the Boundary Commission sits, and the alleged ambiguity cannot be left to the tender mercies of the British nominee on the commission' (which is what happened ultimately). If there were differences of interpretation of the Article between the British and Irish governments, then, he argued 'some sort of arbitration must be agreed upon, and such arbitration must take place before the commission is set up. There must be no ambiguity or alleged ambiguity in the terms of referee of the commission.'[31]

Hugh Kennedy, the Free State Attorney General, disagreed with O'Higgins' suggestion, arguing that 'the terms of reference of the Boundary Commission were set out in the treaty in specific form', that they do not call for 'any interpretation from either government before the commission is constituted', and 'that it will be for the commission to interpret its terms of reference when it proceeds to business'. He noted the Free State did 'not admit that any ambiguity exists or that any question of interpretation can arise'; and that the British government had not 'suggested any ambiguity exists or that it favours an interpretation different from ours'. The only ones raising the question have been the 'Northern Eastern people' who 'refuse to take part in the commission'. He doubted 'the wisdom' of O'Higgins' proposal, as it was 'based on the assumption that there is some ambiguity which we have always denied and cannot now admit'. As for arbitration on the true interpretation of the terms of reference, Kennedy asked who would be the parties to the arbitration, two or three governments, and who would choose the arbitrators? If the same parties that would nominate the Boundary Commission were to choose the arbitrators, he wondered, 'how are we any better off than we would be before the commission?' On the matter of specific areas to be transferred, like Counties Fermanagh and Tyrone, Kennedy thought they, the Free State government, 'should not allow ourselves to be pinned to this position'. The area claimed was not yet defined, hence the need for the commission. He thought that by not committing themselves to any specific forecast of the area to be transferred, the more open they kept the matter, then 'the greater margin we have to work upon'.[32] What happened was just the opposite.

Cosgrave seemed to accept Kennedy's reasoning as the Free State government insisted that an 'essential preliminary to conference about details of any kind must be the establishment of the commission...so that agreement, approximate agreement, or the cases in conflict could be brought under its legal powers without delay'. The government was confident that the right of option by the inhabitants of areas would be best facilitated by the commission, as it was guaranteed by the treaty article and it was the duty of the governments 'to see that no obstacle is placed in the way of having this right exercised'.[33]

O'Higgins acknowledged that the British had said their government could not be the interpreter of Article 12. But he thought the chairman of the commission, who would be the nominee of the

British government, 'ought not to be allowed to do' what the British government cannot do. While there possibly might not be disagreement on the meaning of the article, he remained suspicious in view of Birkenhead's pronouncements and the tone of the 'leading British newspapers'. Therefore, he said the Free State should take 'steps to ascertain whether there was disagreement'. If there were disagreements, he asked if the Free State was 'prepared to allow the matter at issue to be decided, as it will in fact be decided, by the vote of one of those government's nominees, [i.e. the British] on the commission'.[34] The domination of the commission by the British-appointed chairman would bear out O'Higgins' anxieties.

A last effort to bypass the commission was a meeting at Chequers on 31 May 1924 to which Prime Minister MacDonald had invited Cosgrave and Craig. However, little was agreed upon. Then a few days later the search for a dominion figure to act as chairman succeeded. The original choice, the former Canadian Prime Minister, Sir Robert Borden, would not take the position unless both governments in Ireland would have appointed representatives. But on June 4, Richard Feetham, a justice of the Supreme Court of the Union of South Africa, accepted the post. Feetham had studied at Oxford with Lionel Curtis. In South Africa both were among Alfred Milner's celebrated 'kindergarten' of imperial civil servants and both were dedicated to imperial unity.[35] However, the Northern Irish government continued to refuse to appoint a member, and the Northern Irish Governor General could not be persuaded to act on his own in making an appointment. A question arose as to the commission's competence to act in the absence of a representative appointed by the government of Northern Ireland. Could the Crown instruct the Governor General of Northern Ireland to appoint the representative, or make the appointment itself, since the method for forming the commission had been stipulated by statute (or treaty)? The British Cabinet decided to ask the Judicial Committee of the Privy Council for a ruling.[36] At the same time the British government persisted in hoping that some arrangement might yet be made between Cosgrave and Craig, which would obviate the need for the commission. Statements by both men had encouraged Prime Minister MacDonald to think as much.[37]

But the firm position taken by O'Higgins inhibited any willingness on Cosgrave's part to settle for less than the commission.[38] Instead, Cosgrave suggested that, while awaiting the Privy Council ruling, the commission chairman, Feetham, and the Free State representative,

MacNeill, undertake preliminary organizational work and collect statistical information. MacDonald thought Craig also should appoint someone to 'join in the preliminary studies' which, while essential, would not be the commission itself.[39] However, O'Higgins said MacDonald's suggestion was inappropriate, as it turned an 'arbitration' process into one of 'conciliation'. He noted that the Free State proposal, which would have had 'the two members of the commission who have been appointed' taking part in work that was 'an obvious preliminary to the operation of the treaty clause', contrasted with MacDonald's proposal, which involved 'participation by a person nominated by a government which has stated repeatedly and in all the moods and tenses that it will have nothing to do with the treaty clause'. A proper reply to MacDonald, according to O'Higgins, would note that the existing boundary had been 'purely arbitrarily drawn in 1920'. It would emphasize that the treaty called for no coercion 'of whatever area would be found to be homogeneously or predominantly Orange and unionist', but that it had equally provided 'that wherever a majority of inhabitants desired inclusion in Free State jurisdiction those wishes would be respected subject to any necessary correction by economic or geographic factors'. He 'found no willingness in Sir J. Craig or his government to recognise that it is the wishes of the inhabitants themselves which must be the deciding factor'. He thought open conferences 'have repeatedly failed and hold no promise of future success', and that future conferences should concern themselves with 'devising the best means to settle this question by the simple democratic test of a census of the adult population and ascertainment of their choice of jurisdiction'.[40]

While awaiting the ruling of the Judicial Committee of the Privy Council[41] on the matter of appointing a Northern Irish member of the Boundary Commission, the British government on July 25 asked the same body whether the rulings of the three members of the commission would have to be unanimous. The assumption had been that the minority member would be the Northern Irish nominee. On July 31, the Judicial Committee issued its ruling. It concluded that the commission would not be valid without a Northern Irish representative; that the Crown could neither instruct the Governor General of Northern Ireland to appoint a representative in default of advice from the Northern Irish government, nor make an appointment on the advice of the British government; and that if a commission was duly established a majority vote would prevail.

Because of the ruling by the Judiciary Committee new legislation had to be passed empowering the British government to appoint a representative for Northern Ireland. But the Irish Free State considered the Anglo-Irish Treaty an international treaty and not simply a piece of legislation subject to alteration by the parliament of one of the signatories. To overcome this concern the British government provided Cosgrave with a letter indicating its intention to introduce the legislation at Westminster with the expectation that the Free State parliament would pass similar legislation refining the treaty. The Free State concurred and the Dáil passed the legislation, but not until after Labour Party leader Thomas Johnson had argued that complying with the British request for Irish legislation to change the treaty would violate the Irish constitution, which was 'bound by the limitations of the treaty'. But if it was 'conceded that we are free to alter our constitution and to pass legislation which will be repugnant to several distinct sections of the treaty as well as to one', then he suggested 'that we should have a Bill introduced not merely to alter this Article XII of the treaty... but that we should have a larger and more extensive Bill altering that treaty in several other respects as well'.[42]

Besides securing the compliance of the Irish, the MacDonald government was anxious that the Conservative Party might oppose the measure, especially its majority in the House of Lords, which then would have required going to the electorate. The 'die-hards' placed great pressure on the Conservative leadership to block its passage. However, the party leader, Baldwin, and most of the more realistic leaders in the party realized that going to the country on the issue of the Lords and the Irish border would be disasterous for the party. This became the case especially after the party was blessed with the anti-communist issue resulting from an Anglo-Soviet treaty and a letter by a Soviet official encouraging worker mutiny in Britain. An election held on 29 October as a consequence of Liberal withdrawal of support for MacDonald resulted in the Conservatives gaining 413 seats, which was 211 more than all others.[43]

### O'HIGGINS' SECOND THOUGHTS

During this period O'Higgins' position had reflected the standard Free State aspirations for Irish unity, or, as a minimum, a significant territorial award by the Boundary Commission. On 25 August he stated in *Reynold's Newspaper*: 'All that the Boundary Commission can do is to make less unfair a division of the country which in itself is thoroughly bad.' But he saw no other course open than the use of the Boundary Commission 'while the Northern government maintains its attitude of refusal to consider any question of union while at the same time refusing to recognize the wishes of the inhabitants as the proper criteria for settling boundaries'. Three weeks later he replied to a letter from Derry nationalists that 'No sane person can doubt the ultimate unity of Ireland', but in the meantime, he regarded it as his trust 'to see that, just as force is not being used to keep within our State areas whose inhabitants dislike its jurisdiction, so areas whose inhabitants desire it and passionately resent their present plight shall not be forcibly kept out'. In a statement in the *Westminster Gazette* on October 2 he repeated the insistence that there be significant boundary changes reflective of popular sentiment: 'The choice lies between political unity and secession, but attached to the privilege of secession was the proviso that if that course were chosen the area seceding must be shown to be homogeneously desirous of it.'[44] This statement came following the 8 September publication by Winston Churchill of Lord Birkenhead's 1922 letter to Balfour stressing the limited mandate of the Boundary Commission. (Interestingly, later correspondence of Birkenhead was less absolute in restricting the mandate.) The release of the letter was Churchill's way of regaining entry to the Conservative Party through the pro-Unionist 'die-hards'.[45]

Evidence of O'Higgins' continued expectation of boundary revision was his forwarding in early September to members of the Executive Council a memorandum prepared by the North Eastern Bureau about the prospective procedures of the Boundary Commission. The memorandum and his accompanying note assumed that plebiscites would have to be taken in some areas, but were uncertain as to what units would be used for such. He would have preferred the Poor Law Unions rather than Electoral Divisions as the units for plebiscites. A further issue would be the determining of when plebiscites should be held. He was apprehensive about having them wherever requested by a stipulated portion of the inhabitants of an area, as that could open the door for plebiscites in homogeneously Orange areas. It would be better to ask for plebiscites in those Poor Law Unions where the 1911 census showed Catholic majorities.[46]

Soon afterwards O'Higgins developed second thoughts about the

efficacy of a commission. On September 25 he sent to the Executive
Council a memo from a member of the North Eastern Boundary
Bureau that was doubtful of 'the advantages to be gained' from the
Boundary Commission.[47] The document suggested that the Free State
make a new offer to settle the boundary issue with the Northern
government independent of the commission. The Free State
government could acknowledge that, even though their right to have
the commission had been established, they were willing 'to make one
more attempt to reach an agreed settlement'. Taking the line that it was
'a matter to be settled among Irishmen', they could 'get the discussion
focused on our proposals'. Even if rejected, the Free State position
would be 'immensely strengthened... in the eyes of the world', and
then, when the commission began to meet, the government would 'be
able to go ahead with much greater confidence' by being able to 'point
back to an offer made by us and rejected by the other party'.

The memo was prescient in suggesting reasons why a commission
decision might turn out to be disadvantageous from the nationalist
perspective:

a. the results of the commission were uncertain and 'its findings may
   prove much less favourable than most of us imagine'. It
   anticipated that the Free State would get parts of south Down,
   much of south Armagh, southern and western Fermanagh, bits of
   Tyrone, but might lose some of Donegal. It doubted the
   nationalist population of central Tyrone would be transferred,
   and it was probable that the Free State 'could gain almost the
   same result by negotiations as by the commission';
b. the commission would 'leave a large number of nationalists,
   probably the majority of those in the six counties, still under the
   Northern government';
c. the ability to alleviate gerrymandering and other disabilities
   would have been lost;
d. there was 'a terrible risk of bloodshed during the course of the
   commission and the carrying out of its findings';
e. at the end of the commission's work Irish unification would be
   'further off than ever', as the number of nationalists in Northern
   Ireland would have been reduced, and the 'reduced Northern area
   may attach itself still more closely to England'.

Any negotiations that would be in place of the Boundary
Commission would have to deal not just with the boundary but the

general questions of relations of North and South, as well as 'restoration of proportional representation', the 'reversal of gerrymandering', 'disbandment of the Specials, release of prisoners', nationalist entry into the Northern parliament and co-operation in local administration, the waiving of the Article 5 treaty requirement that the Free State bear a proportionate share of the Imperial Debt at the date of the signing of the treaty, an improved customs arrangement between both parts of Ireland, and 'some system of joint government, giving an opportunity of advance to fuller union later'.[48]

Four days later O'Higgins submitted another memorandum elaborating on the first proposal. Anticipating another British effort to avoid the commission, he asked whether the Free State 'ought not to be the first in the field with a reasonable offer calculated to command support in England and even to some extent in the North-East'.[49] He was sceptical that 'a settlement imposed by an external arbitrator', the Boundary Commission, could be 'as satisfactory as one reached by agreement among Irishmen', and noted that the Boundary Commission would not deal with 'the alleviation of the condition of those of our supporters (probably the majority) who would still be left in Northern Ireland' or with 'the future relations between North and South'. An alternative conference could concern itself with 'real peace and friendship between North and South', the formation of an all-Ireland authority with members of the respective parliaments proportionate to population, the transfer of reserved powers held in Westminster to either Northern Ireland or to the all-Ireland authority to control external affairs, customs and excise, income taxes (but not necessarily their collection), and to meet alternately in Dublin and Belfast, with a single Governor General appointed in turn by the respective governments, the restoration of proportional representation for local government in Northern Ireland, the reversal of gerrymandering, the disbanding of the Specials, and entry of Northern nationalists into the Northern parliament.[50]

The Executive Council considered the memo and appointed a committee to examine the proposals and make recommendations as to an offer that could reasonably be made after the appointment of the Northern member of the Boundary Commission.[51] The committee established by the Executive Council included figures like J.J. McElligott, the Assistant Secretary in the Department of Finance; D. O'Hegarty, the Secretary to the Executive Council; J.A. Costello, a barrister, soon to become Attorney General and much later Taoiseach; and E. Stephens, the Secretary to the North-Eastern

Boundary Bureau. It returned an extensive report that discussed various offers that could be made to the Northern government in lieu of the Boundary Commission. Five different plans of union were suggested: a federal system with two separate local legislatures and a federal legislature; a subordinate parliament for Northern Ireland; joint sittings of both existing legislatures; an elected Central Council of Ireland; and an elected Central Assembly. This exercise in constitution making, which was the work of some of the more talented people in the Free State, was considered by the Executive Council later in the month, but no decision was made as to whether an offer should be made to Northern Ireland.[52]

No doubt, their disinclination to act on the recommendations was prompted by a letter from Eoin MacNeill, who argued that any offer of a settlement other than the Boundary Commission 'should not go beyond general terms sufficient to convey a notion of the character of the proposals to the ordinary public mind, and should not attempt to sketch out the working details', which is precisely what the special committee had done. MacNeill went on to say that the publication of a detailed scheme 'as a preliminary to conference, would be altogether fatal', as public opinion in both parts of Ireland and in Britain 'would be easily confused about details, and even those most friendly to a national settlement would be led into endless controversies'.[53]

Ultimately, the Free State made no suggestion to settle the boundary question other than through the commission and the British then appointed Joseph R. Fisher as the third commissioner. He was a sixty-nine year old Northern Irish barrister and a fully committed Ulster Unionist who probably was recommended privately by Craig.[54] The Boundary Commission held its first meeting on 6 November 1924.

WORKING THE COMMISSION

The expectations of nationalists were destined for disappointment because the commission interpreted its mandate as implying that 'Northern Ireland shall continue to exist as a province of the United Kingdom'. It started 'its examination of the whole question on the basis of the division marked by the existing boundary', and treated 'that boundary as holding good where no sufficient reason ... is shown for altering it'. The commission did have the power 'to shift the existing boundary in either direction', 'the wishes of the inhabitants' were 'to be a determining factor', and its work was 'not limited to a mere correction of irregularities in the present boundary', but it contemplated no wholesale reconstruction of the map and it was 'not to reconstitute the two territories, but to settle the boundaries between them'. When the boundaries had been determined, Northern Ireland must 'still be recognisable as the same provincial entity'. Furthermore, it was 'the duty of the commission to overrule the wishes of inhabitants, whether for or against transfer, where the result of giving effect to such wishes would be incompatible with economic or geographic conditions'. Boundary changes based on the wishes of the inhabitants were not to take place 'unless the majority in favour of the change appears to be a substantial majority'. In determining areas that should be subject to transfer in response to popular wishes, the commission should select 'the smallest area which can be fairly entitled, having regard to its size and situation, to be considered separately, and with regard to which separate data are available'. Accordingly, it was free to not use existing political units like counties in marking out 'convenient units of area in light of the three factors which it was required to take into account – wishes of the inhabitants, economic and geographic conditions'.[55]

These premises appeared in the final report. They were adapted from a memo given to the members by the chairman on 11 September 1925 to which no objection was made,[56] which suggests that the commission was dominated by the chairman. His judicial career and his control of the secretariat of the commission made that dominance understandable. On the other hand, the Free State commissioner, Eoin MacNeill, was an academic rather than a jurist, had neither staff nor any say in the appointment of the commission's staff, and was serving as Minister for Education at the same time he was on the commission. The Northern Irish commissioner, Fisher, being a barrister, was professionally more appropriate for the work than MacNeill, and unlike MacNeill, appears to have not adhered to the commission's decision at its very first meeting that its proceedings be confidential.[57]

The visits by the commission to the effected areas of Northern Ireland began with a fortnight's tour in December 1924 in Armagh, Enniskillen, Newtownstewart, and Derry. Formal hearings on Down and Armagh were held in March, on Fermanagh in late April and early May, on Derry from May 14 to June 5, and on Tyrone from June 6 to July 2, 1925. The record showed that the nationalist position was not unheard. The commission also had hearings, both at the outset of its work on December 4 and 5, 1924 and at the conclusion of its investigation on August 25, 1925 specifically dealing with representations by spokesmen, including the Free State Attorney General, about its mandate and about whether territories could be transferred out of the Free State.

Significantly, the British may have had some anxieties about potential disorder and turmoil if the commission made significant territorial changes favourable to the Free State.[58] The Colonial Office invited the Free State government to a conference regarding 'arrangements necessary in order to enable the determination of the Boundary Commission to take effect with the least possible inconvenience to the public'.[59] At the conference, held in the Dominion Office in London on July 28, O'Higgins, J. O'Byrne (who had become Attorney General upon Kennedy's appointment as Chief Justice of the Supreme Court), and James MacNeill (the High Commissioner for the Free State in London) met with permanent British civil servants. O'Higgins was particularly concerned about the discharging and disarming of the B and C Specials, the auxiliary forces linked to the RUC, in transferred territories, as the transfer was to take place at, or immediately after, the moment of determination of new boundaries. He inisisted it was 'important that this should be done, by the Northern Irish or British authorities, and not by the Free State authorities'. O'Higgins obviously wanted to minimize the prospects of confrontation with the more sectarian Specials.[60] At a second conference on October 29, O'Higgins acknowledged the wisdom of advance warning and delay, and 'urged that there should be no hurry to withdraw British troops' from transferred territories as they should have the task of disarming the B and C Specials. He even thought it well for British troops to be available, even after the final transfer, 'to act in aid of Free State civil power if necessary'.[61] O'Higgins' report on the conference prompted the Free State Cabinet to conclude that 'the Governments concerned were now as prepared as they were likely to be to take over the administration of the territories in question'.[62]

## MORNING POST LEAK, DÁIL REACTION AND MACNEILL'S RESIGNATION

Alas, within a week, on 7 November 1925, the *Morning Post* reported the prospective award with accompanying maps.[63] The newspaper's report accurately indicated that while territory and population would be transferred from Northern Ireland to the Free State, territory and population would also be transferred the other way. The major territorial gains for the Free State would be in south Armagh and border areas of Fermanagh and Tyrone, while a portion of Monaghan and larger portions of Donegal would be transferred to Northern Ireland.

Reaction was swift. On November 11, in the Dáil, Thomas Johnson inquired whether the Boundary Commission had asked the Executive Council or the government of Northern Ireland for facilities to determine by plebiscite the wishes of the inhabitants within one jurisdiction regarding transfer to the other. If the request had not been made, he asked if the Executive Council would take steps to inform the Boundary Commission, before the announcement of their decision, that Article 12 of the treaty required consent of the inhabitants. Cosgrave replied to the question in the negative, adding that Executive Council believed and had told the commission that Article 12 did not empower it to transfer territory out of the Free State. When Johnson asked if Cosgrave assumed the inhabitants of areas subject to transfer had been consulted as to their wishes as the treaty obliged, Cosgrave dismissed the question as hypothetical, but insisted that the ascertaining of the wishes of the inhabitants 'falls within the province of the Boundary Commission'.[64]

Cosgrave, O'Higgins and Blythe had a meeting with some Cumann na nGaedheal members and with a delegation from East Donegal, an area liable to be transferred to Northern Ireland. They also received a letter from Cahir Healy, a Northern nationalist MP who had been interned by the Northern Irish government between 1922 and 1924, asking whether the Executive Council and representatives from the people affected would be consulted before the report was signed. He was told that it was not a requirement that the Executive Council be told of the proposal before its being issued and the decision as to signing the report was a matter to be determined by the Free State member on the commission, Eoin MacNeill. In response to a request by the secretary of the Boundary Commission for a conference 'to discuss certain matters arising out of the imminence of the publication of the commission's report', the Executive Council decided to send the Attorney General to London on November 19 to press 'for a full copy of the full records of the commission to be given to his government', and to state that his government favoured 'the immediate publication of all evidence given before the commission'. The British government suggested that the British and Free State governments 'meet beforehand to discuss the matters which were to be the subject of discussion at the conference'. The pre-publication meeting with the commission was postponed until 24 November. Intervening developments before then made an inter-governmental conference even more urgent.[65]

In the Dáil on November 19, Deputy Denis McCullough, Cumann na nGaedheal for Donegal, raised the issue that Johnson had a week earlier, that the Boundary Commission be told that inhabitants of transferred areas should be consulted. He and P.J. McGoldrick, also a Cumann na nGaedheal deputy for Donegal, reiterated the basic expectations of most nationalists, that the commission award should set a significant transfer of territory in one direction only. They professed satisfaction with Cosgrave's answer that the suggested transfer of Free State territory would not 'be permitted to reach any stage that would forebode or contemplate possible acceptance of or permission for the perpetuation of such an outrageous atrocity'. Unconsciously advancing a self-fulfilling prophecy, McGoldrick even asserted 'Much better the present border than any change' that would shortchange the self-determination of nationalist majorities on the Northern side of the border.[66]

In an attempt to calm scepticism about the imminent award and to ready an attack on it if the scepticism proved valid, Cosgrave repeated the expectations of the Executive Council that the treaty did not empower any transfer of territory from the Free State. He tried to downplay the *Morning Post* report, even asserting that it would be inconceivable for the commissioners, 'as a judicial authority' and with a 'reputation for impartiality and honour', to approve a decision such as the paper had suggested. He admitted some deputies were apprehensive and noted how 'a most scandalous campaign of intimidation and misrepresentation' had been waged during the setting up of the commission, and a 'most indecent and flagrant violation of judicial procedure' had been indulged in, as 'important personages in public life, both in Great Britain and in the Six Counties, assisted in the endeavour to influence the court'. Were the commission a court of justice he suggested, such behaviour would have warranted 'imprisonment for flagrant contempt'. But until he had proof to the contrary, Cosgrave preferred to believe that the commissioners were 'men who place a value on impartial justice, that they will respect the considerations which have been laid down for their guidance and direction, and that they will not allow outside considerations to sway them from the paths of judicial honesty'. But if they had allowed themselves to be so intimidated, they would 'have dishonoured themselves and they will have sullied before the nations of the world the reputation for judicial impartiality of which the British Commonwealth is so jealous'. If that was the case, even the securing of advance information by the *Morning Post* would have to be explained and 'the British government, which has so far, with the utmost punctiliousness, fulfilled its obligations under Article 12 of the treaty, could not, of course, escape moral responsibility for the action of its nominees [Feetham and Fisher]'.[67]

At the very time of this Dáil discussion, MacNeill had landed in London for his final meeting with the commission. Unaware of MacNeill's impending resignation, Cosgrave had sent a letter advising him of the debate and giving him a line to follow in anticipated continued deliberations. He reported to him the views of a Tyrone delegation that favoured having no report in preference to one which, even if it transferred Tyrone to the Free State, did not also transfer south Down, Newry, south Armagh, south Fermanagh and Derry.[68] But two days later, on November 21, MacNeill, after returning on the ferry to Dun Laoghaire, and consulting with his Executive Council colleagues, formally submitted his resignation to Feetham. Cosgrave used the resignation to suggest that the other commissioners had allowed themselves to be swayed in the discharge of their judicial duty 'by the threats and political influences which have been brought to bear upon them'. The Free State ministers would follow this line in subsequent negotiations with the British to inhibit the publishing of the award.[69]

MacNeill spoke for himself the following Tuesday, November 24, in the Dáil, explaining his resignation. He noted that he had viewed his appointment to the commission as that of 'a plenipotentiary', and 'not purely and simply the representative of a government nor... an advocate for a particular point of view'. In addition, he had agreed with the other commissioners that the 'proceedings should be confidential'. He then reported on the commission's travels and interviews, which were followed by the assessment and classification of evidence, after which 'the commission came to the point of deliberation, of giving effect to the terms of the treaty and to the evidence laid before it'. Up to then, he insisted, 'no question of the principles of interpretation had formally arisen', although such might have been presumed from the form of questions addressed by commissioners to various witnesses.

He admitted the assertion of the other commission members that they 'had agreed to sink individual differences of opinion for the purpose of arriving at a unanimous award', and that all three would sign it. That agreement was not to imply unanimity 'as to principles of interpretation upon which the award was to be based', nor 'the manner in which the principle should be applied in detail', but was made simply to 'provide the least possible fuel for renewed, perhaps embittered, controversy'. Furthermore, the agreement for all three to sign had been reached 'at a very early stage of the deliberations of the commission, following the taking of evidence, and before there was any formulation of an award in whole or in part'. At the time he had viewed Article 12 as implying the making of an award in response to popular wishes and as a correction of the Act of 1920. But Feetham, on the contrary, had held 'that the Act of 1920, and time that had elapsed, had created a *status quo* which should only be departed from when every element and every factor would compel us to depart from it'. MacNeill insisted Feetham believed that if the adherence to popular wishes would seriously reduce 'the extent of territory under the jurisdiction of Northern Ireland' and 'so place the government of Northern Ireland in a distinctly less advantageous position than it occupied under the Act of 1920' those popular wishes were to be overridden by 'political consideration', a position to which he had 'never assented'.

He noted the absence of debate among the commissioners about 'the principles of interpretation' or the 'application of such principles', and recalled that details had come to them 'in a very gradual and piecemeal manner.' He 'was at fault' and was 'remiss' in failing 'to appreciate the circumstances' and in his not demanding, requiring, and challenging 'at the earliest convenient stage, a discussion of the general principles of interpretation and a decision upon those principles'. 'A better politician and a better diplomatist, if you like, a better strategist' than he was 'would not have allowed himself to be brought into that position or difficulty'. As a result, the commission had worked 'until a complete boundary line had been presented to us', and 'a draft award was actually in existence'. That was October 17. Since then, he had come to the conclusion that it 'would not be possible' for him to defend the award. Although he was Minister for Education and a member of the Executive Council, he regarded his action as a member of the Boundary Commission as entirely his own responsibility. Since he had mistakenly assumed at the outset of the commission that the award would be made on 'reasonable and consistent principles', it would be inappropriate for him to continue in the government 'which will have the future responsibility for dealing with this particular matter', and he resigned as Minister for Education.[70]

Afterwards, Thomas Johnson asserted that the Executive Council, even if not kept informed of developments within the commission by MacNeill, shared responsibility for the unsatisfactory turn of events, especially as statements by the Executive Council had suggested that it was satisfied with the way things were developing. He feared parts of Donegal and Monaghan were going to be assigned to Northern Ireland and that six county residents who had expected to join the Free State were 'being placed in the position now of absolute hopelessness'. He believed the Dáil had a right 'to demand from the Ministry a complete statement of their views and of their position in this matter'.[71]

O'Higgins acknowledged in theory Johnson's point about the ideal of having held a plebiscite in affected areas. However, the commission was not empowered to call for such, and for the Executive Council to have demanded such would have further delayed the commencement of the commission, as requisite legislation would have to be passed. However, short of a plebiscite, he suggested a valid alternative would have been the 1911 census returns. As for Johnson's criticism of the conduct of the Executive Council, O'Higgins asked: 'What have we left undone that we ought to have done? We have taken every step in accordance with our treaty of peace with Britain and our conduct in relation to this commission compares favourably with the conduct of any other party concerned.' He noted that the Executive Council had only become aware of the full extent of the situation three days before, and he appealed against 'hasty and ill-considered decisions'. Since the Executive Council had the responsibility of dealing with it, he insisted they 'must not be challenged hastily or brusquely for a statement of policy on this whole matter'. The government had done no wrong to merit withdrawal of confidence. He asked that it be given time to consider the situation 'in all its bearings, to weigh it very fully, to form our best judgment on courses and their possible reactions'.[72]

His appeal to the Dáil bought the appropriate time and within two weeks the government would be able to present a substitute settlement in place of the feared commission award. That settlement would be the consequence of an intergovernmental conference at which O'Higgins would display his adeptness as a diplomat. The settlement would save the Free State in its greatest crisis since the Civil War.

On November 26 Cosgrave met with Prime Minister Baldwin, Foreign Minister Austen Chamberlain, Home Secretary William Joynson-Hicks, and Dominion Secretary L.S. Amery. He presented the Free State position that 'the proposed line went against the spirit of the undertaking embodied in the treaty' and called for a new conference between representatives of the British Cabinet and the Free State's Executive Council to find 'a saner and better solution'. He urged that the Boundary Commission 'not issue their award either now or at any time'.

Chamberlain sought to correct the expectations of the Free State with regard to the commission. He said the British participants in the original treaty conference had never accepted the Irish demands 'for a vote by counties or by local government areas, or for a plebiscite in some form or another', and had always spoken of 'an adjustment', and not 'the drawing of a new boundary apart from and independent of the existing boundary'. He even insisted that 'every British signatory spoke of territory being given not by Ulster to the Free State, but by the Free State to Ulster'. He added that neither Collins nor Griffith had objected when such positions were taken by the British signatories in the debate on the treaty in the House of Commons. L.S. Amery was unsure the award could be blocked without legislation and said he had voted for the treaty in parliament because 'no lawyer would regard it as meaning other than an adjustment' of the existing boundary.

Cosgrave argued that the then British Prime Minister (Lloyd George) had referred to county and local areas 'as within the ambit of the discussion of the boundary'. He emphasized that the Irish would not have asked for the commission and would have endeavoured to settle the matter directly with Sir James Craig if the mandate had been only to rectify the boundary. Baldwin reminded Cosgrave that the commission had been imposed 'on an extremely reluctant Ulster', and that, had the award been more favourable to the Free State, Cosgrave would have expected them 'to impose it on Ulster', with which Cosgrave agreed. While he was aware of Irish popular outrage, he could not compel Ulster. However, recognizing

Cosgrave's difficulty, he would urge Craig to meet Cosgrave. He would also ask the commissioners to withhold their report pending a possible alternative agreement being reached. Chamberlain, almost to offset Unionist suspicion for his having signed the treaty, added that the Conservative Party had voted 'to impose upon a reluctant Ulster acceptance of the verdict of this commission whatever it might be'. Therefore it was impossible for them 'now that the verdict is alleged to be unduly and unexpectedly favourable to Ulster' to accept 'any agreement which would deprive Ulster of the commission's finding except with the consent of Ulster'.[73]

Two days later, on November 28, O'Higgins, accompanied by Patrick McGilligan, the Minister for Industry and Commerce, and John O'Byrne, the Attorney General, met Baldwin. The Boundary Commission had already sent its secretary with the report of their award to the intergovernmental meeting and Feetham had proposed to release it on December 7. O'Higgins declined to read the award and indicated that the Executive Council would be certain of defeat in the Dáil were they to approve the commission proposals. The ensuing crisis would lead eventually 'to a break-up of the state based on the treaty'. Even if the existing boundary was kept, along with a few concessions from Craig, such as prisoner release, members of his own party would vote against the government. He insisted that no one in the Free State would regard the award to be 'in accordance with the wish of the people subject to geographic and economic considerations', and he thought it could not 'lead to anything but hate and the starting of the old fires between the peoples'. While the Free State would comply if the award was granted, it could not pretend to its people that the treaty had been fulfilled, and might have to consider an approach to the League of Nations over the issue.

Baldwin said it would have been better if the commission had never been formed, but it had been set up. Had the report gone another way, against Northern Ireland, the Free State 'would have expected us to carry it through even by force of arms'. To set up another commission because the first was unsatisfactory would be impossible, as any award would cause trouble. However, the British government wanted, so far as it could, to help the Free State government 'in a difficult domestic position'. Baldwin outlined three alternatives: let the commission deliver its judgment, accept the existing boundary, or set a new boundary by agreement of the two governments. He added that Craig had said he could accept either the award or the existing boundary.

O'Higgins held that just maintaining the existing boundary was insufficient, even with the release of a few nationalist prisoners being held in the North, unless there was also 'some substantial alleviation for the nationalists of the North-East' who 'had no proper representation under the Northern government either in Parliament or in local administration', and were 'kept down by an army of special constables paid and maintained by the British government'. However, he thought the Cosgrave government might be able to ride out the storm if they could not get 'substantial relaxation for the Catholics in the North-East' along with the present boundary, as the disappointment of those hoping to have been transferred to the Free State would be offset by the improved position of those nationalists so geographically positioned as to be unlikely to be transferred out of Northern Ireland in any circumstances.[74]

The next day Baldwin met with Craig and told him that he was going to tell the Free State group that if they could not take the old boundary they must take the new, and that the sooner the publication of the award the better.[75] When actually meeting with the Irish representatives, he reassured O'Higgins, who had not yet read the commission's documents, that the award was not exactly the same as reported in *The Morning Post*, and suggested that the Free State got the best of it. But O'Higgins replied that the 'trifling inaccuracies' in *The Morning Post* award did not affect him, as any award 'leaving Newry and its economic hinterland within Northern jurisdiction' could not be an award based on evidence. To him, Newry was 'the acid test of the commissioners' desire to act on their terms of reference'. As for Baldwin's suggestion that the Free State should be better to have seen the award before it was published, O'Higgins replied that because of the unlikelihood of the report being in accordance with the terms of reference 'the less contact they had with the commission the better'.

Baldwin gave the area and population statistics to O'Higgins, noting a net gain of 134,048 acres and 23,725 people for the Free State, and a boundary shortened by 51 miles. He observed that English opinion 'would be disposed to regard the award as fair'. O'Higgins replied that the commission had sought to preserve 'the political unity of Northern Ireland' based on the 1920 Act, which should not have been a consideration, as the commission had been set up 'for the express purpose of determining how much of Northern Ireland was to be allowed to remain outside the Free State'.

At that point Sir James Craig was brought in to the meeting and

O'Higgins was told to put his views to him. O'Higgins said it might be found distasteful, but Craig replied 'that if their discussions were to be of any value all the cards must be put on the table'. O'Higgins then asserted that the Free State 'had always regarded the commission as set up for no other purpose but to see how much of Northern Ireland was entitled to be excluded from the rest of Ireland', rather than a minimal boundary adjustment since Lloyd George had suggested that 'Tyrone and Fermanagh could not remain part and parcel of political Ulster'. The Free State should have protested when the view was expressed in the House of Commons that the boundary correction 'was a small and innocent thing, just a dinge here and a bulge there along the existing line', but it was preoccupied at the time with the Civil War. He also acknowledged that the Free State had not objected that a plebiscite had not been taken to ascertain the wishes of the people, as that would have required legislation that would have delayed things. Instead, they would have accepted the 1911 census as 'a fair basis for deliberations'. If the Free State were to accept the present boundary, even if accompanied by the release of a few prisoners in Northern Ireland (who had already served four of their ten years' imprisonment), it would not be able to stay in office for a day. The only kind of deal with which the government might be able to survive would be the maintenance of the *status quo* along with 'some substantial improvements in the lot of the minority in Sir James Craig's area'. He pointed to the coercion of the minority by the 45,000 Specials and insisted that 'the conditions in the constituencies of the North East which deprive nationalists of their due representation must be changed'.

Craig regarded O'Higgins' historical account as accurate, but added that he and his colleagues had never done anything other than to 'emphasise to the Free State that they were living in a fool's paradise as to what the outcome of the commission would be'. O'Higgins interjected that Craig's boycott of the commission had strengthened Free State expectations that it would work to the advantage of the nationalists. Craig said that he had told Michael Collins early in 1922 to consider whether or not he might be worse off if a commission finding turned out to be unsatisfactory. Collins had agreed that a round table conference between himself and Craig might be a better alternative. That never came about. Also, when Craig asked the Free State about the prospects of transfer of territory to the North, their only reply was to not discuss such a contingency. He had told Ramsay MacDonald 'that great harm was being done in the South by the people there being brought up to believe that they would get great advantages from the commission'.[76]

After lunch, Craig and O'Higgins met together alone for more than half an hour. Subsequently, Craig met with Baldwin, Tom Jones, and Sir John Anderson. He reported on his conversation with O'Higgins and suggested dropping Article 5 of the treaty, which obliged the Free State to meet its proportionate share of the existing Imperial debt, as a way to help the Free State government ride out the political storm that the maintenance of the existing boundary would raise. He saw no reason why the Free State should not be released from the debt obligation, as he thought it would never be collected at any rate. As for the release of prisoners in Northern Ireland, he himself would not order it, but would defer to any decision on the matter made by Home Office experts in Whitehall. In return for his efforts to induce the British to lessen the Irish debt obligation, Craig asked two favours from O'Higgins: one was to define the shore of Donegal as the boundary with Derry to avoid the aggravating division of the waters of Lough Foyle; and the other was to drop the Council of Ireland, that pan-Ireland remnant of the 1920 Act which still applied to certain services in Northern Ireland, but not to the Free State. O'Higgins would agree to transfer the Council of Ireland functions to Northern Ireland and would ask his colleagues about the Donegal–Derry boundary. Craig himself was indifferent on the question of the Boundary Commission award as opposed to the existing boundary, but thought that the transfer of Council of Ireland services would be valuable to Northern Ireland.

When he again met with the Free State representatives, Baldwin was reluctant to raise hopes regarding Article 5, but would have to discuss it with the Chancellor of the Exchequer, Winston Churchill. O'Higgins reiterated that, to satisfy the Free State government's supporters, he had to return with either concessions for Catholics, which Craig would not give, or the dropping of Article 5 obligation toward the Imperial debt. He announced Cosgrave would return to England in a couple of days to continue the discussion. In the meantime the conferees issued a statement, agreed to by Craig, that the existing boundary was to be undisturbed, that the debt obligations were to be waived for a set period, that both governments in Ireland had equal rights regarding the navigation of Lough Foyle and that Derry should have free trading facilities through Lough Foyle, that the decisions of the British government regarding convicted prisoners in Northern Ireland would be accepted by the Northern

Irish government, and that the administration of Council of Ireland services in Northern Ireland would be transferred to the government of Northern Ireland.[77]

Two days later, prompted by a request by O'Higgins to Baldwin, the Secretary of the British Cabinet wrote to the Boundary Commission that the ongoing discussions of the Free State and the British government 'might be seriously impaired by the publication at this moment either of the determination of the commission or any other official forecast of that determination'. The commission, through its secretary, indicated its willingness to postpone the issuance of its determination pending future instructions from both governments.[78]

A full-scale conference got underway when Cosgrave returned to London and joined O'Higgins and O'Byrne in negotiations with Churchill, Salisbury, and Birkenhead for the next three days about possible financial concessions to the Free State in return for their acceptance of the existing boundary change. Cosgrave described the difficult fiscal and economic situation of the Free State, such as reduced British investment, an adverse trading balance, large numbers of uneconomic land holdings and lowly paid agricultural labourers, small old-age pension, and an inability of the government to fund unemployment insurance.

O'Higgins added that the Free State government could survive politically on the basis of the present border only if they got either 'an amelioration of the conditions under which the nationalists were at present living in North-East Ireland' or some other concession that could 'deaden in the twenty-six counties the echo of the outcry of the Catholics in North-East Ireland'. He would have preferred the former, having in mind the correction of such sources of Catholic grievance as the sectarian auxiliary police force, the abolition of proportional representation in local elections, and the employment of gerrymandering. However, he made 'no headway on these lines in his discussions with Sir James Craig'. Therefore, he asked Baldwin if 'he could make a contribution beyond the meagre offer of Sir James Craig' to accept any request from the British to release some political prisoners. When Baldwin asked what direction might such a contribution take, he answered that the 'amelioration for the Catholics in Northern Ireland would have been preferred', but a solution 'might lie in the direction of a modification of Article 5 of the treaty'.

Churchill argued that the British government had strictly adhered to the treaty and had carried out the conditions of Article 12 and thought the commission's tentative award was 'very much what he had expected and meant when he signed the treaty'. As for Article 5, the final sum of which was yet to be determined by arbitration, it 'was impossible to forecast the result of the arbitration under that article'. The British Treasury thought that an arbitrator might award £155,000,000, which would mean an annual annuity of £8,250,000 for 60 years. 'It would be a very serious step for a British government to renounce on behalf of the British taxpayer so substantial a claim' at a time when 'retrenchments were being pressed in education, health services, unemployment allowances and the armed forces'. He believed there would be 'an explosion of public opinion if the British government were to abandon Article 5 although they had carried out to the letter the terms of Article 12'.

Cosgrave replied that the maintenance of peace between both parts of Ireland ought to 'be of importance to the British government'. He thought an arbitrator would arrive at a lower obligation on the part of the Free State, possibly less than £6,000,000, although he wondered if they could pay even that sum, as they 'had not succeeded in existing circumstances in balancing their budget and they would not be able even to maintain services at the figure estimated in this year's budget'. He rhetorically assumed the British government 'did not wish to see the Free State bankrupt'.

Salisbury said the British government 'took a rigid view of the obligations of Article 5, but he fully understood, and indeed sympathised with Free State anxiety in regard to the position of Roman Catholics in Northern Ireland'. He wondered if the Free State government might not look bad if it accepted being relieved of the fiscal burden of Article 5 in place of gaining relief of Northern Catholic grievances. O'Higgins acknowledged that the Free State government 'would be open to the taunt of having sold the Roman Catholics in Northern Ireland', but could survive with the existing border, either by obtaining relief for the Northern Catholics or by securing 'the elimination of Article 5'. He reminded them that de Valera had referred to Article 12 and had been warning the people to expect a similar shock to that received by the commission award when arbitration would take place under Article 5. O'Higgins also noted the £21,500,000 in military expenses the Free State had encountered as a consequence of the Civil War, as well as the great amount of material destruction and compensation still to be paid, as a further justification for waiving Article 5.[79]

When the conference resumed after a late afternoon adjournment,

Birkenhead noted the domestic political difficulties that would be created in Britain if Article 5 were to be wiped out altogether. He made clear he had no authority to make any offer to the Irish ministers, but wondered if a moratorium for a certain number of years might be of assistance in their difficulties. Salisbury said that as trustees for the British public they had no right to give up the claim, but would 'agree to give further time for the financial settlement'. Even Churchill, the political realist, softened his line and thought it 'desirable to consider the question not only strictly from the financial point of view'. That broader perspective might make it possible 'to go some distance, but not as far as the Free State desired'. He also suggested that Craig, for his part, might be able to do something toward 'amelioration of the lot of Catholics in Northern Ireland', but also 'not as much as the Free State wished'.

When Salisbury enquired about the actual oppression of Catholics in Northern Ireland, O'Higgins pointed to their minimal role in the administrative life of the country, the closing of judicial positions to them, and their small numbers in the RUC, all of which contrasted with the comfortable position of Protestants in the Free State. Cosgrave noted, in view of Article 12 of the treaty not being workable, his government would acquiesce in the boundary *status quo* in return for an abandonment of the Article 5 obligations, hoping that 'by surrendering some immediate advantage' they might 'obtain something of far greater value in, say 20 years'. That something would be 'a better feeling between the North and the South, by eliminating the disputes and distrusts that existed', and hope 'for the possibility in the future of their becoming one country with the same political outlook'. Churchill said 'the maintenance of the existing boundary was in every way preferable to the marking out of a new boundary by the Imperial commissioners', which 'would only stereotype existing differences' and impede any ultimate Irish unification. O'Higgins believed that the Free State government could only survive if 'the territorial *status quo*' remained, if there was 'the release of the prisoners to which Sir James Craig had agreed', and 'if Article 5 were to disappear'.[80]

The group met for the third time that day at 6:15 pm, this time joined by Craig. Salisbury said the government continued to oppose writing off Article 5, but could 'consider proposals for postponing payment under that Article'. He and his colleagues had 'been very much impressed by the feeling in the Free State...that the Roman Catholics in the Six Counties were not receiving fair treatment', and, whether valid or not, 'the mere fact that such a feeling existed did great harm to the interests of good government'. He asked Craig 'whether any steps could be taken to improve the position of Catholics in Northern Ireland', being anxious 'not only to eliminate injustice, which was not, of course, admitted, but to destroy the feeling that injustice existed'. Craig replied by noting relatively minor advances such as the entry of two nationalists into the Northern parliament, the official aspiration that one-third of the RUC be Catholics, the appointment of a Catholic as a stipendiary justice, the appropriate apportionment of unemployment relief, and the impartial administration of the widows and orphans pension scheme. Churchill then suggested as a settlement: the abrogation of Article 12, a moratorium on Article 5, a liaison officer for the Northern Catholics, and periodic joint consultation between both governments. Even Craig feared the inadequacy of such a proposal 'might in the present circumstances be a source of embarrassment to Mr Cosgrave'. Churchill then adjourned the meeting and scheduled another for noon the next day.[81]

When the conference assembled the next day Churchill concluded that since Craig was not amenable to concessions on Northern Catholics the only option was a financial concession. Craig had proposed a mitigation of the Free State portion of the Imperial debt to a specified sum, in return for which the Free State would increase by 10% the compensation awarded by the courts in post-truce damage claims. Cosgrave thought that even the suggested sum of £20,000,000 was too much for the Free State and thought that the obligation should be 'limited by the capacity of the Irish Free State government to pay'. O'Higgins suggested applying the Colwyn Principle,[82] which allowed tax revenues from Northern Ireland to be used to meet local expenses before being applied to the expected Imperial contribution, to the Irish Free State's obligations.

Discussion continued about the appropriate portion of national expenditure that should be directed toward paying off debt, with comparisons being made with other nations, and whether a moratorium would be advantageous to the Free State. O'Higgins thought a moratorium would offer no political advantage to the Free State, as the popular view was that, even after a moratorium, the arbitration decision would be as disappointing as the Boundary Commission. Salisbury reminded the Free State ministers that inability to arrive at some settlement would make the award of the Boundary Commission inevitably operative. O'Higgins said 'it was impossible to forecast the consequences that would flow' from the publication of the award, but it was safe 'to say that no good would come to the British government or the Free State government or the government of Northern Ireland from such a situation'. However, he hoped that 'an opportunity of obtaining durable peace between Northern Ireland and the Free State', would not be lost simply 'because the British government were not willing...to forego phantom millions of money that they could never hope to obtain'.[83]

After the meeting had adjourned for lunch, Cosgrave and O'Higgins met privately with Churchill. When they subsequently rejoined the others, Churchill placed on the table two alternatives suggested by Cosgrave: the fixing of the Irish portion of the Imperial debt at £6,000,000 to be paid over an agreed period or the waiving of Article 5 in return for the Free State repaying to Britain any compensation payments on damages in Ireland, as well as increasing by ten per cent the court awards on post-truce damages being paid by the Free State. While Salisbury indicated his inability to accept either proposal, Churchill agreed to present them to the British cabinet that evening. Birkenhead acknowledged 'the unfortunate economic situation of the Free State and to the undesirability of fixing payments which they could not possibly hope to discharge'.[84] In the Cabinet meeting Churchill advanced the Irish case, noting that a settlement was of paramount interest since the collapse of the Free State into the hands of the republicans would mean not just the loss of Article 5, but also the £1,750,000 being received for RIC pensions and £3,500,000 being received in land annuities.[85]

Later that evening Churchill reported to the Irish that the Cabinet had accepted in principle the proposal to drop Article 5 in return for the proposal on compensation. Cosgrave welcomed the decision and said it would 'go far to cement the friendship of the two peoples', and that the proposed arrangement 'showed a spirit of neighbourly comradeship which had never before been revealed'. He thought the 'active cooperation of Sir James Craig in promoting this spirit was also most welcome'. O'Higgins thought the British Cabinet's acceptance of compensation payments and the dropping of the Article 5 obligation rather than have a moratorium on it was 'better for the Executive Council' of the Free State, as it could be presented that they 'were prepared to shoulder their own burdens arising out of the disturbances in Ireland'. Similarly, Cosgrave was hopeful that, while Craig would be able to announce that he had given nothing away, 'it was clearly understood between them that every effort would be made to promote goodwill between North and South'. O'Higgins promised on behalf of the Executive Council 'that what seven men could do to clothe the agreement with the spirit of friendship should be done, and that they would also use what influence they possessed to induce the Nationalist members in Ulster to take their place in the Northern parliament'.[86]

The next day a formal agreement was composed. O'Higgins sought to include a paragraph indicating that if the governments of the Free State and Northern Ireland were to enter into an agreement for the political union of the island, that British and Free State governments would 'respectively promote such legislation and take such steps as may be necessary to give effect to such agreement'. But Churchill was doubtful of incorporating it into the agreement in view of 'the possible opposition of eminent ministers', and Cosgrave agreed that it not be pressed. It was also agreed that the three Prime Ministers were to meet the Boundary Commissioners and formally request the suppression of the award, with a possibility of its being published later as a matter of historical interest.[87]

## DÁIL DEBATE ON TREATY REVISION

In the Dáil debate on the legislation that would confirm the agreement, the Treaty (Confirmation of Amending Agreement) Bill, Cosgrave said the failure of the commission 'to achieve the results for which it was constituted', was not the fault of the government. It had done everything possible 'to ensure that the commission should be fully cognisant of our claims and should be in complete possession of all the requisite information'. But when the publication of the ultimate award had become imminent, at which point it would have become 'legal and binding', the Executive Council was faced with two alternatives: to have accepted the award with the transfer of territory in both directions, or 'to resort to the arbitration of force'. Either way 'pointed straight to disaster and chaos', and not just for the Free State, as both Sir James Craig and the British government feared them. But a basis for peace was found. That was contained in the present Bill. 'Although political separation is an accomplished fact', the recent conference was 'a manifestation of a genuine desire for united effort for the common good' that would 'in time lead to the voluntary acceptance of closer and more tangible bonds of union' and 'justify our decision to put this barren question of the boundary behind us'. While the agreement did nothing for the Northern minority, he noted the treaty had already placed them under the jurisdiction of the Northern government. Even though the Free State had carried out all the provisions in the treaty that it had been hoped would assist them, things had worked out in a way 'the signatories could not possibly have foreseen'. However, he believed that the one 'real security' for the minority would be 'the good will and neighbourly feeling of the people among whom they live', next to which 'written guarantees are scraps of paper, and sometimes irritating scraps of paper which kill in spirit what they profess to secure in words'.

He celebrated the agreement's removal of the fiscal obligation of Article 5 of the treaty, which had 'hung over us as a menace to our credit, a hindrance to borrowing for development, a deterrent to our business expansion and a not unlikely cause of friction between the two countries'. In return the Free State had assumed the damages cost of the British in Ireland since 21 January1919 and the liability of £5,000,000 compensation 'for damages suffered by our own people'. The agreement's increase in awards for damages between the truce to the end of the Civil War – which he regarded as a Free State responsibility – was justified since awards made had compared 'unfavourably with the awards for damage suffered pre-truce'. The transfer of powers regarding railways, fisheries, and the diseases of animals from the Council of Ireland to Northern Ireland was also appropriate since those powers applied only to Northern Ireland, even though half the representatives on the council were from the Free State. Northern Ireland could not have looked on the operation of the council 'as anything but irritating interference', and 'in abandoning the Council of Ireland, the Free State will lose nothing. It will gain goodwill.'[88]

Professor William Magennis, until then a member of Cumann na nGaedheal, was the foremost critic of the agreement in the Dáil. He challenged not the patriotism of Cosgrave and his colleagues, but 'their capacity and confidence and their negligence'. Even Eoin MacNeill's adherence to the confidentiality of the commission was not an excuse for their unawareness of how the award would turn out since they had appointed him and allowed him 'to go on until there was no way out'.[89] As for the removal of the Article 5 fiscal obligation, he doubted if there would have been any. 'Whatever Imperial claim could be made under the categories of national debt and war pensions' would be offset by such a 'gigantic counter-claim' that Ireland would be found to be 'the creditor nation'. All the Free State got from the agreement was the 'border as it was' and a specified debt of 'some millions'. Ulster got a 'boundary of its own choice', 'a transfer of the reserved powers', and the ending 'of what irritated them so exceedingly – the prospect of the Council of Ireland' without 'the provision for later unification' that the council had implied.[90] He could scarcely applaud those who achieved the agreement, as he asked 'Where is the proof that the men who muddled the boundary question were the only possible negotiators?' While he might be told that he is an old fool with 'his eyes on the ends of the earth', he insisted his eyes were 'upon the border and upon the Irishmen who are sacrificed through this permanent border line'. He wanted to make sure it was on record that 'there were some among the representatives of the people who did not forget that they were Irishmen and that they had a duty to all Irishmen and not to those that lived south of a line drawn artificially by an alien government'.[91]

O'Higgins spoke after Magennis and delivered one of his most eloquent addresses. He repeated the account of how the Boundary Commission, or more specifically, two of its members, took the view of its mission to be one of adjusting an existing line, whereas the Free State and its member 'had the conception that considerable tracts of territory might be transferred from one jurisdiction to the other'. As for the position that the Executive Council bore collective responsibility for the actions of MacNeill as a Boundary Commissioner, he suggested the same presumption would imply that Feetham should have kept the British government similarly informed. He drew a distinction between MacNeill's role as a member of the Executive Council and as a member of the Boundary Commission, and asked if a non-member of the Executive Council had been appointed to the commission, would he have 'reported frequently to the Executive Council' and kept it informed of all his doings?[92]

Magennis had implied that had the Executive Council done its job properly 'there would be no boundary at all and no nationalists cut off from the jurisdiction of their choice'. But, in fact, even if the Boundary Commission had done the best from the Free State perspective, 'there would be a boundary, and north of that boundary there would be a minority. It would be a smaller minority proportionately than that which at present exists within the Six County area. The difference for them would be that they would be a smaller and more helpless minority within the enclave than they now are.' While he sympathized with those who hoped for a commission award to put them within the jurisdiction of their choice, he argued that given the ways things developed 'it was in the interests of the whole country that this proviso of Article 12 should be allowed to lapse and that other and saner solutions should be sought for the tangle that had arisen'. He asked if it was saying too much 'to assert that the interests of the whole country must be above and before and beyond what seemed to be the immediate interests of the inhabitants of a particular set of square miles up there, in and around the border area'?

Suggestions had been made prior to the London conference to repudiate the treaty rather than accept the unsatisfactory award. But taking such a course because of dissatisfaction with the way Article 12 was construed would be 'plunging the fortunes of this state and of this people back once more into the melting pot'. Instead, they negotiated with those whom Magennis had called sarcastically 'our good friends, the British'. In contrast to that embittered tone, he asserted:

> Hate, whether between individuals or between peoples, is a barren thing, and I am not ashamed to say here what I have said and will say again out through the country, that I believe there ought to be friendly relations and relations of neighbourly comradeship, not merely between our people and the people of the north-east, but between our people and the people of the neighbouring country which is a co-equal state with ours within the British Commonwealth of Nations. And so mere cheap gibes about 'Our good friends, the British,' and so on, are rather out of place and must not be taken, and should not be taken, as a serious contribution to this grave question.[93]

As to the abolition of the fiscal obligations in Article 5, he noted that differences between the two governments would have made arbitration inevitable. While he could not say with certainty what the result of such arbitration would be, he did note that the critics of the state, upon hearing of what the Boundary Commission award would have been, had warned of how massive would be the arbitration settlement of the Article 5 obligation. Now, because of the agreement, that threat, whether real or imaginary, was gone.[94]

Admittedly, the original idea behind the Council of Ireland was as 'a body forming a kind of overhead link of union'. But since the treaty, it was 'a very different matter' and had 'a kind of mutilated and lopsided existence'. It was to have members from both the Free State and Northern Ireland, but would deal only with limited services within Northern Ireland. A deputy had suggested such a body was an irritant, 'useful in creating deadlocks and one to obstruct and make trouble'. But the agreement had been framed 'to work away from a state of mind when things are valuable when they are irritants, because one can obstruct with them, and make difficulties with them'. Instead, 'the net result of this agreement will be that we will draw nearer to our fellow-countrymen in the North-East and they to us'.[95]

In depicting the agreement as bearing the seeds of peace and construction for the people of the island, he observed that:

> It is the easy thing, the obvious thing, to sneer, to suggest that we were cowed, intimidated, or coaxed or cajoled by the statesmen of other countries into signing this agreement. It is always easier to believe ill of the neighbour's child than to believe good of him. It is always easier to believe that you have been sold, that you have been let down, that people took their price, whether in flattery or in cash, or in some other way; but, in the end, people have, simply, faced with a grave situation, to do what they believe in their inmost heart and soul and mind to be the right thing, and to chance the sneers of spatted hillsiders and armchair patriots and the jibes of those who think that the real statesmanship is for the perpetuation of hatred. We stand, not for the perpetuation of hatred, but for the rooting up and elimination of the old hatreds, old furies, and the quenching of old fires; we stand for peace and sanity and construction in this country, and peace between neighbours.[96]

### REPUBLICAN DIVISIONS AND ATTEMPT AT RIVAL COALITION

The Boundary Commission crisis had coincided with significant signs of a dissent within Sinn Féin ranks over the question of abstentionism. Labour Party leader Thomas Johnson tried unsuccessfully to capitalize on this in an effort to gain a majority in the Dáil for no-confidence in the government. The understanding of the situation requires an appreciation that the Sinn Féiners viewed the Free State government as illegitimate, and regarded the second Dáil Éireann as the *de jure* government. However, they were pragmatic enough to allow the ranks of anti-treaty members of the Second Dáil to be joined by those additional abstentionists elected to the Third and Fourth Dáils. The increased group was considered their *de facto* government, which was called Comhairle na dTeachtaí (Council of Deputies). More pragmatic Sinn Féiners, like Gerry Boland, Frank Aiken, Seán Lemass, Seán T. O'Kelly, and de Valera himself, were giving thought to entering Dáil Éireann, which they considered illegitimate, but to which they had been elected, if the obligatory oath to the King was removed.

But these compromising tendencies prompted more purist republicans to move a resolution at a 17 November 1925 Sinn Féin Árd Fheis that would disallow such moves, but de Valera's opposition resulted in a compromise resolution asserting that policy had not changed, but that no subject was barred from discussion other than the unacceptability of the oath and the partition of Ireland.[97] But the purists had prevailed a couple of days earlier, November 14 and 15, at the first General Army Convention of the IRA since the Civil War, which voted that 'the Army of the Republic severs its connection with the Dáil [that is, Comhairle na d'Teachtaí] and acts under an independent Executive'.[98] In the same spirit the Army Convention amended its constitution to allow the Army Council, the permanent governing body of the Army, to determine who was 'the de facto government of the Republic'.[99] The Army Council forbade any of its members or members of the GHQ staff from entering 'the Parliaments of "Northern" or "Southern" Ireland, or advocate the entrance of these bodies with or without the Oath of Allegiance'.[100]

Because of the increasing inclination of some Sinn Féiners to turn to pragmatic politics, Thomas Johnson of the Labour Party summoned a meeting on the morning of December 8 of all elected members of Dáil Éireann, including the abstentionists, to gather in the Shelbourne Hotel to discuss the proposed treaty revisions. He hoped that the abstentionists might be induced to enter the Dáil, where, in combination with Labour, Redmondites, Farmers, breakaway Cumann na nGaedheal members, and some independents, they might be able to block the measure and force the Executive Council from office. However, when the Sinn Féin members met in a private caucus, the majority opposed entering the Dáil, although Gerry Boland and Austin Stack were sympathetic. De Valera was unable to decide which way to move, and the prospective opposition coalition failed to materialize.[101]

## CONTINUED DEBATE

Sinn Féin's continued abstention guaranteed the Dáil's approval of the agreement, but not before several more sessions of debate. One critic of the agreement was Labour deputy Daniel Morrissey from

Tipperary, who noted how Southern loyalists were to get an added ten per cent compensation for damages between the truce and the end of the Civil War, but there was nothing additional for Northern nationalists, 'who were driven out of their homes . . . who were driven from their work . . . driven out of their business'. He considered those who applauded being 'forgiven a debt, under Article 5, that we did not owe', to be 'the greatest political *amadans* that ever postured in Irish history'.[102] Support for the agreement came from Major Bryan Cooper, who recalled his having warned more than a year earlier that 'whatever the Boundary Commission decides we shall not get all that we expect'. He saw the cancellation of Article 5 as fortunate. Judging by the wartime expenditures of the other dominions, he feared that in any settlement by arbitration the Free State was 'liable to lose' and 'have an undoubted millstone round our necks when we go into the money markets and when we want to develop our country'.[103]

Thomas Johnson, the Labour leader was sceptical of the 'new spirit, this new atmosphere of friendship and brotherhood', that the Executive Council had claimed existed between both governments in Ireland, arguing that 'the claim of the Northern government which they have insisted on from the beginning has not changed in any degree'. He described the mentality of the elements 'that go to make up the Ulster Unionist Council' as one of 'contempt' towards the people of the South and the West. He saw no alternative to the treaty unless the Northern government would 'consider alternatives within the unity of Ireland'. Instead, there had been 'an absolute refusal to confer on any condition which will pre-suppose an Irish unity'.[104] Johnson may have been correct on the last point, but from a unionist perspective the Southern presupposition of Irish unity made good will and co-operation impossible.

In his closing speech on the issue O'Higgins sought to rebut those who depicted a dire situation for the nationalists left in the Six County area. He asked them to imagine the situation if the Boundary Commission award had been more to their liking. There would have remained 'an area, smaller, no doubt, standing out from your state system, containing a smaller proportion of nationalists – a more homogeneous area, a more embittered area, because of the loss of territory and the friction that there had been in the course of the transfer'. Critics sought to indict the Executive Council because of 'its inability to compel a majority of the members of the Boundary Commission to bring in an award after our own heart'. But other parties had a different conception of the commission's terms of reference, and the Executive Council should not be indicted for failure to compel acceptance of its interpretation. Besides, the Executive Council did not have the right to bargain Article 5 for Article 12 before the commission was established and for so long as 'there was a real prospect or a real hope or chance' for their interpretation to prevail. But it had become another thing once those hopes were gone, and accordingly, the Agreement ensued.[105]

The measure passed and the boundary remains to this day. Aside from a couple of meetings between the Prime Ministers in the 1960s, the expected goodwill between the two governments of both parts of Ireland never materialized until the hopeful developments at the end of the twentieth century. The explanation for the delay is beyond the scope of this book, although the replacement of the Cumann na nGaedheal government in 1932 did not facilitate better relations between both parts of Ireland.

## NOTES

1. Kevin Matthews, *Fatal Influence: The Impact of Ireland on British Politics, 1920–1925* (Dublin: University College Dublin Press, 2004), pp. 63–9.
2. *Ibid.*, pp. 71–4.
3. *Ibid.*, pp. 77–8.
4. *Ibid.*, pp. 84–5.
5. Birkenhead to Balfour (3 March 1922), reprinted in *Ibid.*, pp. 288–90; Geoffrey J. Hand, 'MacNeill and the Boundary Commission', *The Scholarly Revolutionary*, ed. F.X. Martin & F.J. Byrne (New York: Harper & Row, 1973), pp. 204–8.
6. Matthews, *Fatal Influence*, p. 96.
7. 'Final Report' (26 February 1926), *North-Eastern Boundary Bureau*, 1–5, S4743, NA.
8. *Cabinet minutes* (31 January 1923), NA, C 1/39.
9. *Ibid.* (12 May 1923), NA, C 1/105.
10. Matthews, *Fatal Influence*, p. 92.
11. *Ibid.*, pp. 114–15.
12. William T. Cosgrave to Stanley Baldwin (9 June 1923), NA, S 1801/C.
13. Geoffrey J. Hand, 'MacNeill and the Boundary Commission', pp. 210–15.
14. Thomas Jones, *Whitehall Diary,* vol. III, p. 221; Devonshire (Secretary of State for the Colonies) to T.M. Healy (Governor-General of the Irish Free State) (25 July 1923), NA, S 1801 H.
15. Devonshire to Healy (22 September 1923), *Ibid.*
16. Healy to Devonshire (8 October 1923), NA, S 1801 H.
17. James MacNeill to Kevin O'Higgins (2 November 1923), NA, S 1801 C.
18. Matthews, *Fatal Influence*, pp. 22–5
19. 'Conference on Boundary Commission' (28 January 1924), NA, S 1801 D.
20. 'Rough Notes on Conference in President's room with the Governor-General' (30 January 1924), NA, S 1801 D.

21. The Council of Ireland had been a feature of the Government of Ireland Act of 1920, which had partitioned Ireland. It called for representatives of both parts of Ireland to come together to deal with matters of mutual concern and offered some hope of eventual political unification. The Anglo-Irish Treaty of 1921 had allowed for the Northern Irish government to opt out of the Free State, but had stated that the Government of Ireland Act still applied there, which meant that the Council of Ireland had nominal authority in Northern Ireland over matters like railways, fisheries, and disease of animals, but no authority in the Free State.
22. 'Outline of Proposal for Consideration' (2 February 1924), NA, S 1801 D.
23. Jones, *Whitehall Diary*, vol. III, p. 226.
24. 'Notes on the Proposals Made at the London Conference' (2 February 1924), NA, S 1801 E.
25. Healy to Thomas (15 March 1924), NA, S 1801F.
26. Thomas Jones to Lionel Curtis (30 March 1924), Jones, *Whitehall Diary*, ud. III, pp. 227–8.
27. Thomas to Healy (1 April 1924); Healy to Thomas (7 April 1924), Thomas to Healy (10 April 1924), NA, S 1801N.
28. Jones, *Whitehall Diary*, vol. III, p. 229.
29. Birkenhead's speech was part of an effort by him and other British signatories to overcome Unionist and 'Die-hard' Conservative distrust they had earned because of the treaty. Matthews, *Fatal Influence*, p. 159.
30. Statement by Kevin O'Higgins, Howth (6 May 1924), NA, S 1801 R.
31. K. O'Higgins to W.T. Cosgrave (7 May 1924), NA, S 1801 R. Also in UCDA, *Blythe Papers*, P24/129 (9).
32. H. Kennedy to W.T. Cosgrave (9 May 1924), NA, S1801 R.
33. Memo, undated NA, S 1801 R.
34. K. O'Higgins to W.T. Cosgrave (10 May 1924), NA, S 1801 R; also, UCDA, *Blythe Papers*, P24/129 (6).
35. Matthews, *Fatal Influence*, p. 154.
36. J.H. Thomas to T. Healy (23 May 1924), NA, S 1801 H; Jones, *Whitehall Diary*, vol. III, pp. 231–2.
37. R. MacDonald to W.T. Cosgrave (27 May 1924), W. T. Cosgrave to R. MacDonald (28 May 1924), R. MacDonald to W. T. Cosgrave (2 June 1924), NA, S 1801H.
38. Jones, *Whitehall Diary*, vol. III, p. 231.
39. T. Healy to J.H. Thomas (3 June 1924), R. MacDonald to W.T. Cosgrave (6 June 1924), NA, S 1801H.
40. K. O'Higgins to W.T. Cosgrave (10 June 1924), NA, S1801 H.
41. The ruling had been delayed by the desire to include jurists from the dominions on the Privy Council Judicial Committee. One, the Chief Justice of Australia, did not arrive for a month.
42. *Dáil Éireann*, VIII (12 August 1924), 2,420.
43. Kevin Matthews, 'Stanley Baldwin's "Irish Question"', *The Historical Journal*, 43, 4 (2000), pp. 1,027–49.
44. NA, S 1801 P.
45. Matthews, *Fatal Influence*, p. 175.
46. K. O'Higgins to the members of the Executive Council (3 September 1924), NA, S 1801 J.
47. K. O'Higgins to Executive Council (25 September 1924), UCDA, *McGilligan Papers*, P35b/138 (1).
48. 'Notes on Possible Offer to Northern Ireland', UCDA, *McGilligan Papers*, P35b/138 (2).

49. K. O'Higgins to Executive Council (29 September, 1924), UCDA, *McGilligan Papers*, P35b/138 (3).
50. 'Draft Outline of Possible Offer to Northern Ireland', *McGilligan Papers*, P35b/138 (4).
51. *Cabinet Minutes* (1 October 1924), NA, C 2/131.
52. 'Report of Committee appointed to consider an Offer to the North-East' (22 October 1924), UCDA, *McGilligan Papers*, P35b/139; *Cabinet Minutes* (27 October 1924), NA, C 2/140.
53. Eoin MacNeill to the Members of the Executive Council (24 October 1924), UCDA, *McGilligan Papers*, P35b/ 139.
54. Hand, 'MacNeill and the Boundary Commission', pp. 222–9; Jones, *Whitehall Diary*, vol. III, pp. 232–5.
55. *Report of the Irish Boundary Commission 1925*, Intro. Geoffrey J. Hand (Shannon: Irish University Press, 1969), pp. 28–32.
56. *Ibid.*, pp. 65-8.
57. *Ibid.*, pp. xi–xii.
58. Jones, *Whitehall Diary*, vol. III, p. 236.
59. *Cabinet Minutes* (10 July 1925), NA, C 2/207.
60. 'Notes of A Meeting…to Discuss Administrative Steps to be Taken to Give Effect to the Determination of the Irish Boundary Commission' (28 July 1925), NA, S 4563A.
61. Hand, 'MacNeill and the Boundary Commission', pp. 245–6.
62. *Cabinet Minutes* (2 November 1925), NA, C 2/223.
63. It is generally assumed that the leak originated from Justice Fisher, who had reassured Lord Edward Carson that most of Northern Ireland would remain intact. Hand, 'MacNeill and the Boundary Commission', pp. 250–1.
64. *Dáil Éireann*, XIII (November 11, 1925), 113–14.
65. *Cabinet Minutes* (10, 13, and 18 November 1925), NA, C 2/224, 225, 226.
66. *Dáil Éireann*, XIII (November 19, 1925), 625–6.
67. *Ibid.*, 634–40.
68. Hand, 'MacNeill and the Boundary Commission', p. 256.
69. *The Times*, November 23, 1925, p. 13, quoted in Hand, 'MacNeill and the Boundary Commission', pp. 257–8.
70. *Dáil Éireann*, XIII (November 24, 1925), 796–804.
71. *Ibid.*, 805–8.
72. *Ibid.*, 810–14.
73. Irish Boundary Commission. Draft Notes, Conference at No. 10 Downing Street (26 November 1925), C.A./H./48, 1st Meeting; NA, S 4720 A.
74. Cabinet Committee on Irish Affairs. Meeting Between the Prime Minister, Mr O' Higgins, Mr McGilligan and Mr O'Byrne at Chequers (28 November 1925), I.A/ (25) 6, NA, S 4720 A.
75. Jones, *Whitehall Diary*, III, p. 239.
76. Cabinet Committee on Irish Affairs, Statements at meeting between Prime Minister and representatives of Free State and Northern Ireland (29 November 1925, AM), I.A. (25) 7, NA, S 4720 A.
77. Jones, *Whitehall Diary*, III, pp. 242–3.
78. O'Higgins to Baldwin (30 November 1925), Correspondence between Secretary to the Cabinet and Secretary, Irish Boundary Commission (1 December 1925), C.P. 512 (25), NA, S 4720 A.
79. Irish Boundary Commission. Notes of Conference at Treasury (1 December 1925, at 12 noon), C.A./H./48, 2nd Minutes, NA, S 4720 A.
80. Irish Boundary Commission. Notes of a Conference at the Treasury (1 December 1925, 4 PM), C.A./H./48, 3rd Minutes, NA, S 4720 A.

81. Irish Boundary Commission. Notes of a Conference at Treasury (1 December 1925, 6:15 PM), C.A./H./48, 4th Minutes, NA, S 4720 A.
82. A committee of arbitration, chaired by Lord Colwyn, had reduced the Imperial contribution for 1922–4 and established the principle for subsequent years.
83. Irish Negotiations, Notes of a Conference at Treasury (2 December 1925, 12:15 pm), C.A./H./48, 5th Minutes, NA, S 4720 A.
84. Irish Boundary Commission, Notes of Conference at Treasury (2 December 1925, 3:50 pm), C.A./ H./ 48, 6th Minutes, NA, S 4720 A.
85. Jones, *Whitehall Diary*, vol. III, p. 245.
86. Irish Boundary Commission, Notes of a Conference at Treasury (2 December 1925, 7:45 pm), C.A./H./48, 7th Minutes, NA, S 4720 A.
87. Irish Boundary Commission, Notes of a Conference at Treasury (3 December 1925, 10:45 am), C.A./H./48, 8th Minutes, NA, S 4720 A.
88. *Dáil Éireann*, XIII (7 December 1925), 1,299–314.
89. *Ibid.*, 1,315–22.
90. *Ibid.*, 1,327–30, 35.
91. *Ibid.*, 1,349–50.
92. *Ibid.*, 1,352–7.
93. *Ibid.*, 1,358–63.
94. *Ibid.*, 1,364–5.
95. *Ibid.*, 1,366–7.
96. *Ibid.*, 1,369–70.
97. Tim Pat Coogan, *De Valera* (London: Hutchinson, 1995), p. 378.
98. Oglaigh na hEireann, Report of General Army Convention (14 and 15 November 1925), UCDA, *Blythe Papers*, P24/165; Richard English, *Radicals and the Republic* (Oxford: Clarendon Press, 1994), pp. 66–8; Donal ÓDrisceoil, *Peadar O'Donnell* (Cork: Cork University Press, 2001), pp. 40–1.
99. Constitution of Oglaigh na hEireann, amended by General Army Convention (14 and 15 November 1925), UCDA, *Blythe Papers*, P24/ 165.
100. Oglaigh na hEireann, Statement by the Army Council (20 November 1925), *Ibid.*, P24 /165.
101. J. Anthony Gaughan, *Thomas Johnson* (Dublin: Kingdom Books, 1980), pp. 235–6; T. Ryle Dwyer, *De Valera: The Man & the Myth* (Dublin: Poolbeg, 1991), p. 138.
102. *Dáil Éireann*, XIII (8 December 1925), 1,419–23.
103. *Ibid.*, 1,426–33.
104. *Ibid.*, 1,467–9, 1,476, 1,483–6.
105. *Ibid.* (15 December 1925), 1,928–33.

# 8

# O'Higgins as a Diplomat

O'HIGGINS SERVED THE Free State in a diplomatic capacity by his attendance at Imperial conferences and at the League of Nations. While he had come only for the foreign policy sessions of the Imperial conference in London in October 1923 (at which the Free State representatives had got their feet wet in Commonwealth politics),[1] he was more involved in the League of Nations meeting in Geneva in September 1925. His letters to his wife indicated some disenchantment with international diplomacy, especially the attitude of the big powers. Soon after arriving he noted 'that the assembly will be unsensational – and possibly somewhat shorter than usual' because the British and the French were 'out to discourage much discussion of the really important thing – the Protocol for the Pacific Settlement of International Disputes – because they are engaged in delicate negotiations over that very matter'.

Within a few days his scepticism intensified:

> I have had enough of Geneva and the League... 'Security, Disarmament, Arbitration' is a wonderful trilogy if it didn't mean – security in my ill-gotten gains, disarmament for the other fellow, and arbitration with court well packed. But I fear it does mean all these things, my little one, at present, and that the time is not yet when nations, like individuals, will lay aside the stone axe and submit themselves to a code. Still the direction is right and I suppose that a big idea has to be talked about for a long time, sincerely and insincerely, before it becomes a fact.[2]

Later he gave a more conclusive analysis:

> On the whole I am, I fear, inclined to be mildly cynical about this 'League of Nations' without denying that it has certain advantages.

> Personal contact between representatives of governments is good. It breaks down prejudices and insularities. A certain amount of humanitarian work of a broadly international aspect has been achieved through the instrumentality of the League. On the other hand, while there is unlimited lip service to idealism and abundant use of such abstract terms as 'Justice', 'Truth', 'Right', etc., a crafty Imperialism can breathe quite freely in the atmosphere of the Salle de la Reformation and here as elsewhere 'God is on the side of the big battalions'.

He was cynical about his British counterparts:

> Lord Robert Cecil is the fine flower of Geneva. He has an episcopal manner, he exudes High Church mortality, his eyes look through you into a better world, and he is, in my humble judgment, the biggest blackguard in an Assembly which contains a fair sprinkling of them. He is a useful type to the British – the 'sword and Bible' type. His sanctimonious exterior conceals an utterly cynical, ruthless, cold-hearted Imperialism. He is the High Priest of Humbug and Hypocrisy. Amery is here...to protest his willingness to carry 'the white man's burden' in any corner of the globe, and Austen [Chamberlain] – the stage Englishman – monocled, wooden, stupid – and successful.

In summary, he warned:

> Don't let anyone convince you that the League, whatever its germs and possibilities, is a temple of Justice where great and small can meet on equal terms and only Right prevails. It simply imposes the necessity for hypocrisy – 'vice's tribute to virtue' – but once that is paid, once the high sounding formula is found, then '*sicut erat in principio, etc.*'[3]

### IMPERIAL CONFERENCE, 1926

O'Higgins' participation in the Imperial conference in London in October and November 1926, was more enthusiastic. At it he sought to advance the concept of Ireland being a distinct dominion, comparable to Australia, Canada, New Zealand, and South Africa, as well as the notion of the autonomy of dominion governments from the British government. Those ambitions for a clear definition of dominion autonomy and equality of status were in line with a memorandum written for a 1921 Imperial conference by General Smuts, the South African Prime Minister, but which was not discussed then. One issue was whether the Governor General in a dominion should be a viceroy of the King or a representative of the British government. The latter would imply inequality of status. In Ireland's case, Governor General Tim Healy's autonomy from the British government and the role of the Free State in his selection would suggest that the Free State had a position in advance of other dominions, even if not formally acknowledged by dominion document or legislation. Lord Balfour, who presided over the 1926 conference, had hoped that J.B. Hertzog, Smuts's successor, would not revive his aspirations. L.S. Amery, the Secretary of State for Dominions, appears to have concurred with Balfour in his having dropped from Prime Minister Baldwin's opening speech to the gathering a paragraph that called for a clarification of 'the status now possessed by several units of the empire, as free and equal nations under one common crown, each independent, but all interdependent'. However, Hertzog was determined on his predecessor's aim, although the Australian and New Zealand Prime Ministers were unsympathetic and the Canadian, Mackenzie King, was too unprepared after a constitutional crisis in Canada, to play a major role. O'Higgins accordingly emerged to occupy a significant part in the ultimate outcome of the conference.[4]

O'Higgins' confidence in achieving his objectives was manifest in a letter written early in the conference to his wife: 'The *work* side is growing more interesting and important – and because we are raising everything we can think of, I feel we are likely to pull off something.' In another letter he elaborated further, noting his own ascendancy over FitzGerald in the activities: 'I want to be here while our "status" push lasts because they will stand more from me than from Desmond whom they dislike. We have made substantial headway and are likely to make more next week.' A few days later he confidently boasted: 'We are making headway. Though it's ourselves that say it we are by far the best team in the conference – bar one – and one would need to have been here in '23 to realize the *vast* change in our position.' Toward the end he took satisfaction in noting that 'We have done quite well all around, and in constitutional matters have made quite definite and important progress. It is recognized that this is by far the most important Imperial conference which has yet been held and we can claim to have left our mark all over its proceedings.'[5] In his study of Ireland within the Commonwealth, David Harkness noted that despite the presence of Desmond FitzGerald, the Minister for External Affairs, it was to O'Higgins 'that the brunt of conference negotiation was to fall'. FitzGerald, for all his courage and culture, 'lacked the dynamism required for such a job', and O'Higgins 'was developing a keen enthusiasm for foreign affairs and a ready appreciation of the value of Commonwealth membership'.[6]

The specific achievements as reported in the summary of the conference proceedings included changes in the title of the King. Previously it was: 'George V, by Grace of God, of the United Kingdom of Great Britain and Ireland and of the British Dominions beyond the Seas King, Defender of the Faith, Emperor of India.' Now it became, thanks to the insertion of what was called O'Higgins' comma: 'George V, by Grace of God, of Great Britain, Ireland and the British Dominions beyond the Seas King, Defender of the Faith, Emperor of India.' The insertion of the comma made Ireland appear in the same status as the other dominions and not uniquely linked to Britain.

Another advance toward dominion autonomy from the British government was the acknowledgement that the Governor General of a dominion was the representative of the Crown, 'holding in all essential respects the same position as is held by His Majesty the King in Great Britain, and that he is not the representative or agent of His Majesty's government in Great Britain or of any department of that government'.

The conference also asserted that 'it would not be in accordance with constitutional practice for advice to be tendered to His Majesty by His Majesty's government in Great Britain in any matter appertaining to the affairs of a dominion against the views of the government of that dominion', and asked that it 'be placed on record that the constitutional practice is that legislation passed by the parliament at Westminster applying to a dominion would only be passed with the consent of the dominions concerned' (The 1931 Statute of Westminster would give legislative confirmation to this expression of Commonwealth opinion made at the conference). These conclusions grew from a request by the Irish Free State representatives for an elucidation of constitutional practice in view of the 1921 Anglo-Irish Treaty's having defined the position of the Irish Free State in relation to the Imperial parliament and government as being like 'that of the Dominion of Canada'. Free State requests for dominion autonomy were met at the conference in all matters except the matter of judicial appeals to the Privy Council, and even on that question 'the right was reserved to bring up the matter again at the next Imperial conference'.[7]

In his retrospective commentary on the conference, the Dominions Secretary, L.S. Amery, argues that the role in these matters of O'Higgins and the Irish Free State should not be magnified out of proportion. While not depreciating O'Higgins' influence, Amery insisted that the way to the advancement of dominion autonomy had been readied by the attitude of his own sympathetically disposed department: 'there was hardly anything in the outcome of those recommendations which had not been prepared beforehand and largely drafted in the Dominions Office and indeed to a very considerable extent by myself personally. The conception of complete equality of status is one for which I had worked for many years before 1926'.[8] But this seems more hindsight than the actual aim of the government at the time of the conference (see p. 235). More authentic was the commentary by the correspondent for *The Irish Times*, who reported that O'Higgins 'had made a name for himself' as he 'has impressed his colleagues in two ways – first by his economy of words and his knack of putting his point of view into the condensed compass of an incisive phrase, and second, by his insistence on essentials'. Another commentator described O'Higgins as 'perhaps the most vital and the ablest figure among all the assembled political leaders of the dominions (which included the likes of J.B. Hertzog of South Africa and MacKenzie King of Canada); and his personal activity and decided ideas concerning the lines upon which dominion rights ought to be developed, set the pace, to a great extent, for the spokesmen of the other dominions'.[9]

### O'HIGGINS' DUAL MONARCHY PROPOSAL

The Imperial conference gave occasion for O'Higgins to press another aim – a formula for Irish unification which he hoped might be amenable to the Northern Irish and the British governments. Early during the conference he wrote to his wife that he had met with Lord Edward Carson, whom he found 'very friendly'.[10] Later, on his own impulse O'Higgins visited Carson at his residence and confronted him with a proposal for the unification of Northern Ireland and the Irish Free State as the Kingdom of Ireland, a concept that would be anathema to an Irish republican, but might be acceptable to an open-minded unionist. Carson expressed interest, promised to do nothing to impede it, but thought it premature.[11] The following day O'Higgins visited the Dominion Secretary, L.S. Amery, reported on his visit to Carson and presented his proposal in great detail to not-inhospitable attention. The proceedings of the conference and the visits to Carson and Amery filled O'Higgins with extraordinary optimism about the prospects of Irish unification as a 'Kingdom of Ireland'. He wrote to his wife:

> Lord, if only people at home had a true sense of their interests they would seize the opportunity of next year's election to steam-roll the irregular elements and go full steam ahead for a united Ireland and a dual monarchy. If only they could be got to realize how injurious to real progress events like those of last Sunday are. [On 14 November 1926 two Garda were killed in IRA attacks on twelve unarmed police barracks in the Free State. See chapter 6, pp. 181–3.] Given a fair chance and decent standards amongst our people, the thing would be practical politics within five years. If things were going right one could talk straight to men like Birkenhead and Churchill here and Craig and Anderson in the North East and the 'Kingdom of Ireland' would be within sight – instead of which we have lousy futile Anglophobia militating alike against unity and *complete* formal independence.[12]

Despite Carson's amiable reception and Amery's apparent interest, O'Higgins' project was premature and ultimately irrelevant. This is apparent from a memo submitted by Amery to the British Cabinet about his meetings with O'Higgins, both during the conference and in a subsequent luncheon engagement a month later. He reported that at the first meeting O'Higgins told him of his meeting with Carson and of Carson's having 'not been at all unsympathetic' though inclined to regard it as premature. Amery went on to say that he himself 'personally sympathized entirely with the general idea', but thought that Sir James Craig also would think it 'premature' and that it would be wise 'in being guided by Sir James's judgment on that point'.

Amery had also indicated to O'Higgins that it was in the power of the Free State to remove 'certain sentimental obstacles to the Union of Ireland'. They were 'the Sinn Féin Flag [the tricolour], the abolition of the King's head on stamps and coinage, the extravagance of the Irish language cult, etc.' O'Higgins replied that he 'was not himself a fanatic about Gaelic', thought the King's head could be readily restored 'once Ireland was a Kingdom again', and that there would be no difficulty in replacing the tricolour with a new flag having 'a harp and crown on a blue ground', as most in the Free State saw the Union Jack as 'a party emblem'. He would also accept the unionist Lord Londonderry, 'or almost anyone else who commended himself to the North', as the Viceroy of the projected Kingdom of Ireland.

In the subsequent meeting O'Higgins indicated Cosgrave's anxiety that the proposal not be put by the Free State to Northern Irish Prime Minister James Craig, which 'involved the transfer of a part of the present United Kingdom', without the consent of the British Prime Minister to such a conversation. Accordingly, Amery took O'Higgins to see Baldwin, to whom he expounded on his proposal and noted the altered relationship between Great Britain and Ireland that it would cause. Amery asked how the relationship would be different, aside from Northern Ireland being transferred to a United Ireland that would be called the Kingdom of Ireland rather than the Free State. O'Higgins pointed out that the United Ireland would not merely 'be described as the Kingdom of Ireland, but there should be a separate kingdom, in other words a dual monarchy', much like that of Austria and Hungary before the First World War.

This was more than Amery had understood from their first conversation. He thought it opened up a much wider question and reversed 'the whole principle upon which the constitutional relations of the empire had been defined at the conference'. That principle had allowed 'the freedom of action of the several governments held together by the unity of the Crown, in virtue of which all British subjects throughout the empire shared a common nationality and a mutual loyalty'. But, he insisted, the dissolution of the common nationality and the unity of a single Crown as its emblem 'would affect the whole conception of Imperial unity'.

O'Higgins appreciated 'the theoretical advantages of admitting the unity of the Crown', but noted 'sentiment in Ireland would not be quite met as long as they were British, and not Irish subjects'. Instead, he suggested a special permanent treaty of alliance. Then, in the situation of a war, there would be more ready support from the Irish than if they were asked to involve themselves 'as subjects of the same Crown'. Amery argued that such obligations already existed on the Irish on the basis of both the terms of the Anglo-Irish Treaty of 1921 and their dominion status. However, he had no objection to a special treaty between Ireland and Britain in view of their geographic proximity, which might also 'make it easier for Northern Ireland to come in'. In summary he 'expressed sympathy with all the proposals he had in view, even possibly to the extent of a separate coronation in Dublin, as long as the fundamental unity of the Crown and the practical and sentimental consequences flowing from it throughout the empire were not prejudiced'.

In his memorandum Amery admitted the question might not come up practically for a long time and that Ulster's point of view would have to be considered, and it was 'not at all likely that Ulster would be prepared to accept anything which impaired in any way the unity of the empire or the world-wide status of British subjects which its citizens at present enjoy'. But he did find interesting 'the direction in which Irish opinion is working, and the extent to which the Free State leaders are prepared to go for the sake of Irish unity and stability'. He thought O'Higgins was fearful 'of what may happen in Ireland when the present government finally exhausts its popularity', and was hopeful that Irish unification would 'make any return to power of the extremist faction impossible'.[13]

The Foreign Secretary, Austen Chamberlain, was quite concerned about the impression O'Higgins might have drawn from his conversation with Amery, as O'Higgins' suggestion appeared to run 'directly counter to all that was said and done at the Imperial conference' and that O'Higgins and Craig should be informed 'before the matter goes further, that it is not a proposal which we can countenance'.[14] At that point Amery immediately retreated from any impression of sympathy for O'Higgins' proposal. He insisted that he had 'left Mr O'Higgins under no possible doubt' that he regarded his suggestion of a 'dual monarchy' with separate Irish citizenship 'as directly contrary to the principles agreed upon at the Imperial conference and as unacceptable'. Furthermore, he had written to Craig, warning him of the danger raised by the matter. Craig had replied 'he was entirely opposed *ab initio* to any form of union with the Free State'.[15]

A handwritten memorandum attached by G.G. Whiskard, a principal civil servant in the Irish office that was under Amery, noted certain economic factors that would irritate Northern Ireland: 'The I.F.S. is quite definitely the poorer part of Ireland; and its present taxation is substantially higher and the standard of the social services substantially lower in the I.F.S. than in N.I. N.I could hardly be expected to accept a change which would mean either higher taxation or a lower standard of living or both.' The memorandum also argued that the cessation of Northern Ireland's payment of its Imperial contribution that would follow acceptance of O'Higgins' proposal would mean a loss of five million pounds to the British exchequer, 'a fact which would seriously diminish the popularity of the change with the British taxpayer'![16] In the discussion of the matter at a Cabinet meeting a month later the Prime Minister informed his colleagues 'that nothing more was likely to be heard of this proposal'.

O'Higgins' proposal can, in retrospect, be seen as both premature and anachronistic. He was premature in his effort to appreciate and even appease diversity of tradition within the island of Ireland, and in his awareness of the mutuality of interests, institutions, and traditions of the two islands. All of this is manifest in the complex, multi-tiered structures emerging from the Good Friday Agreement of 1998. However, his suggestion was anachronistic in seeing monarchy as the institution that could overcome those diversities. Republicanism had become too strong a feature of a Catholic Ireland that historically and psychologically should have a monarchist temperament. On the other hand, Northern unionism, which was psychologically more republican, had for the tactical reasons of asserting separation from Catholic 'theocracy' accepted a monarchist position. But even more anachronistic from the perspective of the twenty-first century were the British anxieties about a dual monarchy endangering Commonwealth unity and loss of revenue from Northern Ireland to the British exchequer.

DÁIL REACTION TO IMPERIAL CONFERENCE REPORT

While the Dáil reaction to the Imperial conference report was ultimately favourable, the outspoken criticisms by many deputies suggested the enormous difficulties O'Higgins' dual monarchy idea would have had gaining acceptance if presented publicly in Ireland. Labour Party leader Thomas Johnson was concerned that the report would 'fix in the minds of the participants' and other countries 'this idea of the diplomatic and military unity of the British empire', as well as the notion that its members, while 'within their respective spheres sovereign', were as a whole 'to be treated as a unit when dealing with non-British nations'. He acknowledged the conference admitted the equality of status of the members with final and complete authority 'over their own internal affairs'. But he insisted there remained a distinct inequality in function in external affairs that left 'Great Britain with the controlling hand'. Recalling that the Irish Free State had entered the League of Nations as 'a fully self-governing state with international rights', he feared the conference report would detract from that status since the dominions, of which the Irish Free State was one, had earlier entered the League as part of the

British Empire. The ultimate test for his acceptance of the conference report would be whether non-British nations were 'prepared to recognize the neutrality of the dominions' in the case of war.[17]

Professor William Magennis was unhappy at the affirmation of Ireland's dominion status at the conference since 'the Irish Free State was never established as a dominion', but 'that we were not a colony that had grown to statehood, but that we were a state of long, in fact, of ancient, standing'.[18] Furthermore, O'Higgins' comma in the royal title may have distinguished the Irish Free State from Great Britain, but it also separated the Irish Free State from Northern Ireland, a separation 'as complete, as thorough, as any separation can be made in political matters'.[19]

Farmers' Union deputy Patrick Baxter from Cavan said the conference report had 'not brought any measure of satisfaction whatever to the nationalists of this country'. He asked 'how free we are in our dealings with foreign peoples and with matters here at home. Are we at liberty to say good-bye tomorrow to the British Empire, if we choose?' With regard to the matter of the King's title, he regarded it as unreal, since nationalists believed that 'the United Kingdom of Great Britain and Ireland did not exist'.[20]

O'Higgins sought to rebut the criticisms, especially those of Magennis and Baxter. He suggested that Baxter had been 'under the illusion that we went to London recently to negotiate and conclude a treaty with Great Britain'. But 'a treaty was made five years ago' and they went as 'representatives of the government of the state which is based upon that treaty of five years ago'. Noting that Magennis described the treaty as having been signed under duress, he argued that the point worked both ways. He would not venture to speculate, 'whether or not there was any degree of duress on the British signatories, whether or not it embodied their *summum bonum*, their ideal conception of Anglo-Irish relations'. What was done at the conference was to raise matters that had appeared 'incompatible with the conception of complete co-equality of status'.

O'Higgins sensed in the speeches of Baxter and Magennis an understandable state of mind, that of 'those amongst us who cannot realize their freedom and are unable to raise their heads and look their fellow man in the face, and say we are a free people. The whine of the slave was in those two speeches.' He reasserted the formal status acknowledged by the conference about the relation between Britain and the dominions: 'autonomous communities within the British Empire equal in status in no way subordinate one to another in any aspect of their domestic or external affairs'. On the matter of the separation of the Irish Free State from Northern Ireland by reason of the change in the royal title, he wondered if Magennis was under 'the illusion that the day before the conference began Ireland was a single political entity and that the day on which it ended it was two political entities'. In fact, 'the relations between the Irish Free State and Northern Ireland remain unaffected by anything that happened at the Imperial conference'.[21]

Desmond FitzGerald then spoke on the matters raised by Thomas Johnson – the contradiction between the Irish Free State's participation in the League of Nations as a sovereign state and her membership of the British Empire. He insisted that their entry into the League as 'a fully self-governing state' was 'not incompatible with the term "dominion" as now used', as 'the use of the term "state" does not conceal "dominion status"'. The report to the Assembly on the entry of the Irish Free State had noted 'that the Saorstát was a dominion forming part of the British Empire upon the same conditions as the other dominions already members of the League'. As for Johnson's concern about the Irish Free State becoming involved in a British war, he reiterated that 'the only government empowered to advise the King on affairs of this state is this government'. Obviously, since whether we are at peace or war 'is pre-eminently an affair of this state', then 'presumably the King cannot declare war on behalf of us except on the advice of this government'.[22]

Aside from the rhetorical objections raised by Baxter and Magennis, and the more substantial ones raised by Johnson, the issues did not raise much difficulty, and ultimately became irrelevant through external evolution of the character of the Commonwealth itself and, of course, the internal political developments within Ireland, including neutrality in the Second World War and the secession from the Commonwealth in 1949. The same evolution made O'Higgins' dual monarchy proposal anachronistic. The greatest value of the latter was the essential notion that any unity of Ireland was to be based on consent by the populations of both parts, the central tenet of the modern peace process.

## KEVIN O'HIGGINS AND LADY LAVERY

A matter of great speculation, especially in recent years with the publication of her biography, has been the relationship between

O'Higgins and Hazel Lavery, the American wife of portrait artist Sir John Lavery.[23] She played a significant diplomatic role for the Irish Free State, as their hostess and provider of entry to British society, during the original treaty negotiations and for several years afterwards, including the period of the Boundary Commission controversy. She was a socialite from a wealthy American family named Martyn that had British roots and some uncertain connection with Norman settlers in medieval Connaught. When staying with her widowed mother in Brittany, Hazel fell in love with the widowed Lavery. In face of opposition from her mother, however, the romance failed. Within a couple of years she was married to a young American physician, Edward Trudeau. He died a few months after the wedding while she was pregnant. A year after enduring a difficult pregnancy and the birth of her daughter, Alice, Hazel was back in Europe where Lavery again pursued her hand over her mother's objections. This time, however, Hazel resisted John and instead became attached to an American diplomat, Len Thomas. Their impending matrimony had maternal blessing, but Thomas never came to Chicago where the marriage was to have taken place. Two years later she returned to Europe yet again. When her mother died there in June 1909 she married the Belfast-born and Catholic Lavery the following month at the Brompton Oratory, London's second largest Catholic place of worship. She also followed her ten-year-old daughter Alice in converting to Catholicism in 1914.

She very quickly occupied a central role in fashionable London society comparable to, if not surpassing, her husband's renown as a painter. Her circle of friends and/or guests included H.H. Asquith, Winston and Clementine Churchill, Duff Cooper, Shane Leslie, George Bernard Shaw, and Lord Londonderry. T.P. O'Connor, the Irish Parliamentary Party MP for Liverpool, influenced the couple to sympathize with the home rule cause. By 1916 John Lavery began doing portraits of Irish figures, political, ecclesiastical and social, and later that year painted a canvas of the passing of Roger Casement's death sentence. From then the couple's identity with the Irish nationalist cause was clear, even while they maintained a circle of friends, like Lord Londonderry, of very different political persuasion. When the treaty negotiations were under way, Sir John (who had been knighted in 1918 for his wartime artistic work) did portraits of many of the participants from both sides in the negotiations.

The guest with the most desired status on Hazel's list was the still mysterious and elusive Michael Collins. From his first appearance at

Lavery's studio to sit for a portrait, she became attached to him in a relationship that had a sort of princess–peasant character, although the insurgent leader was too well read and intelligent to be limited to such a label. Collins had become engaged to Kitty Kiernan the day before he went to England for the negotiations, and regardless of the affectionate tone of his letters to Hazel, which included even poetry, and her devotion to him, the relationship may well have been innocent, but pragmatic, as he saw her as extremely helpful in the painful stages of getting as much autonomy for the new state as possible. But her remarkable inclination to show affectionate letters she received from various men, especially men like Collins, fuelled suggestions of an affair, which anti-treaty elements cherished. Her shock at Collins' death assumed almost irrational grief as she had to be persuaded not to wear widow's attire and she made daily pilgrimages to the grave site until she returned to England.

By mid-1923 Hazel Lavery and Kevin O'Higgins had become very close, beginning an extensive and frequent correspondence that lasted until his death. He had first met the Laverys while with Collins in the negotiations about the implementation of the treaty and the transfer of governmental power to the Provisional Government in early 1922. She had passed on to him the outrage of Lord Kenmare about the Free State soldiers' behaviour in Kenmare that year. In 1924 she wrote to Winston Churchill regretting that he seemed to be backing Ulster against the Irish Free State on the boundary question (this was about the time he was releasing Birkenhead's 1922 letter minimizing the mandate of the commission) and enclosed a speech by O'Higgins at Oxford.[24] The years 1923 through 1927 gave O'Higgins numerous occasions to be in London, particularly with regard to the Boundary Commission or the Imperial conferences. He encouraged others in his government, particularly Desmond FitzGerald, to take full advantage of the hospitality and assistance of the Laverys. John and Hazel Lavery also frequently visited Ireland, including a stay at O'Higgins' home in 1923 when attending the Dublin Horse Show. They also were guests many times at the Viceregal Lodge in Phoenix Park.

From all this, rumours flourished about a romantic connection between O'Higgins and Lady Lavery. His earlier biographer, Terence de Vere White, downplayed both that and her relationship with Collins. De Vere White repeated the claim that some romantic passages in Collins' letters to her that were shown to others had been 'interpolated in a woman's handwriting'. He then went on to suggest that 'O'Higgins was destined to take the place of Collins in Lady Lavery's romantic imagination.'[25] But Sinéad McCoole's 1996 biography of Lady Lavery drew in part upon a hitherto unknown cache of letters and materials in the attic of the home of Lady Lavery's late daughter, Alice Gwynn, that included several letters from O'Higgins. Reportedly he had written to her over 300 times, as she herself noted in a letter in which she expressed annoyance at alleged critical commentary on her by O'Higgins' widow. Lady Lavery wrote that she might send Mrs O'Higgins 'half a dozen of the three hundred odd letters I have received from her husband bearing *in no complimentary* manner on married life in general and his own in particular'.[26] However, of the 300 letters, only thirty have survived, as Hazel Lavery destroyed most of them, and of those surviving, there are only fragmentary remains. 'Hazel cut up the letters, in some cases keeping just the envelope or leaving just the corner of a letter with the date. The only complete letter is the first one O'Higgins wrote to her. Apart from this, the most complete letter is about 12 lines. Most of the references are those that illustrate O'Higgins' love.'[27] McCoole does conclude that O'Higgins' letters contrasted with 'his public persona' as 'deeply religious' and suggest he was 'beset by his love for Hazel' and estranged 'from his wife and young family', but she carefully never asserts that the relationship was adulterous.[28]

Significantly, Una O'Higgins O'Malley, his daughter, acknowledged that her 'young and over-stressed father had indeed become enamoured of the lovely Lady Lavery' and that the letters revealed by Sinead McCoole were 'indisputable'. She felt prompted by the revelations to make a public apology in both the press and the radio for the suggestion in de Vere White's book 'that Hazel Lavery had fabricated the story – an allegation which had deeply hurt her daughter Alice (Trudeau) Gwynn...for which I felt the need to express regret.'[29]

The suggestion that a major political leader had been romantically attracted to someone other than his wife did not have the shock effect it would have had a generation earlier, as Ireland of the late twentieth and early twenty-first centuries had become quite used to sexual scandal involving public figures, including clergy. A social liberalism had replaced an earlier puritanism as the national orthodoxy even celebrated the absence of condemnation of the private behaviour of public figures. On the other hand, there appeared to be a certain quiet delight in the suggestion that a pillar of social conservatism and devout Catholicism like O'Higgins might have lived a double life. But, whether from a liberal attitude that sexual misconduct ought to be irrelevant or from a liberal delight in embarrassing the orthodox, the suggestion of O'Higgins having become enamoured of Lady Lavery quickly advanced to the suggestion of adultery, of her being his mistress, or, as one less sympathetic commentator would assert, 'a sultry affair with Hazel Lavery'.[30]

However, going by the only evidence at hand, the parts of letters that have survived, it is not conclusive that the relationship had reached a physical level. Admittedly, in November 1924 O'Higgins could say to Lady Lavery that she was 'the sweetest and most wonderful influence' in his life. The following month, shortly after he had suffered the death of a twelve-day-old son, he commented about his 'poor stunned brain' and that there was 'no happiness for me without you', but also the prayer and lament 'God help me. I loved the highest when I saw it and Fate has placed it out of reach. You have been so sweet with me.'[31] One could interpret the second letter as meaning that as much as he loved her, the consummation of the same was out of reach because of his religious and moral scruples. Later letters in late 1926 and early 1927, when the Laverys were in America, might imply a physical relationship, but given the style of the times and the type of correspondence she received from many others, too much should not be read into them. For instance: 'I am lost and desolate without you...I want you...all the enchantments...sight and sounds and the touch of you', and 'you are my life and my breath my sun and air and wind'. In May 1927, readying for a gruelling election campaign in which the governing party would remain in power, he lamented 'I am so unhappy and I want you, want you, want you'.[32]

One reviewer of the McCoole book suggested the relationship should be interpreted as 'a deep romantic friendship and some flirtation', but not adultery.[33] No doubt, at a minimum, it could be interpreted as an emotional infidelity to Brigid O'Higgins. Such infidelity, however, would have been an understandable failure for a young man drawn from the innocent social circles of middle and upper-middle class Catholic Ireland of the early twentieth century into the vortex of London high society in the 1920s, who was also overwhelmed with public problems and personal tragedies far beyond his years. The latter included the murder of his father in January 1923, his first child being born because of the Civil War in government buildings, where the families of officials had to reside, the death of a son in November 1924 two weeks after birth, and the agony of involvement with the execution of his best man. O'Higgins' involvement with Hazel Lavery no doubt enhanced his rapid political maturation and broadening. Her societal glamour, social ease, mobility, etc., was like nothing he had experienced before and made him the victim of infatuation, in which he was seemingly drawn to qualities in her, which he either did not have, but wished to have; or did have, and suppressed in himself. In either event, his infatuation with her amounted to a desire for something (or someone) he could not have, but with which he would remain almost irrationally preoccupied. Had he actually been involved in a sexual affair, it seems likely it would have had some other repercussions on his life, whether in his family or in his position, especially since the affair would have involved such a departure from his central values. The fact that these did not appear suggests that the relationship did not become physical.

Naturally, admirers of O'Higgins would have preferred to dismiss any consideration of even the romantic attachment, but the letters, as few as they are, make that undeniable. However, the relationship, especially if it did not become physical, could be interpreted as evidence of almost medieval chivalry on his part.

### NOTES

1. D.W. Harkness, *The Restless Dominion: The Irish Free State and the British Commonwealth of Nations, 1921–1931* (New York: New York University Press, 1970), p. 54; Richard Egan, 'A Kingdom of Ireland? Kevin O'Higgins, the Irish Free State and its relations with the British Commonwealth of Nations', UCDA, MA thesis, 2002.
2. Kevin O'Higgins to Brigid Cole O'Higgins, from Geneva, 1925, *O'Higgins Papers*, Book 5. In the same letter, he spoke disparagingly of American observers of the League: 'There are a lot of Americans here buzzing around like bluebottles – darting in and out of the Assembly and its committees. If America is not *in* the League she is all around it unofficially and semi-officially. They are a terrible tribe – terrible in their crudeness, in their ignorance, in their appalling self-complacency.' He and Desmond FitzGerald were given lunch by the Americans at which he gave a talk. Although 'it was difficult to take them seriously', he 'tried to get in a certain amount of publicity about the North-Eastern situation rather in the way of exposition than comment'.
3. Kevin O'Higgins to Brigid Cole O'Higgins, from Geneva, m.d. 1925, *O'Higgins Papers*, Book 5.
4. Egan, 'A Kingdom of Ireland?', pp. 42–7.
5. Kevin O'Higgins to Brigid Cole O'Higgins, October–November, 1926, *O'Higgins Papers*, Book 5.
6. Harkness, *The Restless Dominion*, p. 87.

7. *Imperial conference 1926, Summary of Proceedings* (London: His Majesty's Stationery Office, 1926), pp. 15–18.
8. Amery, L.S., *My Political Life* (1953), II, p. 385, quoted in Hyam, Ronald and Martin, Ged, 'The Irish Free State and the Evolution of the Commonwealth, 1921–1949', *Reappraisals in British Imperial History* (Toronto: Macmillan of Canada, 1975), pp. 214–15.
9. Harkness, *The Restless Dominion*, pp. 90–1. *The Irish Times*, 8 November 1926 and Denis Gwynn, *The Irish Free State, 1922–1927* (Dublin: Macmillan, 1928), p. 112.
10. Kevin O'Higgins to Brigid Cole O'Higgins, October 1926, *O'Higgins Papers*, Book 5.
11. De Vere White, *Kevin O'Higgins*, p. 225.
12. Kevin O'Higgins to Brigid Cole O'Higgins, 17 November 1926, *O'Higgins Papers*, Book 5.
13. 'Proposed Creation of a Kingdom of Ireland', *Memorandum by the Secretary of State for Dominion Affairs* (13 December 1926), C.P. 416, PRO DO 117/51.
14. *Memorandum by the Secretary of State for Foreign Affairs* (18 December 1926), *Ibid*.
15. *Note by the Secretary of State for Dominon Affairs* (22 December 1926), *Ibid*.
16. *Ibid*.
17. *Dáil Éireann*, XVII (15 December 1926), 734–50.
18. *Ibid*., 757-60.
19. *Ibid*. (16 December 1926), 887–90.
20. *Ibid*., 891–4.
21. *Ibid*., 895–9.
22. *Ibid*., 905–10.
23. Sinead McCoole, *Hazel: A Life of Lady Lavery, 1880–1935* (Dublin: Lilliput, 1996).
24. Lady Lavery to Winston S. Churchill (10 November 1924), *Churchill Papers*, CHAR 2/136/30–34.
25. De Vere White, *Kevin O'Higgins*, p. 93.
26. McCoole, *Hazel*, p. 143. Hazel Lavery to Thomas Bodkin (19 February 1929).
27. Sinead McCoole to author, 25 February 1997.
28. McCoole, *Hazel*, p. 128.
29. Una O'Higgins O'Malley, *From Pardon and Protest. Memoirs from the Margins* (Galway: Arlen House, 2001), p. 14.
30. John Regan, 'Review of *Hazel: A Life of Lady Lavery, 1880–1935*', *The Irish Times* (11 September 1996), p. 12; Regan, *The Irish Counter-Revolution*, pp. 217, 267; Uinseann MacEoin, *The IRA in the Twilight Years: 1923–1948* (Dublin: Argenta Publications, 1997), p. 136.
31. Kevin O'Higgins to Hazel Lavery (4 November 1924 and 17 December 1924), McCoole, *Hazel*, pp. 118–19.
32. Kevin O'Higgins to Hazel Lavery (27 November 1926 and 4 February 1927 and 6 May 1927), *Ibid*., pp. 128–9.
33. Charles Lysaght, *Irish Historical Studies*, xxx, 120 (November 1997), pp. 629–32.

# 9

# Liquor, Censorship, Divorce, Women Jurors, and Constitutional Revision

### INTOXICATING LIQUOR ACT 1924

W ITH A PERSPECTIVE not dissimilar to many current commentators on the Irish social situation, O'Higgins saw intemperance to be at the root of such challenges to social stability as disorderly behaviour, indebtedness, petty crime, and family abuse. Accordingly he directed considerable police energy to enforcing existing liquor legislation and advanced new legislation to regulate more tightly the drink trade. As was inevitable whenever a government attempts to regulate public behaviour or interferes with substantial economic interest such as that of the brewers, distillers, and publicans, that commitment cost him and his party severely in terms of popularity. He desired new legislation because he regarded the existing legislation governing the drink trade, which had been passed under British rule, as inadequate. He thought the magistracy, during the twenty or more years of Irish Parliamentary Party ascendancy in local government, had tended to be over-generous in issuing liquor licences, paying more heed to that substantial source of support for the Parliamentary Party, the drink trade, than to social concerns.

The Dáil had passed legislation prior to its dissolution in the summer of 1923 that limited the general hours of opening for the drink trade from 9 am to 9:30 pm, extended the powers of the police and the courts, increased fines, and established tougher criteria for the issuance of new licences for sale of liquor. The Seanad had rejected the same, but the Dáil overcame their rejection on 29 April 1924. But before the measure had been forwarded to the Governor General for his signature, O'Higgins, on 30 May 1924, introduced a more comprehensive measure calling for uniform hours of sale throughout the country, no opening hours on Sundays other than the existing 2 to 5 pm in the cities of Dublin, Cork, Limerick and Waterford, and the extension of the universal closing on Christmas to be extended to Good Friday and St Patrick's Day.[1] The colourful practice of allowing the sale of drink at any hour to *bona fide* travellers (those who had travelled more than three miles) would continue, but henceforth not between 7 am and 1 pm on Sundays and at no time on the three holy days. It also increased penalties for illegal sales by unlicensed premises or 'shebeens' and the sale of intoxicating liquor on credit or to those less than 18 years of age would be prohibited. Girls under 18 would not be allowed to work as barmaids. 'Mixed trading', that is the sale of anything in the licensed premises other than food being consumed on site, tobacco, matches, and table water, would be prohibited after 25 September 1925. The hours for serving drink in private clubs would be made identical to those of public houses, except for allowing sale between 1 and 10 pm on Sundays and the three holy days.[2]

O'Higgins said the bill was 'somewhat more comprehensive' than the still-unsigned measure of the previous year. He admitted, however, that the Bill did not deal with the central problem, that there were 'far too many licensed establishments'. He hoped a commission would be established 'to go into the question of how best the number of licences might be reduced', as most would agree 'that 15,000 public houses in the Saorstát' (one for every 200 people, in contrast to one for 400 in England and one for 695 in Scotland) was 'far in excess of the reasonable requirements of the inhabitants'. Pending a report from such a commission, the proposed measure was 'a reasonable measure of temperance reform'.[3]

The Intoxicating Liquor Bill provoked extensive and varied opposition, even from within the ranks of the government's own supporters and from ordinarily friendly independents. Paradoxically, the leader of the opposition, Thomas Johnson of the Labour Party, supported the legislation, but thought it should have been more severe.[4]

An example of populist, self-serving opposition was that of deputy John Daly for Cork East, whose political designation was Independent Labour and who was a publican. He did 'not agree with the general terms of this Bill at all', although he did agree with the minister that 'a girl under the age of eighteen should not be allowed inside any counter for her health's sake'. If young girls were not allowed to work behind bars, he noted 'we will have better athletes in the country, for the girls will make better mothers'. He objected to concessions allowed to the cities, such as the three hours of opening on Sundays. On the other hand, if these were given to the rural places, it would almost make him 'fall into line with the Minister for Justice'. Not allowing the sale of liquor to *bona fide* travellers until one o'clock on Sundays was 'a great hardship on the people in country districts', as the people from where he came from, especially those coming into town from the country, 'can hardly go to Mass at all without a drop'. He elaborated that 'from time immemorial' the farmers had travelled to church from more than three miles and 'put up their horses in the stables...built for them years ago by our fathers'. As an improvement for Sunday openings, he suggested, 'that a country public house should get permission to open for three hours, say, from eleven until two. We have Mass at 12 o'clock. You would have an hour before Mass and an hour after.' He went on to lament that 'Alas, we are asked not to taste a tint of drink on St Patrick's Day. Our fathers would turn in the grave if they heard it. Many of them got their heads smashed on St Patrick's Day, and it would not be a St Patrick's Day unless they came home half "boozed".'[5]

The criticisms of another Independent Labour deputy, John Lyons, from Longford–Westmeath, were similar: too early a Saturday closing would prompt drinkers to take drink home, where children might get the taste of it. Lyons even argued that 16-year-old girls should be able to serve in a bar. The teenage barmaid served three years without pay as an apprentice for which 'privilege' her parents would have to pay a fee. Only after that would she make any money to compensate her parents 'for having reared her'. The proposed legislation, which would delay the beginning of her apprenticeship until she was 18, would keep her from being able to make any money until she would be 21. But by then 'some lucky or unlucky man' would come along and 'the barmaid gets married', leaving the parents uncompensated, although in most cases they were 'poor people who cannot afford to send their children to a university in order that they may become priests, doctors, or solicitors', and whose only alternative had been 'to put them inside a counter and let God do for them as God did for themselves'.[6]

A more thoughtful objection came from deputy Bryan Cooper, independent for Dublin, reflective of a different class bias than that of country publican Daly or Lyons. He criticized the Bill for its 'rather excessive rigidity', as it did not make 'enough allowance for exceptional cases'. The Bill treated all licensed houses on the same basis, but he thought it to be 'rather ridiculous to apply exactly the same standards to the Shelbourne Hotel and to a public house, say, in Clifden, or Cahirciveen'. He thought there should be a variety of types of licenses, including a distinct one for hotels, for restaurants, and for clubs, in addition to the traditional licenses for public houses and for off-license sales, with flexible rules for the different types of licenses. Cooper regarded the 'uniform rigidity' of the Bill as 'due to the minister's Napoleonic cast of mind', as he believed 'the minister would derive great pleasure from feeling that on every Saturday night at twenty-five minutes past 9 o'clock the last tumbler is being emptied in every public house in Ireland; at twenty-eight minutes past 9, all over Ireland, that thousands of mouths are being wiped after the last drink, and that at thirty minutes past 9 the keys in the locks of thousands of public houses are grating'.[7]

The difficulties O'Higgins had in achieving his desired legislative goals were manifest in the objections of many deputies in his own party. Patrick McGoldrick, Cumann na nGaedheal deputy for Donegal, for instance, thought that the limited Sunday *bona fide* rules should also apply on St Patrick's Day, rather than the absolute prohibition of sale. He regarded the attempt to impose structural separation between the liquor trade and other trade, that is, the effort to stop 'mixed trading' within the same premises, as being based on 'the greatest myth that could possibly be invented, that mixed trading promoted intemperance'. Another Cumann na nGaedheal, Louis J. D'Alton, deputy for Tipperary, opposed the linking of the national festival, St Patrick's Day, with Christmas and Good Friday, and asked why the Irish people should be told that they could not enjoy it the same way other nationalities do and as the Irish do in London, where re-unions attended by prominent people 'continue until an advanced hour in the morning'?[8]

Opposition within the ranks of the government party forced O'Higgins to allow a free vote on the issue of mixed trading.[9] He was further disappointed in the committee stage when an amendment dropping complete closing on St Patrick's Day passed fifty to thirty-three. While he admitted 'it was customary to refresh the tender plant of patriotism in the local taverns' on that day, he questioned, 'whether that particular brand of patriotism, which needed to be so refreshed, was good for the country'.[10] Then further consideration of the measure was postponed until after the summer recess. The Governor General finally signed the 1923 legislation making it the operative law for the duration.[11]

When the Dáil resumed consideration in October, numerous amendments were advanced.[12] The most decisive amendment was that moved by John Daly, supported by Patrick Shaw, Cumann na nGaedheal deputy for Longford–Westmeath and Richard H. Beamish, an independent business deputy for Cork City and a brewer who had accepted the Cumann na nGaedheal whip, which would drop the section requiring a structural separation for the sale of liquor in houses of mixed trade. Although reconciled to defeat on the issue, O'Higgins justified such regulations for the trade, describing the holders of liquor licences as 'monopolists' to whom the Dáil should be able to say that women and children 'going in on other business should not be put into the position of having to force their way into a shop through men drinking their pints', and men, going in on other business, should 'not be subjected to the temptation of prolonging their stay and spending more time and more money than they had intended to spend by being subjected to the temptation of refreshing themselves'. The existing situation had arisen from the shortsightedness of the magistrates of the old regime who had 'dealt out licenses to their friends or neighbours in a light-hearted, irresponsible, foolishly genial kind of way'. The man who received one of those licenses quickly discovered 'there was scarcely enough business to go around', and as a result, had a local carpenter put up another counter, with which he could proceed 'to traffic in other commodities'.[13] Since O'Higgins had allowed a free vote on the issue, the amendment was carried by a vote of forty to eleven. In his negative vote O'Higgins was joined only by Desmond FitzGerald and Eoin MacNeill in his own party, and significant independents such as Bryan Cooper and Darrell Figgis, Trinity College members Ernest Alton, William Thrift, and James Craig, Businessmen's Party members William Hewat and John Good, and Thomas Johnson, the Labour Party leader.[14]

The Seanad was favourable to the legislation; some members even demanded that it be more stringent. Senator Douglas successfully moved to reverse the Dáil's removal of the requirement for complete closing on St Patrick's Day from the Bill.[15] The Seanad also voted twelve to eight to include the requirement for structural separation of trades in mixed houses, although O'Higgins, while agreeing that mixed trading was an evil, opposed the amendment as it might endanger the rapid passage of the whole bill.[16] As expected, the Dáil rejected the Seanad's amendments to close public houses on St Patrick's Day and to require structural separation in mixed trading houses. Richard H. Beamish noted how easy it was for the Senators, 'with their cellars full of wines and spirits and plenty of soda water', to discuss the issue, while the 'ordinary workman, farmer or labourer with very little money in his pocket cannot afford to order in the drink which is probably enjoyed in Senatorial houses'.[17]

## INTOXICATING LIQUOR ACT 1927

In 1925 O'Higgins appointed an Intoxicating Liquor Commission to inquire into what he regarded as the central problem: 'whether the existing number of licenses for the sale of intoxicating liquor is in excess of reasonable requirements'. If they were in excess, the commission was 'to make recommendations by which an adequate reduction may be effected on an equitable basis', and 'to review the state of the law regulating the sale and consumption of intoxicating liquors'. J.J. Horgan, the chairman of the Cork Harbour Board, a coroner for County Cork, and a strong Parliamentary Party supporter before the First World War, was the chairman of the commission. Other members were three TDs: Richard Wilson, Farmers' Union deputy for Wicklow; Sir James Craig, MD, Independent for Trinity College; and Seamus Murphy, Cumann na nGaedheal deputy for Louth; two Labour Party Senators: John O'Farrell, the party leader in the Seanad, and Mrs Eileen Costello, from Tuam and an early Gaelic League activist; J.J. McElligott, a civil servant who was Assistant Secretary, and later Secretary in the Department for Finance, and ultimately Governor of the Central Bank and Director; and Very Rev. J. Flanagan, the administrator of the Pro-Cathedral in Dublin.[18]

The commission recommended that the law and the classification of licenses be simplified and the number of licenses be reduced so that there not be more than one for every 400 inhabitants in any local court district. District Courts would determine which licenses were not to be renewed because of superfluity and local compensating authorities would determine the amount to be awarded non-renewed licenses on the basis of the difference of the value of the house with and without the license. The compensation would be financed by a levy 'on all remaining license holders' in the same district. The commission also recommended three categories of hours of operations: in exempted cities, that is Dublin, Cork, Limerick and Waterford, hours would be 10 am to 3 pm and 5pm to 10 pm on weekdays, but with a 9:30 pm closing on Saturdays; in towns of over 5,000 population the hours would be the same, except there would be no midday closing from 3 pm to 5 pm; everywhere else, the weekday opening and closing would be an hour earlier, that is, from 9 am to 9 pm, and an 8:30 pm closing on Saturday. The four cities could keep their Sunday opening hours of 2 to 5 pm, but elsewhere there was to be no Sunday traffic other than *bona fide* traffic, that is, the serving of a customer who had travelled a certain distance. On Sundays that would be limited to the hours of 1 to 3 pm and 5 to 7 pm, and would not be allowed in the four cities at all. The distance required to establish that one was a traveller was to be extended from three to six miles, and from the cities to ten miles. The Sunday rules would apply to St Patrick's Day. The commission did not share O'Higgins' concern about mixed trading, in which it saw no evidence of abuse consequent from the mixed trading.[19]

On 8 February 1927 O'Higgins introduced legislation that generally adhered to the recommendations of the commission. Since a general election was imminent, it was an inopportune time to bring forward a measure likely to generate considerable opposition, particularly from within the Cumann na nGaedheal Party. But the most celebrated opponent of the measure was William Redmond, the son of the late Parliamentary Party leader, who was an independent deputy for Waterford. Among his many objections was that the ten-mile limit for *bona fide* customers from cities meant that the citizens of the city of Waterford would not be able to get a drink in the resort town of Tramore which was less than ten miles away.[20]

A predictable populist criticism of the legislation came from the same two Independent Labour TDs, who had opposed the 1924 measure, John Daly for Cork East and John Lyons for Longford–Westmeath. Combining concern for the publican with allegations of class bias, John Daly saw the change from three to ten miles minimum requirement to qualify as a *bona fide* traveller able to order drink as proof that the legislation was 'a class Bill, a rich man's Bill'. While that requirement could easily be met by the man with a motor car or a bicycle, it would be inconvenient for the man who would have to walk to where he would get the refreshment he would want after a week of work. He interpreted the required closing in the middle of the day in cities as 'only a trap for the police to catch the publican'.[21] Reasoning on the assumption that home drinking was done by the wealthy, John Lyons noted there was 'nothing in the Bill to prevent a man taking a case of whiskey or stout to his own home and drinking it night and day, even on Sundays, Christmas Day and Patrick's Day'. But the Bill would 'prevent the ordinary man who has to earn his living by the sweat of his brow, from getting a drink when he requires it', which implied the workers only drank in public houses.[22]

Despite vigorous opposition, signs of the measure's ultimate passage came when Cumann na nGaedheal members such as P. W. Shaw for Longford–Westmeath, P.J. Egan for Leix–Offaly, and George Wolfe for Kildare, fell into line in support. They did ask, however, for certain modifications in the Bill, such as having the state as well as the surviving licensees contribute to the compensation burden.[23] But Thomas Johnson, the Labour Party leader, thought the Bill ought to be withdrawn for the very reason that there would be concessions such as those requested by the likes of Shaw, Egan, Wolfe, and Beamish.[24]

O'Higgins displayed some flexibility in accepting requests by his party colleague, P.J. Egan for Leix–Offaly to split the difference between the Bill's 8:30 pm Saturday closing in rural areas and the requested 9:30 pm closing and to allow mixed-trade establishments to be able to sell non-intoxicating products at 9 am.[25] Another interesting display of flexibility, or, more likely, awareness of possible defeat, was O'Higgins' willingness to make the vote on the proposed two-hour midday closing for the four cities a free vote, not binding on government supporters. Fearing that the 3 to 5 pm closing would be defeated, O'Higgins indicated he would accept a one-hour closing, but that the mixed trade houses would also have to close for that one hour, which would not be the case if there was a two-hour closing.[26] An amendment that called for a one-hour closing from 2:30 to 3:30 pm carried by a free vote, although O'Higgins himself voted against it. He would have preferred a two-hour break, but accepted the shorter midday break since his experience was 'that you have got to ask twice what you want and then there will be enthusiasm and unanimity almost in favour of the thing you want'.[27]

On the issue of the *bona fide* trade, that is the ability to sell intoxicants to legitimate travellers during hours when liquor ordinarily could not be sold, O'Higgins was unresponsive to amendments that would have given the privilege to the cities on Sundays, in addition to their privilege of having limited hours of regular service, from 2 pm to 5 pm. Aware of the abuse connected with the *bona fide* traffic, however, he wondered if it might 'not be worthwhile, a good exchange, to accept a limited uniform opening throughout the state [on Sundays] in exchange for the complete abolition of the *bona fide* traffic'. But his offer was not taken up.[28] He also accepted amendments lessening the distance requirement to determine if a traveller could be served liquor to five rather than ten miles from cities and to three rather than six miles in rural areas.[29]

The legislation allowed the removal of endorsements from licenses, that is, indications that the law had been violated on some matter by the holder, if it could be demonstrated that the offence provoking such was of a trivial nature. But the removal could only be authorized by a Circuit Court judge. O'Higgins did not want to vest the power 'in the lower court, nearer to the people, subject to forms of pressure from which a Circuit Court Judge is somewhat more remote, the same degree of discretion' as would be vested in the latter. He knew 'the hundred and one forms of pressure that can be brought to bear on justices – on the relatives of justices, aye, beyond the forbidden degrees of kindred – when a licensing prosecution is pending'. Accordingly, 'if there is to be any discretion in the District Court', he wanted it 'to be of the most limited character'.[30]

Another issue was what would be the territorial unit for drawing revenues from surviving licensed premises to finance the compensation for those licenses declared redundant. Patrick Baxter, Farmers' Union deputy for Cavan, moved to have the territorial unit changed from the 340 licensing areas to the twenty-six counties of the Irish Free State. William Davin, Labour deputy for Leix–Offaly, preferred instead to regard the entire Free State as a single unit. Professor Magennis feared that if the total cost of compensation was to be borne by the local unit, it would mean that 'because that district has suffered in the past this fearful infliction of too many facilities for the drinking of intoxicants it will be further penalised by the survivors having to bear an undue share of the compensation'. O'Higgins acknowledged that 'administrative convenience would lie entirely in the direction of the state unit or any larger unit' than in the 340 districts called for by the Bill. But he pointed out that extinction of licenses would proceed where there was the greatest redundancy, and that there would be a great outcry if most of the extinctions were in one end of a county and the traders in the rest of the county would have to pay 'without benefit'. As to Magennis's point that the individual in the area with greatest redundancy was the least able to pay for the compensation, he noted that, 'where redundancy is greatest the individual unit is least valuable and the burden will be proportionately small'. That is, the amount to be raised from surviving units to compensate the closed houses would not be as much.[31] The bill was approved by the Seanad, with minor technical amendments and one of substance, which would make St Patrick's Day one of complete closing comparable to Good Friday and Christmas Day.[32] This time the Dáil accepted a St Patrick's Day closing, but not until after hearing complaints by deputy (and publican) John Daly, that, unlike Good Friday, which was 'a day of sorrow', St Patrick's Day 'should be observed, I think, as a day of joy in this country'.[33]

The passage of the legislation has to be seen as a tribute both to O'Higgins' practicality as measured by his willingness to compromise on issues like the length of the midday closing and his political courage in being willing to take up the issue on the virtual eve of a general election in which his own party would suffer significantly in no small part because of the legislation.

## DIVORCE AND CENSORSHIP

Kevin O'Higgins' position on the indissolubility of marriage in Ireland and literary and artistic censorship – issues that some regard as the defining marks of both the Irish Free State and subsequent Irish governments up until the last quarter of the twentieth century – did not deviate from the prevailing orthodoxy, although he was not as outspoken on these matters as he had been on other issues.

With regard to the divorce issue, O'Higgins spoke briefly seconding a motion by President William T. Cosgrave to inhibit consideration of Bills of Divorce by the Oireachtas. Matrimonial issues in Ireland at the time were still governed by the Matrimonial Causes Marriage Act passed by the Westminster parliament in 1870. The Act had established a Court for Matrimonial Causes and Matters to deal with matters of divorce *a mensa et thoro* (that is, separation from bed and board), suits of nullity of marriage, and other matrimonial matters that previously were under the jurisdiction of the Ecclesiastical Court of the Church of Ireland. Unlike a comparable Act for England passed in 1857, the Act affecting Ireland did not enable the new court to decree the dissolution of a marriage, which meant that divorce in Ireland could only be granted by a private Act of parliament, or, after 1922, by the Oireachtas. Since the Free State parliament had not yet established standing orders on matrimonial matters, private bills on such could be introduced to the Dáil. In anticipation of such happening, President William T. Cosgrave moved that the Joint Committee on Standing Orders be requested to submit additional standing orders to 'prevent the introduction of Bills of Divorce *a vinculo matrimonii*. He had no doubt 'that the majority of the people in this country regard the bond of marriage as a sacramental bond which is incapable of being dissolved'.[34]

In O'Higgins' brief remarks seconding the motion, he said the basic question was whether 'the Dáil believes that it is within its competence to consider a Bill which purports to dissolve the marriage tie so that the parties will be free to re-marry'. He himself did not believe it had, nor did he think the great majority believed it had. Accordingly, he considered it 'a saving of the time of the Oireachtas' to vote on 'a matter like this in the abstract' once and for all, rather than 'have a farce perpetuated from time to time' of having futile private Bills of divorce being symbolically introduced.[35]

While O'Higgins did not play a central role in the discussion of the issue, other than supporting Cosgrave, his attitude on divorce corresponded to the prevailing popular view of the period. This is borne out by the arguments of two Protestant members of the Dáil who took opposing views on the specific motion. Professor William Thrift, who sat for Trinity College (Dublin University), opposed the measure 'with very great reluctance'. His personal views were 'against the setting up of any facilities to obtain divorce'. However, he feared the motion had 'the effect of imposing on the whole population the religious views of the majority of the population'. He regarded as 'one of the essential principles of the constitution' the guarantee of 'freedom of conscience and the free profession and practice of religion', and noted how in the past those whose conscience permitted them to divorce and remarry 'were able to do so by a certain by-law in accordance with civil law'. He also feared that the 'passing of this motion will raise up one more barrier against a possible union between the North of Ireland and the South of Ireland'.[36] On the other hand, George Wolfe, a Cumann na nGaedheal deputy for Kildare, supported the resolution. He alluded to experience in other countries where divorce had worked to loosen the bonds of marriage. He feared that the freedom Thrift had been anxious not to curb 'may degenerate into licence', and argued, 'that it is the giving of the facilities for loosening the marriage tie which has increased the demand for the dissolution of marriage'. With regard to the Northern people, he did not believe it was an issue 'that will prevent us from coming together', for 'a big number of them are as much against divorce as we are'.[37] The measure passed by acclamation, but during the Seanad consideration, William Butler Yeats opposed it with his celebrated defence of the Anglo-Irish as a proud people who could not be dismissed.[38]

Further evidence of O'Higgins' identity with the social and cultural conservatism of the period was his May 1925 proposal to broaden the existing Censorship of Films Act. The original Act itself had established an official censor for films to be shown within the Free State. However, the measure did not extend to the advertisements for films. O'Higgins, as a consequence, sought 'to extend the censorship to these posters and advertisements in connection with the film trade'. The advertisements were usually 'either actual photographs extracted from the films' or were 'posters which may or may not represent actual incidents in the film'. The latter possibility, provocative advertising suggestive of more than the film actually contained, had disturbed a number of people, especially clergymen, and was thought to have done 'considerable harm'.[39]

Evidence of the prevailing approbation at the time of censorship were the remarks of Thomas Johnson, who regretted that it was not also applied to printed advertisements. He noted that 'the exploitation of the new science and art of pictorial presentation by means of moving pictures is in the hands of people ... who have not any long-established tradition of decency', like the ordinary publishing world for whom censorship would be inappropriate. He feared there was

> within the world of films, on the exploitation side – that is, on the publication side – a large number of people who are prepared to use their opportunities to excite curiosity of an unpleasant kind and that the facts are whatever we might like in this matter, that that must be restrained and that the censorship will be bound to apply to advertisements which are not merely pictorial.[40]

Later in the year Patrick O'Duffy, Cumann na nGaedheal deputy for Monaghan, asked about the advisability of 'an official censor to deal with the imported Sunday and weekly newspapers', which he regarded as 'indecent'. O'Higgins replied that existing legislation provided ample powers 'to deal with the sale and distribution of obscene literature', but he believed the deputy was using the word 'indecent' in a very wide sense, and 'was afraid there are serious difficulties in the way of the state interfering to enforce a censorship such as the deputy requests'. What the deputy objected to was 'a matter more for public opinion than for an official or officials appointed by the state'.[41] His response suggested O'Higgins had no objections to censorship, but had a commonsensical disposition about the limitations and practicality of such efforts.

In 1926 and 1927, however, O'Higgins took steps that led to, in retrospect, a most embarrassing institution that contravened common sense. He appointed a Committee on Evil Literature on 12 February 1926 to consider in the interest of public morality extending 'the existing powers of the state to prohibit or restrict the sale and circulation of printed matter'. On the committee were two deputies, independent Prof. William Thrift representing Trinity College and Thomas O'Connell, Labour, from Galway. Other members were Very Reverend James Dempsey, a Catholic priest, Rev. J. Sinclair Stevenson, a Protestant clergyman, and Robert Donovan, UCD Professor of English.

The committee reported to O'Higgins on 28 December 1926 that they had invited various organizations of a religious, educational and youth character to submit evidence or delegate witnesses. Among the groups who did so were the Irish Christian Brothers, the Irish National Teachers' Organization, the Dublin Christian Citizenship Council, the Catholic Truth Society, representatives of booksellers and newsagents, the Department of Posts and Telegraphs, Customs and Excise, and the Garda. Different witnesses raised concern about such matters as the ineffectiveness of existing legislation because of 'the narrow technical meaning attached by the courts to the terms indecent and obscene', 'the wide circulation in Ireland of imported newspapers' that emphasized sensationalism 'of an immoral and degrading character', advertising of books and pamphlets 'advocating' contraceptives and the circulation of pseudo-medical books advertising the same and other remedies for sexual diseases and disorders, the use of those advertisements to obtain mailing lists for selling 'indecent' materials, 'the circulation of books, novels, and magazines, containing fiction of a demoralizing kind', and 'the sale of indecent pictures and photographs'.[42]

The committee reported that, 'all of the witnesses advocated a new definition of the terms [indecent and obscene] so as to include not only what was grossly "indecent" and "obscene", but what was generally demoralising and offensive in sexual matters to the moral ideas of the community generally'. The committee recognized the difficulty in applying the criminal law, except where the standard for testing the offence was absolute, acknowledging that 'ideas of decency vary, not merely between country and country, but between individual and individual'. They added that 'in the case of publications it is possible to distinguish between those which are written with an obviously obscene intent, and those into which the gross or indecent enters only incidentally as reflecting the reality of life', but they noted that 'it cannot be easy for a judge or magistrate in applying the criminal law with its penalties to draw a definite line'. Accordingly, the committee thought the remedy for the Irish Free State should 'be sought in a scheme of prevention, rather than the application of the criminal law' since so many of the publications complained about were imported and because 'any part of their contents taken separately could not be regarded as a breach of the law', even though 'taken as a whole are obviously designed to cater for a morbid taste and curiosity, and to satisfy an unhealthy sensationalism'.

They had in mind weekly British newspapers 'in which the sensational crimes, divorce cases and prosecutions for sex offences of the week preceding publication are collected in a mass and provide three-fourths of the matter for reading contained in the papers'. Newsagents, booksellers, and stationers had indicated a 'readiness to abstain from the sale of any publication which the authorities might warn them was of a demoralising character'. Therefore, rather than wait until the publication arrived at the ports of the Irish Free State, the committee suggested extending to the Minister for Justice, assisted by 'a permanent committee . . . of nine to twelve persons representative of the religious, educational and literary or artistic opinion of the Irish public', the power 'to prohibit generally the circulation of future issues of any newspaper, magazine or other publication where it is found to be usually of a debasing or demoralising kind'. That committee would advise the minister, whose authority would be final. The report alluded to examples in Canada, South Africa, and Australia, where undesirable publications were prohibited entry at the frontier. Significantly, the grounds for prohibition were to 'be strictly limited to the case of publications undesirable from the point of view of public morality' so that censorship would not be exercised because of 'the political or economic opinions expressed or advocated'.[43]

Another area of concern to the committee was 'propaganda in favour of the limitation of families by the unnatural prevention of conception'. They noted that, at that time, twenty-four American states made such publications a crime, as did Canada and New Zealand. Some witnesses had said that support of the contraceptive propaganda was 'beginning to exist in the Saorstát', and the practices recommended were being 'followed by a limited number of persons'. Accordingly, 'it would be an unwarranted interference with individual liberty to prohibit the practices'. But there was the issue of 'the dangers consequential upon a propaganda conducted indiscriminately, the books and pamphlets of which are uncontrolled in their contents and distribution, and are scattered abroad among the young and unmarried as well as among those married and of mature age'. These dangers were even acknowledged by witnesses 'who maintained a reserved attitude upon the question of the total prohibition'. To that end, the committee recommended prohibiting the publication of advertisements 'relating to any complaint or infirmity arising from or relating to sexual intercourse, or to nervous debility or female irregularities, or which might reasonably be construed as relating to any illegal medical treatment or illegal operation'.[44]

Lastly, the committee turned to the matter of books. They recognized that even in the classics, ancient and modern, there were 'subjects indelicate and indecent', but agreed that 'scarcely anybody proposes to ban the classics'. Protection should be provided 'from literary influences pernicious to the immature' not by state censorship, but by that exercised in 'the home, the school, and through the spiritual director'. Literature can never be restricted 'to writings that meet the standard to be observed in works intended only for the youth and the maiden'. On the other hand, 'many contemporary writers exercise a licence much less controlled by concern for the accepted moral standards than did their predecessors. In their choice of subject and in the mode of treatment there are far less reserve and reticence than were formerly observed.' The only existing limitation would be if the matter was 'obscene' in the technical sense in which the law was authoritatively interpreted. The committee recognized the difficulty in framing a law 'prohibiting books of an immoral tendency that would not impose restrictions on authors from which literature has ever been free', but believed 'it ought not be difficult for a group of citizens selected for their culture, good sense and respect for morality to recognise books written with a corrupt intent, or aiming at notoriety and circulation by reason of their appeal to sensual or corrupt instincts and passions'.[45]

O'Higgins received and passed on to the Executive Council the report of the committee and its recommendations that would require legislation, and asked approbation 'to proceed with a bill, to be introduced in the Autumn [after the forthcoming national elections], giving effect to the recommendations'. Among the specific recommendations were: 'a wider definition of the terms indecent and obscene'; legislation restrictive of reporting of marital and sexual courts matters; the creation of a board 'to advise the Minister for Justice as to any publications that, in the opinion of the board, are demoralizing', whose circulation he could prohibit; 'prohibition of the sale or circulation, except to authorised persons, of birth control publications'; search warrants not needing 'previous proof that an offence against the Obscene Publication Act has been committed'; increased penalties, and inclusion of advertisements for contraceptives as an offence in the Indecent Advertisements Act, 1889; power for the Customs and Postal authorities 'to stop the importation and circulation of publications prohibited'; and extending the definition of indecent and obscene to 'prints, photographs and postcards'.[46]

The legislation was not passed until 1929, two years after O'Higgins' death. It is questionable whether the zealous character of the censorship board created by that legislation reflected the more thoughtful, but admittedly scarcely libertarian, position of the committee itself or of O'Higgins.

JURIES BILL

In 1927 O'Higgins was the central figure advancing a position that, from a twenty-first century perspective, would be regarded as politically incorrect, but again scarcely out of keeping with prevailing Irish opinion in the 1920s. The issue was women as jurors. British legislation in 1919 had extended the duty of serving on juries to women as well as men. That law continued to apply in the Irish Free State until 1924 when legislation allowed women to exempt themselves from jury duty. In 1927 O'Higgins introduced a Juries Bill with a provision to exclude women altogether from jury duty, that is, to return to the pre-1919 situation. His justification for the proposal was administrative rather than ideological. He did not argue that 'women are incapable of rendering reasonably good service on juries'. Rather, he thought it not worth 'all the administrative expense', that is, to go through 'the process of putting all women on the jury list, sending them circulars, asking them whether they wish to serve or not, and then attempting to provide separate accommodation in the courts for women jurors', if most exempted themselves from service. He insisted that 'the great bulk of women are unwilling, most reluctant, to serve on juries', and noted that fewer than forty women had served among the thousands of jurors in the year 1925. He also alluded to 'extremely unpleasant cases...cases of indecent assault, of rape, and, occasionally, of sodomy', which contained matters 'one would not like to discuss with the feminine members of one's own family', and on that basis the exemption of women officials or stenographers from duty in such cases ought also apply to jurors.[47]

His proposal met with severe criticism. Thomas Johnson insisted that the constitutional position was that 'privileges and obligations must go together for all citizens', and that 'jury service is one of the corollaries of voting power'. He acknowledged that there were 'many cases in which one would not like to have women serving as jurors', but 'if a woman in the dock or a woman in the witness box has to suffer all the indignities, indelicacies and indecencies that come out in court...it is not too much to expect a woman in the jury box to undergo the same ordeal'. He saw the proposal as 'undesirable' and 'creating another sense of grievance amongst one sex in the community – one half of the citizenship of the country'. While ninety-nine per cent of the women would be glad to be relieved of the duty, the same would apply to men, 'though they would not agree that it would be a desirable thing to abolish the jury system altogether'.[48]

Major Bryan Cooper also objected to the Bill. He was willing to give some weight to the argument about financial and administrative convenience, but found the existing situation, which 'does not compel any woman who wishes to avoid jury service to serve', as 'fairly satisfactory'. It 'give an opportunity to those women who realise their responsibilities as citizens to serve, and it further gives them an opportunity of educating their own sex', so that in the future there may be, 'not five per cent, but fifteen per cent or twenty per cent of qualified women asking to be allowed to serve as jurors'. He also thought it advantageous to have women on juries, particularly in the unpleasant cases, such as rape, where the one witness was the victim, a woman. 'It is very much easier for a woman to tell whether or not another woman is telling the truth than it is for a man.'[49]

Professor William Magennis was especially condemnatory of O'Higgins' position. Noting that the minister did not 'exclude men because men do not like service', he argued that O'Higgins was 'trying to hide from the public' his real motive for excluding women. It was not their dislike of serving, but rather his dislike for activist women. Suggesting that O'Higgins had introduced 'a lot of sentimentality that did duty in the Victorian age, by which men and women are discriminated between', Magennis did not accept the principle of the 'supposed delicacy of soul or spirit' underlying this discrimination. He noted the contradiction in the tendency of a younger man 'to be selected for the jury and the capable woman excluded because she is a woman'. The same principle justified the exclusion of women stenographers from court and the next step would be 'to exclude women from membership of the Dáil'.[50]

O'Higgins returned to the argument that administrative expenses did not make it worthwhile to collect the relatively few women willing to serve as jurors. The only alternatives in his mind were to go back to the 1919 legislation or to accept his proposal: 'It has got to be compulsory jury service for women citizens on a position of complete parity with men, or it has got to be exemption'.[51]

Deputy W.A. Redmond argued that 'under the existing law women are entitled to practically all the advantages of citizenship, and it would be a retrograde step to legislate in the direction proposed, namely, that they should be immune from some of its disadvantages'. He continued: 'If women are eligible for taxation I say that they are as eligible for taking their part and performing their duties by serving upon juries.'

In response, O'Higgins argued that it was 'not any use pretending that the question of women jurors does not present much greater difficulties than the question of jury service for men'. The difficulties were such as to 'make the service that one could secure thereby administratively not worth while'. He hoped the state would be spared 'the task of vetting and sifting the innumerable grounds for exemption that may be pleaded by women, grounds more numerous, more intricate, and more compelling than can be devised by the most subtle male shirker'. He further argued the exemption of women was no more a disadvantage than the exemption from jury duty granted to the Governor General or members of the Oireachtas. Wondering whether the great question of equality of status was 'in fact involved', he suggested that Redmond should 'recognise the distinction between equality and identity'. The present issue was one in which the proposition, 'that there can be equality of status without identity of function,' was profoundly true. He did not consider it 'an infringement of the principle of equality of status to say that, all things considered – and there are many things to consider – one is prepared to dispense women from the burden of jury service'.

After noting the overwhelming majority of women secured exemption as a consequence of the 1924 Act, he did recognize, 'here in and around Dublin there are a small number of women ... who say that the state should compel the ninety-seven per cent of women who shrink from the duty of jury service and all the strain – physical, mental and nervous – that it involves, to serve, in order, forsooth, to vindicate this great principle of equality of status'. But those women willing to undertake the duty were exceptional. It was 'scarcely reasonable' for them to insist for ninety-seven per cent of their unwilling sisters 'to do it'.

O'Higgins would object to any barrier 'to the woman of capacity who feels an aptitude for a particular line of life entering that line of life', but asked that there be recognized 'the distinction between an outlet for an individual woman, for the capacity and talent and aptitude of an individual woman, and this proposal to impose on all women of the state a duty which is onerous and unpleasant even for male citizens, and which inevitably would be ten times more onerous and more unpleasant for the woman citizen'. He also did not accept the position 'that it is merely Victorian to suggest' that certain cases would be 'more unpleasant for women than they are for the man'.[52]

Later, O'Higgins advanced, but 'without enthusiasm', an amendment based on his consultation with Independent deputy Sir James Craig for Trinity College, which would allow women whose sex was their only disqualification to volunteer their names for jury service, that passed.[53]

During the Seanad consideration, O'Higgins put forward an alternative to either including all women, but allowing easy exemption, or excluding all women, but allowing voluntary inclusion. That would establish two categories of persons exempted from jury duty. Persons in the first category would be absolutely exempt, while those in the second could apply for inclusion on the jury register. Women would be among the groups in the second category.[54] The suggestion, after minor revision of the lists of exempted, was ultimately accepted by the Seanad and the Dáil. Examples of those absolutely exempted from jury duty included the Governor General, the members of the

Oireachtas, the defence forces, the Garda, court employees, public employees, clergymen, lighthouse keepers, barristers and solicitors, and illiterates, and those 'who from lunacy, imbecility of mind, deafness, blindness or other permanent infirmity are unfit to serve as jurors'. The second category of exempted, who were 'entitled to serve on application', included women, peace commissioners, doctors, vegetarians, dentists, pharmacists, professors or teachers, masters of vessels, licensed pilots, journalists, and civil engineers.[55]

## CONSTITUTIONAL AMENDMENTS

As in the debate on the original Free State constitution in 1922, O'Higgins played a major role in presenting to the Dáil and Seanad various constitutional amendments in late 1926 and early 1927.

For the first eight years of the Irish Free State its constitution could be amended by ordinary legislation. Since a general election would have to be held by mid-1927 and there existed a possibility of a different group coming to power, the government was anxious to achieve some refinement of the constitution beforehand while utilizing the easier procedure. Concern was prompted in July 1925 when the Ceann Comhairle, Michael Hayes, wrote to Cosgrave suggesting the establishment of a committee of judges and representatives of both houses of the Oireachtas to propose refining amendments. Insisting the amending should not be postponed until after the general election, he argued the incumbent Dáil was the most appropriate body for correcting the constitution since it contained 'almost all the members of the original Cabinet which presented a draft constitution to the constituent assembly in 1922'. He feared waiting for a new Dáil might 'be a very changed assembly' and need 'quite a long time – at least a year – to settle down into an understanding of the constitution and an atmosphere in which constitutional amendments could be discussed', by which time the eight year period of amending by ordinary legislation 'would be very near its close'.[56]

The President and the Executive Council acted on Hayes' suggestion five months later, on 19 December 1925, by appointing a committee to advise on amendments to the constitution. Hayes was made the chairman. Other member were O'Higgins, Blythe, the Minister for Finance, J.J. Walsh, the Minister for Posts and Telegraphs, John O'Byrne, the Attorney General, Senator Douglas, and E.M. Stephens, the Secretary for the Executive Council. The committee held fifteen confidential meetings between 6 January and 6 May 1926. It agreed not to consider any prospective amendments dealing with relations to other members of the Commonwealth or to those articles in the constitution, 'the insertion of which was, in 1922, deemed necessary for the carrying out of the treaty'. The committee 'took the view that the constitution should specifically provide only for fundamental matters, leaving questions of detail, or of carrying out the principles of the constitution, to ordinary legislation'.

Most of the recommendations made by the committee were not advanced by the government nor by the Dáil committee that examined potential amendments prior to consideration by the entire body. Many of those not advanced were designed to weaken populist features of the constitution, such as the initiative, the referendum, and the popular election of senators; to strengthen the executive, such as allowing a government that had lost its majority in the Dáil to ask for a dissolution; and to give the courts broader grounds for summary and *in camera* trials in security matters. Of these, only the repeal of the initiative and the referendum and the change in the manner of selecting senators would ultimately enter the constitution.[57]

There were four amendments advanced for Dáil and Seanad consideration. The first advanced, Amendment No. 2, provided for the automatic return to the Dáil of the incumbent Ceann Comhairle, and was justified on the basis that in his role as Speaker he had had to absent himself from partisan politics and accordingly would be in a difficult position in presenting himself for re-election in his constituency in the next general election. Because of the electoral system of single transferable vote in multi-seat districts, a gentlemen's agreement between the parties about not contesting the seat of the Speaker, as was the practice in Britain, would not be practicable in the Irish Free State. It met minimal opposition, but Thomas Johnson, the Labour leader, opposed the measure for various reasons. There were the more general grounds 'that the constitution ought not be amended lightly and easily', and that 'the constitution itself assumes that changes will not be made in the constitution without very strong reason'. Therefore, he believed a change 'ought not to be made merely on the initiative of a minister'. He also thought a constitutional change affecting the legislature should be formulated by a committee on which the Seanad would be represented, prior to the Bill being introduced.

O'Higgins defended the amendment by reiterating the point that, upon being selected the Ceann Comhairle was debarred 'from further part in active controversial politics ... from being in any true or effective sense the spokesman of his constituents and the guardian of the interests of his constituents'. While in Britain the speaker's seat was taken care of by a gentlemen's agreement between parties, such was impossible in the Free State because of the electoral system of proportional representation. As for the argument that the constitution ought not be lightly altered, he recalled that the 'constitution was drafted by a number of persons who candidly recognised that not one amongst them had any very close experience either of parliamentary life or of departmental administration'. It was because they recognized the limitations of their own work and the inevitability of 'sins of omission and sins of commission' and of certain matters being passed over and other matters dealt with imperfectly, the original constitution committee sought 'the greatest possible elasticity' by inserting 'a provision that for eight years after the constitution would come into operation it would be possible to alter it by ordinary legislation'.[58]

Johnson also opposed Amendment No. 3, which ended the constitutional requirement that the election be a public holiday. He was also anxious, as were other deputies, that if election days were not to be holidays, that there be an extension of the hours of polling so that 'there may be opportunities given to men employed in the daytime to record their votes after their day's work is over'. O'Higgins was pleased that there was general approval of the measure and he said the request for extension of the voting hours was a matter for future consideration.[59]

Amendment No. 4, which extended the maximum life of the Dáil to five years, met no objection other than a suggestion by Johnson that the constitutional maximum should be longer than the statutory maximum, so as to allow flexibility in an emergency situation to extend the life of the Dáil without having to go through the amending process.[60] In the committee stage, O'Higgins accepted an amendment increasing the maximum life to six years.[61]

Amendment No. 5 would allow the size of the Executive Council to be increased by up to four additional members, whose nominations would be in lieu of external minister nominations. The existing constitution limited the number of members that the President could nominate to the Executive Council to seven, although he could also nominate up to four others as external ministers, responsible individually to the Dáil, rather than collectively like the Executive Council. O'Higgins argued the amendment gave latitude and elasticity to the President, as the external minister idea had proved 'not as valuable a constitutional idea as we once thought it would be'. Theoretically the external ministers were individually responsible, but for the fact that 'every one of them has to run to the Minister for Finance for the funds to implement... his policy'. Since Finance was necessarily within the Executive Council, the 'single responsibility of extern ministers' and their aloofness from the Executive Council and its works and pomps was 'largely theoretical'. Johnson opposed this amendment as well, arguing that 'sufficient time has not been given to the experiment' of external ministers, which had been proposed 'so eloquently by the Minister for Justice to the Dáil when we passed the constitution'. O'Higgins said the experiment of external ministers had failed because the Dáil and the general public had made a 'a definite refusal to discriminate' between matters within the purview of the Executive Council and those 'administered by the external ministers'.[62]

The Seanad accepted Amendment No. 2 after a slight alteration suggested by Senators O'Farrell and Farren. They had feared that the amendment might enable the automatically returned Speaker to be regarded as an addition to, rather than one of, the members ordinarily elected from his constituency. If the automatically returned member would not then be re-elected as Speaker, that constituency would be over-represented. To prevent this they proposed limiting the number of members elected from the Speaker's constituency to one less than usual. The Dáil accepted the senatorial revision.[63] The amendments ending the public holiday character of polling day and extending the maximum life of the Dáil met with no senatorial objection.[64] But during the consideration of Amendment No. 5, Senator Patrick Kenny, a champion of Irish industrialization and of the Irish language movement, interpreted the measure, which allowed the increase in the size of the Executive Council and the dispensing of external ministers, as a slight on the Seanad since its members could not be on the Executive Council. He noted that senators had been nominated because of their 'useful public service' and/or 'special qualifications or attainments', whereas Dáil members simply represented 'constituencies determined by law' and did not have 'any special qualifications'. The Seanad shared this annoyance as it approved a motion by Sir John Keane, a barrister, Director of the Bank of Ireland, and a JP and High Sheriff for Co. Waterford, that the Dáil be asked for the formation of a joint committee from both houses to correct the constitutional barrier to senators being on the Executive Council.[65]

O'Higgins successfully urged the Dáil to disregard the request, which he interpreted as a Seanad threat to block the original amendment unless its wishes were granted. He also opposed the concept of making senators eligible for the Executive Council on its own merits. He noted that none of the sixty senators, whether the thirty-one who were elected, the twenty-seven who were nominated, or the two co-opted, had been chosen 'with a view to their being anything else than members of a second chamber, a second chamber with powers of revision, powers of criticism, powers of suggestion, and even powers – maximum powers – of delay'. None had been selected with consideration of 'the possibility of their becoming members of a body which is collectively responsible to the people for major matters of administration, for the handling of the finances of the country, for the bigger issues of policy, domestic and international, that may arise'. He regarded it as 'a wrong thing, an unsound thing for the Dáil or the country to say that persons who have been elected in the peculiar circumstances in which senators were elected should even be eligible to become members of the Executive Council'.[66]

Later Senator Kenny moved to refine Amendment No. 5 to make senators eligible for Executive Council membership. A more amenable O'Higgins promised to discourage government opposition to such a resolution and assured him that he 'would be glad to see the resolution passed', but doubted if the Dáil would agree. Kenny then withdrew his motion and the original amendment passed.[67]

## NOTES

1.　The existing law allowed Saturday hours of 7 am to 10 pm in large towns and 7 am to 9 pm elsewhere.
2.　Mary Frances McKenna, 'Reform of the Intoxicating Liquor Laws in the 1920s', MA Thesis, University College Dublin, 1995, 27–31; *Dáil Éireann*, VII (30 May 1924), 1,662–5.
3.　*Ibid.* (19 June 1924), 2,712–8.
4.　*Ibid.*, 2,731–5.
5.　*Ibid.*, 2,719–22.
6.　*Ibid.*, 2,747–54.
7.　*Ibid.*, 2,723–30.
8.　*Ibid.*, 2,737–46.
9.　*Ibid.* (24 June 1924) 2,915.

10. *Ibid.*, VIII (2 July 1924), 310–14.
11. *Ibid.* (14 and 17 July 1924), 1,109–11, 1,535–6.
12. *Ibid.*, IX (22 October 1924), 29–32, 35–6, 46, 63–6.
13. *Ibid.* (28 October 1924), 305–11.
14. *Ibid.*, 330.
15. *Seanad Éireann*, III (27 November 1924), 1,179–95.
16. *Ibid.* (28 November 1924), 1,251–66.
17. *Dáil Éireann*, IX (10 December 1924), 2,319–34, 2,354–7.
18. *Irish Independent* (4 February 1925).
19. *Report of Intoxicating Liquor Commission*, NA, S 4251.
20. *Dáil Éireann*, XVIII (16 February 1927), 544–52.
21. *Ibid.*, 554–5.
22. *Ibid.*, 557–60.
23. *Ibid.*, 552–3, 555–7, 561–2, 581–2.
24. *Ibid.*, 584–92.
25. *Ibid.* (3 March 1927), 1,246–9.
26. *Ibid.* (2 March 1927), 1,173, 1,180–2, 1,184, 1,195–6, 1,199–12,00.
27. *Ibid.*, XIX (23 March 1927), 117–130.
28. *Ibid.*, XVIII (3 March 1927), 1,283–85, 1,308–9, 1,315–17.
29. *Ibid.*, 1,320–22.
30. *Ibid.* (16 February 1927), 530–1; (4 March 1927), 1,349–50, 1,372–4, 1,377–8, 1,379–85.
31. *Ibid.*, 1,387–97.
32. *Seanad Éireann*, VIII (27 April 1927), 899, 904, 924 and 934.
33. *Dáil Éireann*, XIX (12 May 1927), 2,437–45.
34. *Dáil Éireann*, X (11 February 1925), 155–9.
35. *Ibid.*, 173–5.
36. *Ibid.*, 159–63.
37. *Ibid.*, 163–5.
38. *Seanad Éireann*, V (11 June 1925), 426–82.
39. *Ibid.*, XI (1 May 1925), 725–8.
40. *Ibid.* (15 May 1925), 1,634–40.
41. *Ibid.*, XIII (3 November 1925), 5–6.
42. *Report of the Committee on Evil Literature*, 3–5, NA, S 5381.
43. *Ibid.*, 8–12.
44. *Ibid.*, 13–15.
45. *Ibid.*, 16–18.
46. K. O'Higgins to Executive Council (16 March 1927), NA, S 5381.
47. *Dáil Éireann*, XVIII (15 February 1927), 466–9.
48. *Ibid.*, 477–8.
49. *Ibid.*, 479–81.
50. *Ibid.*, 483–4.
51. *Ibid.*, 489–90.
52. *Ibid.* (23 February 1927), 751–8.
53. *Ibid.*, XIX (22 March 1927), 24–30.
54. *Seanad Éireann*, VIII (9 April 1927), 792–8.
55. *Dáil Éireann*, XIX (12 May 1927), 2,430–1. The Juries Act dealt with many other less controversial, but highly technical matters such as the summoning of jurors, the challenges of jurors to be allowed, the compensation for jurors, etc.
56. Michael Hayes to William T. Cosgrave (21 July 1925), NA, S 4650.
57. *Amendments to the Constitution Committee Report* (6 May 1926) 5–6, NA, S 4650/1
58. *Dáil Éireann*, XVII (1 December 1926), 394–408.

59. *Ibid.*, 410–14.
60. *Ibid.*, 416–17.
61. *Ibid.*, 496–7.
62. *Ibid.*, 418–28.
63. *Ibid.* (23 February 1927), 282–8; *Dáil Éireann*, XVIII (11 March 1927), 1,817–20.
64. *Seanad Éireann*, VIII (2 February 1927), 137–40.
65. *Ibid.*, 141–57.
66. *Dáil Éireann*, XVIII (2 March 1927), 1,150–2.
67. *Ibid.*, 753, 777–80.

# 10

# The Last Months

INTERNAL PROBLEMS IN CUMANN NA NGAEDHEAL

Cumann na nGaedheal's prospects in the June 1927 general election were mixed. In November 1924 and March 1925 by-elections abstentionist Sinn Féiners had won four of fourteen seats that were originally held by the government. A year later, however, the government gained two seats in by-elections, occasioned by the death of independent Darrell Figgis and the disqualification of an abstentionist Sinn Féin TD from Leix–Offaly. But that gain was offset by the withdrawal from the party of two other TDs, Denis McCullough, the former head of the IRB who was elected for Donegal in the November 1924 by-election, and Professor William Magennis, one of the TDs for the National University of Ireland, because of their displeasure at the settlement of the Boundary Commission issue.[1]

A split occurred within Sinn Féin, but it did not benefit the government. De Valera had withdrawn from the party after his proposal to enter the Free State Dáil – should the oath not be required – was rejected at a special Árd Fheis in March 1926. Two months later, he founded a new party, Fianna Fáil, and was joined by the more politically astute members of the movement. In the June 1927 general election only a handful of Sinn Féin candidates ran, while de Valera's movement drew the support of the overwhelming majority of the previously Sinn Féin voters. He also gained the support of many in the electorate who had accepted the treaty, but who had grown dissatisfied with the government. An analysis of the electoral returns from the earlier by-elections, which preceded the formation of Fianna Fáil, suggests a decided electoral swing toward the left (or republican) position, even if not necessarily supporting the more purist and armed perspective of Sinn Féin/IRA.[2] While Cumann na nGaedheal had increased its percentage of votes in the by-elections, Sinn Féin did even more so. The fact that there were few candidates from other parties did not help the government. Also, dissatisfied Cumann na nGaedheal members were potential Fianna Fáil supporters.

The dissatisfaction of the more nationalist elements in Cumann na nGaedheal ranks coincided with the strengthened position of O'Higgins within the government during the Army and Boundary Commission crises. Paradoxically it was the very success of the government's security policy, which lessened the likelihood of a resumption of Civil War or disorder in general and insured the endurance of the treaty, that allowed some of its supporters to conclude that the time had come to advance an irredentist agenda not achieved by the treaty. O'Higgins and Cabinet colleagues like Desmond FitzGerald, Patrick McGuinness, Ernest Blythe, and Patrick Hogan, with the apparently resigned approval of Cosgrave, had placed more emphasis on governmental stability, juridical and civil service professionalism, and fiscal rectitude, than on the pursuit of the irredentist, cultural nationalist, or socio-political objectives of some in the party ranks. The evidence was the increased reliance on professional civil servants, especially the likes of Gordon Campbell, Secretary to the Department for Industry and Commerce, and J.J. McElligott, Secretary to the Department of Finance, as well as the opposition of most cabinet members and the economically orthodox civil servants to protective tariffs. An exception, Minister for Posts and Telegraphs, J.J. Walsh, withdrew from politics prior to the second 1927 election.[3]

Cumann na nGaedheal's hopes to reach out to non-party members, especially to the right, were complicated when Captain William Redmond, the son of the late Irish Parliamentary Party leader, and an independent member for Waterford, resurrected a version of the old party. Called the National League, it ran thirty candidates and won eight seats in the June 1927 election. Closely identified with the vintners and license holders, Redmond had vigorously opposed the intoxicating liquor legislation and saw the overtaxing of the liquor trade as 'killing the trade of the breweries and distilleries and also the barley-growing farmers'. He also played the 'green card' against the government, arguing that the nation 'had suffered defeat – bitter, humiliating, damaging defeat – in great national claims for freedom for a united Ireland'. The 'weak, vacillating, and unintelligent handling' of Irish claims by Cosgrave and colleagues had reduced Ireland 'to a plight little better than if she had submitted to the Government of Ireland Act of 1920'. A few weeks later, well into the campaign, he asserted that Cumann na nGaedheal 'had not given them good government. They had given them officials and more officials, and schemes of expenditure and taxes, and sheriffs to collect them'. But while he was attacking the government from the right for its fiscal irresponsibility, it was its very fiscal restraint that had hurt it on its leftward or more nationalist flank.[4]

Another right of centre political grouping whom Cumann na nGaedheal failed to successfully court was the Farmers' Union, even though that group's leader, Denis J. Gorey, TD for Carlow–Kilkenny, had urged colleagues to follow him in joining Cumann na nGaedheal. He had argued that fusion with Cumann na nGaedheal would afford 'the representatives of the agricultural industry the opportunity of becoming by the most direct route and in the shortest time, a real influence in the life of the country'. He feared either the anti-treatyites getting a majority and causing inevitable trouble with England, or there being a coalition of a number of small parties, collectively having a majority, but with 'no definite policy either agricultural or political... united merely in the common ground of opposition to the government at present in power'. The result would only be 'constant general elections, with the consequent insecurity and the consequent depreciation of credit'.[5] However, his appeal fell on deaf ears as the Farmers' Union ran thirty-eight candidates and won eleven seats.[6]

*The Irish Times* endorsed the Cumann na nGaedheal government for re-election and warned of the effect of a multiplicity of parties in a contest between the government and the anti-treatyites. Fearing the disorder of continental politics, it believed Cumann na nGaedheal, 'with all its defects of policy and outlook', was 'the only bulwark of the country against chaos'.[7] Since the next five years were 'likely to be a most important period in Irish history; the debris of revolution has been cleared away; solid foundations have been laid, but the real task of nation-building has yet to be tackled', it concluded 'that the national interests demand the continuance of Mr Cosgrave and a majority of his ministers at the head of affairs'. But the paper did not rule out coalition, doubting that 'the restraining influence of a parliamentary coalition would hamper the nation's progress'.[8] A week later, even more resigned to the unlikelihood of the government getting an absolute majority, the paper hoped for a successful anti-Fianna Fáil coalition since there was 'nothing to choose between the policies of the Farmers' Union and the government' aside from differences on protection and agricultural matters, and Captain Redmond and friends, 'in most essentials', were 'pursuing the same policy as the government'.[9]

## THE ELECTION

In the election campaign, the government assumed its very record was sufficient to get voter support, in spite of rank and file alienation. Fianna Fáil, on the other hand, was especially well prepared for the election. Its party organization combined highly disciplined centralization with mass popular involvement. Its leaders concerned themselves with electoral politics more than republican doctrine as they mixed irredentist and republican rhetoric with populist themes such as unemployment, emigration, small farmer poverty, and lower middle-class discontent. Lastly, they successfully raised funds from domestic national collections, from Irish business interests desirous of protectionist policies, and from that perennial source of support for irredentist Irish nationalism, Irish America.[10]

The campaign rhetoric of Fianna Fáil leaders mixed pragmatism and ideology. Frank Aiken waved the extreme nationalist flag in Dundalk when he described the Free State parliament, that is, the Dáil, 'as a collection of people who broke every promise that they had ever made, and who, when England cracked the whip, always obeyed at once'. The way to make Ireland free was 'to kick out the present bunch, who stood for England and not for Ireland'.[11] When de Valera arrived in Queenstown, now Cobh, from a successful fundraising trip to America, he proclaimed 'our people in the United States are ready to support us again, as they did in the past, if we stand together'. Indicating their anxiety to get into the Dáil, he saw the oath as the barrier, since 'those who believed in right were met at the door with an oath, which made them repudiate the right of the Irish people to be free'. If it were not for that oath the popular representatives would be able to get together and 'frame a national policy'. In discussing that ideal national policy he evoked populist grievances:

> They should make the customs barriers sufficiently strong to protect their industries and to defeat foreign competition ... if they were to make their country self-supporting they must have employment for

their people. Fianna Fáil stood for protection for their industries. They did not want to make Ireland a bullock ranch for England or even a pleasure ground for tourists, but to make it a home for as many happy Irish families as possible.

A week later in Nenagh, County Tippperary, he demonstrated the practical electoral strategy of Fianna Fáil by asking the voters to give them a majority, for 'if they had that they would enter the Dáil and work for their country'. A few days before the election, in Kilfenora, County Clare, de Valera indicated that, even as a minority, they were willing to enter the Dáil to 'use the foreign machinery', but only on the condition that they did not have to go on their knees to a foreign king: 'We are prepared to go in there to sit with other representatives, and use that foreign manufactured machine for the purposes of the Irish people, provided we can do so holding the principles we are holding.'[12]

O'Higgins commented on de Valera's claims about his American support: 'The wretched leader of a wretched faction...goes to America begging for money for a minority party within the state, and the people who subscribed that money know as much – probably less – about the political situation here as I do about the political situation in America.' Turning to the matter of Northern Ireland, he thought that de Valera's followers 'had no solution for the problem of the North-East except simply another round with England'. Insisting that the problem 'could not be solved by force', he offered as an alternative 'building up the resources of the country, increasing efficiency in administration, and reducing taxation until the people of the Six Counties come to an appreciation of the fact that it would be in their own interest to be part and parcel of the Free State'. Later in the campaign he repeated his ideas on how to achieve Irish political unification. At Athlone he proclaimed:

> You will only get this entire country with a single political system by agreement, and I believe that you will get that agreement only by going ahead and building up conditions here that will constitute an attraction to the good people who have been led to believe that the greatest disaster that could happen to them would be to be included in a single political system with the rest of their countrymen.

The next day at Carrickmacross, County Monaghan, he repeated the theme that the solution for the boundary problem was not 'by the strong hand, or by force; it would only be solved by agreement'. He noted: 'Anyone can vault on to a platform and denounce England, but we have got to do our business and face facts, think matters carefully over and do the best you can for the country.'[13] As might be expected, such strong rhetoric guaranteed that O'Higgins' campaign appearances were met by hecklers, and often resulted in fights, arrests, and baton charges by the Garda.[14]

The Cumann na nGaedheal government received the support of the *Irish Statesman*, the weekly of George Russell ('AE'). Warning that the only certainty from a Fianna Fáil majority would be 'that the severance between Northern Ireland and the Free State would be as complete as it would be possible to imagine', the paper concluded 'that the government party, though it has some poverty-stricken minds in office, has at its service much better brains than any of the others. It has laid down the foundations of reforms which in the nature of things only begin to have their effect within the next decade'. Expecting 'that in ten years' time the country will be reaping the full harvest' of these reforms, it was appropriate 'that those who sowed the seed should be allowed to look after the harvesting'.[15]

In looking at the political alternatives, the paper concluded that presently 'not one of the several parties contain a group who have given evidence, either as critics or constructive statesmen, of anything like the competence of Messrs. Cosgrave, O'Higgins, Hogan, Blythe and McGilligan'. The paper could not imagine any of the alternative parties

> grappling with civil war with the same fearlessness as the ministers did, or pursuing with the same moral courage policies they believed in, and which they knew would cause a great deal of temporary unpopularity, policies health-giving in the long run as the bitter draught the physician orders. The superseding of inefficient councils, the determined prevention of jobbery in public appointments, the necessary insistence on payment of rates and annuities, the curbing of the drink traffic, the taming of the physical-force men – all these and many more things they did – created enemies in every part of Ireland, and only men of character would have faced the unpopularity.[16]

A month later, the opinion of the *Irish Statesman* was especially laudatory of the government:

> We believe that the country was extraordinarily fortunate that the Irish revolution turned up men with so much moral courage and

ability. They took over the country when everything was chaotic and they have made it as peaceable as any country in the world. They are hardworking. The Dáil follows breathless behind their activities. The Civic Guards, the Courts of Justice, the Land Act, the liquor legislation, the great electricity enterprise, the introduction of sugar beet, the elimination of jobbery in the civil service and local administration, the recasting of government activities from the forty odd boards into co-ordinate and logical departments, the putting down of civil war, all these stand as monuments to the capacity of these young men. We confess we cannot imagine any combination of leaders of the various oppositions having the vigour or moral courage or the capacity to have faced difficulties in the same speed or solved them with the same measure of success.[17]

However, most of the electorate were not readers of the *Irish Statesman*. The government was not able to draw support from the right, that is, those who supported the Farmers' Union or the old Parliamentary Party supporters drawn to Redmond's National Group. At the same time a significant portion of the Cumann na nGaedheal rank and file began to accept the more nationalist message of Fianna Fáil. Many others were drawn to its populist message of protectionism. The job of defending unpleasant, but necessary, policies in an election campaign was a thankless task. O'Higgins grasped a sense of the futility in a letter to Lady Hazel Lavery early in the campaign: '...it is so miserable to have to pretend that I haven't a wish in the world except to win the elections which is absurd and suggests a convict clamouring for heavier balls of lead about his ankles'. On the day after the election he wrote to her asking: '...is it all worth while, I wonder? this brick-laying of ours? Will some fool come along some day when you and I are dead and kick the fabric of our rearing into dust and nothingness. Or will Ireland go forward from strength to strength to find at last Unity and Peace – peace for her fevered soul?'[18]

The outcome of the election was as bad as could be imagined from the government's perspective, short of Fianna Fáil gaining a majority or winning the greatest number of seats. Out of 153 seats, Cumann na nGaedheal got only 47 (including the Ceann Comhairle), down from 63 in the 1923 election, while Fianna Fáil got 44.[19] O'Higgins astutely analyzed the consequences of the outcome. Beside the bad effect on national credit, he feared the Northern Irish unionists would 'feel justified and self-righteous. They will feel again that safety lies in aloofness in isolation. We will never get unity until our people consciously and deliberately relegate Separation and Anglo-phobia (as distinct from Independence) to the waste paper basket'.

He was annoyed at Redmond and the Farmers. He believed that with their support the government would have gotten sixty seats and de Valera would have been held to thirty. If that had happened there would be cheaper credit and five years of development, after which they 'could have talked to the North about unity'. There might have developed 'a final settlement with Britain on the basis of the "Kingdom of Ireland" – a dual monarchy, with possibly, some defence agreement between the two Kingdoms'. But as a result of the election they 'can only hold on like grim death to what has been won, and even that is going to be difficult'. He found it 'an irony that Right-Wing elements here' – the Redmondites and the Farmers' Union – 'have gone near to destroying the treaty!'[20] He reiterated many of the same themes in a public statement that the 'insecurity and instability' consequent on the election results were 'the joint gift to the state of the National League, the Farmers' Union, and the independent candidates'.[21]

## THE FIFTH DÁIL ÉIREANN

There remained some uncertainty about who would form a govern-ment when the Dáil would meet, especially if the forty-four Fianna Fáil deputies decided to take their seats. Potentially they, along with the twenty-two Labour votes, the eight Redmondites, and some Independents, could have put together enough votes to form a government. Much depended on how de Valera and followers would finesse the required signing of the admittance document required by Article 17 of the constitution that each deputy did 'solemnly swear true faith and allegiance to the Constitution of the Irish Free State as by law established', and 'be faithful to H.M. King George V, his heirs and successors by law in virtue of the common citizenship of Ireland with Great Britain and her adherence to and membership of the group of nations forming the British Commonwealth of Nations'.

While the *Irish Statesman* found the situation 'more difficult and critical for the pro-treaty parties than it was in 1923', it was reassured by 'the fact that there is now no danger of an appeal to physical force'. Sinn Féin, the only group still claiming 'the right to upset constitutional verdicts by violence' had become almost completely extinct. As for the prospects of de Valera's participation in the Dáil or a government, it doubted 'whether all the units of his motley regiment are prepared to remain another spell of years in a wilderness where there is no prospect of either manna or quail'.[22]

De Valera had issued a celebratory statement about the election, suggesting that Fianna Fáil's only opponents were Cumann na nGaedheal. He applauded the accomplishment of Fianna Fáil in view of its being 'a youthful organization founded less than thirteen months before the day of the poll, the enforced exile of the majority of its young adherents, the terrorisation of the electorate by repeated threats, and the unscrupulous campaign of calumny conducted by its opponents'. He insisted that if a referendum were held on the single issue of the oath, the 'infamous penal legislation would be repudiated by an indignant nation'. He insisted: 'In accordance with the mandate given to them, the Fianna Fáil deputies will claim their seats.' He was confident the people would not tolerate 'their being barred by the imposition of the penal oath'. Two days later he asserted that under 'no circumstances whatever will Fianna Fáil deputies take any such oath'.[23]

When the Dáil met on June 23 the Fianna Fáil leaders refused to sign the required oath and were denied admission. Cosgrave was nominated as President of the Executive Council, but before being elected he indicated his willingness to accept an adjournment should any of the other parties wish to hold discussions about forming an alternative ministry. But if he became President he would not preside over a caretaker government. He did not interpret the results of the elections as a popular demand that he abandon his programme. Furthermore, he had 'no intention of tampering in any way with the treaty', particularly Article 17 requiring the oath, since 'as long as the treaty remains neither this House nor any other assembly can remove the obligation which the treaty imposes upon elected representatives', and noted that the treaty could only be altered 'by agreement with Great Britain, ratified by legislation on both sides'.[24]

Thomas Johnson said the Labour Party would oppose Cosgrave because the government's policy towards the working classes had been one 'of reduction of the standard of living, a reduction of wages, a reduction of comforts, and a removal and declining of the social and ameliorative enactments'.[25] Captain Redmond, on the other hand, thought it 'the primary duty of the largest party in the house to take the initial steps to form a government'. While his own party could not vote for Cosgrave and would abstain, they would 'support whatever government is brought into existence in the carrying out of the public work of this state through its services', while retaining 'our right of criticism and of opposition'. Patrick Baxter, the new leader of the Farmers' Union, on the other hand, said his party would vote for Cosgrave, as would independent Bryan Cooper with 'the hope that the government will be slightly more responsive to public opinion and to the opinion of the Dáil'.[26]

In what would be his last speech in Dáil Éireann, O'Higgins attacked the National League, the Farmers, and Labour for not having put forward enough candidates to form a majority. 'The only party taking that risk was the party to which I belong, and one other party which is not represented here [Fianna Fáil]'. Observing that many editorials suggested Cograve would be irresponsible to not form a government and that all other parties had refused 'the responsibility of government', he said Cumann na nGaedheal, although a mathematical minority of the Dáil, was 'not shirking that responsibility'. However, he hoped that 'the people should learn from this position a constitutional lesson, learn for future guidance that it is a cynical thing, a fundamentally deceptive thing, for a party to dangle spectacular programmes before it while not seeking a majority in parliament by which to put those programmes into operation', an attack on minority or sectional parties that have continued in Irish politics. He also sought to rebut some of Johnson's remarks about the social indifference of the government by pointing to housing construction, with more being built in Dublin between 1922 and 1927 than between 1890 and 1921, beet sugar development, harnessing of the Shannon for electricity, and other sources of employment such as arterial drainage and road work. He recalled that Cumann na nGaedheal had been 'careful to disclaim before the electorate any capacity in working miracles'. He boasted that 'within the limits of our resources we had done as much as men could do by legislation and administration to deal with the social evils that we found in our midst'. He rebuked Fianna Fáil, who:

> were so eloquent in the country some fortnight or three weeks ago. All the fine promises have faded out. The party that was to end partition, the party that was to halve taxation, the party that was to have every man sitting down under his own vine trees smoking a pipe of Irish-grown tobacco are not here today.[27]

With the support of the Farmers' Union and a few independents, Cosgrave got a majority. Labour voted against him, while the National Group and a few independents abstained. He presented to the Dáil the names of nine ministers who would serve with him in the Executive Council. The expanded number, and the absence of external ministers, had been permitted by the recently approved constitutional amendments. General Richard Mulcahy was back in the government, with the encouragement of O'Higgins, as Minister for Local Government and Health.[28] Desmond FitzGerald, in poor health at the time, was moved from External Affairs to Defence. O'Higgins, while continuing as Vice President of the Executive Council and Minister for Justice, took on the additional portfolio of External Affairs. Cosgrave rejected any suggestion that the change in FitzGerald's position was because of incompetence. If there had been such, he would not have appointed him to Defence. He had hesitated to give O'Higgins two posts since he had 'been one of the most hard worked of all the ministers', but had been reassured that O'Higgins' work had lessened in the Ministry of Justice, and that 'he would be able to take on the work of the Ministry of External Affairs'.[29]

One of O'Higgins' first functions as Minister for External Affairs was to attend an international conference in Geneva on naval disarmament. He acknowledged that the Irish Free State interest in the matter was 'to keep the constitutional position right and allow no inroads or unhealthy precedents', that is, any departures from the autonomy asserted by the Free State and the Dominions in the Imperial conferences. He did not expect anything of significance to be agreed to, but suspected the British and the Americans were 'anxious to sign *something* to give the appearance of progress in limitation of armaments'. Desirous to be home, he wrote to his wife that he wished he could leave the conference but feared, if he left and some agreement was reached, he would have to return 'to sign on behalf of the Free State', as 'the phraseology of the document will be of importance to us and Canada and South Africa', whom he thought had 'not yet learned to take a stand on their own' and 'only see things when they are pointed out to them'. At any rate he was 'feeling much less the leavings of an election campaign than . . . four days ago' and was able to swim every morning and had toured mountains and railways.[30]

O'Higgins was back in Dublin by the end of the following week, making his last appearance in Dáil Éireann on July 8.

THE END

The following Sunday, July 10, while walking alone from his home to a noon Mass at the parish church in Booterstown, O'Higgins was shot several times by three men. They had been waiting in a stolen car parked near where O'Higgins would turn from Cross Avenue on which his home, Dunamase, was located, on to Booterstown Avenue where the church was. The incident was only a few hundred yards from his residence. Some accounts suggest one or two others may have acted to signal his approach to the gunmen. At any rate, as one or more of the gunmen approached him, O'Higgins ran across Booterstown Avenue and sought entry into the gates of a residence called Sans Souci. By that time all three assassins had opened fire on him. He fell and one continued firing at him while standing over him. The assassins then left.

Eoin MacNeill, whom the gunmen passed running towards their car, was one of the first to arrive on the scene. O'Higgins remained conscious, although wounded seven times, including a wound in front of the right ear, and suffering a great loss of blood. His first remark to MacNeill was 'I forgive my murderers'. He also told MacNeill to tell his wife Brigid that he loved her eternally. He also gave him instructions regarding certain papers on his person. Several others then came on the scene including a doctor who had been at Mass and Canon Breen, the pastor of the church, who gave the last rites and who also heard him assert 'I forgive them all'. An ambulance came which took him to his nearby home where he survived, under the attention of two Dublin surgeons, for nearly five hours.

In the last hours he expressed concern for his governmental colleagues, his affection for his wife and his two young daughters, three-year old Maeve and five-month old Una, and forgiveness for his enemies. Present was his colleague and very close friend who often stayed in his home in Dublin, Minister for Agriculture, Patrick Hogan. Even Police Commissioner Eoin O'Duffy called and was told by O'Higgins to 'Continue on the same lines'.[31]

Extremely important for the future evolution of constitutional democracy in Ireland was the immediate condemnation of the act by Eamon de Valera, who stated: 'The assassination of Mr O'Higgins is murder, and is inexcusable from any standpoint.' He added that he was 'confident that no republican organization was responsible for it, or would give it any countenance', as it was 'a crime that cuts at the root of representative government'.[32] Despite that condemnation of the assassination, a less generous, but not unique, attitude was reflected in the retrospective commentary by C.S. Andrews, an adjutant to republican leader Liam Lynch during the Civil War and later the director of Bord na Mona and executive chairman of CIE: 'It would be hypocritical to pretend that the death of O'Higgins caused a tear to be shed by any republicans; nor were many shed by the general public or his colleagues. He was not a well-liked man. The assassination was worse than a crime, it was a mistake.'[33]

Although many suspects were interrogated, the assassins were never caught. In such an environment and with no answer being found, numerous conspiracy theories developed. In his memoir of the period, James Hogan, who had been Director of Intelligence for the National Army during the Civil War, a Professor at UCC and brother of Patrick Hogan, O'Higgins' close friend and colleague, reported that the police intelligence agency headed by David Neligan believed the assassination was the work of an extremist wing within republicanism centred on Frank Ryan, George Gilmore, and Seán MacBride.[34] Others suggested that aggrieved persons from either side in the Army mutiny dispute might have been responsible. It was claimed by Fianna Fáil member and later President of Ireland, Seán T. O'Kelly, who was supported by later Fianna Fáil Minister for Justice, Gerard Boland, that former members of the CID, the predecessor of the Special Branch of the Garda Síochána, who had been subjected to disciplinary action by O'Higgins, were responsible.[35]

It was only fifty-eight years later, with the appearance of the biography of Harry White, a Belfast republican activist of the 1930s and 1940s, that the identity of the killers was revealed. Archie Doyle was the first to fire at O'Higgins, while Bill Gannon and Timothy Coughlan joined in the assault as O'Higgins lay on the ground mortally wounded. Doyle remained a republican activist and gunman for many years after, and ambushed a Garda sergeant in Dublin in 1942. He served as a clerk in the Office of Public Works and was a building manager for Woolworths. He died in the early 1980s. Coughlan was killed in an exchange of shots following an attack on a police undercover agent in January 1928. Gannon was later involved with Saor Éire, a left-wing republican organization of the 1930s that included the likes of Seán MacBride and Peadar O'Donnell. He organized and recruited for the Irish unit of the International Brigade that fought on the republican side in the Spanish Civil War. When Gannon died in 1965 his burial had an official honour guard because of his being a veteran of the War of

Independence.[36] Peadar O'Donnell, the last surviving member of the 1920s IRA Executive, confirmed the account of their identity. He claimed that the IRA Army Council had been informed of the names of the killers by its own intelligence section soon after it had happened. He, however, insisted the assassination was against the policy of the IRA Army Council, and that the assassins 'were part of a little group in the IRA that behaved in the manner of the Invincibles[37] in the 1880s... They thought the IRA was not being active enough toward the Cosgrave regime, and thought they would create an incident that would bring about a confrontation'.[38]

The same Peadar O'Donnell told O'Higgins' daughter, Una, at a chance meeting long after the event, that it had been

> a terrible thing about your father's death. We [in the IRA] had paid £1,000 dáily for the transcripts of the Imperial Conference of 1926 and we could not fault him [O'Higgins] nor the rest of the delegation on what they did then for Ireland. He was the main inspiration, and what he did all came out in the Statute of Westminster. He should have been let do his job – but then we Irish can never pull together.

Una O'Higgins O'Malley also reported on her correspondence with Roger Gannon, the son of one of her father's assassins. He told her of his father's deathbed account of the event and of the impression O'Higgins, when he had been shot, had made on him in expressing forgiveness and lamenting that too much blood had been shed. Gannon had been one of Michael Collins' gunmen in the shootings of British agents on the morning of Bloody Sunday in November 1920. Collins had instructed his men to never leave their victims in agony, but to finish them off, especially if they might be able to identify their assailants. However, the words of forgiveness, of understanding of why they did what they had done, and of hope that it be the last of killings, uttered by the severely wounded O'Higgins, inhibited the gunmen from completing their task. They left, even though they thought O'Higgins knew them. Bill Gannon told his son that 'afterwards his whole life had been haunted by this happening'.[39]

Remarkably, on the sixtieth anniversary of the assassination, a Mass was offered for the repose of the souls of both the victim and his killers in the very Booterstown church towards which O'Higgins was heading for Mass that fateful day.[40]

O'Higgins' body lay in state in the Mansion House Monday and Tuesday, and was then removed to the Church of St Andrew,

Westland Row, where the funeral Mass took place on Wednesday, July 13, with burial afterwards in Glasnevin Cemetery. In a three-quarter hour meeting of the Dáil on Tuesday, July 12, tribute to the slain Minister was paid by the President and the leaders of the Labour Party, the Farmers' Union, the National League, and several independents. Johnson noted 'his intellectual competence...an honest and fair opponent', who in 'the crowded years of his apprenticeship in statescraft' had 'packed a journeyman's work both in the quantity and quality towards making secure the foundations of this young state'. Farmers' Union leader Patrick Baxter said: 'Kevin O'Higgins always did what he considered best for Ireland. He loved his country well and the splendid gifts that God endowed him with he used unsparingly in his country's service.' Redmond said that no differences of opinion prevented him from realizing O'Higgins' 'earnestness and constancy of purpose, the richness of his intellectual equipment, his courage and the unremitting labour which he gave to his work; these and the breadth of his conceptions and his grasp of principles and details held a rich promise of a fully developed career, for they marked him with the stamp of greatness'. Independent Bryan Cooper noted 'his astonishing precocity'. O'Higgins was only thirty years of age when Cooper first knew him, yet 'he had the ripe wisdom, the balanced judgment, and the sure determination of a man twenty or thirty years older'. O'Higgins, when asked by Cooper to explain this maturity, had answered that '1922 and 1923 counted for ten years each in the lives of most of us'.[41]

Similar tribute was paid at the same time in the Seanad. Typical were the remarks of Senator Jameson, who had become acquainted with him during the deliberations between the Provisional Government and representatives of Southern unionists and/or 'non Sinn Féin' Irish, specifically with regard to the establishment of the Seanad. The impression O'Higgins had made was that 'his vision of the future was clear and just'. They 'saw his great statesmanship, his great moral bravery, and...that what he said he would he would do, no matter what the cost when it came to the doing'.[42]

A comparable message appeared in William T. Cosgrave's grave-side oration the next day at Glasnevin, after the funeral procession from St Andrew's:

> To his capacity as a constructive statesman and an administrator no
> testimony is needed. From disorders, the combined result of long
> misgovernment, revolt and revolution, in a few years time under his

direction arose a new and stable edifice of public order and public peace. His example of duty, sanity, energy and enterprise will inspire our nation till the end.[43]

Two editorial tributes from rather diverse journals capture the finest points of O'Higgins. The *Irish Statesman* said:

> His name will be remembered as one of the great architects of the new state along with Griffith and Collins. While others were concerned with economic reconstruction, his imagination seems primarily to have been concerned with the moral architecture of the Free State, the establishment of justice and peace.[44]

The English Catholic weekly, *The Tablet*, paid tribute to another aspect of the man. Depicting him as a 'great Irishman and great Catholic and great Christian', it noted that he 'spoke and acted as a saint and hero, not through a Three Hours but a Five Hours Agony last Sunday afternoon'. While his 'life-blood was ebbing away', he confessed 'his faith in personal immortality', 'paid reverent heed' to priestly ministrations, 'made his will and gave directions for the carrying on of labour in the fields from which he himself was called away', and 'sent practical messages to many a colleague and friend'. But what was 'most memorable of all memorable things in this Good Death was his insistent saying: "I forgive them all. I forgive my enemies"'.[45]

To play upon another theme in Irish history, blood sacrifice, which Pearse evoked to inspire the Easter uprising, O'Higgins' murder can be seen as the martyrdom that forced a course of events that would make Ireland democratically whole. On July 20 the government proposed a constitutional amendment requiring Dáil candidates to declare before nomination their intention, if elected, to take the prescribed oath, 'and to make provision for the failure of a member of the Oireachtas so to take such oath'.[46] Confronted with this, de Valera and Fianna Fáil on August 11 were able to rationalize their signing the document containing the oath and take their seats in the Dáil. Five days later the tie-breaking vote of the Ceann Conmhairle saved the government in a Labour motion of no confidence. In an election called for the following month, both Cumann na nGaedheal and Fianna Fáil gained at the expense of the other parties, but there was enough support from the Farmers and the independents to give Cumann na nGaedheal another four and a half years of power, during which time Fianna Fáil evolved from its 'slightly constitutional status' to one whereby it took power by electoral mandate and without resistance from the incumbent government. In that sense O'Higgins' mission of guaranteeing the endurance of democratic constitutionalism in Ireland was achieved.

In a letter to O'Higgins' widow after the assassination, Yeats proclaimed: 'What can one say but that the country has lost the man it needed, its great builder of a nation.' He found consolation in the thought that 'when men write the history of this generation they will tell his life and know that all is told'.[47] Hopefully this volume will contribute to that expectation.

NOTES

1. Walker, *Parliamentary Election Results*, pp. 116–25.
2. Regan, *Irish Counter-Revolution*, p. 243.
3. Mary E. Daly, *Industrial Development and Irish National Identity 1922–1939* (Syracuse: Syracuse University Press, 1992), pp. 14–15, 28–9; Regan, *ibid.*, p. 275.
4. *The Irish Times* (2 and 27 May 1927).
5. *Ibid.* (7 May 1927).
6. Walker, *Parliamentary Election Results*, pp. 117–25.
7. *Irish Times* (20 May 1927).
8. *Ibid.*, (24 May 1927).
9. *Ibid.*, (3 June 1927).
10. Richard Dunphy, *The Making of Fianna Fáil power in Ireland 1923–1948* (Oxford: Clarendon Press, 1991), pp. 76–83.
11. *The Irish Times* (2 May 1927).
12. *Ibid.* (10 and 16 May and 4 June 1927).
13. *Ibid.* (16 May and 2, 3 June 1927).
14. *Ibid.* (23 May and 7 June 1927).
15. *Irish Statesman* (5 March 1927).
16. *Ibid.* (2 April 1927).
17. *Ibid.* (7 May 1927).
18. Kevin O'Higgins to Lady Hazel Lavery (6 May and 10 June 1927), quoted in McCoole, *Hazel*, pp. 129–30.
19. Abstentionist Republicans got 5, Independent Republicans got 2, Labour got 22, the Farmers got 11, the National Group got 8, and there were 14 Independents.
20. Kevin O'Higggins to Frank McDermott (17 June 1927), *McDermott Papers*, NA, 1065/1/2, quoted in Regan, *Irish Counter-Revolution*, p. 271.
21. *The Irish Times* (15 June 1927).
22. *Irish Statesman* (18 June 1927).
23. *The Irish Times* (15 and 17 June 1927).
24. *Dáil Éireann*, XX (23 June 1927), 11–15.
25. *Ibid.*, 15–19.
26. *Ibid.*, 19–24.
27. *Ibid.*, 25–30.

28. Conversation between Richard Mulcahy and Michael Hayes (22 October 1964), UCDA, *Mulcahy Papers*, P7D/78, cited Regan, *Irish Counter-Revolution*, p. 272.
29. *Dáil Éireann*, 5 (23 June 1927), 59–60.
30. Kevin O'Higgins to Brigid O'Higgins (30 June 1927), *O'Higgins Papers*, Book 5.
31. *The Irish Times* (11 July 1927), *Irish Independent* (11 and 12 July 1927), *Dublin Evening Mail* (11 July 1927), de Vere White, *Kevin O'Higgins*, pp. 240–2.
32. *Irish Independent* (12 July 1927).
33. C.S. Andrews, *Man of No Property* (Dublin: Lilliput Press, 2001, 1st pub. 1981), p. 80.
34. Patrick Hogan, 'Memoir, 1913–1937', in *James Hogan: Revolutionary, Historian and Political Scientist*, ed. Donnchadh Ó Corráin (Dublin: Four Courts Press, 2001), p. 202. All three sought to move republicanism in a left-wing direction in the late 1920s and 1930s. Ryan led the Irish contingent of volunteers fighting in defence of the Republic in the Spanish Civil War, became a prisoner and subsequently worked with the Third Reich, where he died, in trying to promote insurrection in Ireland during the Second World War. Gilmore visited the Soviet Union in pursuit of aid for the IRA, helped set up a rival left-wing Republican Congress to advance a workers' republic, and recruited volunteers for the Spanish republican cause. MacBride founded a radical republican party after World War Two, Clann na Poblachta, whose electoral success ironically resulted in his becoming a successor of O'Higgins as Minister for External Affairs in 1948.
35. Brian Quinn, 'Secrets of State', *Irish Independent* (3 February 1981).
36. Proinsias MacAonghusa, 'The O'Higgins Mystery Solved', *Sunday Press* (5 October 1985).
37. The Invincibles were a breakaway group of Fenians whose assassination of Chief Secretary, Lord Frederick Cavendish, and Undersecretary, Thomas Burke, in Phoenix Park on 6 May 1882 nearly jeopardized the Kilmainham Treaty, the political settlement between Parnell and Gladstone the month before.
38. Fergus Pyle, 'O'Higgins assassination against IRA policy', *The Irish Times* (7 October 1985).
39. O'Higgins O'Malley, *From Pardon and Protest*, 14–15.
40. Una O'Higgins O'Malley, 'Bricklayer of the Nation', *The Irish Times* (6 June 1992).
41. *Dáil Éireann*, XX (12 July 1927), 755–62.
42. *Seanad Éireann*, IX (12 July 1927), 9–10.
43. *Garda Review* (August 1927), pp. 903–4.
44. *Irish Statesman* (16 July 1927).
45. *The Tablet* (16 July 1927).
46. *Dáil Éireann*, Vol. XX (20 July 1927), 809–10.
47. *Uncollected Prose by W.B. Yeats*, collected & ed., John P. Frayne and Colton Johnson (New York: Columbia University Press, 1975), II, p. 476.

# Bibliography

ARCHIVES

NATIONAL ARCHIVES

Dáil Éireann
Dáil Éireann, Local Government
Provisional Government
Cabinet
Department of Taoiseach
Department of Justice

BRITISH DOCUMENTS AVAILABLE IN NATIONAL ARCHIVES

Cabinet Committee on Irish Affairs
Correspondence between Secretary to the Cabinet and Secretary,
Irish Boundary Commission
Irish Boundary Commission. Notes of Conference at Treasury; Draft
Notes, Conference at No. 10 Downing Street

PUBLIC RECORDS OFFICE

Cabinet Papers, 'Proposed Creation of a Kingdom of Ireland',
*Memorandum by the Secretary of State for Dominion Affairs*
*Memorandum by the Secretary of State for Foreign Affairs; Note by
the Secretary of State for Dominion Affairs*

NATIONAL LIBRARY

*Rev. Patrick J. Doyle Papers*

UNIVERSITY COLLEGE DUBLIN ARCHIVES

*Blythe Papers*
*Cumann na nGaedheal/Fine Gael Papers*
*FitzGerald Papers*
*Kennedy Papers*
*Healy Papers*
*Mulcahy Papers*
*McGilligan Papers*


PRIVATE COLLECTION

*O'Higgins Papers* (Since research for this book was done these papers have been given to University College Dublin Archives.)


PUBLIC DOCUMENTS

*Dáil Éireann*
*Dáil Éireann, Debate on Treaty*
*Dáil Éireann, Private Session*
*Seanad Éireann*
*Imperial Conference 1926, Summary of Proceedings*


WRITINGS BY O'HIGGINS

*Civil War and the Events Which Led to It* (Dublin: Talbot Press, 1922). 'The Quenching of Our Shining Light', in *Arthur Griffith: Michael Collins* (Dublin: Martin Lester, n.d.).


NEWSPAPERS

*Dublin Evening Mail*
*Garda Review*
*Irish Independent*
*Irish Statesman*
*The Irish Times*
*The Nationalist and Leinster Times*
*Sunday Independent*

*Sunday Press*
*The Tablet*


THESES

Egan, Richard. 'A Kingdom of Ireland? Kevin O'Higgins, the Irish
    Free State and its relations with the British Commonwealth of
    Nations' (UCD: MA thesis, 2002).
Lynch, James Eoin. 'Operations and conduct of the Free State Army
    Command during the Irish Civil War' (UCD: MA thesis, 1996).
McGoey, Gillian. 'The assassination of Kevin O'Higgins and its
    implications for law and order policy in the Irish Free State'
    (UCD: MA thesis, 1996).
McKenna, Mary Frances. 'Reform of the Intoxicating Liquor Laws
    in the 1920s' (UCD: MA thesis, 1995).


SECONDARY SOURCES

ARTICLES

Akenson, D.H. and Fallon, J.F. 'The Irish Civil War and the Drafting
    of the Free State Constitution', *Eire–Ireland*, 5: 1 (Spring, 1970),
    2 (Summer, 1970), and 4 (Winter, 1970).
Costello, Francis J. 'The Irish Representation to the London Anglo-
    Irish Conference in 1921: Violations of Their Authority or Victims
    of Contradictory Instructions?' *Eire–Ireland*, XXIV: 2 (1989).
Daly, Mary A. 'Local Government and the First Dáil', in Brian
    Farrell (ed.), *The Creation of the Dáil* (Belfast: Blackwater, 1994).
Egan, Richard. 'Kevin O'Higgins, the Tullamore Realm Trial and the
    ideas of a complex revolutionary', *Journal of the Offaly Historical
    and Archaeological Society*, Vol. 2 (2004).
Hand, Geoffrey J. 'Introduction', in *Report of the Irish Boundary
    Commission 1925* (Shannon: Irish University Press, 1969).
Hand, Geoffrey J. 'MacNeill and the Boundary Commission', in F.X.
    Martin and F.J. Byrne (eds), *The Scholarly Revolutionary* (New
    York: Harper & Row, 1973).
Hart, Peter. 'Michael Collins and the assassination of Sir Henry
    Wilson', *Irish Historical Studies*, XXVIII, 110 (November
    1992).
Hawkins, F.M.A. 'Defence and the role of Erskine Childers in the

treaty negotiations of 1921', *Irish Historical Studies*, XXII, 87 (March 1981).

Hogan, Patrick. 'Kevin O'Higgins: An appreciation', *An t-Óglach* (October, 1927).

Hopkinson, Michael. 'The Craig–Collins Pacts of 1922', *Irish Historical Studies*, XXVII, 106 (November 1990).

Hyam, Ronald and Martin, Ged. 'The Irish Free State and the Evolution of the Commonwealth, 1921–1949', in *Reappraisals in British Imperial History* (Toronto: Macmillan of Canada, 1975).

Keane, Ronan. 'The Voice of the Gael: Chief Justice Kennedy and the Emergence of the New Irish Court System', *The Irish Jurist*, XXXI (1996).

Knirck, Jason. 'Afterimage of the Revolution: Kevin O'Higgins and the Irish Revolution', *Éire–Ireland*, XXXVIII, 3–4 (Fall/Winter 2003).

Matthews, Kevin. 'Stanley Baldwin's "Irish Question"', *The Historical Journal*, 43, 4 (2000).

McColgan, John. 'Implementing the 1921 Treaty: Lionel Curtis and Constitutional Procedures', *Irish Historical Studies*, XX, 79 (March 1977).

O'Bierne-Ranelegh, John. 'The I.R.B. from the treaty to 1924', *Irish Historical Studies*, XX, 70 (March 1976).

Regan John. 'Review of *Hazel: A Life of Lady Lavery, 1880–1935*', *The Irish Times* (11 September 1996).

Regan, John M. 'Kevin O'Higgins, Irish Republicanism and the Conservative Counter-Revolution', in *Laois: History & Society* (Dublin: Geography Publications, 1999).

Regan, John M. 'The Politics of Utopia: Party Organization, Executive Autonomy and the New Administration', in Cronin, Mike and Regan, John M. (eds), *Ireland: The Politics of Independence, 1922–1949* (London: Macmillan, 2000).

Towey, Thomas. 'Hugh Kennedy and the Constitutional Development of The Irish Free State', *The Irish Jurist*, XII (1977).

Towey, Thomas. 'The Reaction of the British Government to the 1922 Collins–de Valera Pact', *Irish Historical Studies*, XXII, 85 (March 1980).

Valiulis, Maryann Gialanella. 'The "army mutiny" of 1924 and the assertion of civilian authority in independent Ireland', *Irish Historical Studies* XXIII, 92 (November 1983).

Valiulis, Maryann Gialanella. 'Power, Gender and Identity in the Irish Free State', *Journal of Women's History* 6, 4; 7, 1 (1995).

BOOKS

Amery, L.S, *My Political Life* (London: Hutchinson, 1953).

Andrews, C.S. *Man of No Property* (Dublin: Lilliput Press, 2001).

Brady, Conor. *Guardians of the Peace* (Dublin: Gill and Macmillan, 1974).

Brown, Stewart J. and Miller, David W. (eds), *Piety and Power in Ireland: 1760–1960* (Notre Dame: University of Notre Dame Press, 2000).

Callanan, Frank. *T.M. Healy* (Cork: Cork University Press, 1996).

Campbell, Colm. *Emergency Law in Ireland, 1918–1925* (Oxford: Clarendon Press, 1994).

Canning, Paul. *British Policy Towards Ireland, 1921–41* (Oxford: Clarendon Press, 1985).

Coogan, Tim Pat. *De Valera: Long Fellow, Long Shadow* (London: Hutchinson, 1993).

Cronin, Mike and Regan, John M. (eds), *Ireland: The Politics of Independence, 1922–49* (London: Macmillan, 2000).

Cruise O'Brien, Conor. *Parnell and His Party, 1880–1890* (Oxford: Clarendon Press, 1957).

Curran, Joseph M. *The Birth of the Irish Free State 1921–1923* (Alabama: University of Alabama Press, 1980).

Daly, Mary E. *Industrial Development and Irish National Identity 1922–1939* (Syracuse: Syracuse University Press, 1992).

Dunphy, Richard. *The Making of Fianna Fáil Power in Ireland 1923–1948* (Oxford: Clarendon Press, 1991).

Dwyer, T. Ryle, *De Valera: The Man & the Myth* (Dublin: Poolbeg, 1991).

English, Richard. *Radicals and the Republic* (Oxford: Clarendon Press, 1994).

Farrell, Brian (ed.), *The Irish Parliamentary Tradition* (Dublin: Gill and Macmillan, 1973).

Farrell, Brian (ed.), *The Creation of the Dáil* (Belfast: Blackwater, 1994).

Garvin, Tom. *The Evolution of Irish Nationalist Politics* (Dublin: Gill and Macmillan, 1981).

Garvin,Tom. *1922: The Birth of Irish Democracy* (Dublin: Gill & Macmillan, 1996).

Gaughan, J. Anthony. *Thomas Johnson* (Dublin: Kingdom Books, 1980).

Gaughan, J. Anthony (ed.), *Memoirs of Senator James G. Douglas,*

*Concerned Citizen* (Dublin: University College Dublin Press, 1998).

Gilbert, Martin. *Winston Churchill: 1916–1922, The Stricken World* (Boston: Houghton Mifflin, 1975).

Gwynn, Denis. *The Irish Free State, 1922–1927* (Dublin: 1928).

Harkness, D.W. *The Restless Dominion: The Irish Free State and the British Commonwealth of Nations, 1921–1931* (New York: New York University Press, 1970).

Hopkinson, Michael. *Green Against Green* (New York: St. Martin's Press, 1988).

Jones, Thomas. *Whitehall Diary, vol III* (London: Oxford University Press, 1971).

Kee, Robert. *The Green Flag* (first published London: Weidenfield and Nicolson, 1972; London: Penguin Books, 2000 edition).

Keogh, Dermot. *The Vatican, the Bishops and Irish Politics 1919–1939* (Cambridge: Cambridge University Press, 1986).

Kotsonouris, Mary. *Retreat from Revolution, The Dáil Courts, 1920–24* (Dublin: Irish Academic Press, 1994).

Lee, J.J. *Ireland; 1912–1985* (Cambridge: Cambridge University Press, 1989).

Lyons, F.S.L. *John Dillon* (London: Routledge & Kegan Paul, 1968).

Macardle, Dorothy. *The Irish Republic* (first published London: Victor Gollancz, 1937; Dublin: Irish Press Edition, 1951).

Maher, Jim. *Harry Boland* (Dublin: Mercier Press, 1998).

Martin, F.X. & Byrne, F.J. (eds), *The Scholarly Revolutionary* (New York: Harper & Row, 1973).

Matthews, Kevin. *Fatal Influence: The Impact of Ireland on British Politics, 1920–1925* (Dublin: University College Dublin Press, 2004).

McBride, Lawrence W. *The Greening of Dublin Castle: The Transformation of Bureaucratic and Judicial Personnel in Ireland, 1892–1922* (Washington, D.C.: Catholic University of America Press, 1991).

McColgan, John. *British Policy and the Irish Administration, 1920–22* (London: George Allen and Unwin, 1983).

McCoole, Sinead. *Hazel: A Life of Lady Lavery, 1880–1935* (Dublin: Lilliput Press, 1996).

MacEoin Uinseann. *The IRA in the Twilight Years: 1923–1948* (Dublin: Argenta Publications, 1997).

Mitchell, Arthur. *Revolutionary Government in Ireland* (Dublin: Gill and Macmillan, 1995).

Moody, T.W. and Martin, F.X. (eds), *The Making of Irish History*

(Dublin: Mercier in association with Radio Telefís Éireann, 2001 ed.).

Ó Corráin, Donnchadh (ed.), *James Hogan: Revolutionary, Historian and Political Scientist* (Dublin: Four Courts Press, 2001).

ÓDrisceoil, Donal. *Peadar O'Donnell* (Cork: Cork University Press, 2001).

O'Halpin, Eunan. *Defending Ireland. The Irish State and Its Enemies Since 1922* (Oxford: Oxford University Press, 1999).

O'Higgins, Thomas F. *A Double Life* (Dublin: Town House, 1996).

O'Higgins O'Malley, Una. *From Pardon and Protest. Memoirs from the Margins* (Galway: Arlen House, 2001).

O'Sullivan, Donal. *The Irish Free State and Its Senate* (London: Faber and Faber, 1940).

Paseta, Senia. *Before the Revolution: Nationalism, Social Change and Ireland's Catholic Elite, 1879–1922* (Cork: Cork University Press, 1999).

Regan, John M., *The Irish Counter-Revolution 1921–1936* (Dublin: Gill & Macmillan, 1999).

Sullivan, T.D. *Recollections of Troubled Times in Irish Politics* (Dublin: Sealy, Brynes & Walker, 1905).

Townsend, Charles. *The British Campaign in Ireland, 1919–1921* (Oxford: Oxford University Press, 1975).

Valiulis, Maryann Gialanella. *Portrait of a Revolutionary: General Richard Mulcahy and the founding of the Irish Free State* (Dublin: Irish Academic Press, 1992).

Walker, Brian M. (ed.), *Parliamentary Election Results in Ireland, 1918–1992* (Dublin: Royal Irish Academy, 1992).

Yeats, W.B. *Explorations* (New York: Macmillan, 1962).

Yeats, W.B. *Uncollected Prose* (New York: Columbia University Press, 1975).

# Index